BERLIN
METROPOLIS

BERLIN
METROPOLIS
JEWS AND
THE NEW CULTURE
1890–1918

Emily D. Bilski

With essays by Sigrid Bauschinger, Inka Bertz, Emily D. Bilski, Barbara Hahn,
Peter Jelavich, Paul Mendes-Flohr, Peter Paret, Chana C. Schütz

University of California Press
Berkeley | Los Angeles | London

The Jewish Museum | New York
Under the auspices of The Jewish Theological Seminary of America

Front Cover:
(Detail) Lesser Ury
At the Friedrichstrasse Station [Am Bahnhof Friedrichstrasse], 1888
Figure 99

Back Cover:
Ludwig Meidner
Apocalyptic Landscape [Apokalyptische Landschaft], 1913
Figure 126

(Detail) page *viii*:
Construction of the Kaiser-Wilhelm Bridge, 1887

(Detail) page *xii*:
Alexanderplatz and Dirckenstrasse, 1911

This book has been published
in conjunction with the exhibition

**Berlin Metropolis:
Jews and the New Culture,
1890-1918**

The Jewish Museum, New York
November 14, 1999–April 23, 2000

A checklist of the exhibition is available on
request from The Jewish Museum.

Exhibition Curator Emily D. Bilski
Project Director Mason Klein
Project Assistant Aliza Edelman
Exhibition Designer Joel Sanders
Catalogue Design 2x4, New York City
Catalogue Editor Sheila Friedling

University of California Press
Berkeley and Los Angeles, California

University of California Press, Ltd.
London, England

Library of Congress Cataloging-in-Publication Data

Berlin metropolis: Jews and the new culture, 1890-1918 / Emily D. Bilski, ed.
p. cm.

Catalogue of an exhibition held at The Jewish Museum, New York,
November 14, 1999–April 23, 2000.

Includes bibliographical references and index.
ISBN 0-520-22241-5 (alk. paper).
ISBN 0-520-22242-3 (paperback: alk. paper)
1. Art, German—Germany—Berlin. 2. Art, Modern—19th century—Germany—Berlin. 3. Art, Modern—20th century—Germany—Berlin. 4. Jewish artists—Germany—Berlin.
I. Bilski, Emily D.
N6885.B43 1999 99-32029
700'.89'924043155--dc21 CIP

Printed and bound in Canada
08 07 06 05 04 03 02 01 00 99
10 9 8 7 6 5 4 3 2 1

The paper used in this publication meets the minimum requirements of
ANSI/NISO Z39.48-1992 (R 1997) (*Permanence of Paper*).

Contents

vi   **Donors to the Exhibition**

vii **Lenders to the Exhibition**

ix   **Foreword**
     Joan Rosenbaum

xiii **Acknowledgments**
     Emily D. Bilski

2   **Introduction**
     Emily D. Bilski

14   **The Berlin Jew as Cosmopolitan**
     Paul Mendes–Flohr

32   **Modernism and the "Alien Element" in German Art**
     Peter Paret

58   **The Berlin Moderns: Else Lasker-Schüler and Café Culture**
     Sigrid Bauschinger

102 **Images of Identity and Urban Life: Jewish Artists in Turn-of-the-Century Berlin**
     Emily D. Bilski

146 **Max Liebermann as a "Jewish" Painter: The Artist's Reception in His Time**
     Chana C. Schütz

164 **Jewish Renaissance—Jewish Modernism**
     Inka Bertz

188 **Encounters at the Margins: Jewish Salons Around 1900**
     Barbara Hahn

208 **Performing High and Low: Jews in Modern Theater, Cabaret, Revue, and Film**
     Peter Jelavich

236 **Chronology: 1890–1918**

255 **Selected Bibliography**

257 **Index**

264 **Contributors**

265 **Photography Credits**

Donors to the Exhibition

Berlin Metropolis: Jews and the New Culture, 1890–1918 has been sponsored by

Deutsche Bank ◪

Significant support has also been provided by The Lucius N. Littauer Foundation; the National Endowment for the Arts; and the Consulate General of the Federal Republic of Germany; with additional funding from Arnhold & S. Bleichroeder, Inc.; Schroder & Co., Inc.; OFFITBANK; Deutsche Beteiligungs AG; the New York Council for the Humanities and the National Endowment for the Humanities; Fanya Gottesfeld Heller; the Norman and Rosita Winston Foundation; the New York State Council on the Arts, a State Agency; and other generous donors.

Endowment support has been provided by the Fine Arts Fund, established at The Jewish Museum by the National Endowment for the Arts and the generosity of Andrea and Charles Bronfman, Melva Bucksbaum, Barbara Horowitz, Betty and John Levin, Lynn and Glen Tobias, Bunny and Jim Weinberg, and the Estates of Ruth Roaman Epstein, Francis A. Jennings, Charles J. Simon, and Leonard Wagner.

The catalogue was published with the aid of a publications fund established by the Dorot Foundation.

Lenders to the Exhibition

Albright-Knox Art Gallery,
Buffalo, New York.

The Art Complex Museum,
Duxbury, Massachusetts

The Art Institute of Chicago

Leo Baeck Institute, Jerusalem

Leo Baeck Institute, New York

Alan and Ruth Barnett

Joseph D. and Beate Becker

Beinecke Rare Book
and Manuscript Library,
Yale University

Berlinische Galerie,
Landesmuseum für Moderne Kunst,
Photographie und Architektur

Bibliothèque nationale de France,
Paris

Bineth Gallery, Tel Aviv

Carnegie Museum of Art, Pittsburgh

Deutsche Bank AG, Frankfurt am Main

Firma Vera Eisenberger K.G.

The Marvin and Janet Fishman
Collection, Milwaukee

Galerie St. Etienne, New York

Georg Kolbe Museum, Berlin

Collection of Oscar and Regina Gruss

Hamburger Kunsthalle

Busch-Reisinger Museum,
Harvard University Art Museums

Fogg Art Museum,
Harvard University Art Museums

The Alex Hillman Family Foundation

Indiana University Art Museum

The Israel Museum, Jerusalem

Collection of Peter Jelavich,
Austin, Texas

Stiftung Jüdisches Museum, Berlin

Jüdisches Museum,
Frankfurt am Main

Krefelder Kunstmuseen

Kunstbibliothek, Staatliche Museen
zu Berlin–Preussischer Kulturbesitz

Kunsthalle Bremen

Kunsthalle zu Kiel

Kunstkreis Berlin GbR

Kunstmuseum Düsseldorf

Kupferstichkabinett, Staatliche
Museen zu Berlin–Preussischer
Kulturbesitz

Landesmuseum Mainz

The Leonard A. Lauder Collection

Library of Congress,
Washington, D.C.

The Los Angeles County
Museum of Art. The Robert
Gore Rifkind Center for German
Expressionist Studies

Werner and Gabrielle Merzbacher

The Metropolitan Museum of Art

Moderna Museet, Stockholm

Munch-museet, Oslo

Museum of Fine Arts, Boston

Museum der bildenden
Künste Leipzig

Museum Ludwig, Cologne

Museum Ostdeutsche
Galerie Regensburg

National Gallery of Art,
Washington, D.C.

Nationalgalerie, Staatliche
Museen zu Berlin

Print Collection, Miriam and
Ira D. Wallach Division of Art,
Prints and Photographs.
The New York Public Library

Rare Books Division,
The New York Public Library

Collection of Peter Paret

Collection of Suzanne Aimée Paret

Philadelphia Museum of Art

Max Reinhardt Archives, Special
Collections, Binghamton University
Libraries, State University of
New York at Binghamton

The Robert Gore Rifkind Collection,
Beverly Hills, California

Saarland Museum, Saarbrücken

The Saint Louis Art Museum

Barbara Slifka

Sylvia Slifka

Solomon R. Guggenheim Museum,
New York

Staatsgalerie Stuttgart

Stiftung Stadtmuseum Berlin

Städtische Galerie im Lenbachhaus,
Munich

Stedelijk Museum, Amsterdam

Axel Springer Verlag AG, Berlin

Stiftung Deutsche Kinemathek,
Berlin

Tel Aviv Museum of Art

Theaterhistorische Sammlung
der Universität Köln

Richard S. Zeisler Collection,
New York

Private Collections

Foreword

Joan Rosenbaum
Helen Goldsmith Menschel Director
The Jewish Museum

The Jewish Museum is proud to present *Berlin Metropolis: Jews and the New Culture, 1890–1918*, an exhibition and publication that continue the Museum's tradition of exploring the intersection of art and Jewish culture in its public presentations. Starting in the mid-nineteenth century, Jewish emancipation offered new possibilities for acculturation, assimilation, and professional mobility, including the opportunity for Jews to emerge for the first time as professional artists in the urban art centers of the world. Previous Jewish Museum exhibitions have focused on Jewish artists and the social milieus in which they worked in Paris, Rome, Moscow, London, and New York.

Berlin Metropolis is a highly focused exhibition encompassing a short period of twenty-eight years; yet it takes a broad interdisciplinary approach, embracing the profound transformations that occurred in Berlin as it developed into a major world cultural center. Illuminated in both the book and the exhibition—through the art, artifacts, and essays—is the atmosphere of cosmopolitanism and change that characterized the city during this extraordinary period. In spite of a continuing undercurrent of anti-Semitism, this environment nurtured the "new culture" that brought Jews into the mainstream of all that was developing in the visual arts, film, theater, literature, and publishing.

In 1999, as we take a retrospective look at Berlin at the turn of the last century, particularly in the context of a Jewish museum, there is an inevitable emotional and moral resonance. It is likely that readers and viewers of *Berlin Metropolis* will have an acute awareness of the cataclysmic events that took place in Germany not so long after 1918, including the Nazi rise to power in the Third Reich, the Second World War, and the Holocaust. The great, vital, culturally forward city of Berlin was destroyed, and all but a few of its Jews were exterminated or forced to flee. The culture of modernism that had flourished in Berlin at the beginning of the twentieth century was later regarded, during the Nazi period, as "degenerate." Looking back at this history, we are aware of the lives and careers that were curtailed and wonder about what could have evolved had there been no Holocaust. At this moment in 1999, we are also cognizant of the energy and expansion pervading the reunified new German capital, not unlike the turn-of-the-century cosmopolitanism that is explored in its diverse perspectives in *Berlin Metropolis*. In a sense, something of that cosmopolitan spirit is being reborn with the globalization of the turn of this century. Today, however, the building, expansion, and revitalization that brought Jews into the "new" Berlin of the early 1900s include a commemoration and memorialization of

Berlin's distinguished Jewish history through the creation of new museums, exhibitions, and memorials, and, to some extent, a renewal of Jewish life in the city.

Berlin Metropolis, in a way, also contributes to the renewal of Berlin Jewish life as it brings into focus—through new scholarship, a rich and complex exhibition, and a wide-ranging interdisciplinary catalogue—an extraordinarily creative period in history. *Berlin Metropolis* is thus for The Jewish Museum a centennial commemoration that is both a celebration and a memorial.

The exhibition and publication focus attention and offer insight into the works of Jewish artists, writers, intellectuals, collectors, and cultural figures whose vision, creativity, and engagement with modernist art and ideas are not well known in the United States. Viewers and readers are introduced to important artists such as Lesser Ury, Max Liebermann, Ludwig Meidner, and Jakob Steinhardt, among others; the poet Else Lasker-Schüler; and to publishers, gallery owners, and dealers such as Herwarth Walden and Paul and Bruno Cassirer. Additionally, we are presented with the new theatricality of Max Reinhardt; the emergence of film as an innovative form of popular culture; and the importance of alternative public spaces such as the café, theater, cabaret, and gallery, where people of diverse social and cultural backgrounds could meet and exchange ideas.

Congratulations to Curator Emily D. Bilski for her superb curatorial skills in envisioning this project; for her definitive role in conceptualizing the catalogue, for which she has written an important essay; and for succeeding in bringing together an ambitious array of art, artifacts, and scholarly interpretation. She was aided by the generous advice and distinguished scholarly contributions of an international group of art and cultural historians represented in this excellent book; and by the Jewish Museum staff who, during the four years of this project, worked exceptionally hard to ensure its realization and success. I thank all those who worked closely with Emily Bilski for their valuable contributions, their diligence, and their good spirit.

The Museum reached well beyond its own walls to gather the contents of the exhibition, which number approximately 250 works that have been borrowed from more than 70 private and public collections throughout the world (listed on page *vii*). Many thanks for their loans to my museum colleagues and also to the private collectors who have been so cooperative and generous.

Berlin Metropolis rests not only upon the wisdom of its scholars, the dedicated work of museum staff, and the good will of collectors, but it also requires the generosity and commitment to The Jewish Museum of donors who support the project budget. We are most grateful to all of the corporations, individuals, and foundations, listed on page *vi*, who have enabled this exhibition and catalogue to come to fruition. I offer my great thanks for their very generous support to Deutsche Bank, the exhibition's lead sponsor, as well as The Lucius N. Littauer Foundation, the National Endowment for the Arts, the Consulate General of the

Federal Republic of Germany, Arnhold & S. Bleichroeder, Inc., Schroder & Co., Inc., OFFITBANK, Deutsche Beteiligungs AG, the New York Council for the Humanities and the National Endowment for the Humanities, Fanya Gottesfeld Heller, the Norman and Rosita Winston Foundation, the New York State Council on the Arts, and other generous donors. Important endowment support has been provided by the Fine Arts Fund, established at The Jewish Museum by the National Endowment for the Arts and the generosity of Andrea and Charles Bronfman, Melva Bucksbaum, Barbara Horowitz, Betty and John Levin, Lynn and Glen Tobias, Bunny and Jim Weinberg, and the Estates of Ruth Roaman Epstein, Francis A. Jennings, Charles J. Simon, and Leonard Wagner. This catalogue has been published with the aid of a publications fund established by the Dorot Foundation. These diverse donors have contributed to the creation of a scholarly, innovative, and richly textured cultural and aesthetic experience.

Finally, my gratitude goes to The Jewish Museum's Board of Trustees, chaired by Robert J. Hurst, who not only sustain the basic operations of the Museum, but who also support projects that further the Museum's mission and offer original and enlightening exhibition experiences to the public. We hope that our efforts at the Museum can live up to the extraordinary legacy of creativity left to us by the diverse artists and cultural figures whom we encounter in *Berlin Metropolis*.

Acknowledgments

The idea for this project was born during a trip to Berlin in 1987. During the intervening years, many friends, consultants, colleagues, lenders, and funders have supported our efforts to present our vision of Berlin Metropolis to an American public. I want to express my profound gratitude to the many individuals and institutions without whose generosity the exhibition and this book would never have been possible. Foremost among them is Joan Rosenbaum, Director of The Jewish Museum, who has championed this project from its inception, and whose insight and intelligence have helped shape and refine it. I am grateful for her unstinting personal support; after I moved to Jerusalem, she encouraged me to pursue this project as a guest curator.

As a guest curator living on another continent, I have benefited greatly from the good will, cooperation, and dedication of my colleagues at The Jewish Museum. A number of people who are no longer at the Museum worked diligently on the exhibition during its formative stages: Eric M. Zafran, former Deputy Director of Curatorial Affairs; Julia Goldman, Jane Becker, and Melissa Sprague, former exhibition assistants; Jonathan Maack, research intern; and Heidi Zuckerman Jacobson, former Assistant Curator, the first Project Director, who enthusiastically shepherded the exhibition during 1997–98. I thank each of them for their contributions to this project.

Mason Klein, Assistant Curator and Project Director, has had the enormous task of overseeing all aspects of the exhibition and catalogue, which he has accomplished with wisdom, grace, and consummate professionalism. Exhibition Assistant Aliza Edelman has handled a myriad of complicated tasks with tremendous skill and verve. Thanks to them both for their scholarly input, intelligent advice, and extraordinary dedication. It has been a great pleasure to collaborate with them on Berlin Metropolis. Aliza has been ably assisted by intern Sarah Timmins DeGregory. We have been extremely fortunate to have Katharina Garrelt as a special intern on the project; her knowledge of German art and her impeccable command of the German language have greatly benefited our project. Alexandra Nocke expertly handled numerous research and administrative tasks in Berlin with persistent good humor. Thanks to her and to Mira Goldfarb Berkowitz for creating the Chronology that enhances this book. I thank my friend Norman L. Kleeblatt, Curator of Fine Arts, and the other members of his department for their assistance and for providing Mason, Aliza, and myself with a home in the Museum. Ruth Beesch, Deputy Director of Program, has been the exhibition's enthusiastic advocate; I am grateful for her skillful management and for her calm support throughout.

Sheila Friedling has done a masterful job of editing this book, working with all the authors on the development of the manuscript and with the designers to produce a cohesive volume. My thanks for her diligence, erudition, and devotion to this project. Thanks as well to Janice Meyerson for her invaluable assistance.

Michael Rock and David Israel of 2 x 4 have created an evocative design for the book and the exhibition graphics. I am grateful for their creativity, hard work, and cooperative spirit. Thanks are also due to Deborah Kirshman, Laura Paulini, and Mari Coates at the University of California Press for their expertise in publishing this book.

As a project that spans a number of disciplines in the humanities, we have relied greatly on an extraordinary group of academic consultants. In the initial phase, Charles W. Haxthausen of Williams College and Thomas Y. Levin of Princeton University made significant contributions to the conceptualization of the exhibition; I am grateful for their personal encouragement and ongoing support of the project. I also thank Danielle Rice at the Philadelphia Museum of Art for her input.

My deep appreciation goes to the authors of the essays in this catalogue for illuminating many facets of the art, literature, and performing arts of Wilhelmine Berlin, as well as the cultural history of Jews in Germany: Paul Mendes-Flohr; Peter Paret; Sigrid Bauschinger; Chana Schütz; Inka Bertz; Barbara Hahn; and Peter Jelavich. Each of them also has made a significant contribution to the development of the exhibition itself. Peter Paret has been an extraordinarily generous and energetic champion of this project; thanks to his commitment, our presentation of entire sections of the exhibition have been immeasurably enriched. Paul Mendes-Flohr—my fellow Jerusalemite—has tirelessly supported this project. My thanks for the many conversations that have enriched my understanding. Thanks to Peter Jelavich, readers and New York audiences will encounter the world of Berlin theater, revue, and cabaret. I am grateful to him for making this ephemeral material available to us and for his patience in responding to endless queries. Sigrid Bauschinger was instrumental in our ability to borrow and publish certain works and graciously answered my questions about literature. Barbara Hahn has made significant suggestions concerning the conceptual framework of the exhibition, and I thank her as well for our illuminating conversations in Berlin. Inka Bertz has been generous with her time for many years of discussions, and I thank her for sharing her insights into the Berlin Jewish Renaissance and related issues of Jews and modernity; more recently, as Curator at the Berlin Jewish Museum, she has been helpful in identifying artifacts for this exhibition. My first friend in Berlin was Chana Schütz. Since 1987 we have had an ongoing conversation about the issues presented in this exhibition and catalogue, and I have turned to her dozens of times with questions or ideas to test out. My gratitude for her unfailing and inventive responsiveness.

Research in Berlin was greatly facilitated by a stint as a fellow at the Einstein Forum in Potsdam during August 1997. I thank former director Gary Smith and his staff for all their efforts on my behalf. Many people in Berlin graciously took the time to share their considerable knowledge and expertise. I thank Sigrid Achenbach, Curator at the Kupferstichkabinett; Ingeborg Becker, Curator at the

Bröhan Museum; Mayan Beckmann of Galerie Pels-Leusden; Janos Frecot, Director of the Photography Collection at the Berlinische Galerie; Anita Kühnel, Curator of posters at the Kunstbibliothek; Peter Mänz at Stiftung Deutsche Kinemathek; Jörg Schweinitz; Annette Seeler at the Käthe Kollwitz Museum; J. Michael Semler and Nina Senger at Villa Grisebach; Hella Zettler, of the Photography Collection at Stiftung Stadtmuseum Berlin; Angelika Wesenberg, Curator at the Nationalgalerie.

Research was primarily conducted at the Kunstbibliothek in Berlin; I thank the staff for all their assistance. In Jerusalem, the Jewish National and University Library has proven an invaluable resource. My gratitude to Margot Cohn of the Buber Archive; and to Shelly Benvenisti and her staff, who have made the General Reading Room a haven for researchers. In Bad Homburg, Dieter Kortenjan, Librarian at the Stadtbibliothek, graciously went out of his way to facilitate my research. I learned a tremendous amount from the Collection of Prints and Drawings at the Tel Aviv Museum of Art and from Curator Edna Moshenson. Meira Perry-Lehmann, Curator of Prints and Drawings at The Israel Museum, and Associate Curator Ruth Apter-Gabriel and their staff graciously made their collection available for study.

I have benefited greatly from conversations with the following friends and colleagues who directed me to important sources and offered invaluable advice: Götz Adriani, Sharon Assaf, Gitte Hartmann, Hans Otto Horch, Wolfgang Iser, Jürgen Kocka, Ute Kruse, Gerhard Kurz, Daniella Luxembourg, Elhanan Motzkin, Wolfgang Nowak, Gunther and Ingrid Osterle, Rivka Saker, and Valerie Zakovitch. Emily Braun and Judith Wechsler read drafts of my essay and made helpful suggestions, for which I thank them.

Along with Joan Rosenbaum, I would like to offer my personal thanks to the private lenders and staffs of the lending institutions; not only have they agreed to part with their works, but they have been most generous in sharing expertise and documentation. In addition to the names that appear on page *vii*, I want to thank the following colleagues: Douglas G. Schultz, Director, of the Albright-Knox Art Gallery, Buffalo, New York; Francis Archipenko Gray and Valerie Tekavec, Archivist, at the The Alexander Archipenko Archive; Charles Weyerhaeuser, Director, and Catherine Mayes at The Art Complex Museum, Duxbury, Massachusetts; James N. Wood, Director; Suzanne Folds McCullagh, Curator of Earlier Prints and Drawings; and Jay Clark, Assistant Curator of Prints and Drawings, at The Art Institute of Chicago; Hendrik Budde and Christoph Schwartz at the Berliner Festspiele; Jean-Pierre Angremy, President; Hélène Fauré, Loans Officer; and Roland Schaer at the Bibliothèque nationale de France; Brigitte Kuhl at the Bundesarchiv, Koblenz; Didier Schulmann at the Centre Georges Pompidou, Paris; Carol Kahn Strauss, Executive Director; Renata Stein, Curator; and Diane R. Spielman, Public Services and Development Coordinator, at the Leo Baeck Institute, New York; Shlomo Mayer at the Leo Baeck Institute, Jerusalem; Vincent Giroud, Curator of Modern Books and Manuscripts, Beinecke

Rare Book and Manuscript Library, Yale University; Joanna Webber at the Yale University Art Gallery; Jörn Merkert, Director; Ursula Prinz; and Wiebke Hess of the Berlinische Galerie, Landesmuseum für Moderne Kunst, Photographie und Architektur; Rodi Bineth, Director of the Bineth Gallery, Tel Aviv; Richard Armstrong, The Henry J. Heinz II Director, and Monika Tomko, Registrar, at the Carnegie Museum of Art, Pittsburgh; Friedrich Pfäfflin, Director; Michael Davidis; and Brigitte van Helt at the Deutsche Schillergesellschaft, Schiller-Nationalmuseum, and Deutsches Literaturarchiv, Marbach am Neckar; Friedhelm Hütte; Britta Färber; and Ariane Grigoteit at the Deutsche Bank AG, Frankfurt am Main; Vera Eisenberger and Jeno Eisenberger of the Firma Vera Eisenberger K.G.; Hildegarde Bachert and Jane Kallir of the Galerie St. Etienne in New York; Ursel Berger, Director, and Josephine Gabler of the Georg Kolbe Museum; Uwe Schneede, Director; Jenns Howoldt; and Anne Barz, Registrar, at the Hamburger Kunsthalle; James Cuno, Elizabeth and John Moors Cabot Director; Peter Nisbet, Curator; and Tawney L. Becker, Curatorial Assistant, at the Busch-Reisinger Museum, Harvard University Art Museums; William D. Robinson, Curator of Drawings at the Fogg Art Museum, Harvard University Art Museums; Mary Claire Altenhofen, Research Librarian, at the Harvard University Fine Arts Library; Mrs. Alex Hillman and Emily Braun, Curator, at The Alex Hillman Family Foundation; Adelheid M. Gealt, Director; Kathy Foster, Curator of Nineteenth- and Twentieth-Century Art; and Janice Dockery, Registrar, at the Indiana University Art Museum; James Snyder, Director; Stephanie Rauchum, David Rockefeller Curator of Modern Art; Elaine Varady, Department of Architecture and Design; and Tanya Zhilinsky at The Israel Museum, Jerusalem; Georg Heuberger, Director; Annette Weber; and Johannes Wachten at the Jüdisches Museum, Frankfurt am Main; Michael Blumenthal, Director; Inka Bertz, Curator; and Gisela Märtz, Registrar, at Stiftung Jüdisches Museum, Berlin; Gerhard Storck, Director, and Julian Heynen, Vice-Director, at the Krefelder Kunstmuseen; Bernd Evers, Director, and Anita Kühnel at the Kunstbibliothek, Staatliche Museen zu Berlin–Preussischer Kulturbesitz; Wulf Herzogenrath, Director and Andreas Kreul at Kunsthalle Bremen; Hans-Werner Schmidt, Director, and Beate Ermacora at Kunsthalle zu Kiel; Hans Albert Peters, Director; Martina Sitt, Chief Curator of the Department of Old Master Paintings; and Dorothea Nutt, Registrar, at Kunstmuseum Düsseldorf; Rolf Budde and Janet Reinhardt at Kunstkreis Berlin GbR; Gisela Fiedler-Bender, Director, and Brigitte Jänsch at Landesmuseum Mainz; Leonard A. Lauder and Emily Braun, Curator, of the Leonard A. Lauder Collection; James H. Billington, Librarian of Congress, and Tambra Johnson, Exhibitions Registrar, at the Library of Congress; Graham W. J. Beal, Director; Stephanie Barron, Senior Curator, Modern and Contemporary Art; Carol S. Eliel, Associate Curator of Twentieth-Century Art; Christine Vigiletti, Assistant Registrar; and Susan Trauger, Librarian, at The Los Angeles County Museum of Art, The Robert Gore Rifkind Center for German Expressionist Studies;

Wolfgang Eberl and Sonja Mayer at the Franz Marc Stiftung; Susanne Kähler of the Graphische Sammlung, Museum für Kunst und Gewerbe Hamburg; Werner and Gabrielle Merzbacher; Philippe de Montebello, Director; William Liebermann, Jacques and Natasha Gelman Chairman, Twentieth-Century Art; Ida Balboul, Research Associate, Twentieth-Century Art; George R. Goldner, Drue Heinz Chairman, Drawings and Prints; Colta Ives, Department of Drawings and Prints; and Dorothy Kellett, Department of European Paintings, at The Metropolitan Museum of Art, New York; Björn Springfeldt, Director, and Lena Granath, Registrar, at Moderna Museet, Stockholm; Arne Eggum, Director, and Petra Pettersen, Assistant Curator, at Munch-museet, Oslo; Herwig Guratzsch, Director, and Claudia Klugmann, Exhibition Secretary, at the Museum der bildenden Künste Leipzig; Malcolm Rogers, Director; Sue Welsh Reed, Associate Curator; and Karin L. Otis, Office of Rights and Reproductions, Photographic Services, at the Museum of Fine Arts, Boston; Jochen Poetter, Director; Evelyn Weiss, Vice-Director; and Gerhard Kolberg, Curator of the Sculpture Collection, at the Museum Ludwig, Cologne; Axel Feuss, Director, at the Museum Ostdeutsche Galerie Regensburg; Earl A. Powell III, Director; Stephanie Belt, Head, Department of Loans; and Mary Lee Corlett, Loan Officer, at the National Gallery of Art, Washington; Dieter Honisch, Director; Angelika Wesenberg, Curator; and Barbara Büstrin, at the Nationalgalerie, Staatliche Museen zu Berlin; Roberta Waddell, Curator of Prints; Paula Baxter, Director, Art and Architecture Division; and Eileen Coffey, Loan Administrator, Registrar's Office, Print Collection, Miriam and Ira D. Wallach Division of Art, Prints and Photographs, The New York Public Library; Virginia Bartow, Curator, Rare Books Division, The New York Public Library; Ruth Ofek at The Open Museum, Israel; Anne d'Harnoncourt, Director; Anne Tempkin, Muriel and Philip Berman Curator of Twentieth-Century Art; Joseph J. Rishel, Curator of European Painting and Sculpture; and Nancy Wulbrecht, Registrar for Outgoing Loans, at the Philadelphia Museum of Art; Jeanne Eichelberger, Head, Special Collections and Preservation, and Herbert Poetzl at the Max Reinhardt Archives, Binghamton University Libraries, State University of New York at Binghamton; Robert Gore Rifkind; Beverly Hills, California; Ernst-Gerhard Güse, Director, and Ernest W. Uthemann, Curator of Modern Painting and Sculpture, at the Saarland Museum, Saarbrücken; James D. Burke, Director; Sidney M. Goldstein, Associate Director, and Diane Vandegrift, Assistant Registrar, at The Saint Louis Museum of Art; Friede Springer and Rainer Laabs of Axel Springer Verlag AG, Berlin; Thomas Krens, Director; Lisa Dennison, Deputy Director and Chief Curator; Ellin Burke, Outgoing Loans Registrar; and Kim Bush, Photography Department, at the Solomon R. Guggenheim Museum, New York; Alexander Dückers, Director; Sigrid Achenbach, Curator; and Anita Beloubek-Hammer, Curator, at the Kupferstichkabinett, Staatliche Museen zu Berlin–Preussischer Kulturbesitz; Christian von Holst, Director; Karin von Maur, Vice Director; and Karin

Hämmerling, Registrar, at Staatsgalerie Stuttgart; Reiner Güntzer, Director; Dominik Bartmann; Thomas Wellmann; and Hella Zettler at Stiftung Stadtmuseum Berlin; Helmut Friedel, Director, and Annegret Hoberg at Städtische Galerie im Lenbachhaus, Munich; R. H. Fuchs, Director, and H. C. Bongers, Deputy Director, at the Stedelijk Museum, Amsterdam; Werner Sudendorf and Peter Mänz at Stiftung Deutsche Kinemathek, Berlin; Mordechai Omer, Director and Chief Curator; Nehama Guralnik, Curator of Modern and Contemporary Art, and Ahuva Israel, Associate Curator; Edna Moshenson, Curator of Prints and Drawings, and Emanuela Caló, Assistant Curator; Shraga Edelsburg, Registrar; and Yaffa Goldfinger at the Tel Aviv Museum of Art; Elmar Buck, Director, and Gerald Köhler at Theaterhistorische Sammlung der Universität Köln; Herbert Pogt at the Von der Heydt-Museum, Wuppertal; and the Else Lasker-Schüler-Gesellschaft, Wuppertal.

I also want to thank the following colleagues who graciously facilitated loans: Sotheby's London; Jeffrey Deitch; Josefa Bar-On Steinhardt; Ulrike Marquardt; Matthias Eberle and Margreet Nouwen.

Exhibition designer Joel Sanders has taken on the challenge of interpreting the cultural spaces of fin-de-siècle Berlin for museum visitors at the turn of our century. With the assistance of Christoph Müller-Roselius, he has accomplished this with style, intelligence, and creativity. Judith C. Siegel contributed her great expertise in communicating complex ideas within the exhibition idiom. Judy also played a critical role in the creation of the film that accompanies the section on Berlin cinema; we were fortunate to have Ingrid Scheib-Rothbart as our expert consultant on this film, which was admirably produced by Michael Schaffer. The public programs have been created by Aviva Weintraub, Director of Media and Public Programs, with a day-long symposium organized together with the Nexus Institute in Tilburg, The Netherlands; my thanks to Aviva and to Rob Riemen and Kirsten Walgreen of Nexus. I am grateful to Sue Davis Mellin, Director of Development, for her tremendous efforts on behalf of *Berlin Metropolis*.

The hard work and professionalism of my colleagues at The Jewish Museum have made *Berlin Metropolis* possible. My heartfelt thanks to the following individuals and their staffs: Thomas Dougherty, Deputy Director for Administration and Finance; Donna Jeffrey, Controller; Christine Byron, Registrar; Al Lazarte, Director of Operations; Marc Dorfman, Deputy Director for External Affairs; Elana Yerushalmi, Director of Program Funding; Andrew Ingall, Coordinator of Broadcast Archive; Alessandro Cavadini, Audio-Visual Coordinator; Anne Scher, Director of Communications; Grace Rapkin, Director of Marketing; Marcia Saft, Director of Visitor and Tourist Services; Barbara Treitel, Manager of Visual Resource Archive; Carol Zawatsky, Director of Education; Debbie Schwab, Director of Retail Operations; Marilyn Davidson, Manager of Product Development and Licensing; Linda Padawer, Director of Special Events.

Finally I want to thank my family for their help in matters both large and small: Berthold and Vicki Bilski, and Mark and

Tracey Bilski. Every project at The Jewish Museum involves
an element of self-discovery. While working on this project I
rediscovered books and prints given me by my grandmothers—
Minnie Rosenak and Alice Bilski—which helped me enormously
to understand Berlin Metropolis and the world of Max Liebermann,
Lesser Ury, Hermann Struck, and Martin Buber. The spirit of
Berlin 1900 has been present in my life also due to the furniture,
linens, and books of another woman—whom I never knew—
my husband's grandmother, Paula Motzkin. The cabaret programs
that she never threw away, the family photos taken by Franz
Pfemfert, have personalized those years for me. I thank my sons
Theo and Alex for their equanimity vis-à-vis a traveling mother
and several summers spent in German kindergartens. My husband, Gabriel Motzkin, remains my most cherished advisor.
I have relied on his profound knowledge of German history and
philosophy, and most important, on his love and support.

Emily D. Bilski

Introduction

Emily D. Bilski

(opposite)
(Detail) Alexanderplatz, 1906
Photograph: Max Missmann

In the summer of 1882, Carl and Felicie Bernstein returned
from Paris to Berlin with a group of Impressionist paintings.
Advised by Carl's Parisian cousin, Charles Ephrussi, the editor
of the *Gazette des Beaux-Arts*, the Bernsteins, who had originally
immigrated to Berlin from Russia, had acquired works by Manet,
Monet, Sisley, and Pissarro. These works formed the core of the
first collection of Impressionist art in Berlin, and, indeed, in all
of Germany. Had the Bernsteins been reclusive or aloof, their collection might not have had a significant impact; but the Bernstein
home was the site of a weekly salon, frequented by artists such
as Adolph Menzel, Max Klinger, and Max Liebermann, as well as
by historians and critics such as Theodor Mommsen and Georg
Brandes. A year later, in October 1883, the wider public had an
opportunity to view these paintings when they were included in
an exhibition of Impressionist works at the Berlin Galerie Fritz
Gurlitt. Thanks to the Bernsteins' enthusiasm, many Berliners
were afforded their first encounter with Impressionism.

Much of the creation and dissemination of modernism in
Berlin between 1890 and 1918, the years encompassed by this
exhibition and book, was characterized by personal convictions
and passions expressed in semi-public salons, culturally dissident
media, and alternative performance and exhibition spaces. Wilhelm
II (1859–1941), who became emperor in 1888, had a deep personal interest in issues of art and culture. He exerted his power
to its fullest in order to advance his own nationalist agenda and
conservative cultural tastes. Though avid in his advocacy of modern
science and technology, Wilhelm II (FIG. 1) fought vociferously
against the new artistic movements. Berlin's extraordinary emergence as a significant capital of modernism during the reign of
Wilhelm II must be viewed against the background of the
regime's intense hostility and active struggle against cultural
modernism.

How were dissident, unofficial artistic movements able to
succeed in making Berlin so central a place of modern culture?
Modernism's advocates devised inventive ways of circumventing
the emperor's control, exemplified by the National Gallery's acquisition of Impressionist and Post-Impressionist art during the
directorship of Hugo von Tschudi. In 1897, Tschudi was the first
museum director in the world to acquire a painting by Cézanne.
Only a few years previously, in 1894, the French state had refused
to accept a number of Impressionist works, including works
by Cézanne, that had been bequeathed by the artist Gustave
Caillebotte. Tschudi could not have succeeded without the financial backing of a critical group of patrons and collectors of modern
art who purchased or donated artworks to the National Gallery
that the state would never have approved.[1] For example, the Manet
still life visible on the left in the Bernstein's music room (see
FIG. 165) was bequeathed by Felicie Bernstein (1850–1908) to
the National Gallery. The Bernsteins were Jewish, as were many
of the collectors and patrons of modern art in Berlin, notably the
painter Max Liebermann and the industrialist Eduard Arnhold.[2]

Figure 1
Vilma Parlaghy
Kaiser Wilhelm II, 1895
Oil on canvas, 51^{15}/$_{16}$ x 35^{7}/$_{16}$ in.
(132 x 90 cm)
Nationalgalerie, Staatliche Museen
zu Berlin

The elective affinity between Jews and modern culture has been a controversial subject since the last third of the nineteenth century, and continues to provoke debate. The representation of Jews engaged in modernist movements in numbers far exceeding their proportion of the population has served both as a rallying cry for anti-Semites and a source of ethnic pride for Jews. The fantasy that modern culture is dominated by Jews was a centerpiece of anti-modern and anti-Semitic thought at the turn of the last century; it reached its obscene conclusions in Nazi cultural policy. The perception of an innate connection between Jews and modernism resulted in many non-Jewish modernists being labeled as Jewish—for example, in the "Degenerate Art" exhibitions mounted during the Third Reich. In contemporary America, where religious practice is no longer the lodestone of Jewish identity for many Jews, pride in the cultural and artistic achievements of Jews in the past provides a vehicle for a positive Jewish identification.

It is thus not surprising that this subject arouses passions on many fronts. Scholars, including those represented in this book, rightly point out that most Jews were not modernists and that many modernists were not Jews. Peter Gay made this point and cautioned against the reading of the Jew as the archetypal modernist in 1978: "It is sheer anti-Semitic tendentiousness, or philo-Semitic parochialism, to canvass the great phenomenon of Modernism from the vantage point of the Jewish question."[3] Moreover, the very terms used in the discussion are seen as problematic. In a recent exchange on the role of Jews in modernism in fin-de-siècle Vienna, Ernst Gombrich expressed his discomfort with the classification of people as "Jews" or "Gentiles," lamenting that "we lack a term to designate all individuals of Jewish ancestry, and thus we cannot but use basically racist terminology." Gombrich cited a text where the art writer and gallerist Serge Sabarsky imagined that Jewish patrons of art in Vienna "would turn in their graves if they knew of this classification, however well intentioned."[4]

How can we evaluate the role of Jews in modern Berlin culture without employing tainted discourse and at the same time avoiding a celebratory display of self-congratulation? And why venture into this minefield at all? First of all, it is important to state that there is nothing innately Jewish about an attraction to modernism; the role played by Jews in the creation and dissemination of modernism is rather a function of specific historical and sociological circumstances. Although these conditions are discussed in a number of the essays in this book, it seems worthwhile to outline them briefly here.

The emancipation of German Jewry—the granting of civic equality, although Jews were still excluded from certain professions, including the civil service—was a slow and gradual process, beginning in the late eighteenth century, and essentially complete only during the Weimar Republic. Furthermore, Jews were integrated into German society not through the political system, but through their economic success as well as their interaction with German culture. The ideology of this kind of cultural integration was known as *Bildung*, the individual pursuit of humanistic culture as an ideal. In contrast to the slow process of Jewish emancipation, the process of economic modernization in German society was the most rapid the world had seen up to that time. An essentially agrarian society in 1850 was transformed into one of the world's most advanced industrial nations by 1890. Because they had left their villages for the cities approximately one generation before other Germans, Jews played a central role in this process, and some Jews had become quite prominent in German economic life by the 1890s.

Despite the many opportunities available to Jews during this period, there were still important areas of German public life from which they were excluded, such as the court, the military, the state bureaucracy, and, to a large degree, the universities. Thus Jews tended to gravitate to the free professions. Denied access to the official public spheres, they turned to the less organized alternative public spheres that characterize urban life, such as the newspaper, the journal, the art gallery, the café, the theater, and the political group. At this juncture in German history, Jews were fully Germans, yet still social outsiders. The men and women involved in modernism were members of the transitional generations of German Jewry: far enough removed from the insular life of the traditional Jewish community, well-versed in German culture, yet not completely assimilated into German society. As Frederic Grunfeld has written:

> . . . it was precisely this problematic stratum of "marginal Jews"—the so-called *Grenzjuden*—which supplied most of the artists and intellectuals who helped to create the most exciting epoch in German intellectual history. The very precariousness of their position astride the two cultures gave them an extraordinary vantage point from which to survey the European cultural landscape.[5]

Georg Simmel offers an illuminating perspective on this issue in his essay "Der Fremde" (The Stranger) of 1908, defining the stranger "not . . . as the wanderer who comes today and goes tomorrow, but rather as the person who comes today and stays tomorrow." Simmel writes about the stranger as an individual who, although a full-fledged member of the group, is both "outside it and confronting it," and, as a result, attains a particular kind of objectivity that constitutes "a positive and specific kind of participation."[6]

Those Jews who embraced modernism certainly demonstrated an open-mindedness and a cosmopolitan attitude, perhaps resulting from an exposure to diverse cultures. Carl and Felicie Bernstein came from Russia, lived in Berlin, and had family in Paris, embodying a cosmopolitanism that was not unusual in Jewish families, which often included branches in different countries. This kind of internationalism was not common in Germany during that period, especially outside the aristocracy. Furthermore, any new movement provides an entry point for those members of society outside the elites. In Germany, a Jew could rise to full professor in the university only in the newest disciplines. In the United States, similar forces were at work; for example, until quite recently, Jews were well represented on the boards of museums of modern and contemporary art, but much less so on those of the major traditional art museums.

The initial impetus for this exhibition and book was a fascination with those Jews in turn-of-the-century Berlin who had an enormous impact on the creation and dissemination of modern art, literature, theater, and film, and our desire to make their work better known to an American audience: the work of artists Max Liebermann, Lesser Ury, Ludwig Meidner, and Jakob Steinhardt; Liebermann's role as founder of the Berlin Secession; the diverse activities of the cousins Paul and Bruno Cassirer as gallerists, publishers, and leaders of the Secession; the publisher, art dealer, poet, composer, and cultural impresario Herwarth Walden (born Georg Lewin), who promoted avant-garde art and literature through his journal *Der Sturm*, exhibitions mounted at his gallery of the same name and elsewhere in Europe, and through numerous publications, postcards, and performances; the poetry, dramas, prose works, and paintings of Else Lasker-Schüler (Walden's first wife), who stood at the center of a group of avant-garde artists and writers who met, performed, and exchanged ideas in the cafés of Berlin; the theatrical innovations of directors Otto Brahm and Max Reinhardt; the pioneers of early film, such as Ernst Lubitsch; and the quest for a modern Jewish art and culture undertaken by the philosopher Martin Buber and artists like Lesser Ury and E. M. Lilien. Whereas culture during the period of the Weimar Republic exerts a great deal of fascination in the United States and has been the subject of many exhibitions and publications, the Wilhelmine period, which was the true birthplace of German modernism, remains little known.

But as research progressed, the story that emerged was not one of solitary pioneers of modernism, but rather one of groups of talented individuals who had a passionate commitment to what was innovative and interesting, and, above all, to what represented quality in the arts; and who were determined to further that art and bring it to a wider public. In this project, Jews and non-Jews were partners, forming close professional and personal relationships. The Berlin Secession would hardly have been possible without the efforts of Max Liebermann and Paul and Bruno Cassirer, but it also would have been inconceivable without Walter Leistikow and August Gaul. Thus an effort was made in the exhibition and publication to show and discuss works of art that demonstrate the achievement of these artists and also document their close ties with one another; a good example is the intimate scene of the daughters of Paul Cassirer and Walter Leistikow drawing together, observed and recorded by Max Liebermann (FIG. 2).

Figure 2
Max Liebermann
**Suse Cassirer and Gerda
Leistikow**, n.d.
Charcoal on paper, 4¾ x 7⁵⁄₁₆ in.
(12 x 18.5 cm)
Collection of Peter Paret

It became apparent that modernism in Berlin was the product
of many unofficial places of cultural creation and presentation,
where people worked together to advance a shared goal. These
alternative spaces became sites in which individuals of disparate
backgrounds and inclinations would meet and exchange ideas.
Perhaps the most striking example of such an encounter is that
between the Jewish artist E. M. Lilien and the German nationalist
writer Börries Freiherr von Münchhausen in the context of the
group Die Kommenden (see FIG. 144); Münchhausen was
looking for an illustrator for his book of poems *Juda* (1900),
and engaged Lilien, who had recently arrived in Berlin from
Munich. It is one of the paradoxes of the Wilhelmine period
that Lilien established his reputation as the Zionist artist *par
excellence* by illustrating the ballads of a right-wing writer with
anti-Semitic leanings.

The decision thus was made to organize the exhibition and
catalogue around the "alternative" public spheres and spaces where
this culture was created and presented: art galleries, the Berlin
Secession, artistic and literary journals, the cafés, the cabarets and
experimental theaters, and the new medium of film. Furthermore,
Berlin itself, the recently emerged metropolis, became a character
in the drama of the exhibition. From the mid-nineteenth century,
Berlin experienced both physical and population growth at a dizzy-
ing pace. (The population grew from 412,154 in 1849 to 825,937
in 1871, when Berlin became capital of the Reich. By 1895 its
population had more than doubled, to 1.7 million; and in 1905 the
population had reached 2,040,148.) Alluding to the instability and
dynamism of the times, Karl Scheffler concluded his 1910 book on
the city with the critical observation that Berlin was fated "always
to be in the process of becoming and never to be."[7]

Both the turbulent atmosphere generated by such rapid change and the physical features of the new city, as well as the way in which urban dwellers interacted with their environment, exerted a profound influence on the creation of modern forms in the arts. The vitality and energy of urban life, its heterogeneity, and the rapid and manifold stimuli assaulting the city dweller in the form of crowds, urban transportation, and the barrage of images and texts from store displays, kiosks, newspapers, advertisements, and posters are reflected in the art and literature of Berlin during these years. The German sociologist Max Weber posited a connection between the technology of the modern city and modern artistic forms when he declared in 1910 that "the distinctive formal values of our modern artistic culture could only have come to be through the existence of the modern metropolis, the modern metropolis with its tramways, underground railways . . . display windows, concert halls, and restaurants, cafés, smokestacks . . . and the wild dance of impressions of sound and color."[8]

In the exhibition galleries of The Jewish Museum, we wanted to create spaces that suggest something of the flavor of the gallery, café, cabaret, and theater spaces of turn-of-the-century Berlin. The essays in this book also examine these spheres of cultural activity from multiple perspectives, exploring the development of new art and cultural forms, the role of Jews in Berlin's modernist movements, and their partnerships with other modernists—Jewish and gentile, German and non-German. A number of important figures are viewed in various contexts in different essays. Indeed, given the polymath talents as well as various cultural projects of people such as Liebermann, Cassirer, and Walden, the reader may gain a sense not only of the wide range of their activities, but also of the fluid network of relationships that supported the growth of modernism. For example, Max Liebermann is presented as a founder and organizer of the Secession, as an artist, and as one whose work was evaluated in the Wilhelmine era in terms of his identity as a Jew.

Paul Mendes-Flohr's essay, "The Berlin Jew as Cosmopolitan," analyzes the cosmopolitan culture of Berlin, examining the role of Jewish intellectuals and the ethic of *Bildung* in the emergence of modern ideas and the modern metropolis. His presentation of the discourse current at the time about Jews and modernism, particularly the debate surrounding Moritz Goldstein's article "The German-Jewish Parnassus" re-creates the context in which Jewish engagement with modernist movements occurred. Peter Paret's essay, "Modernism and the 'Alien Element' in German Art," explores the complex issue of Jews and German modernism from the standpoint of both critics and supporters. His nuanced discussion of what constituted modernism in the fine arts brings to light the cultural politics and critical aesthetic issues of the day, focusing on individuals and institutions that were leading creators or disseminators of modern art—in particular, the Berlin Secession and its president, the artist Max Liebermann, as well as the gallerists and publishers Paul and Bruno Cassirer. Sigrid

Bauschinger discusses the Cassirers from a slightly different perspective, that of modernism in literature—particularly its creation and promotion in Germany. Her essay also presents the extraordinary activities of the cultural impresario Herwarth Walden, through his journal and gallery *Der Sturm*, and examines the work and life of the poet Else Lasker-Schüler. The important roles of alternative groups, such as Die Kommenden and the Neue Gemeinschaft, as meeting places for artists and writers creating the new culture and the significance of the café as a site for artistic and intellectual exchange are major themes woven through her essay, "The Berlin Moderns: Else Lasker-Schüler and Café Culture." In "Images of Identity and Urban Life: Jewish Artists in Turn-of-the-Century Berlin," I discuss the Jewish and urban works of Max Liebermann, Lesser Ury, Ludwig Meidner, and Jakob Steinhardt in an attempt to understand the interaction between urbanism and Jewish identity in their artistic expression. In her essay, "Max Liebermann as a 'Jewish' Painter: The Artist's Reception in His Time," Chana Schütz addresses Liebermann's art in the context of the discourse current at the time on the nature of a "Jewish" artist and the relationship between art and Jewish identity. The notion of a modern Jewish art and culture, the movement supporting its emergence—the Jewish cultural renaissance—and the relationship of this movement both to Zionism and to German modernism is the subject of Inka Bertz's essay, "Jewish Renaissance—Jewish Modernism." One of the least-examined alternative spheres in the Wilhelmine period has been that of the salon, the subject of Barbara Hahn's essay, "Encounters at the Margins: Jewish Salons around 1900." Led primarily by cultivated Jewish women of the upper bourgeoisie, the salons presented an opportunity for artists, writers, and intellectuals to congregate and exchange ideas. Women played a prominent role in the organization and activities of these cultural spaces, which provided a significant alternative to formal sites, such as the university, from which women were excluded by virtue of their gender or religion. Finally, Peter Jelavich's essay, "Performing High and Low: Jews in Modern Theater, Cabaret, Revue, and Film," focuses on pioneers of the performing arts such as Otto Brahm, Max Reinhardt, and Ernst Lubitsch. In addition to exploring issues of modernity within these innovative forms of art and entertainment, Jelavich considers the ways in which themes of the metropolis and Jewish identity were expressed in these media. Jelavich's discussion of Jewish theater audiences, who supported modernist performances regardless of whether they actually liked the results, offers another important gloss on the relationship of Jews to German modernism.

Throughout the book, the tensions in Wilhelmine culture between Jewish assimilation and anti-Semitism, between opportunity and restriction, between acculturation and a lingering sense of "otherness" and difference, are brought to light.

In the final analysis, the Jewish support and engagement in modernism may not have been primarily an issue of modernism per se, but rather of a personal commitment to quality and to the art that moved and inspired. This is evident in Paul Cassirer's response to the painter Carl Vinnen's pamphlet *Ein Protest deutscher Künstler* (1911), a protest of German artists against what they viewed as the manipulation of the German art market in favor of modern French art. In his contribution to the pamphlet entitled *Deutsche und französische Kunst* (German and French Art, 1911), Cassirer replied:

> Why did I have to speculate with French paintings? Tell me that, Herr Vinnen. Why not just as easily with German works? Wouldn't that have been more pleasant for me? I'll answer the question: because I regard bringing French art to Germany as a cultural deed. But even that wasn't the real reason. Simply, because I loved Manet; because I recognized Monet, Sisley and Pissarro as powerful artists, because Degas was among the greatest masters, and Cézanne the bearer of a philosophy of life.[9]

Apart from the public advocacy of personal artistic passion and taste, another theme that can be traced through this book is the struggle to define Jewish identity in the modern period and to find an appropriate artistic language with which to express this modern identity. It could be argued that an attraction to modernism was itself an expression of the new possibilities available to Jews in post-emancipation Germany, and that embracing the new art constituted a rejection of tradition that was also a declaration of emancipation from the bonds of traditional Judaism and the Jewish community. Yet it is noteworthy how much of the work produced by Jews during this period explicitly addressed the issue of Jewish identity. Else Lasker-Schüler used word and image to construct elaborate Orientalist fantasies in which she and her friends are the dramatis personae. The artists E. M. Lilien and Hermann Struck also looked to the East—to the people and landscapes of Palestine—for images of authentic Jews. Lesser Ury mined the Hebrew Bible for models of a new heroic Jewish type. Max Liebermann's few paintings with Jewish themes portray the intimate sphere of family life or capture the bustling activity of the Jewish Quarter in Amsterdam. Each of these artistic idioms found its inspiration in a distant time and place. It was only in the "popular" arts of film and cabaret that artists seemed ready to construct a Jewish identity of the here-and-now. In his directorial debut, *Schuhpalast Pinkus* (*Pinkus's Shoe Palace*, 1916), Ernst Lubitsch stars in the role of Sally Pinkus, a Jew in contemporary Berlin who employs his wits and a keen understanding of marketing to make his fortune in the retail shoe business. Lubitsch's characterization of Sally Pinkus incorporates gestures, language, and types of behavior that were part of the repertoire of Jewish stereotyping; it is Lubitsch's genius to turn these negative stereotypes on their head by presenting them as positive traits. Lubitsch demonstrates a self-confidence that is familiar from our own time: Sally Pinkus in 1916 Berlin would not have been out of place in one of the "Jewish" skits of "Saturday Night Live" shown in New York in the 1980s.

Lubitsch created the character of Pinkus in the midst of the First World War, which irrevocably brought Wilhelmine culture to an end. Wilhelm II's Jewish subjects greeted the outbreak of the war with the same enthusiasm and patriotic fervor as other Germans. The small number of pacifists notwithstanding, most Germans saw the war as an opportunity to unify a society that had become divided along class, economic, and ideological lines. For Jews in particular, the war promised to eliminate the remaining barriers to their complete integration into German society; Jews fighting alongside their fellow Germans, they believed, would eradicate lingering anti-Semitism. Max Liebermann signed the "Declaration of the Ninety-Three," which rejected the Allied charge of German aggression, and subsequently received his first decoration from the Prussian state. Despite his age and deteriorating health, Paul Cassirer volunteered for military service in August 1914 and received the Iron Cross for bravery the following month; he is depicted as the officer on the right in Max Beckmann's *Two Officers* of 1915 (FIG. 3).

The artists associated with the Berlin Secession expressed their allegiance to the national cause in a new journal founded by Cassirer in August 1914—*Kriegszeit* (Wartime)—in which artists interpreted the war. As the war progressed, *Kriegszeit* depicted the horrors endured by the soldiers and the anxieties of those on the homefront; yet it retained its patriotic tone. But by 1916 the stalemate on the Western Front, the mounting casualties, and the growing economic crisis had produced a shift in mood. Demobilized and returned to Berlin in 1916, Cassirer

Figure 3
Max Beckmann
Two Officers (Zwei Offiziere), 1915
Drypoint, 4¼ x 7 in. (10.8 x 17.8 cm)
Collection of Peter Paret

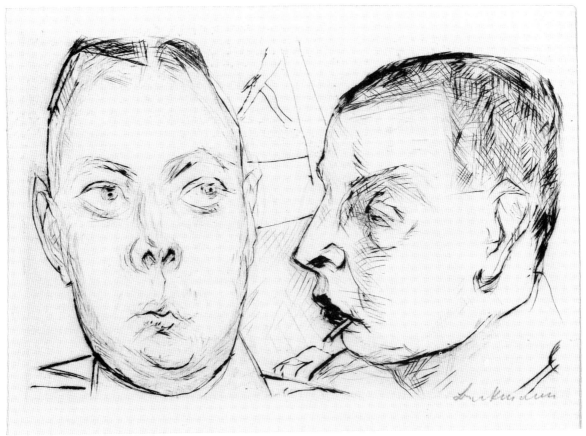

Der Bildermann

Herausgegeben
von
Paul Cassirer

N⁰ 18

20. Dezember, 1916
ERSTER JAHRGANG

DONA NOBIS PACEM!

Figure 4
Ernst Barlach
Dona Nobis Pacem!
From *Der Bildermann* 18,
20 December 1916
Lithograph, 16 x 13¼ in.
(40.6 x 33.6 cm)
Print Collection, The Miriam and
Ira D. Wallach Division of Art,
Prints and Photographs.
The New York Public Library.
Astor, Lenox, and Tilden Foundations

decided to replace *Kriegszeit* with a new periodical, called *Der Bildermann*, that would communicate a desire for peace. *Der Bildermann* included a variety of works depicting daily life in Germany, pacifist appeals, and trenchant social commentary. Eventually it ran into trouble with the censors; the issue of 20 December 1916, with Ernst Barlach's poignant prayer for peace "Dona Nobis Pacem!" (FIG. 4), was the last to appear.

The war decimated the ranks of the avant-garde in Europe; Franz Marc and August Macke, who had been closely associated with *Der Sturm*, were both killed on the Western Front. Ludwig Meidner and Jakob Steinhardt returned from active duty, but their wartime experiences left an indelible impression (see FIG. 198). Meidner's *Battle* of 1914 (PLATE 7) is a scathing critique of the war. For many Jewish soldiers who served on the Eastern Front, the war unexpectedly brought German Jews into direct contact with the shtetl communities of Eastern Europe. This encounter with an unassimilated Orthodox Jewish community served as a catalyst for a return to more traditional forms of Jewish expression, especially pronounced in the art of Jakob Steinhardt. (Compare, for example, FIG. 114 with FIG. 156.)

For the Jews of Germany, the greatest disillusionment was caused by the 1916 census of Jews serving in the army—the *Judenzählung*. Ostensibly taken in response to allegations that Jews were shirking military service, the census confirmed that Jews were in fact performing their patriotic duty. When the army refused to release the exonerating data, German Jews experienced a profound sense of betrayal. It was as if the bubble of the Jewish-German symbiosis had been burst.

The end of the war ushered in a new chapter in German history and in the relationship of Jews to their country. On the one hand, with the end of the empire and the introduction of democratic reforms, the last legal restrictions to the full participation of Jews in German society were lifted; it was only in the Weimar period, for example, that Liebermann could be elected president of the Prussian Academy of Arts. On the other hand, political divisions and extreme nationalist tendencies had been exacerbated by the war and by Germany's defeat; expressions of anti-Semitism became increasingly virulent and violent. These developments would have severe repercussions for the Weimar Republic and for the future of Germany and the Jews.

Notes

1. For the specific manner in which each of these works was acquired, see *Manet bis Van Gogh: Hugo von Tschudi und der Kampf um die Moderne*, ed. Johann Georg Prinz von Hohenzollern and Peter-Klaus Schuster, exh. cat. (Berlin and Munich: Nationalgalerie and Neue Pinakothek, 1996); for the Cézanne acquisition, see cat. no. 59.

2. See Barbara Paul, "Drei Sammlungen französischer impressionistischer Kunst im kaiserlichen Berlin: Bernstein, Liebermann, Arnhold," *Zeitschrift des deutschen Vereins für Kunstwissenschaft*, 42, no. 3 (1988): 11–30. Paul notes (p. 11) that nearly all Berlin collectors of Impressionism were Jewish.

3. Peter Gay, *Freud, Jews and Other Germans: Masters and Victims in Modernist Culture* (Oxford and New York: Oxford University Press, 1978), p. 21.

4. Ernst Gombrich, "The Visual Arts in Vienna circa 1900: Reflections on the Jewish Catastrophe," *The Art Newspaper*, 73 (September 1997): 28, 29. Gombrich's remarks were made in response to an article by Steven Beller, "Was bedeutet es 'Wien 1900' als eine jüdische Stadt zu bezeichnen," in *Zeitgeschichte*, 23, no. 7–8 (1996): 274–80.

5. Frederic V. Grunfeld, *Prophets Without Honour: A Background to Freud, Kafka, Einstein and Their World* (New York: McGraw-Hill, 1979, 1980), p. 5.

6. Georg Simmel, "The Stranger," in *The Sociology of Georg Simmel*, trans. and ed. Kurt H. Wolff (New York: The Free Press, 1964), pp. 402–4.

7. Karl Scheffler, *Berlin: Ein Stadtschicksal* (1910; reprint Berlin: Fannei & Walz, 1989), p. 219.

8. Cited in Lothar Müller, "The Beauty of the Metropolis: Toward an Aesthetic Urbanism in Turn-of-the-Century Berlin," in *Berlin: Culture and Metropolis*, ed. Charles W. Haxthausen and Heidrun Suhr (Minneapolis: University of Minnesota Press, 1990), p. 43.

9. Paul Cassirer in *Deutsche und französische Kunst*, ed. Alfred Walter Heymel (Munich: Piper, 1911); cited in Peter Paret, *The Berlin Secession: Modernism and Its Enemies in Imperial Germany* (Cambridge, Mass.: Harvard University Press, 1980), p. 195.

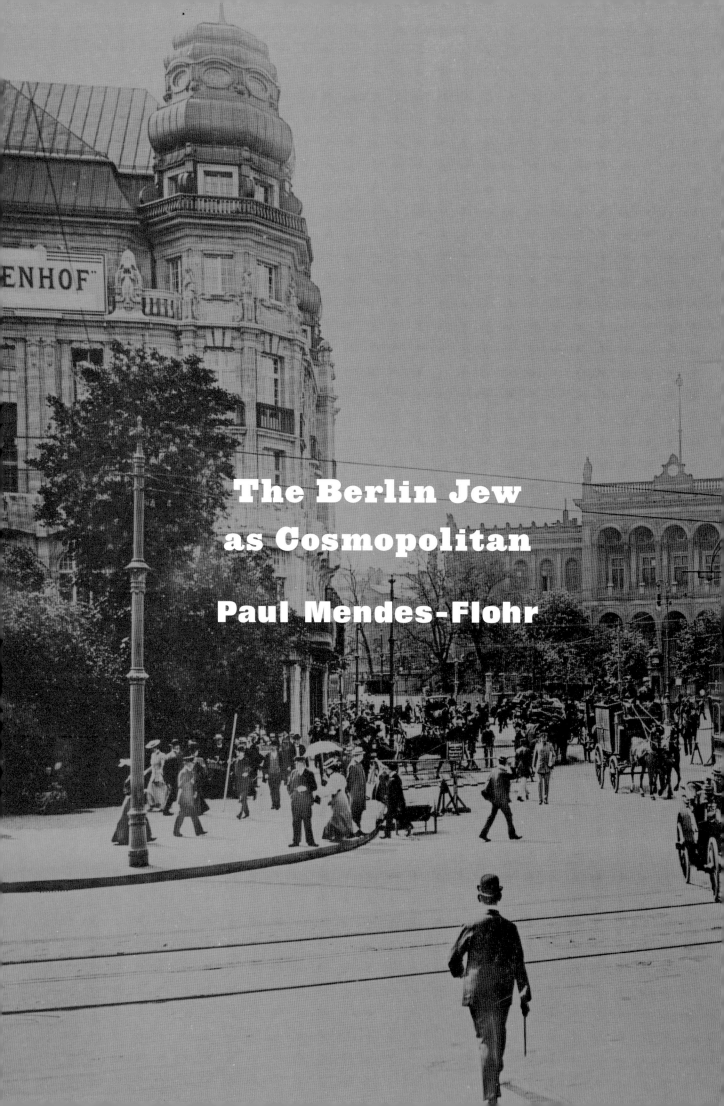

The Berlin Jew
as Cosmopolitan

Paul Mendes-Flohr

With the dismantling of the ghetto, the Jews of Central Europe rushed to drink of the waters of German culture. Emancipated Jewry's passionate adoption of the ethic of German *Bildung*— the studied cultivation of high culture and aesthetic refinement— also elicited a dedicated pursuit of higher education. They did so in numbers so disproportionate to their actual representation in the population of Germany and elsewhere in Central Europe, and with such success, that Albert Einstein is said to have remarked that it was as though the Israelites had spent the past two millennia of the exile preparing for their university entrance exams.[1] The march of Jews on the citadels of German culture gave birth to another quip: "Doktor ist ein jüdischer Vorname" (Doctor is a Jewish first name).[2]

The Ideal of *Bildung*

The energetic entrance of the Jews into the *Bildungsbürgertum*— the educated bourgeoisie—of Central Europe witnessed a spectacular efflorescence of Jewish creativity. Under the aegis of German *Kultur*, Jews contributed to all spheres of modern culture. Children and grandchildren of rabbinic scholars or of impoverished peddlers often found themselves at the forefront of European science and letters. But cruel misfortune overtook German Jewry: less than 150 years after the death of Moses Mendelssohn, who inaugurated Jewry's romance with German culture, demonic forces arose, determined to expunge the Jews from the midst of "Aryan" civilization. The flower that once was German Jewry was torn at its roots and trampled underfoot with a Manichaean fury. In view of the Holocaust, nostalgic sentiment and an inconsolable grief have led many to extol and unwittingly mystify the cultural achievements of German Jewry. Celebrating the Jewish intellectuals of Germany and Central Europe, George Steiner hails them as "meta-rabbis," observing that:

> The Jewish element had been largely dominant in the
> revolutions of thought and of sensibility experienced
> by Western man over these last one hundred and twenty
> years. . . . Without Marx, Freud, or Kafka, without
> Schönberg or Wittgenstein, the spirit of modernity,
> the reflexes of argument and uncertainty whereby
> we conduct our inner lives, would not be conceivable.[3]

The treatment of the Jewish intellectuals of modern Germany and Central Europe as the prophets of modernity—or as one study has it, "prophets without honor"[4]—is animated by an understandable affection and a profound sense of loss; but it is hardly illuminating. For one, this approach, shared by many, makes the facile assumption that "Jewish genius" was unique— and somehow glosses over the Kants, the Hegels, the Nietzsches, the Jungs, the Thomas Manns, the Beethovens, the Bruckners. Moreover, in eulogizing German Jewry's cultural and intellectual creativity as a singular accomplishment, it tacitly, and sometimes

(opposite)
(Detail) Potsdamer Platz, 1907
Photograph: Max Missmann

not so tacitly, appeals to the allegedly superior intelligence of the Jews. On purely methodological grounds, one is obliged to endorse Peter Gay's demand, when in a fit of exasperation he exclaimed: "There is a historical and sociological study that desperately needs to be undertaken: that of stupid Jews."[5]

The ramified cultural achievements of German Jewry nonetheless demand an explanation. The poet Heinrich Heine suggested that it had something to do with Judaism's faith in a transcendent, universal deity, which engendered a cosmopolitan sensibility. In an essay from 1832 he observed:

> Europe is raising itself up to the Jews. I say "raising itself up," for from the very beginning the Jews bore within themselves the modern principle, which is only today becoming palpably manifest among the peoples of Europe. . . . The Jews adhered only to the law, the abstract idea, like our more recent cosmopolitan republicans, who respect as their highest good not the land of their birth or the person of their prince, but only the law. Cosmopolitanism, it might truly be said, sprang from the soil of Judea; and Christ, who . . . was truly a Jew, had actually established a propaganda of world citizenship [*eine Propaganda des Weltbürgertums*].[6]

Although these observations are not free of apologetic hyperbole, they serve to focus our attention on the affinity between the Jewish intellectual and the cosmopolitan spirit that distinguished German urban culture.

Jews and the Cosmopolitan Spirit

In the heat of a polemic on the sudden prominence of the Jews in the urban landscape of Germany, the nineteenth-century historian Heinrich von Treitschke—who took a decidedly negative view of the Jews' *embourgeoisement*—is reported to have snapped that one knows one has entered a city when one sees a synagogue.[7] This ironic comment was an oblique reference to Berlin's elegant Oranienburger Strasse synagogue, whose towering gilded dome, crowned with a Star of David, claimed a commanding position in the city's skyline (FIG. 5). In the presence of Chancellor Bismarck and a legion of Berlin's notables, the splendid house of worship was dedicated in September 1866 (FIG. 6). Just a few days later, the city would celebrate the triumphant procession of Prussia's troops returning from their victorious battles against Austria, concluding a war that heralded the unification of Germany under the tutelage of Prussia and the royal house of the Hohenzollerns.[8] The dedication of the synagogue thus marked both the emergence of Berlin as the prosperous capital of the new state—the Second German Empire—and the coming of age of the city's Jewish community, whose rapid growth was prominently associated with the city's meteoric rise from a provincial backwater to a vibrant metropolis.

Figure 5
Exterior of the New Jewish Synagogue
(Neue Synagoge),
Oranienburger Strasse, Berlin, 1866

In the decade from 1864 to 1874 alone, Berlin's Jewish population grew from 24,000 to 45,000—a number all the more striking when one recalls that, in 1812, the city's Jewish community numbered only 3,000 souls. The Jewish population would continue to grow with that of the ever burgeoning city.[9] However, their proportion of the city's general population would never exceed 4 percent. Nonetheless, their impact on the economic and intellectual life of Berlin far exceeded the limits of their demographic representation. It was, in fact, the widely perceived disproportionate role of the Jews in the commercial and intellectual life of Berlin—symbolized by the Oranienburger Strasse synagogue—that clearly irked Treitschke.

The quasi-Moorish architecture of the Oranienburger Strasse synagogue (FIG. 6)—which was intended to point to the Golden Age of Jewish life in Islamic Spain, underscoring the ebullient hopes of the Berlin Jewish community—also betrayed in Treitschke's eyes the alien, essentially Oriental, character of the Jews. Indeed, the charge was often made that the Jews were "Asiatic" interlopers. In the first decade of the twentieth century, the social and economic historian Werner Sombart added a special twist to this indictment by arguing that despite their remarkable assimilation, the Jews remained true to their Oriental, nomadic origins, which paradoxically rendered them an urban people *par excellence*.

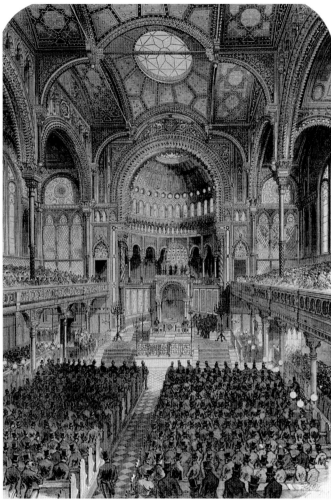

Figure 6
Dedication of the New Jewish Synagogue
(Neue Synagoge),
Oranienburger Strasse, Berlin
From the *Illustrated London News*, 1866

The Jew as Asiatic Interloper

Identifying urban civilization with commercial capitalism and abstract, irreverent intellectuality, Sombart argued in a monograph on the Jews and modern economic life that the harsh, arid climes of their desert origins—reinforced by their nomadic peregrinations in the Diaspora—prepared the Jews for the contemporary city with its rootless, restless commercial and cultural activity.[10] The nomadic shepherd, he stressed—unlike the Germanic farmer, who is concerned with the *quality* of his crops—has a *quantitative* interest in his flock, and thus naturally seeks the incessant reproduction of his sheep. This, Sombart claimed, is the root idea of the capitalistic devotion to "unlimited production."[11] For Sombart, the Jews' desert origins actuated a "chain of tendencies that stressed results, which was to a large extent responsible for the utilization of money for lending purposes, and, indeed, for the whole capitalistic nexus."[12]

Similarly, Sombart argued that the Jews' nomadic provenance provided an explanation for "their extreme intellectuality in which all their peculiarities are rooted."[13] For their primordial desert abode with the "sharp outlines of its landscape in hot, dry countries, its brilliant sunshine and its deep shadows, its clear starlit nights and stunted vegetation" encouraged abstract intellectuality.[14] The seemingly boundless extent of the desert imbued the Jews with a sense of "infinite horizons," which, Sombart reasoned, encouraged both material avariciousness and insatiable intellectual curiosity.[15] The desert's lack of vegetation, Sombart further reasoned, dictated a dependence on the artificial, the contrived. Thus Sombart, positing that their life as nomadic shepherds led the Jews to disdain physical labor, coined the slick epigram—employing two alliterative Hebrew and Yiddish terms—that in the desert the Jews became a people of "*moach* rather than *koach*," of brain rather than brawn.[16] What ultimately characterizes Jewish intellectuality, declared Sombart, is its superficiality: indeed, it is as shiftless as the desert sands. Their intellectual rootlessness, combined with a nomadic adaptability, enables the Jews to place themselves "in another's position,"[17] a capacity for empathy that allows them to excel in journalism, jurisprudence, and theater—the three most distinctive and, to his mind, most troubling expressions of urban culture.

Sombart's jaundiced, sophistic arguments thinly veiled an anti-Semitic animus: the Jews are incorrigibly Jews, an Asiatic clan bent on insinuating themselves through the ploys of urban civilization and subverting the culture and life of the native population. With the learned inflections of a scholar, Sombart joined the chorus of ethnic Germans (despite the fact that his ancestors were Huguenots!) claiming that no degree of assimilation and *Kultur* could possibly dissimulate the fact that the Jews remained fundamentally alien to the pristine ethos and values of the German people. Yet when he first published his thesis in a series of articles in a Berlin newspaper, Sombart was inundated with invitations to lecture on the subject before audiences "recruited mainly from the Jewish intelligentsia" of the city.[18] They were apparently prepared to dismiss or overlook his anti-Semitic innuendos, for they were eager to discuss what had been increasingly regarded as an urgent issue, namely, the apparent dominance by Jews of Germany's, especially Berlin's, commerce and culture.

The issue came to a head in what came to be known as the "*Kunstwart* debate." In March 1912, the prestigious cultural review *Der Kunstwart* (Guardian of Art) published an article entitled "The German-Jewish Parnassus." Written by a young Jewish scholar of German literature, Moritz Goldstein, the article provoked a ramified debate that reverberated for several years throughout the German press. Goldstein obviously touched a raw nerve when he asserted: "We Jews are administrating the spiritual property of a nation that denies our right and our ability to do so."[19]

> Among ourselves we have the impression that we speak
> as Germans to Germans—such is our impression.

BERLINER
TAGEBLATT
MIT·ULK·ZEITGEIST
TECHNISCHE RUNDSCHAU
DEUTSCHE LESEHALLE
MITTHEILUNGEN ÜBER LANDWIRTHSCHAFT
GARTENBAU·U·HAUSWIRTHSCHAFT

But though we may after all feel totally German, the others feel us to be totally un-German. We may now be called Max Reinhardt and have inspired the [German] stage to an unanticipated revival, or as a Hugo von Hofmannsthal introduced a new poetic style to replace the exhausted style of Schiller; we may call this German, but the others call it Jewish; they detect in us something "Asiatic" and miss the German sensibility [*germanisches Gemüt*], and should they—reluctantly—feel obliged to acknowledge our achievement, they wish we would achieve less.[20]

In an editorial presenting a selection of the ninety or so replies—many lengthy manuscripts, mostly by Jews—elicited by "The German-Jewish Parnassus," the editor of *Der Kunstwart*, Ferdinand Avenarius, conspicuously ignored Goldstein's implied criticism of German society's failure to accept Jewish intellectuals as fellow Germans. Instead, he chose to endorse with manifest enthusiasm Goldstein's sweeping characterization of the Jews' putative domination of German culture.

Focusing on Berlin, Avenarius noted that the press (see FIG. 7) was all but a Jewish monopoly and the theater as well—with virtually all the directors and as many of the actors being Jews. He was likewise quick to agree with Goldstein that the musical life of Germany's capital would be unthinkable without the Jews. As a nephew of Richard Wagner, Avenarius, one would suspect, probably did not regard this as a laudable development. He also approvingly cited Goldstein's observation that "even the study of German literature seems to be passing into Jewish hands . . . [and] that not a few guardians of German art realize to their chagrin how many Jews there are among the 'German poets.'"[21] Similarly, in amending an alleged oversight by Goldstein, Avenarius noted that art and art galleries in Germany were increasingly Jewish. Disassociating himself from anti-Semitism, Avenarius nonetheless seemed to have had no compunctions in appealing to popular stereotypes of Jews to explain their emergence as the "administrators of German culture." Asserting that this role is ultimately a matter of power and that "wealth is power," he supports his thesis by simply reminding his readers that "the best seats in the theater, the most luxurious clothes, and the most expensive homes belong to the Jews."[22] Seemingly unable to control his appeal to stereotypic arguments, the otherwise cultured editor adds that he "recently heard claimed that the luxury cars of the train from Berlin to the Riviera are nigh-exclusively occupied by Jews."

Goldstein himself surely did not wish to pander to anti-Semitic sentiment, conceding at the very outset of his article that by raising the issue as he did in the general press, he would doubtlessly tap anti-Jewish feelings. But he was determined to address his fellow *Literatenjuden*, the Jewish intellectuals, and felt he had no other effective forum. Indeed, he turned to *Der Kunstwart*, dedicated to conservative opinion, only after having his article rejected three times by liberal organs that apparently deemed it inappropriate to broach such a delicate issue.[23] Goldstein was undeterred, however. Borne by a sense of urgency, he sought to awaken his fellow Jewish writers from what he believed to be a dangerous complacency and even a studied indifference to "the intolerable and undignified ambiguity" of their position within German society, which viewed their often commanding role in German culture with, at best, a strained tolerance.[24]

The cultural ascendency of German Jewry may have made Germans, Jews and non-Jews alike, nervous, but, from afar, it fascinated many. In an essay of 1919, the American social philosopher Thorstein Veblen lauded what he called "the intellectual pre-eminence of Jews in Modern Europe."[25] With his eye particularly on Germany, he asserted—with palpable admiration—that Jews "count for more than their proportionate share in the intellectual life of Western civilization; and they count particularly among the vanguard, the pioneers, the uneasy guild of pathfinders and iconoclasts, in science, scholarship, and institutional change and growth."[26]

Grenzjuden: At the Boundaries Between Cultures

Postulating that skepticism is the cognitive ground of intellectual innovation, Veblen argued that assimilation placed "gifted" Jews at the margins between cultures—that of their ethnic origin and that of Europe—rendering them ingrained skeptics. There, at the boundary of two disparate cultural universes, they are unable to maintain unquestioned allegiance to either. Upon liberation from the ghetto, Jews embraced the culture of Europe; they learned its languages and adopted its universe of discourse—and yet they remained apart. They were, in a sense, simultaneously insiders and outsiders; while at home in European culture, their origins as outsiders induced a lingering cognitive dissonance, an abiding irreverence that allowed them to assume a position at the forefront of modern inquiry and imagination.

In German, one spoke of *Grenzjuden*—literally "Jews at the border," straddling the boundaries between cultures—which in effect became a popular code word for Jewish cosmopolitans. The Berlin sociologist Georg Simmel (FIG. 8) seemed to have the *Grenzjuden* in mind when he penned the essay "Der Fremde" (The Stranger).[27] A denizen of the modern city, he observes, the stranger is characterized precisely by the paradoxical situation of being both insider and outsider; "the stranger" is thus a person who is "near and far at the same time."[28] Although a "full-fledged member" of the group, the stranger's membership in the group "involves both being outside it and confronting it."[29]

Figure 8
Georg Simmel, ca. 1915
Collection of
Paul Mendes-Flohr

Simmel's essay "The Stranger," published in 1908, is widely viewed as an autobiographical statement. Although a child of parents who had converted before his birth to Christianity, he was universally regarded as a typical Berlin Jewish intellectual. One of the first sociologists to address the specific realities of the modern urban experience, he was consistently treated as an outsider by the German academic establishmment, and not necessarily because of anti-Semitism—which certainly was a factor—but also because they discerned in his work a tendency to affirm the rootless, indeed, cosmopolitan culture of the city. His reflections on "the stranger" may thus be seen as a defense, by way of sociological explanation, of the bold new breed of men and women known as urban intellectuals. Simmel duly cast his reflections on "the stranger" in formal, abstract sociological categories, with no specific reference to intellectuals or Jews (other than some telling asides about the Jews being the classical strangers of medieval Europe). He speaks of the stranger—in contrast to the wanderer, tourist, or inhabitant of a distant land—as one "who comes today and stays tomorrow."[30] The stranger becomes a member of the "host" society, yet remains apart, bearing the marks of his origin. A unique "synthesis of nearness and distance,"[31] the stranger is integrated into the social and cultural fabric of the host society through sharing its "general human qualities";[32] presumably, Simmel means those values and modes of thought borne by enlightened high culture with its decidedly universal orientation. The stranger, however, does not connect "organically" with the host society "through established ties of kinship [and] locality";[33] that is, although the stranger is integrated into the "culture"— or rather, the high culture—of the host society, he is excluded, by choice or rejection, from its primordial culture, or culture of origin. With respect to the latter, the "organic" realm of ethnic sentiment, memory, and aspirations, the stranger remains apart. Because the stranger is "not radically committed to the unique ingredients and peculiar tendencies of the group,"[34] he is able to consider the group's passions and attendant agendas with "objectivity." The stranger is, accordingly, "freer, practically and theoretically; he surveys conditions with less prejudice; his criteria for them are more general and more objective ideals; he is not tied down in his action by habit, piety, and precedent."[35]

The stranger—the Jewish intellectual?—thus often questions notions and objectives that the group tends to regard as self-evident and self-legitimizing. The stranger is understandably deemed a "rebel," one who challenges conventional wisdom and values. There is perforce a persistent tension between the stranger and the host society. At its core, Simmel underscores, this tension is due to the paradoxical fact that by highlighting the "general and more objective" aspects of culture—that is, what is presumably common to all humanity—the stranger, in effect, "stresses that which is not common."[36] Despite his nearness, the stranger thus remains an outsider, a disruptive and hence threatening element in society.

Simmel's somewhat gnomic reference to the stranger's preference for the "general" as opposed to the specifics of primordial culture becomes somewhat more concrete when his reflections are placed in the context of the German society in which he lived. Germany of the Kaiserreich was a society rife with contradictions. It had an advanced and vibrant industrial economy, which in other countries favored the rise of the middle class and liberal political institutions. The dominant political culture of Imperial Germany, however, remained in the hands of the nobility, which placed pre-eminent value on loyalty to the emperor, honor, service, obedience, and the integrity of the German *Volk*—the community of ethnic Germans, to which Romantics ascribed distinctive primordial, if not racial, qualities.[37] Imperial Germany's constellation of power and political values isolated the nation's middle classes, to which the Jews overwhelmingly belonged. Middle-class Jews were further isolated by their single devotion to the ethic of *Bildung*, education in the broad sense of a pursuit of humanistic culture and personal cultural refinement.

Figure 9
Schlossbrücke with view of the Altes Museum, Tiergarten, and Berliner Dom, 1909
Photograph: Max Missmann

Since the Enlightenment—and later, especially under the tutelage of the likes of Goethe, Herder, and Wilhelm von Humboldt—the ambit of *Bildung* was regarded as universal, the assumption being that all human experience is relevant to one's own self-understanding and personal dignity. Thus, in its initial articulation, *Bildung* was grounded in a vision of a "neutral society," a cultural and social space that regarded matters of ethnic origin and religious background to be utterly irrelevant to one's qualifications to enter that space.[38] In principle, *Bildung* and its supporting social structures were open to one and all. Needless to say, Jews were deeply attracted to this inclusive vision of a neutral society.

The appeal of this vision was strengthened by the fact that its principal advocates were also often regarded as the allies of the Jews in their struggle for political emancipation. Even before being granted civic parity and equal rights, as already noted, the Jews eagerly joined the *Bildungsbürgertum*, the educated middle class, which included not only those who earned their social status by virtue of their educational attainments but also those who identified with the values of *Bildung*. And middle-class Jews are said to have become the most passionate supporters of high culture. They filled the concert halls and theaters, purchased art, assembled in their homes libraries honoring the canon of educated Germany, and provided their children with the finest humanistic education.

Figure 10
Potsdamer Platz, 1907
Photograph: Max Missmann

Although the *Bildungsbürgertum* established itself in German society, it did not assume the formative political role that people—certainly Jews—would have expected. Social and political forces conspired to restrict its influence in determining the institutions of governance. Increasingly, Germany's political culture was ruled by those beholden to parochial, national, or, rather, *völkisch* considerations, which even penetrated the ranks of the *Bildungsbürgertum*. Naturally, Jews were among the staunchest defenders of the cosmopolitan—the open, tolerant, "neutral"—image of *Bildung*.

Perhaps there was no more eloquent defense of the world of *Bildung* than that launched by Sigmund Freud. In the midst of the First World War, he defiantly celebrated the cosmopolitan spirit of a Europe that seemed mortally threatened by a xenophobic fury unleashed by the conflict. Evoking the image of the modern museum, which displays works of art and treasures drawn from a multitude of diverse cultures as testimony to the inherent cosmopolitanism of the human spirit, he mused:

> Relying on [a] unity among the civilized peoples [of Europe], countless men and women have exchanged their native home for a foreign one, and made their existence dependent on the intercommunications between friendly nations. Moreover, anyone who was not by stress of circumstance confined to one spot could create for himself out of all the advantages and attractions of these civilized countries a new and wider fatherland, in which he could move about without hindrance or suspicion. . . . This new fatherland was a museum for him, too, filled with all the treasures that the artists of civilized humanity had in the successive centuries created and left behind. As he wandered from one gallery to another in this museum, he could recognize with impartial appreciation what varied types of perfection a mixture of blood, the course of history, and the special quality of their mother-earth had produced among his compatriots in this wider sense. . . . Nor should we forget that each of these citizens of the civilized world had created for himself a "Parnassus" and a "School of Athens" of his own. From among the great thinkers, writers and artists of all nations he had chosen those to whom he considered he owed the best of what he had been able to achieve in enjoyment and understanding of life, and he had venerated them along with the immortal ancients as well as with the familiar masters of his own tongue. None of these great men had seemed to him foreign because they spoke another language—neither the incomparable explorer of human passions, nor the intoxicated worshiper of beauty, nor the powerful and menacing prophet, nor the subtle satirist; and he never reproached himself

on that account for being a renegade towards his own nation and his beloved mother tongue.[39]

The eclipse of a cosmopolitan Europe wrought by the First World War understandably engendered profound disillusionment. For Freud, it actually marked the end of an illusion: "Strictly speaking [our disappointment] is not justified, for it consists in the destruction of an illusion. [For] in reality our fellow-citizens have not sunk so low as we feared, because they had never risen so high as we believed."[40]

Despite this somber conclusion, Freud—like countless other Jews—remained true to the ethic of *Bildung*, with its cosmopolitan vision as well as commitment to the project of advancing human knowledge beyond all borders wrought by prejudice, moral lassitude, national ego, and intellectual conceits.

Der Jude and the Jewish Renaissance

As Freud penned his reflections on the war, a fellow Vienna-born Jew, Martin Buber (FIG. 11), was engaged in planning a journal that would seek to reaffirm the cultural values associated with *Bildung* while addressing the specific problems faced by German Jewry underscored by the parochial emotions and attitudes engendered—or at least, exacerbated—by the war. Inaugurated in April 1916, the Berlin journal was called *Der Jude* (The Jew)—a striking name, which with one bold sweep was meant to capture the seemingly paradoxical commitments of the journal to assert Jewish pride while affirming the ethic of *Bildung*.

Buber's decision to found the journal at this juncture—he had contemplated it more than a decade earlier—was prompted by an unanticipated eruption of anti-Semitism that rudely disrupted the beguiling fraternal mood that had overtaken Germany during the initial hours of the First World War. Heeding the Kaiser's dramatic calls issued with the outbreak of hostilities, for all his subjects, regardless of religious and political affiliation, to unite in defense of the fatherland, Germany seemed united as never before. The flush of patriotism seemed to fuse all Germans—including Jews, who shared in the war effort with unbridled enthusiasm—into one *Volk*. But as the war progressed, the old divisions that buffeted German society resurfaced, and Jews soon found themselves once again the object of public scorn. The ever-mounting anti-Semitism culminated in the humiliating "census" of Jewish soldiers, conducted by the supreme command of the German armed forces, to determine whether they were sharing the patriotic duty in numbers equal to *Urdeutschen*, authentic Germans.[41] Having volunteered in the tens of thousands for combat, many in frontline units, German Jewry was deeply scarred by the deliberate insult. It was in this context that Buber issued his journal.

The very name of Buber's journal, which soon became one of the premier literary and political reviews of its day, sought to

Figure 11
Martin Buber, ca. 1916
Collection of Paul Mendes-Flohr

signal a change in Jewish self-consciousness. Just a generation earlier, the term *Jude* (Jew) would have evoked shame and embarrassment. As a young university student in the 1890s, Buber himself hesitated to utter the word *Jew* in public, for in cultured circles it was then considered somewhat of an obscenity. Hence, to have published less than twenty years later a journal with the words *The Jew* emblazoned on its masthead was nothing short of revolutionary. Founded in the midst of World War I, and at the height of a wave of anti-Semitism, the journal was surely an expression of defiant pride. As Arthur A. Cohen notes in his introduction to the volume of translated selections from *Der Jude*:

> [C]alling the periodical *The Jew* . . . says something about its audience as well as about its [editor]. It would be hard to imagine the postman dropping such a periodical into the mailboxes of American Jews. Yet in Berlin, Vienna, Prague . . . there arrived with relative punctuality each month between April 1916 and 1923 (and irregularly thereafter), wrapped but not concealed, the periodical *The Jew*.[42]

But *Der Jude* was eminently more than a defiant expression of Jewish pride. Buber's journal was also a manifestation of what was called the German Jewish Renaissance, which began to crystallize as early as 1900.[43] (See the essay by Inka Bertz in this book.) Largely centered in Berlin and inspired by Zionism, the Jewish Renaissance promoted a remarkable flowering of Jewish culture, a sustained interest in Jewish matters that found expression in a variety of creative, and often uniquely modern forms, especially fiction and art. Among the array of artists, mostly residing in Berlin, who at the turn of the century began to adapt Jewish themes to their work, were Joseph Budko (1888–1940), E. M. Lilien (1874–1925), Hermann Struck (1876–1944), and Lesser Ury (1861–1931). Much of their work involved the illustration of the many books and periodicals of Jewish interest that appeared in the years before the First World War. The war—the attendant anti-Semitism and, particularly, the encounter with the East European Jewish masses—gave added impetus to the Jewish Renaissance and the ensuing process whereby assimilated or indifferent Jews were assuming an affirmative Jewishness.

The affectionate embrace of a rediscovered Judaism did not lead, in most cases, to a jettisoning of German and European culture. As Walter Benjamin declared in correspondence of 1912 concerning the German Jews' reclaimed Jewishness, "We are bifurcated—Jewish and German."[44] The Jewish Renaissance did not then entail a retreat from *Bildung*; rather, it reflected the valoriza-

Figure 12
Corner of Unter den Linden and
Friedrichstrasse, 1909
Photograph: Max Missmann

tion of Judaism within the project of creating a cultural discourse informed by the diverse historical voices constituting humanity's shared inheritance. In this respect, the Jewish Renaissance sought to reverse the tendency to assume that Judaism was an anachronism or, at best, a private sentiment irrelevant to the larger concerns of the educated European.

Buber himself was emblematic of the *Jewish Renaissance*, a phrase that he, in fact, coined in an essay of 1901.[45] He devoted his prodigious talent to presenting the forgotten or maligned wisdom of the Jewish mystical tradition, pre-eminently that of the Polish Hasidim, but deliberately recast in an aesthetic mode that was compatible with predominant aesthetic sensibilities while resonating contemporary cultural concerns of the *Bildungsbürgertum*. Furthermore, and perhaps more significant, Buber's Jewish reaffirmations and general cultural interests were of one seamless weave. At the same time that he published works on Jewish mysticism, folklore, art, theater, and language, his writings explored similar themes as refracted through other cultures. For Buber, the voice of Judaism was that of a polyphonic chorus. His volume *Ekstatische Konfessionen* (Ecstatic Confessions, 1909), now regarded as one of the seminal documents of German Expressionism,[46] for instance, presents mystical testimonies from pagan and Indian traditions, Christianity, both Western and Eastern, Islam, and Judaism. None is privileged; each mirrors the other, reflecting a universal, albeit variegated, experience. In the pages of *Der Jude*, the blend was more subtle. Although the focus of the journal was perforce on exigent political and cultural issues confronting the Jewish people, its intellectual reflexes remained decidedly that of *Bildung* with its universal human compass.

One of the earliest contributors to *Der Jude* was Franz Kafka, whom Buber personally recruited for the journal. The two had met earlier in Prague, and later in Berlin, where Buber had resided since 1899. Kafka later wrote Buber that those hours they spent together signified "in every respect the purest memory I have of Berlin."[47] In the years before the war, Kafka often visited Berlin and found the city "invigorating."[48] He recorded his impressions in a letter: "As a city Berlin is so much better than Vienna, that decaying mammoth village."[49] And in another letter, he added that he hoped to move to the German capital: "Berlin does me good in every way."[50] Alas, the outbreak of World War I along with personal circumstances did not allow him to realize his dream of joining the myriad of intellectuals drawn to Berlin. His plans constantly postponed, he finally managed to take up residence in the city in 1923, but only for a brief period before his death.

Figure 13
Construction of the U-Bahn
(Underground)
at Alexanderplatz, 1911

Figure 15 *(opposite)*
Lovis Corinth
Portrait of Alfred Kerr, 1907
Oil on canvas,
40¾ x 23 in. (103.5 x 58.5 cm)
Stiftung Stadtmuseum Berlin

A Marketplace for Brash Newcomers

The pull of Berlin, according to Kafka, was due to "its easy life, great opportunities, pleasant diversions, etc."[51] In the decades before World War I, Berlin had become a mecca for aspiring writers, poets, artists, actors, and philosophers from throughout Europe and beyond. Emerging as a metropolis in the nineteenth century and expanding at an unyielding pace, it was more akin to an American immigrant city, with a steady stream of ambitious foreigners—and an endless array of social and intellectual outsiders—flocking through its open gates. The burgeoning amalgam of populations lent the city a restless rhythm, an uninhibited vitality decidedly oriented to the present, and the future, rather than to the past. As Ian Buruma recently noted, "Berlin was always a marketplace for brash newcomers. More than that, among European capitals, Berlin was itself a brash newcomer."[52]

Its conservative critics derisively called the city a new Babylon, wallowing in a directionless, cacophonous decadence. The Jewish literary critic, and later statesman, Walther Rathenau (FIG. 14)—whose family was prominently associated with the economic and cultural development of Berlin—feared that a frenetic, uncontrolled growth (see FIG. 13) would transform his beloved city into "Chicago on the Spree," rife with the destitution and crime of an American boomtown. Although an individual of refined cosmopolitan taste and an advocate of modernism, he was wary of the underside of a hypermodern urbanity. Indeed, together with the writer and Nobel Prize laureate of 1912, Gerhart Hauptmann, and his fellow Berliners of Jewish provenance Maximilian Harden, the editor of the city's most influential literary and political review, *Die Zukunft* (The Future), and the publisher Samuel Fischer, he became one of the leaders of the self-styled "aesthetic opposition" to the vulgarities of Wilhelmine Germany. In particular, they objected to what they perceived to be an insidious alliance between the Byzantine rule of the Kaiser and a rampant urbanization blighting the country and leading to a "mechanization of the spirit" and death of the soul.[53]

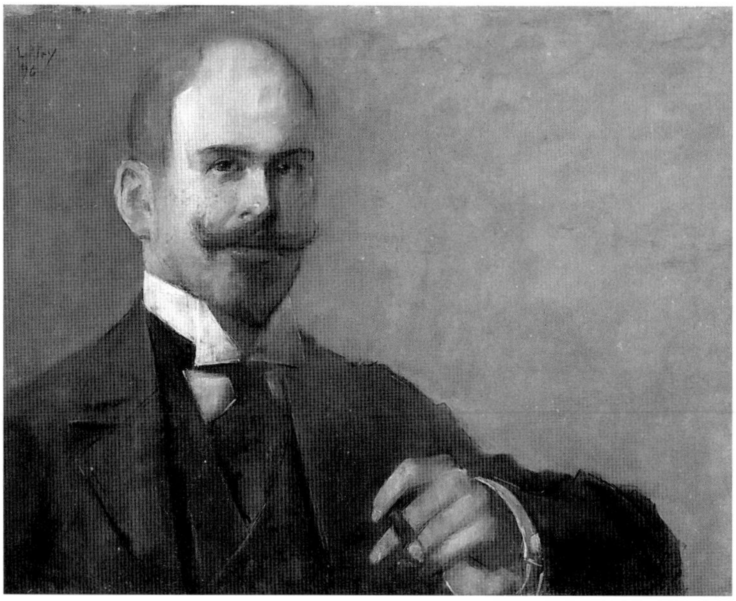

Figure 14
Lesser Ury
Portrait of Walther Rathenau, 1896
Pastel on paper,
18⅞ x 27⅜ in. (48 x 69.5 cm)
Courtesy of the Leo Baeck Institute, Jerusalem

There were others, however, who took heart from the comparison of Berlin with one of America's dynamic urban centers. Like a New World metropolis, sitting on the edge of boundless frontiers, Berlin was said to dwell "utterly in the present,"[54] creating, so to speak, its own history, and a cultural and intellectual landscape that was fluid, protean, and often irreverent. Cosmopolitan by demography and temperament, the city was uniquely hospitable to individuals prepared to explore new horizons, daring iconoclasts, innovative artists and thinkers. Led by inspired "newcomers," many of them Jews, Berlin became a center of European modernism and an energetic avant-garde. As noted by Alfred Kerr (FIG. 15), who hailed from a

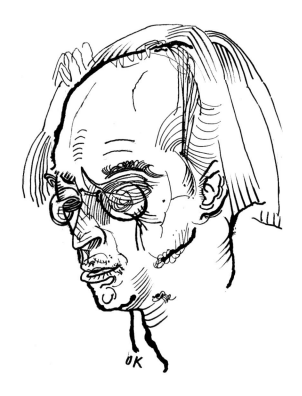

Breslau Jewish family and became Berlin's most prominent—and feared—theater critic, by the early twentieth century Berlin had become "the most important theater city in the world, and also the first in music."[55] To a similar degree, this was true in the arts, journalism, and literature—all endeavors in which Jews abounded. The Jew's singular imprint on Berlin's restless cosmopolitanism was widely perceived by Jew and non-Jew alike. As the historian Peter Gay, himself a scion of a Berlin Jewish family,[56] observed: "Jews, it is said, making themselves at home in Berlin, transformed it, and imprinted upon it something of their rootlessness, their alienation from soil and tradition, their pervasive disrespect for authority, their mordant wit."[57]

The grand patron of Berlin's avant-garde was Herwarth Walden (FIG. 16); born Georg Lewin, his exotic name was given to him by his first wife, the Jewish poet Else Lasker-Schüler. (See the essay by Sigrid Bauschinger in this book.) He was an unapologetic *Grenzverwischer*—an eraser of boundaries—as Jewish cosmopolitans were frequently pilloried. For over thirty years, he tirelessly promoted avant-garde artists and writers, primarily through his journal *Der Sturm* (The Storm), founded in 1910, and his gallery of the same name. With a verbal extravagance befitting his flamboyant manner, he portrayed Berlin as a polyglot, cosmopolitan mesh of cultures:

> Russia lies in West Berlin. Berlin is very large and therefore she is the capital city of the United States of Europe. . . . Is it not a great city, in which Russians live in the west, the Germans in the south and the Italians in the north? A city in which the Germans speak French, the Russians German, the Japanese a broken German, and the Italians English. . . . Berlin is a microcosm of America. Berlin is timeless motion and timeless life. Perhaps the United States of America has a Berlin. But Berlin lacks a United States of Europe. One should establish the United States of Europe as quickly as possible. Not only for the sake of Berlin, but also for the sake of Europe.[58]

These last words of Walden's cosmopolitan vision of Berlin, from today's perspective, resonate with an uncanny prophetic ring.

Notes

1. See Robert Wistrich, "Fateful Trap: The German-Jewish Symbiosis," *Tikkun* 5, no. 2 (March/April 1990): 34.

2. Theodore Wiener, "The German-Jewish Legacy: An Overstated Ideal," in *The German-Jewish Legacy in America, 1938–1988: From Bildung to the Bill of Rights*, ed. Abraham J. Peck (Detroit: Wayne State University Press, 1989), p. 153.

3. George Steiner, "Some 'Meta-Rabbis,'" in *Next Year in Jerusalem: Jews in the Twentieth Century: Portraits of the Jew in the Twentieth Century*, ed. Douglas Villiers (New York: Viking, 1976), p. 26.

4. See Frederic V. Grunfeld, *Prophets Without Honour: A Background to Freud, Kafka, Einstein, and Their World* (New York: Holt, Rinehart and Winston, 1979).

5. Peter Gay, "German Jews in German Culture: 1883–1914," *Midstream* (February 1975): 25; reprinted in Gay, *Freud, Jews, and Other Germans: Masters and Victims in Modernist Culture* (New York: Oxford University Press, 1978), p. 99.

6. Heinrich Heine, "Shakespeare's Mädchen und Frauen," in Heine, *Confessio Judaica: Eine Auswahl aus seinen Dichtungen, Schriften, und Briefen*, ed. Hugo Bieber (Berlin: Welt Verlag, 1925), p. 124.

7. For example, "when one considers the characteristic fact that the most beautiful and magnificent house of worship in the German capital is a synagogue—which, naturally, is not a reproach directed to the Jews but the Christians—then one cannot deny that the Jews in Germany are more powerful than they are in any other country in Western Europe." Heinrich von Treitschke, "Herr Graetz und sein Judenthum" (1879), in Walter Boehlich, ed., *Der Berliner Antisemitismusstreit* (Frankfurt am Main: Insel, 1965), p. 37.

8. See Peter Fritzsche and Karen Hewitt, *Berlin Walks* (New York: Henry Holt, 1994), p. 99.

9. In 1800, the general population of Berlin was approximately 170,000; by the 1850s, the city had 500,000 residents, by 1877 1 million, and 2 million at the turn of the century. At this juncture, the population expanded beyond the city limits. When, in 1920, the surburbs and satellite cities were incorporated within the city, Greater Berlin became a metropolis of 4 million, and thus the third largest city in the world after London and New York.

10. Werner Sombart, *Die Juden und das Wirtschaftsleben* (Leipzig: Duncker & Humblot, 1911); *The Jews and Modern Capitalism*, trans. M. Epstein (New York: The Free Press, 1951), pp. 301–16.

11. Ibid., p. 316.

12. Ibid., p. 246.

13. Ibid., p. 248.

14. Ibid., pp. 312f.

15. Ibid., pp. 313, 316. Indeed, Sombart held that capitalism is primed by an *appetitus divitiarum infinitus*—unlimited lust for gain—whose development, therefore, knows no bounds. It is this conception of capitalism that allowed him to discern its "phenomenological" origins in the life of nomads and their endless wandering in a seemingly boundless desert. Accordingly, he posed the rhetorical question, "Is it not too much to say that nomadism is the progenitor of capitalism?"

16. Ibid., p. 243.

17. Ibid., p. 251. Sombart also ascribed the extraordinarily rapid and successful assimilation of the Jews to their "nomadic" adaptability.

18. Hans Liebeschütz, "Max Weber's Historical Interpretation of Judaism," *Leo Baeck Institute Year Book* 9 (1964): 50.

19. Moritz Goldstein, "Deutsch-jüdischer Parnass," *Der Kunstwart*, 25, no. 11 (1 March 1912): 283.

20. Ibid., p. 286.

21. Ferdinand Avenarius, "Aussprachen mit Juden," *Der Kunstwart*, 25, no. 22 (2 August 1912): 226. See Goldstein, "Deutsch-jüdischer Parnass," p. 283.

22. Ibid., p. 226.

23. See Goldstein's memoir, "German Jewry's Dilemma: The Story of a Provocative Essay," *Leo Baeck Institute Year Book* 2 (1957): 245.

24. Ibid.

25. Thorstein Veblen, "The Intellectual Pre-eminence of Jews in Modern Europe," *Political Science Quarterly* 34 (March 1919); reprinted in *The Writings of Thorstein Veblen: Essays in Our Changing Order*, ed. Leon Ardzrooni (New York: N. Kelley Bookseller, 1964), pp. 219–31.

26. Ibid., p. 223.

27. Georg Simmel, *Soziologie: Untersuchungen über die Formen der Vergesellschaftung* (Leipzig: Duncker & Humblot, 1908), pp. 509–12. Translated in *The Sociology of Georg Simmel*, trans. and ed. Kurt H. Wolff (New York: The Free Press, 1964), p. 402.

28. Ibid., p. 407.

29. Ibid., pp. 402f.

30. Ibid., p. 402.

31. Ibid., p. 404.

32. Ibid., p. 405.

33. Ibid., p. 404.

34. Ibid.

35. Ibid., p. 405.

36. Ibid., p. 407.

37. On the German concept of *Volk*, see George L. Mosse, *The Crisis of German Ideology: Intellectual Origins of the Third Reich* (London: Weidenfeld & Nicolson, 1964), pp. 13–30.

38. On the notion of a "neutral society" as it bears on the Jewish experience of modernity, see Jacob Katz, *Tradition and Crisis: Jewish Society at the Middle Ages* (New York: The Free Press, 1961), chap. 23. Katz later amended the notion, acknowledging that in the light of abiding Christian and primordial sentiments, one could best speak of a "semi-neutral" society sponsored by the German Enlightenment. See Jacob Katz, *Out of the Ghetto: The Social Background of Jewish Emancipation, 1770–1870* (Cambridge, Mass.: Harvard University Press, 1973), chap. 4.

39. Sigmund Freud, "Thoughts for the Times of War and Death" (1915), in *The Standard Edition of the Complete Psychological Works of Sigmund Freud*, ed. James Strachey, in collaboration with Anna Freud (London: The Hogarth Press, 1963), p. 277.

40. Ibid., p. 285.

41. On the census, the so-called *Judenzählung*, see Egmont Zechlin, *Die deutsche Politik und die Juden im ersten Weltkrieg* (Göttingen: Vandenhoeck & Ruprecht, 1969), p. 524.

42. Arthur A. Cohen, Introduction to *The Jew: Essays from Martin Buber's Journal "Der Jude," 1916–1928*, ed. A. A. Cohen, (The University of Alabama Press, 1980), p. 3.

43. See Michael Brenner, *The Renaissance of Jewish Culture in Weimar Germany* (New Haven: Yale University Press, 1996), pp. 11–35.

44. Walter Benjamin to Ludwig Strauss, 11 September 1912, Ludwig Strauss Archives, The National and University Library, Jerusalem.

45. Martin Buber, "Jüdische Renaissance," *Ost und West* 1, no. 1 (January 1901): cols. 7–10.

46. See editor's introduction to Martin Buber, ed., *Ecstatic Confessions: The Heart of Mysticism*, trans. Esther Cameron, ed. Paul Mendes-Flohr (San Francisco: Harper & Row, 1985; Syracuse: Syracuse University Press, 1997), pp. *xiii–xxx*.

47. Kafka to Buber, 29 November 1915, in *The Letters of Martin Buber*, ed. Nahum N. Glatzer and Paul Mendes-Flohr (New York: Schocken, 1991), p. 182.

48. Kafka to Grete Bloch, 18 April 1914, in Franz Kafka, *Letters to Felice*, trans. James Stern and Elisabeth Duckworth (London: Secker & Warburg, 1974), p. 390.

49. Kafka to Grete Bloch, 8 April 1914, *Letters to Felice*, p. 381.

50. Kafka to Grete Bloch, 18 April 1914, *Letters to Felice*, p. 389.

51. Kafka to Max Brod, 5 November 1923, in Franz Kafka, *Briefe: 1902–1924*, ed. Max Brod (Frankfurt am Main: Fischer Taschenbuch, 1975), p. 464.

52. Ian Buruma, "Hello to Berlin," *New York Review of Books*, 19 November 1998, p. 25.

53. See Walther Rathenau, "Die Kritik der Zeit" (1912); reprinted in *Hauptwerke und Gespräche*, ed. Ernst Schulin (Heidelberg: Lambert Schneider, 1977), pp. 17–103.

54. Bernhard von Brentano, *Wo in Europa ist Berlin? Bilder aus den zwanziger Jahren* (1928; reprint, Frankfurt am Main: Suhrkamp, 1987), p. 11.

55. Cited in Grunfeld, *Prophets Without Honour*, p. 27.

56. See Peter Gay's recently published autobiography, *My German Question: Growing Up in Nazi Berlin* (New Haven: Yale University Press, 1998).

57. Gay, "The Berlin-Jewish Spirit," in Gay, *Freud, Jews and Other Germans*, p. 171.

58. Cited in *Berlin Kultur: Identität, Ansichten, Leitbild*, ed. Klaus Siebenhaar and Steffen Damm (Berlin: FAB, 1995), vol. 1, p. 33.

Modernism and the "Alien Element" in German Art

Peter Paret

In 1913, the anti-Semitic publicist Philipp Stauff issued the second volume of his biographical dictionary (FIG. 17) of Jews and their gentile associates, friends, and supporters in Germany. An introduction denounced the Jewish threat to German culture as expressed in one area of the nation's life—the art world. The eleven-page essay, "The Alien Element in German Art, or Paul Cassirer, Max Liebermann, etc.," opened with the pronouncement that "Dealers, critics, and painters, who are strangers in our land and to our blood, stand today at the apex of the fine arts."[1] Cassirer (FIGS. 18, 36), a prominent art dealer and publisher, and Liebermann (FIGS. 20, 22, 23), one of the best-known German painters of the time, personified for Stauff the cultural crisis that was engulfing the country. They and their followers, he charged, were driven by the innate Hebrew motives of greed and cultural hate. They wanted to become rich and penetrate the upper levels of German society; and they intended to destroy the native values by which the Germans had lived since the Teutonic tribes first confronted the Romans. But Jews were merely the first, not the only, target of his indictment. Stauff also attacked the quality of much of the art Jews were imposing on the German public. To praise

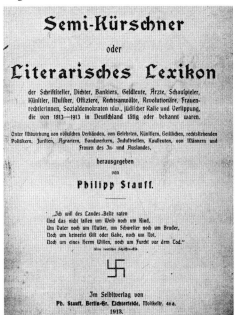

the "boring, unnatural, egg-like faces" of El Greco's figures as inspirations for the modern artist was merely an attempt to drive up prices of his work; Van Gogh's paintings were "childish," some French Impressionists had produced good paintings, but *"very* bad Renoirs and weak Monets" were being palmed off on German buyers. In any case, the great German Realists of the preceding generation were the equals of any foreign master. The pamphlet's third target was Germans who had given in to Jewish seduction.

Stauff took a broad view of Jewish identity. Anyone whose great-grandfather a century earlier had converted to Christianity and married a Gentile remained as much a Jew in his eyes as a recent arrival from the shtetl, and was more dangerous because he might pass as authentically German. But with equal fervor he denounced Gentiles who had married Jews, like Lovis Corinth and Henry van de Velde; who worked for a Jewish publisher, like the editor and critic Karl Scheffler; or who had Jewish friends, like the collector Harry Count Kessler or the museum directors Hugo von Tschudi and Alfred Lichtwark. Either as deluded victims or as men who had sold out, he charged, they belonged to a vast conspiracy, which in the fine arts propagated one form or another of a diseased modernism that expressed international rather than national values.

Stauff's fantasies, which fifteen years later Goebbels reformulated into effective propaganda, were generally dismissed as the rantings of an extremist, even by many Germans who drew a

Figure 18
Georg Kolbe
Portrait of Paul Cassirer, 1925
Bronze, 12⅝ in. (32 cm); base: 4½ x 6⅛ x 7¼ in. (11.5 x 15.5 x 18.5 cm)
Georg Kolbe Museum, Berlin

Figure 19
Adolph Menzel
**Views of Workers
Eating (Essende Arbeiter
in mehreren Ansichten)**,
ca. 1872–1874
Pencil on paper,
10⁷/₁₆ x 14⁹/₁₆ in. (26.5 x 37 cm)
Kupferstichkabinett, Staatliche Museen
zu Berlin–Preussischer Kulturbesitz

Figure 20
Max Liebermann
**Self-Portrait with Brush
and Palette (Selbstbildnis mit
Pinsel und Palette)**, 1913
Oil on canvas,
35 x 28½ in. (89 x 72.4 cm)
Kunstmuseum Düsseldorf

dividing line between themselves and their Jewish fellow citizens. But absurd though it was, in one respect his tract reflected reality. The great majority of modernist artists and their supporters were not Jews. Had Stauff limited his attacks to Jews—even to those who fell within his expansive definition of Jews, like Franz Marc, whose paternal great-grandfather was Jewish—he would have had difficulty making a case for their overwhelming cultural power. Stauff also sensed correctly that Jewish assimilation had progressed further in the fine arts, in literature and music, than in most areas of German life, and that in modernism, with its often self-conscious rejection of tradition, it had found a particularly favorable environment.

Modernism in German art in the decades before 1914 was anything but a simple extension or translation of foreign patterns. The various modernist movements derived from German Romanticism and Realism on the one hand, and on the other responded to foreign influences ranging from the landscapes of Constable and of the School of Fontainebleau to Impressionism, the Symbolism of Böcklin and Moreau, and to such precursors of Expressionism as Edvard Munch. Some avant-garde groups rejected foreign models altogether, others borrowed selectively; the work of none could ever be mistaken as other than German. But to nativists like Stauff, any but the slightest departure from conventional realism seemed un-German, and their criticism added a strikingly violent note to the more commonplace, often unideological, resistance to innovation.

A generation earlier, in 1892, an exhibition of Munch's paintings, sponsored by the Association of Berlin Artists, opened in Berlin. It was the first extensive presentation of the work of a truly revolutionary modernist in the capital; and it caused a sensation, which turned into a major scandal when the conservative majority of the Association forced the show to close after three days. At the time, the outstanding artist in Berlin was Adolph Menzel, a tough, solitary figure then in his seventies, who rarely involved himself in the politics of the art world. We do not know how—if at all—he reacted to Munch's pictures; but he could confront Munch's emotional readings of modern man and woman with a merciless realism of his own, grounded in an earlier, more self-contained aesthetic vision. His powerful images of contemporary life, from high society at court to industrial workers and their machinery (FIG. 19), were the supreme embodiment of what has been called Berlin Realism, which was also the starting point of Max Liebermann's art.[2]

Max Liebermann

Liebermann (FIG. 20) was born in Berlin in 1847, into a prominent Jewish family with connections throughout Central Europe.
An uncle was raised to the nobility in Vienna; a second cousin,
Walther Rathenau, became foreign minister in the Weimar
Republic. The family's great wealth derived from cotton mills;
later, factories making machine parts, girders, and railroad
tracks were added. Throughout his long life—he died in his
eighty-eighth year, in 1935—Liebermann possessed the material
freedom of the very rich. One expression of his wealth was his
art collection, which, apart from works by Rembrandt, Daumier,
and such German contemporaries as Menzel, included paintings
by Cézanne, Degas, Monet, Pissarro, Renoir, Toulouse-Lautrec,
and fifteen paintings, studies in oil, and watercolors by Manet; at
the time it was one of the most important private collections of
Impressionists in the world (FIG. 21). The pictures defined a creative standard that Liebermann—with different gifts and living
in a different culture—tried to emulate in his own way.

Figure 21
The salon in Max Liebermann's
villa at Wannsee, ca. 1930
Photograph: Martha Huth

Figure 22
Max Liebermann in his studio in
the Kaiserin-Augusta-Strasse, 1899
Photograph: Max von Rüdiger

Liebermann was twenty-five when he painted the first work
that set him apart from the mass of young
artists—*Women Plucking Geese*, 1872 (see
FIG. 24). For the next decades, his preferred
theme remained the world of working people—peasants, shoemakers, knife grinders,
carpenters, harbor pilots, laundrywomen,
the inmates of orphanages (see FIG. 25) and
of old-age homes—whom he painted not
as colorful outsiders of the bourgeois world,
nor as victims of capitalism, but as men
and women whose hard work and dignity
demanded respect. His energetic brush-

strokes and uneven laying-on of paint led early critics to condemn
his work as sketchy and unfinished; in his early thirties he began
to paint outside the studio (FIG. 23) and to experiment with a freer
use of color. By his fortieth birthday he was gaining a national
and, in a small way, even an international reputation. In 1888 the
Royal Academy of Arts awarded him its small gold medal; and
Wilhelm von Bode, the future Director-General of the Berlin State
Museums, declared that Liebermann assured the emergence of a
new German art.

Nevertheless, his nonacademic style, the serious sympathy
with which he invested his paintings of the poor, and his liberal
politics made Liebermann a figure of contention in Berlin at the
same time that he was winning major prizes in Paris, Munich,
and Vienna. The environment for the fine arts in Berlin was not
repressive, but neither did it afford much scope for innovation.
Honors, purchases of art by the state, and the major exhibitions—
which still dominated the art market—were controlled or strongly
influenced by the Royal Academy and by the less elitist but in its
leadership equally conventional Association of Berlin Artists,

Figure 23
Max Liebermann in front of his painting
Striding Peasant (Schreitender Bauer),
1894

of which Liebermann was a member. The Prussian cultural bureaucracy included liberal as well as conservative officials; but the sympathies of the young emperor Wilhelm II were with the conservative camp, and as king of Prussia he possessed certain defined powers in matters of cultural policy. Artists who sought important commissions and official honors had to tread cautiously in this environment.

A change became noticeable in the late 1880s. Germany's rapid economic development, a slowly expanding private art market, the emergence of new artists, and foreign influences combined to make the situation of the arts in Berlin more fluid. In February 1892, the young landscape painter Walter Leistikow (FIG. 26) and eight other members of the Association of Berlin Artists formed a group to hold separate exhibitions in addition to the annual salon with its many hundreds, even thousands, of entries of indifferent quality. To broaden their appeal, they invited Liebermann and the well-known painter of Berlin life Franz Skarbina to join them. Leistikow, a close friend of Corinth, who was to write his biography, soon formed an intimate personal and professional alliance with Liebermann, which lasted until his early death in 1908. Under the leadership of the two men, the "Eleven" held a series of shows that were favorably reviewed and helped mobilize the supporters of modernism in the city.[3]

In the gradually changing cultural atmosphere, Liebermann's stature was at last acknowledged. In 1896 the German government allowed him to accept the French Legion of Honor, a decoration he had been offered once before but had been compelled to reject. The following year, the annual Berlin salon marked his fiftieth birthday with a retrospective; he was awarded the great gold medal and the title of professor. In 1898 he was elected to the Royal Academy.

But an event in the same year drove Liebermann openly into opposition to the art establishment, which had just welcomed him as one of its own. The jury of the annual salon rejected one of Leistikow's entries for the 1898 exhibition. The painting— *Grunewald Lake*, 1895, today in the Berlin National Gallery— is one of Leistikow's most emotionally charged landscapes, a work bridging the realms of good regional art and art of universal significance. As the painting was not aggressively revolutionary in conception or execution, its rejection seems to have been motivated by the wish to embarrass one of the leaders of modernism in Berlin. Leistikow reacted by proposing that artists who disagreed with the Association's policies resign and organize their own shows, and Liebermann agreed that the jury's decision might be the provocation needed to persuade people to take a step that had long been considered. A secessionist group was formed in May, and after efforts failed to keep it in the Association as a

Figure 26
Walter Leistikow
**Lake in the Mark Brandenburg
(Märkischer See)**, 1898
Oil on canvas,
29½ x 39⅜ in. (75 x 100 cm)
Kunsthalle zu Kiel

BERLINER SECESSION

IX. AUSSTELLUNG APRIL-SEPTEMBER 1904

KANTSTRASSE 12, TÄGLICH GEÖFFNET V. 9-7 UHR EINTRITTSPREIS M.1

HALTESTELLE DER STRASSENBAHN, HOCHBAHN U. STADTBAHN: ZOOLOG. GARTEN

Figure 27
Wilhelm Schulz
Poster for **Ninth Exhibition
of the Berlin Secession,
April–September 1904**
Lithograph,
26 9/16 x 35 13/16 in. (67.5 x 91 cm)
Kunstbibliothek, Staatliche Museen
zu Berlin–Preussischer Kulturbesitz

semi-autonomous branch, the group became wholly independent. It indicates the stage that assimilation had reached in Berlin culture by the end of the nineteenth century that Liebermann— possibly the only Jew among the sixty-five founding members— was elected president of the Berlin Secession.[4]

The Secessionist Movement

In the 1890s, groups of artists broke away from national and local art associations throughout Central Europe. The secessions they formed were institutional responses to two phenomena before which the existing associations seemed helpless: new developments in painting and sculpture; and an expanding urban society, whose commercial power potentially changed the market for art. All secessions were driven by similar motives, and, broadly speaking, all passed through similar life cycles. Their founders were established artists, or at least artists on the way to recognition, whose aesthetic sympathies and professional interests had come to diverge from those of the conventional majority of Association members. Above all, they did not want their work subjected to conservative juries and submerged in mass exhibitions. The professional standing of the secessionists is also indicated by their financial resources and connections, which allowed them to build their own galleries—as they did, for example, in Vienna and Berlin—and to mount expensive exhibitions that could draw on loans from artists throughout Europe.

In the aggregate, the secessions incorporated most of the modernist tendencies of the time. If a specific direction was not represented among the members of a particular group, it usually appeared in one of the group's shows, the various secessions tending to support one another and to use their shows to disseminate a broad range of modernism. Nevertheless, different styles often clashed, and the conflicts within modernism could be as intense as the conflicts between avant-garde and establishment. Personal antagonisms and aesthetic differences contributed to the secessions' frequent changes of course, and often to their end. Soon after it was formed in 1892, the Munich Secession divided again. Within eight years of its birth, the Vienna Secession split, partly because many members resented the preferential treatment given to one of the group's leading figures, Gustav Klimt. The Berlin Secession struggled through several crises and, after 1914, lost its innovative edge. But these conflicts and even breakups should not be seen as failures. They were natural turning points in the rise and development of creative energies, their diffusion and decline, and their replacement by new forces.[5]

Every secession encountered opposition within and outside the art community, but most were quickly accepted by the cultural bureaucracy and—as in Munich, Vienna, and Weimar—soon received financial support from the state. In Berlin the situation was more complex. The Secession had influential friends in government and the cultural bureaucracy, but also opponents, of whom one of the most openly antagonistic was the emperor. He was driven by an honest attachment to styles of idealized or entertaining realism, and by the belief that art should celebrate the

Figure 28
Thomas Theodor Heine
Poster for **Exhibition of the Berlin Secession, April–September 1912**
Lithograph, 25¾ x 35½ in. (65.5 x 90 cm)
Kunstbibliothek, Staatliche Museen zu Berlin–Preussischer Kulturbesitz

beauty of life. If it addressed the unfortunate or seamy side, art, he thought, became negative, and could even turn into a politically destructive force.

Some forms of modernism did have political characteristics, and modernism as such had long-range political implications, but the Central European secessions were not centers of political art. Only a few members of the Berlin group expressed even social criticism in their work. By background as well as attitude, almost all belonged to the moderate, liberal, or conservative middle and upper-middle classes; several were members of the nobility, like Konrad von Kardorff, son of a leading conservative politician; and although Wilhelm II might not have thought so, until the First World War their work, with rare exceptions, remained apolitical. But with their more selective exhibitions, their lectures and publications, the secessions nurtured a more knowledgeable art public, fostered private patronage, and reduced the artist's dependence on the state. Economically they were a free-market force, and in this sense they *were* political. That the secessions' interest in aesthetic innovation—limited in Munich, much stronger in Vienna and Berlin—was linked with economic self-interest was criticized at the time and worries some interpreters even today. Yet artistic integrity may coexist with the wish to publicize and sell one's work, and artists—small entrepreneurs in a notoriously treacherous market—had good reason to try to improve their situation by banding together. Nor, although opportunities were increasing, was it without risk to cut loose from the traditional centers of patronage and prestige. More than one member of the Berlin Secession lost an official appointment or a purchase by the state because of his membership.

Of the founding members of the Secession, two-thirds are forgotten today. Perhaps twenty still enjoy a regional reputation in Germany, of whom a few—the sculptors August Gaul (FIGS. 138, 139) and Fritz Klimsch, and the Berlin painters Hans Baluschek (FIG. 29), Carl Hagemeister, Franz Skarbina, and especially Walter Leistikow—stand out. Only Max Liebermann remains widely known, and he barely reaches past the cultural boundaries of Central Europe. With the arrival of other artists, the group gained strength. Some, like Lovis Corinth (FIG. 30) and Max Slevogt (FIG. 37), who came from Munich, were drawn to Berlin in part by the new energy the Secession generated. Käthe Kollwitz (FIGS. 32, 170, 171) became a member in 1901; another primarily graphic artist, Hermann Struck (see FIGS. 48, 152, 153), a few years later. Among those who joined subsequently were Lyonel Feininger,

Figure 31
Preparing for the Berlin Secession
exhibition: Executive and Hanging
Committee at work, 1904
Left to right: Willy Döring, Bruno Cassirer,
Otto Engel, Max Liebermann, Walter
Leistikow, Kurt Herrmann, Fritz Klimsch

Figure 32
Käthe Kollwitz
Uprising (Aufruhr), 1899
Etching, approx. 10⅜ x 8¼ in.
(26.5 x 20.9 cm)
Kupferstichkabinett,
Staatliche Museen zu Berlin–
Preussischer Kulturbesitz

Max Beckmann, Ernst Barlach, and Emil Nolde. As early as 1901, corresponding members included Degas, Forain, Hodler, Klinger, Monet, Pissarro, Rodin, Sargent, Steinlen, and Valloton—names that again indicate the diversity of styles represented in the group. In his talk at the opening of its first exhibition, Liebermann declared: "In selecting the works [shown] . . . talent alone, whatever its style, was the determinant. . . . We do not believe in a single, sacred direction in art."[6] It remained the Secession's guiding principle—more difficult to follow as time went on—to maintain this diversity.

Gifts and loans enabled the Secession to build a small gallery, and its first exhibition in the spring of 1899—a survey of contemporary nonacademic German art (including two Swiss painters, Arnold Böcklin and Ferdinand Hodler)—was well received by the critics. Sales of several of the works shown and of the catalogue, which had to be reprinted, also made it modestly profitable. During the next few years, the Secession acquired enough capital to build a larger gallery with a restaurant and a garden on the Kurfürstendamm. Throughout its existence it enjoyed financial stability, its income derived from membership dues, ticket and catalogue sales, and a commission on works sold. From the beginning it was agreed that administering the affairs of the new organization could not be a part-time effort left to volunteers from among the members; and at an early meeting of the founders, Liebermann suggested the appointment as business managers of two cousins, Bruno and Paul Cassirer, who had recently started a gallery and publishing firm in Berlin. The two young men, neither yet thirty, turned down the offer of salaried positions, and proposed instead to handle the Secession's business without pay if given seats on the executive committee and the jury. This brought individuals who were not artists to the artistic leadership, an unusual arrangement that was to serve the Secession well, but also caused it difficulties.

The Cassirers

Liebermann's recommendations of the Cassirers would have been taken by Philipp Stauff as further evidence of Jewish conspiracy and infiltration. In the process of assimilation, the Cassirer and Liebermann families followed basically similar patterns, individual differences notwithstanding. First lumber merchants and estate managers in Silesia, the Cassirers expanded their business activities throughout the nineteenth century, culminating in the factory of high-quality cables that Paul Cassirer's father founded in Berlin. The family

(FIGS. 33, 38) grew very wealthy, although not on the level of the Liebermanns, let alone such Jewish dynasties as the Mendelssohns and the Friedländer-Fulds.[7]

By the end of the nineteenth century, the Cassirers were turning increasingly to the professions in the humanities and sciences. Sociologically, the generation that reached maturity in the 1890s was both in advance of and behind its time. The now widely dispersed family tried to maintain cohesion by such means as family foundations and joint projects—a famous progressive boarding school owed its existence to the Cassirers—but most significantly by marrying within the family. Bruno Cassirer and his cousins Ernst, the philosopher, and Richard, one of Germany's foremost neurologists, married cousins, and the parents of Bruno and Ernst had themselves been cousins. Marriages with Gentiles also occurred, but rarely led to conversions. Liebermann's only child also married a non-Jew, but Liebermann and his wife never completely shed their religious ties. For many of the Cassirers, religion, whether Judaism or Christianity, no longer mattered even in a social sense. Like his father, Paul Cassirer was an atheist.

Before they became partners, Paul Cassirer had published a play and a novel, and worked on the staff of the satirical journal *Simplicissimus*; his cousin had studied art history. Both held firm opinions on art and literature, and since neither was good at sharing authority it soon was apparent that the partnership could not last. In 1901 Bruno Cassirer (FIG. 34) left the Secession and became sole owner of the publishing firm, while his cousin remained manager of the Secession and assumed control of the Cassirer Gallery. Within a few years, Bruno Cassirer built up a small but very strong list in modern literature, art history, and cultural studies. That he also brought out his cousin Ernst's edition of Kant's works in twelve sumptuous volumes scarcely fit into the firm's program, but once again expressed family solidarity. Bruno Cassirer's bibliophile editions illustrated by contemporary artists became famous. Often they were followed by inexpensive editions, which brought avant-garde images and designs to a wider market. Another force in shaping the taste of the educated public was the firm's periodical *Kunst und Künstler* (Art and Artist) (FIG. 35), which appeared from 1902 to 1933, and under Karl Scheffler became Germany's finest journal of art scholarship and connoisseurship, even if its treatment of the most recent directions after Neo-Impressionism was more dutiful than enthusiastic. It was generally regarded as the unofficial journal of the Berlin Secession.

Figure 35
Cover of **Kunst und Künstler (Art and Artist)**, designed by Max Slevogt
Ink on paper,
12³⁄₁₆ x 9⅝ in. (30.9 x 24.5 cm)
Courtesy of Harvard University Fine Arts Library, Cambridge, Massachusetts

Figure 36
Leopold Graf von Kalckreuth
Portrait of Paul Cassirer, 1911
Oil on canvas, 24 x 18⅛ in. (61 x 46 cm)
Stiftung Stadtmuseum Berlin

Figure 37
Max Liebermann
Portrait of Max Slevogt, 1899
Oil on panel,
16⁵⁄₁₆ x 12³⁄₁₆ in. (41.5 x 31 cm)
Landesmuseum Mainz

Figure 38
Max Slevogt
**Portrait of Suzanne
Aimée Cassirer**, 1901
Oil on canvas,
38⁹⁄₁₆ x 59 in. (98 x 150 cm)
Collection Suzanne Aimée Paret

Bruno Cassirer combined his activities as a publisher with running the estate he had inherited from his father and managing a stud farm and harness-racing stable. His colors won the German national cup eight times. Horses like writers, it was said, stimulated his innovative energies. "He was not a thinker," Scheffler wrote in his memoirs after the Second World War, "but totally a man of instinct. In the end, however, everything turned into action."[8] In his social attitudes he was rather conventional, far more accepting of German upper-class values than was his cousin Paul, who early on led an international life, and became increasingly critical of the ethos and style of the Wilhelmine empire.

Paul Cassirer (FIGS. 18, 36) is generally regarded as the principal German champion of Impressionism and Neo-Impressionism at the turn of the century. But even more significant than his efforts to gain recognition for movements that were rapidly becoming historical was his backing and advocacy of a number of artists still at the beginning of their careers. This point is sometimes obscured by his differentiated response to the next great wave of German modernism. He admired the work of some Expressionists, but disliked or was indifferent to that of others, and limited its exposure in his gallery. He valued neither Impressionism nor Expressionism in their totality, but prized individual artists, which made him suspect to ideologues of all stripes.

The gallery he founded with his cousin in 1898 opened with a show of paintings by Liebermann and Degas, and sculptures by Constantin Meunier—a first statement stressing the link between French and German modernism, which became a permanent theme of the gallery, and subsequently of the exhibitions of the Secession. Cassirer was the first in Germany to assemble large representative shows of Van Gogh and Cézanne (FIG. 39). As in France—where Vollard's two Van Gogh retrospectives in 1896 sold only four paintings—few buyers appeared, or, as in Cassirer's first Van Gogh exhibitions in 1901, none at all. But his program of jointly presenting current and recent works with Old Masters, and Germans together with foreigners, had an impact on artists and critics, and gradually on the public.

The gallery filled a cultural vacuum, and within a few years Cassirer had made it the most important venue for nineteenth- and twentieth-century art in Germany. The 1907 fall season illustrates the gallery's scope and depth. It opened in September with a show of 69 Cézanne watercolors, 6 paintings by Matisse, and 34 by Munch. The October show ranged from El Greco, Manet, Monet, and Hodler to Leistikow. January 1908 began with a show of 14 Beckmanns (FIG. 40), 17 Corinths, and 10 paintings by Nolde, who was just becoming known. The February show

Figure 39
Emil Orlik
Poster for the **Cézanne Exhibition at the Cassirer Gallery**, 1910
Lithograph, 26¼ x 36 in. (66.5 x 91.5 cm)
Kunstbibliothek, Staatliche Museen zu Berlin–Preussischer Kulturbesitz

Figure 40
Max Beckmann
Balloon Race (Ballonwettfahrt), 1908
Oil on canvas,
27⁹⁄₁₆ x 31¹¹⁄₁₆ in. (70 x 80.5 cm)
Staatsgalerie Stuttgart

Figure 41
Ernst Barlach
Pulling the Net (Netzzieher), 1906–7
Charcoal and pencil,
4 x 3⅜ in. (10.2 x 8.5 cm)
Collection of Peter Paret

combined paintings by Liebermann and Slevogt with a survey of the work of Alexej Jawlensky, a strong West European accent being added by paintings of Courbet and Renoir. Each exhibition also introduced the work of two or three Central European new-comers.[9] In later years, Cassirer continued to hold retrospective exhibitions, but increasingly interspersed with exhibitions consisting of a few works by many artists. In 1912, in a catalogue marking the fifteenth anniversary of his gallery, he commented on this change with words that express with great clarity his interest in individual quality rather than in the particular artist, style, or aesthetic doctrine:

> The task I faced in 1898 was to introduce a number
> of great artists, who were unknown in Germany,
> to give art lovers and critics an opportunity to become
> acquainted with the personalities of the true leaders
> of the modern movement.
>
> Today the task seems to me quite different. If in
> the past it was necessary to show the personalities of
> particular artists by means of large exhibitions of their
> work—collective and combative exhibitions—today
> the[se] personalities . . . are better known in Germany
> than anywhere else. As long as we had to fight for this
> art—and we fought hard enough during the past fifteen
> years—it was necessary to point again and again to the
> artists' personalities, to their intentions, their theories,
> and their development—and that could be best achieved
> in collective exhibitions.
>
> I always knew that this way of showing art had
> many dangers, especially here in Germany, with our
> pronounced tendency to theorize. Instead of commenting on the finished work, the realization of the artist's
> intention, the viewer was seduced into occupying himself
> with the individual behind the work, with the artist's
> intentions and struggles rather than with the work
> itself—the only thing that really matters in art. And
> so it happened that this new art, which, among other
> things, fought against the anecdotal. . . , intensely
> fostered pleasure in the anecdotal. To occupy oneself
> with the artist's personality rather than with the work is
> at bottom the same thing as occupying oneself with the
> painting's subject matter rather than with the painting.
>
> Friend and enemy claim that my gallery is the gallery
> of Impressionism. In 1898 that was a curse word meaning revolution. In 1912 it is again a curse word, now
> signifying reaction. But just as the single work always
> gives the lie to broad trends and developments in art,
> so an exhibition can demonstrate—as I hope this exhibition [of 108 works by 45 artists] does—that the theorists
> who label my gallery as "Impressionist" are mistaken
> whether they mean one extreme or the other.[10]

Figure 42
Ernst Barlach
**Resting Wanderer
(Ruhender Wanderer)**, 1910
Wood, 8¼ x 25½ x 28⅜ in.
(21 x 65 x 72 cm)
Private collection, United States

Figure 43
Georg Kolbe
Amazone, 1912
Bronze, 14¹³⁄₁₆ x 9¹³⁄₁₆ x 3¹⁵⁄₁₆ in.
(37.7 x 25 x 10 cm)
Georg Kolbe Museum, Berlin

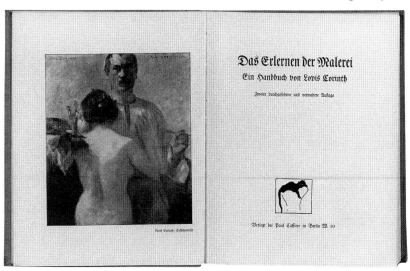

Figure 44
Title page of **Das Erlernen der
Malerei: Ein Handbuch von
Lovis Corinth (Painting:
A Handbook by Lovis Corinth)**
Published by Paul Cassirer,
Berlin, 1908
Collection of Peter Paret

Cassirer strengthened his gallery by offering young artists an annual income in return for exclusive representation of their work. Barlach was supported for three years before he sold his first sculpture (FIGS. 41, 42). Cassirer's entry into publishing was a further source of strength. In 1908 he started the Pan Presse for contemporary graphics and bibliophile editions, which produced several of the most impressive illustrated books of the early twentieth century, among them the facsimile score of Mozart's *Magic Flute* with forty-seven etchings by Slevogt, both in a portfolio and in a bound edition. He also launched a small publishing program in art history, modern literature, and writings by artists (FIG. 44). Among its titles in the next decade and a half were Van Gogh's letters to Theo, Marc's wartime sketchbooks and his letters to his wife, fifteen volumes of poetry by Else Lasker-Schüler, novels and plays by Heinrich Mann, and plays by Kokoschka and Barlach—works of considerable aesthetic variety that went far beyond Impressionism in pursuit of new forms of expression.

Paul Cassirer continued to conduct the business affairs of the Secession, a situation that inevitably led to complaints about conflicts of interest. But he could not have succeeded in his dual role for nearly fifteen years had the Secession and his gallery been competitors rather than allies in a movement to create interest in recent and current art, in providing modernists with a strong professional base, and in selling art— the Secession selling the work of its members, the gallery the work of the artists it represented. Occasionally these were identical; but most members of the Secession were affiliated with other galleries.[11] His most serious conflict of interest, Cassirer once noted, came when he had to divide paintings by Van Gogh among simultaneous shows of the Secession and his gallery. The different structures and policies of the two also guaranteed their autonomy. The gallery expressed the views of one man. The Secession was an artists' cooperative, which, after ten years, had more than 200 members and corresponding members. It was headed by a president, Max Liebermann, known for his energy and decisiveness, and an executive committee on which Cassirer was merely one among a group of colleagues; major issues were voted on by the entire membership. The gallery shows were more frequent, much smaller, and included far fewer artists than the exhibitions of the Secession, which, after the first years, might number 150 participants or more. The Secession and the Cassirer Gallery complemented one another, and between them represented a majority of modernist artists working in Berlin. They were two centers in a spreading modernist network of galleries, critics, publishers, and museum directors, which, within a remarkably few years, had radically changed the situation of the fine arts in Berlin.

The Berlin Secession and Wilhelm II

Modernist artists now had their own institutions, as well as allies throughout society, including the cultural bureaucracy. Opposition nevertheless remained strong, not only on aesthetic but also on ideological grounds: it was claimed that modernism, especially when choosing working-class themes, was subversive. Terms such as *Armeleutemalerei*—paintings of poor people—became catch-phrases in the debates over art. Typical of efforts to bridge the opposing sides, and the difficulty of doing so, was the vote of the Prussian Commission for the Fine Arts in 1903 to buy a Leistikow landscape for the National Gallery. The minister of cultural affairs rejected the recommendation because "Leistikow is organizationally active as leader of the 'secession.'"[12]

Figure 45
Max Liebermann
**Boy on Horse
[Junge auf Pferd]**, 1903
Oil on board,
24¾ x 27⁹⁄₁₆ in. (62.8 x 70 cm)
Sammlung Kunstkreis Berlin GbR

This episode was repeated on a national scale when Wilhelm II (FIG. 1) and the Association of German Artists maneuvered to exclude the Secession from the German art exhibition at the 1904 St. Louis World's Fair. They succeeded, but the emperor's open partisanship led to a debate in the Reichstag in which even some moderates and conservatives deplored the mobilization of monarchical power against a group of artists. "The history of art and culture," one speaker declared, "has shown that art will go its own way despite kings and emperors who want to enchain it."[13] A second consequence was the founding of a national league of progressive art associations, under the presidency of Harry Count Kessler, which further strengthened modernism throughout the country.

In his last important attempt to stem the tide of modern art, Wilhelm II reached far into the senior cultural bureaucracy of the state. For years he had had disagreements with the director of the National Gallery, Hugo von Tschudi, who, in part influenced by Liebermann, was trying to build up the museum's holdings in modern art. In 1908 Paul Cassirer offered Tschudi four nineteenth-century French paintings. Tschudi's acquisition budget was spent, but he bought the works in expectation of a supplemental appropriation. The emperor exploited this irregularity by demanding that Tschudi take a leave of absence, and followed up his advantage by proposing to replace him with the history painter Anton von Werner (see FIG. 50), head of the Association of Berlin Artists and an energetic opponent of modernism. The change was being widely and unfavorably discussed in the press, when the

Figure 46
Lovis Corinth
Poster for an **Exhibition of Lovis Corinth at Salon Paul Cassirer**, 1908
Lithograph, 24¾ x 34⅝ in. (63 x 88 cm)
Kunstbibliothek, Staatliche Museen zu Berlin–Preussischer Kulturbesitz

Figure 46
Lovis Corinth
Poster for an **Exhibition of Lovis Corinth at Salon Paul Cassirer**, 1908
Lithograph, 24¾ x 34⅝ in. (63 x 88 cm)
Kunstbibliothek, Staatliche Museen zu Berlin–Preussischer Kulturbesitz

Figure 47
Max Pechstein
Poster for **Exhibition of Artists Refused by the Berlin Secession—Organized by the New Secession**, 1910
Color lithograph, 27⅜ x 36⅝ in. (69.5 x 93 cm)
Museum für Kunst und Gewerbe Hamburg

London *Daily Telegraph* published an article with comments on foreign and domestic affairs by the emperor. His impulsive statements caused such outrage in Germany that he felt driven to promise greater restraint in the future. The emperor's agreement to retain Tschudi as head of the National Gallery was a first step in the new direction.[14]

Politically, nevertheless, the so-called *Daily Telegraph* Affair had no significant lasting consequences. The executive structure of the Reich, with its ambiguous areas of responsibility, was not modernized, nor did the Reichstag gain greater authority. But in the cultural sphere, the Tschudi Affair, which had become engulfed in the greater scandal, ended in an unintended victory for modernism. Wilhelm II and his conservative allies in the cultural establishment now took some care to appear unbiased in determining the state's support for the fine arts.[15]

By the time the Tschudi Affair erupted, conservative criticism of such artists as Leistikow and Liebermann was, in any case, outdated. The invective *Armeleutemalerei* (see FIGS. 24, 25) could no longer be applied to Liebermann's work, which had gradually shifted to landscapes, portraits, and themes of upper-class life (FIG. 45). His constantly more daring use of color, the freedom of his brushwork, and his fragmentation of line might continue to offend conventional taste; but their power to shock was as nothing compared to the distortions, let alone subject matter, that began to be shown in some galleries. By the middle of the decade, traditionalists, but also members of the Secession, were forced to confront the broadly variegated movement in art that came to be known as Expressionism.

The Old and the New Avant-Garde

Initially the Secession's response was auspicious. In agreement with Liebermann's statement at the Secession's opening exhibition, "we do not believe in a single, sacred direction in art," the jury for the 1908 graphic exhibition chose entries by members of the Brücke, and by Feininger, Kandinsky, Nolde, and Klee. Paintings by Max Pechstein and Alexej Jawlensky were accepted for the summer exhibition the following year. The Secession seemed ready to accommodate an infusion of the newest avant-garde.

Some members nevertheless objected to the jury's choices. Their disapproval of the new works combined with dissatisfaction in the Secession's leadership, which essentially had remained unchanged for a decade. Consequently, Liebermann, Cassirer, and their supporters resigned from the jury and the executive committee in 1908. They were persuaded to return, except Cassirer, who took a six-month leave of absence from the Secession's business

affairs. In the meantime, a new jury, which included Beckmann, rejected the entries of Nolde and the Brücke painters.

A destructive chain reaction set in. Pechstein organized the "New Secession," which held sensational shows in 1910 (FIG. 47) and 1911. Nolde, who imagined that a conspiracy by Liebermann and Scheffler, the editor of *Kunst und Künstler*, robbed him of deserved recognition, accused Liebermann of venality and artistic senility.[16] At a special general meeting, the members voted to expel Nolde from the Secession. Liebermann, who advised against this step, tired of the endless quarrels and resigned as president. He was succeeded by Lovis Corinth, whose stature as artist and dislike of the work of the Expressionist newcomers seemed to make him an ideal compromise choice; but he was unable to

Figure 48
Lovis Corinth
**Portrait of Makabäus–
Hermann Struck**, 1915
Oil on canvas,
31 11/16 x 23 7/16 in. (80.5 x 59.5 cm)
Städtische Galerie im Lenbachhaus,
Munich

restore harmony. The results were mediocre exhibitions in 1911 and 1912. Pechstein's return in 1912, which led to the breakup of the "New Secession" as well as of the Brücke, again indicates the fluid relations between the old and the new avant-garde, but could not stem the Secession's decline. Dissension among members, not surprising in a large and democratic artists' cooperative and exacerbated by the emergence of Expressionism, was pushing the Secession from its institutional leadership of modernism in Berlin.

Its place was taken by an array of new groups, galleries, and periodicals, of which historically the most influential was Herwarth Walden's weekly *Der Sturm* (The Storm). At first a literary journal, *Der Sturm* soon published graphics, beginning with a drawing by Liebermann, but finding its true message in black-and-white works by Kokoschka (FIG. 60), the Brücke (see FIGS. 65, 70, PLATE 4) and Blaue Reiter (see FIGS. 61, 62, 66, PLATES 5, 6, 12) artists, and later—as Walden tired of them—by Futurists (PLATES 8, 15, 16, 18) and Cubists. In March 1912, Walden held the first Sturm exhibition. Others followed, culminating in the First German Autumn Salon of 1913, the most important international exhibition of contemporary art in the waning months of peace.[17]

During this time, the Secession experienced a last, brief return to vitality. Severe illness forced Corinth to resign as president, and in the obvious crisis in which the Secession found itself, the members elected Cassirer president. The exhibition he organized in the summer of 1913 was a powerful reaffirmation of the breadth and riches of modernism, going back to the 1880s. In contrast to Walden's Autumn Salon, Cassirer stressed the historical continuity from Cézanne and Van Gogh to Matisse and such newcomers as Derain, Marquet, and Vlaminck, and from Liebermann and the early Secessionists to Kokoschka, Barlach, and the Brücke. But the Secession's old tolerance had weakened. Thirteen members, whose work the jury had rejected—among them paintings by Corinth's wife, which made Corinth's position difficult— protested the exhibition and forced a split in the Secession. Liebermann, Slevogt, Cassirer, and thirty-nine others resigned and formed the "Free Secession," a gesture of protest that the coming of war soon made meaningless. Except for Corinth, Hermann Struck (FIG. 48), and two or three others, the members who remained were among the weakest of the group.[18] Corinth served as president of the rump secession until his death in 1925, but his continued poor health rendered effective leadership out of the question, and the group faded into insignificance. The acceptance of a broad range of styles, which had been the Secession's strength when it was founded, could not survive in a new, more radical, narrowly programmatic time.

The Secession in Perspective

For fourteen years after its opening exhibition in 1899, the Berlin Secession was a major institutional force in German modernism.

By creating an alternative to the exhibition and patronage policies of the traditional art associations and of the state, the Secession gave artists a new freedom. That this was achieved only after overcoming intense official opposition was a function of Berlin's special character. The city had developed into a center of great economic power, generated and controlled by the bourgeoisie; at the same time it was the capital of a constitutional yet authoritarian monarchy, whose sovereign claimed broad jurisdiction in matters of art. That the Secession was, nevertheless, victorious in its conflict with Wilhelm II helped change the culture of Berlin and of Germany.

In this conflict the Secession had allies, ranging from directors of the state museums to journalists and art dealers. Together and often competing, they created the resources and opportunities necessary for a vigorous art community. They strengthened Germany's links to foreign art; broke down the provincial isolation of artists, museums, and the art public; and helped German artists translate foreign concepts into a native idiom. As in literature and music, a sophisticated modern-art culture developed in Berlin. It survived the First World War and fostered the efflorescence of Weimar, much of which was the work of men and women who were already in the forefront of innovation in 1914.

But although the Secession and its allies were successful at the time, the opposition they faced succeeded in turning art into politics. Before 1914, most modern art in Germany was apolitical— in contrast to the work of officially supported history painters and portrait painters, who celebrated the imperial system—but nowhere in Europe was the issue of modernism politicized to the same extent. The First World War intensified this tendency, until defining certain kinds of art as degenerate and a threat to the nation's values—usually in anti-Semitic terms—became a political weapon in the war against the Weimar Republic.[19]

Jews and German Modernism

From a different perspective, the brief, creative history of the Secession and its allies may be seen as a high point of Jewish assimilation in Germany, an example of the partnership of Jews and non-Jews in an important area of German life. That anti-Semitic attacks on Jews prominent in the arts were not the monopoly of Philipp Stauff and other radical populists, but might come from the ranks of modernism itself, does not negate the fact of integration.

How important were Jews in the rise of German modernism? This touches on the issue of Jewish identity, which can hardly be discussed at length here; a few comments related to Berlin at the turn of the century must suffice. For many Jews in the arts or interested in the arts, the issue posed no difficulty. They felt themselves to be Jews, whether in a religious or nonreligious sense, as did the gentile majority among whom they lived. In a society in which assimilation had passed a certain point, this did not neces-

Figure 49
Interior of the Eduard Arnhold residence

sarily mean that their ideas and feelings about art and its place in German culture and society were uniquely Jewish. Some Jews were influenced by Jewish cultural traditions, others were not. At the time, the concept of race was still widely respected as scientifically sound, but only the more rabid anti-Semites and a few philo-Semitic enthusiasts claimed that genetic inheritance automatically led to a given cultural point of view.

Family background may give us useful evidence for understanding the ideas and behavior of proponents and opponents of modernism in Wilhelmine Berlin. But it is ambiguous evidence, and a complex background makes it more problematical. It is often misleading to characterize someone as a Jew who had both Jewish and gentile ancestors, whose Jewish ancestors had converted to Christianity, who no longer held religious beliefs or followed Jewish customs, and who married a Gentile. Nor did bloodlines of one sort or another determine a person's sense of self. Some Germans of mixed descent felt themselves to be Jews, others did not.

The role of Jews differed in the various facets of modernism. For the Secession's first twelve years, its president, who was also one of its leading artists, was a Jew who was proud of his Jewish identity and traditions even as he valued assimilation. (See the essay by Chana Schütz in this book.) But apart from Liebermann, only a few significant artists of Jewish or partly Jewish origin worked in Berlin, among them Hermann Struck, best known for his graphics (see FIGS. 152, 153); the sculptor Louis Tuaillon; Walter Bondy, a cousin of the Cassirers; the young painters Eugen

Figure 50
Anton von Werner
The Mosse Family Banquet:
Study for Dining-Room Mural
at the Mosse Villa [Das Gastmahl
der Familie Mosse: Entwurf für
ein Wandbild im Speisesaal der
Villa Mosse], 1899
Oil on canvas,
18⅛ x 35 in. (45.5 x 88.7 cm)
Stiftung Jüdisches Museum, Berlin.
Purchased with funds from the
Stiftung Deutsche Klassenlotterie

Spiro and Max Oppenheimer; and, above all, Lesser Ury
(see FIGS 98, 99, 102–6, 108).[20] In the Secession, they never
formed more than a small minority. Jews were equally rare
among the Expressionist avant-garde, unless ethnic identity is
measured by refinements that go beyond the definitions of the
Nuremberg Laws.

Far more dominant was the Jewish presence among the initially small number of gallerists and publishers of modernism.
Bruno and Paul Cassirer and, later, Herwarth Walden exerted a
notable influence on the exhibition, dissemination, and sale of
modern art. As more publishers and art dealers entered the field,
and such long-established Berlin galleries as Gurlitt, Schulte, and
Amsler & Rutthardt expanded their clientele for modern art, the
Cassirers remained first among a growing number of equals.
Their work was supported by influential critics, several of whom
were Jews, although others were not. Jewish journalists could also
be found in the traditional camp.

The buyers and collectors of modern art, finally, fell into two
main groups. Museum directors and curators were state officials,
holding positions to which unconverted Jews were only rarely
appointed. The museum directors pivotal in making modern
art acceptable in Germany—men such as Hugo von Tschudi in
Berlin and later in Munich, Alfred Lichtwark in Hamburg,
Gustav Pauli in Bremen and later in Hamburg—were Gentiles.

Among private collectors and donors the situation was
reversed, especially in Berlin. The major donors of modern and
old art to Berlin museums between the accession of Wilhelm II
and the end of the Weimar Republic have been identified as
almost all belonging to the "German-Jewish high bourgeoisie."[21]
The reasons for their large gifts of works of art and money varied.
Genuine interest and community spirit were motives, as might be
social ambition, although several of the most important Jewish
donors rejected titles of nobility—for instance, Eduard Arnhold,

one of the richest men in Berlin, whom Paul Cassirer advised on his collection (FIG. 49) and who was one of Tschudi's strong supporters.[22] The claim—advanced not only by racists—that Jews had a special affinity for modernism would, however, be difficult to prove. In other European capitals before 1914, wealthy Jews directed their support elsewhere; presumably each city's particular social and cultural configuration helped determine its preferred forms of patronage. And in Berlin, not all wealthy Jews interested in the arts favored modernism. One of Arnhold's peers, the Jewish newspaper magnate Rudolf Mosse, after the Kaiser the richest man in the capital, was a patron and friend of Anton von Werner, the Kaiser's ally in fighting the Secession, and a collector of nineteenth-century history and narrative painting (FIG. 50). Nor are multimillionaires necessarily representative of larger socioeconomic and ethnic groups. There is no evidence to indicate that in 1900 the tastes in art of the average Jewish and non-Jewish professional or businessman differed greatly. On the other hand, the arts provided unusual scope for the individualism and creativity of members of a group still not fully accepted in German society. Those Jews who resented or were unimpressed by norms that found them inadequate could welcome new forms of art for reasons that would not motivate gentile supporters of modernism.

Not ethnic characteristics, however measured, but historical conditions and individual convictions determined the role that Jews played in bringing modernism to Germany. Had there been no Liebermann, Cassirer, or Arnhold, modern art would still have made headway in Central Europe, although the details of the process would have differed. As it was, modernism was fostered jointly by Jews and non-Jews, each depending on the other. Their actions can hardly be identified as representative of this or that ethnic or religious group. Jews took opposing positions in the arts, as did Gentiles, and any effort to define assimilated artists, critics, collectors, and dealers on the basis of their Jewish or partly Jewish origins breaks down as soon as the individual life is studied in detail. The leading figures, especially, with their unique talents, experiences, and goals, rise far above any ethnic typology.

But Jewish participation in Berlin modernism does say a great deal about a larger community that undoubtedly did exist: German society as it was before the First World War. The shifting balance between acceptance and continued anti-Semitism not only conditioned the role of Jewish, partly Jewish, and formerly Jewish participants in the course of modernization; it also points to later stages of German history and, in particular, to the shift in the Third Reich from assimilation to extermination.

Notes

1. Philipp Stauff, "Das Fremdtum in Deutschlands bildender Kunst, oder Paul Cassirer, Max Liebermann usw.," in *Semi-Kürschner*, vol. 2, ed. Philipp Stauff (Berlin, 1913), p. i.

2. On Liebermann's work and his ideas on art, see the valuable although incomplete edition of his writings, *Die Phantasie in der Malerei*, ed. Günter Busch (Frankfurt am Main: S. Fischer, 1978); and the catalogues of two retrospectives, which give a good overview of recent scholarship: *Max Liebermann in seiner Zeit*, ed. Sigrid Achenbach and Matthias Eberle (Munich: Prestel, 1979); and *Max Liebermann—Jahrhundertwende*, ed. Angelika Wesenberg (Berlin: Ars Nicolai, 1997).

3. Corinth's biography *Das Leben Walter Leistikows* (Berlin: Paul Cassirer, 1910) is an empathetic study of the artist in his environment, and representative of the literary talent of many German artists of the time. Liebermann, Leistikow himself, Barlach, Kokoschka, Marc, and—despite his intellectual and moral convolutions—Nolde would be other examples. A good modern biography is Margrit Bröhan, *Walter Leistikow* (Berlin: Ars Nicolai, 1989).

4. The background, founding, and history of the Berlin Secession are discussed in Peter Paret, *The Berlin Secession* (Cambridge, Mass.: Harvard University Press, 1980).

5. A more detailed discussion of the common characteristics of secessions, and of some of the differences between them, may be found in Paret, *The Berlin Secession*, pp. 29–37. Two informative studies of the Munich and Vienna secessions are Maria Makela, *The Munich Secession* (Princeton: Princeton University Press, 1991); and James Shedel, "Art and Identity, The Wiener Secession, 1897–1938," in *Secession*, ed. Eleonora Louis (Ostfildern-Ruit: Gert Hatje, 1997).

6. *Katalog der Deutschen Kunstausstellung der "Berliner Secession"* (Berlin: Bruno and Paul Cassirer, 1899), p. 15.

7. Some comparative figures are given in Rudolf Martin, *Jahrbuch des Vermögens und Einkommens der Millionäre in Berlin* (Berlin, 1913), pp. 11, 26, 50. On Bruno and Paul Cassirer, see Paret, *The Berlin Secession*; Harry Nutt, *Bruno Cassirer* (Berlin: Stapp, 1989); Christian Kennert, *Paul Cassirer und sein Kreis* (Frankfurt am Main: Peter Lang, 1996); and such specialized studies as Eva Caspers, *Paul Cassirer und die Pan-Presse* (Frankfurt am Main: Buchhändler-Vereinigung, 1989); and Walter Feilchenfeldt, *Vincent van Gogh and Paul Cassirer* (Zwolle: Uitgeverij Waanders, 1988). Georg Brühl's history of the family, *Die Cassirers* (Leipzig: Edition Leipzig, 1991), is insufficiently documented and contains factual errors.

8. Karl Scheffler, *Die fetten und die mageren Jahre*, 2d rev. ed. (Munich and Leipzig: Paul List, 1946), p. 193.

9. Catalogue of the Paul Cassirer Gallery, vol. 10 (Berlin: Paul Cassirer, 1907–8).

10. Catalogue of the Paul Cassirer Gallery, vol. 15 (Berlin: Paul Cassirer, 1912–13). In this connection, note also Cassirer's important essay on the economics of art, "Kunst und Kunsthandel," in a collection of essays by various authors defending modern art against conservative attacks, *Deutsche und französische Kunst*, ed. Alfred Walter Heymel (Munich: Piper, 1911). For the background to the volume and a discussion of its contents, see Paret, *The Berlin Secession*, pp. 182–99.

11. The assertion, sometimes encountered in the literature—for example, Walter S. Laux, *Der Fall Corinth* (Munich: Prestel, 1998), p. 17—that all or nearly all members of the Secession were under contract to Cassirer is incorrect, and reveals a misunderstanding of the relationship between the Secession and the gallery. Indeed, the resentment of some members toward those who did have contracts was one of the factors that eventually led to the decline of the Secession.

12. Far from being confidential, the minister's statement was published in the press. See, for instance, the art journal *Kunst für Alle* 19 (1903–4): 152.

13. Paret, *The Berlin Secession*, p. 141.

14. Wilhelm II's conflict with Tschudi is discussed in detail in Peter Paret, "The Tschudi Affair," *Journal of Modern History* 53, no. 4 (1981): 589–618.

15. This did not, of course, signify a true change of heart. The emperor continued to judge art from political and social perspectives. As late as 1913 he noted in a private memorandum: "Certainly we must seek . . . to limit Jewish influence in all areas of art and literature as much as possible." Cited in Hartmut Pogge von Strandmann and Immanuel Geiss, eds., *Die Erforderlichkeit des Unmöglichen: Deutschland am Vorabend des ersten Weltkrieges* (Frankfurt am Main, 1965), p. 38.

16. For a fuller account of Nolde's attack, with its falsifications and anti-Semitic overtones, see Paret, *The Berlin Secession*, pp. 210–16.

17. On Walden and the First German Autumn Salon, see Peter Selz, *German Expressionist Painting* (Berkeley and Los Angeles: University of California Press, 1974), pp. 250–73.

18. Struck's decision to remain in the rump secession did not affect his good relations with Paul Cassirer, who respected him as a serious, if limited, craftsman. Cassirer continued to reprint Struck's work on graphic technique, *Die Kunst des Radierens*, first published in 1908, which he eventually brought out in a revised fifth edition in 1923.

19. Among the many links between the years before 1914 and the Weimar period is Stauff's anti-Semitic dictionary. The 1929 edition continued to denounce Liebermann, who is labeled "a parasite on the body of German character and art, one of the birds of doom of the German spirit, international in outlook, and a servant of the Talmud."

20. Ury, an innovative colorist and brilliant interpreter of urban scenes, was, after Liebermann, perhaps the most distinguished Jewish painter in Berlin. His work was favorably reviewed and sold well; but his extreme shyness and a sense of persecution isolated him among Berlin artists. After initially good relations, he and Liebermann became enemies, which may explain why he did not join the Secession. The rumor that he had added highlights to improve some of the older man's paintings led to a characteristic witticism by Liebermann: "I don't care if people say my paintings are by Lesser; but if he claims his paintings are by me, I'll sue." In 1916, the Paul Cassirer Gallery showed a large retrospective of Ury's work; but despite these and other marks of achievement, permanent success escaped him. Informative comments on the relationship between Ury and the Secession are in Rudolf Pfefferkorn, *Die Berliner Secession* (Berlin: Haude & Spener, 1972); and Werner Doede, *Die Berliner Secession* (Frankfurt am Main and Berlin: Propyläen, 1977). Alfred Werner has published an uneven but interesting essay on this tragic figure, "The Strange Tale of Lesser Ury," in the *Leo Baeck Year Book* 19 (1974): 197–207.

21. Research by Cella-Margaretha Girardet, cited in Peter Paret, "Bemerkungen zu dem Thema: Jüdische Kunstsammler, Stifter und Kunsthändler," in *Sammler, Stifter und Museen*, ed. Ekkehard Mai and Peter Paret (Cologne/Weimar/Vienna: Böhlau, 1993), p. 176.

22. Wolfgang Hardtwig, "Drei Berliner Porträts: Wilhelm von Bode, Eduard Arnhold, Harry Graf Kessler," in *Mäzenatentum in Berlin*, ed. Günter and Waldtraut Braun (Berlin, 1993), p. 44.

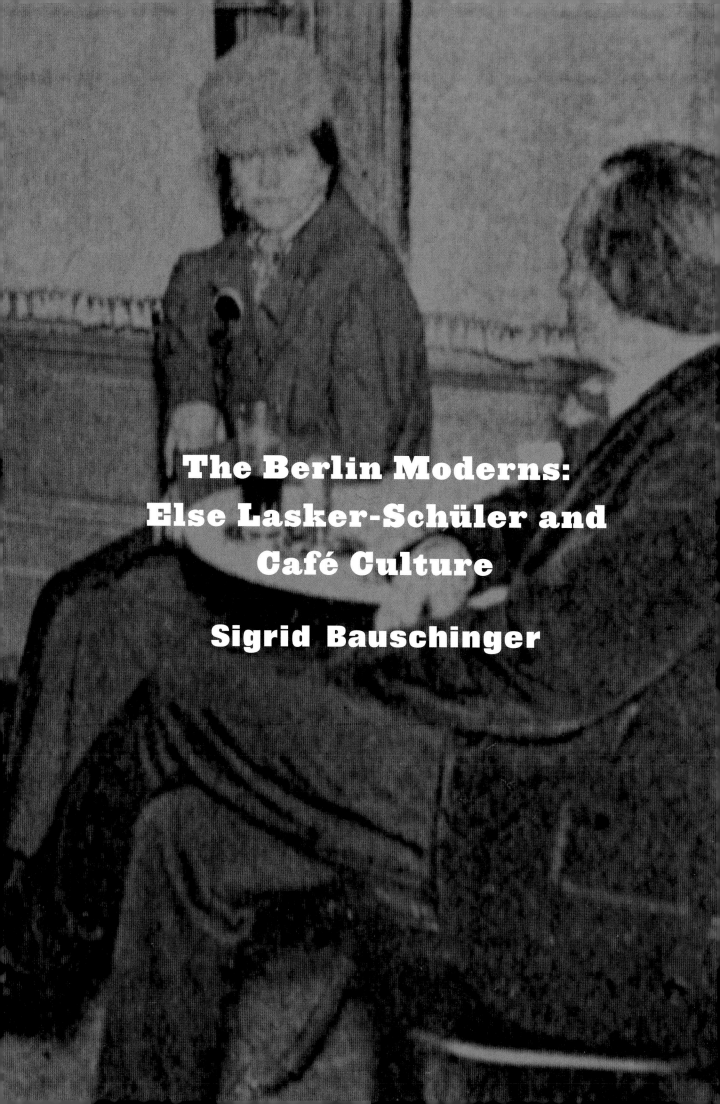

The Berlin Moderns:
Else Lasker-Schüler and
Café Culture

Sigrid Bauschinger

In Berlin during the first two decades of the twentieth century, Jewish literary figures—poets, novelists, editors, and critics, even those who produced rather conventional works themselves—were among the first to discover the innovative new artists, and to encourage and promote their work. Gottfried Benn, whom Peter Gay cites in his essay on the "Berlin Jewish Spirit" as "hardly a sympathetic witness," put it this way: "The overflowing plenty of stimuli, of artistic, scientific, commercial improvisations which placed the Berlin of 1918 to 1933 in the class of Paris, stemmed for the most part from the talents of this sector of the population, its international connections, its sensitive restlessness and above all, its dead-certain—*totsichere*—instinct for quality."[1] This *totsichere* instinct was evident among Jewish critics such as Ludwig Jacobowski and Samuel Lublinski even before the turn of the century. It peaked in such extraordinary champions and disseminators of modern art and literature as Herwarth Walden and Paul and Bruno Cassirer; and it found its incarnation in the poet and artist Else Lasker-Schüler, who stood at the center of Berlin's early modern culture and its common ground, the café.

The Up-and-Coming

Among the very first to recognize the new artistic direction was Ludwig Jacobowski (1868–1900). He had been invited in February 1896 by the twenty-year-old Rainer Maria Rilke (1875–1926) to join his Bund der Moderne (Modern Association). Rilke knew the Jewish writer, seven years his senior, as one who was dedicated to a new literature that would lead beyond the "dilapidated building of Naturalism."[2] While he was still a student, Jacobowski had founded the journal *Der Zeitgenosse* (The Contemporary). During his short life he published eleven volumes of poetry and prose, of which the novel *Werther der Jude* (Werther the Jew, 1892) was the most successful, as well as plays and innumerable literary studies. A stalwart fighter against anti-Semitism, he was also the author of many political articles.

Jacobowski is more important, however, for his efforts in discovering and propagating the "newest" literature.[3] As president of Die Neue Freie Volksbühne (The New Public Theater Association), he introduced Berlin audiences to the plays of Arthur Schnitzler. And as editor of the influential magazine *Die Gesellschaft* (Society), he published many young writers for the first time. In his reviews, he predicted the lasting fame of Rilke and Thomas Mann. During the last months of his life, together with Rudolf Steiner he founded Die Kommenden (The Up-and-Coming), a colloquium of poets who met every Friday at the Casino am Nollendorfplatz to read and discuss their latest works (see FIG. 144). Among the group were quite a few women, most of whom Jacobowski overestimated. One notable exception was Else Lasker-Schüler (1868–1945), whose poems were first published in *Die Gesellschaft* and who was given a forum among Die Kommenden.

(opposite)
(Detail) The "Moderns" at their regular table at the Café des Westens
From *Der Weltspiegel*, Illustrated Biweekly of the *Berliner Tageblatt*, no. 41, 21 May 1905

Figure 51
Else Lasker-Schüler, 1906
Deutsche Schillergesellschaft,
Marbach am Neckar

Her poems were regarded as "new" and "modern" by yet another remarkable Jewish critic, Samuel Lublinski (1868–1910). As early as 1904, he published a critique of the modern Naturalist movement entitled *Bilanz der Moderne*. His *Literatur und Gesellschaft* (Literature and Society, 1910) was the first attempt to write literary history from a sociological point of view. Lublinski recognized, for example, that the women's movement had given women the courage to express their female personality and experiences, and that Lasker-Schüler (FIG. 51), among the many who now dared to bare their innermost feelings and even passions, was the most convincing. "Weltflucht" ("Flight from the World"), from her first collection, *Styx* (1902), is one of the poems that startled those gathered at the Casino am Nollendorfplatz:

> Ich will in das Grenzenlose
> Zu mir zurück,
> Schon blüht die Herbstzeitlose
> Meiner Seele,
> Vielleicht—ist's schon zu spät zurück!
> O, ich sterbe unter Euch!
> Da Ihr mich erstickt mit Euch.
> Fäden möchte ich um mich ziehn—
> Wirrwarr endend!
> Beirrend,
> Euch verwirrend,
> Um zu entfliehn
> Meinwärts!

> Let me go into the boundless,
> Back to myself.
> The autumncrocus of my soul
> Is already in flower,
> Perhaps it's already too late to return.
> I die among you!
> You, who suffocate me with your selves.
> O, to draw threads around me—
> Ending confusion!
> Misleading,
> Confusing you,
> To escape
> Me-wards.[4]

Lasker-Schüler spoke for herself and out of her own experience in poems such as "Sinnenrausch" (Intoxicated Senses) or "Nervus Erotis." Inspired by the vitalism of the Art Nouveau movement, she used its vocabulary, images, and colors—weaving, floating, entwining movements, water and dance metaphors, and an abundance of the color red. Lasker-Schüler would outgrow her Art Nouveau beginnings, as did the others whose work endured. At the turn of the century, however, she had arrived at the forefront of modern literature.

What is the meaning of "modern" in this context? Every era that introduces new themes and forms in literature and art could be called modern. The innovations of the modern period in German literature, which began during the last decades of the nineteenth century—most notably, with the Naturalist plays of Gerhart Hauptmann—intended to challenge "the validity of traditional morality, social thought, and art."[5] For Carl Schorske, who makes the important connection between the Naturalist movement and the growth of urban life, the turn toward the modern occurred in Europe around 1850, ushered in by Baudelaire, the French Impressionists, and Nietzsche. Andreas Huyssen, stressing the political radicalisms of the post-Revolutionary avant-garde, points to the period following the French Revolution when the artist was given a prominent role in constructing the ideal state. This idea was still very much alive in the bohemian subculture around 1900, when artists and anarchists alike rejected the stagnating cultural conservatism of bourgeois society.[6] Peter Gay traces the disdain for the "philistine" even further back, to eighteenth-century Germany, where it was expressed, for instance, in student songs. The passionate "bourgeoisophobe" Gustave Flaubert enunciated this idea in his axiom: "Hatred of the bourgeois is the beginning of all virtues."[7] This pronouncement could just as well have come from Else Lasker-Schüler, echoing through her circle of poets and artists who were flocking to the German capital in ever rising numbers around 1900.

Figure 52
U-Bahnhof Nollendorfplatz, 1909
Photograph: Max Missmann

Why Berlin? The city had expanded in the thirty years since unification, in 1871, in unimaginable proportions. The population nearly doubled between 1880 and 1915, when it reached 1,879,000. One hundred daily newspapers were published in Berlin, many coming out with both morning and evening editions. The city had sixty theaters and twenty-five railroad stations that connected the capital with every region of the empire and beyond (FIG. 52).

Previous German cultural centers, such as Dresden in the eighteenth century and Munich in the nineteenth, could not compete with this magnet that attracted young, hopeful artists and writers who had found in Berlin not only congenial colleagues but also a market. Newspapers were in daily need of brief prose pieces, poetry, book reviews, and art criticism for their arts section, the "Feuilleton." Theaters had to produce new plays. Publishing houses were established, giving employment to editors. Art galleries exhibited the latest works from Germany and abroad.

Outside of Berlin, everywhere was the provinces. Especially from the eastern regions of Prussia, young families, like Ludwig Jacobowski's, moved to the metropolis. Samuel Lublinski chose Berlin as the most promising for his work, as did Else Lasker-

Figure 53
Members of the Neue Gemeinschaft
celebrate the Spring Festival
(Else Lasker-Schüler, Albert Weidner,
Julius Hart, and Peter Hille), 1902
Stadt- und Landesbibliothek Dortmund

Figure 54
Herwarth Walden (born Georg Lewin),
1903

Schüler's husband, the physician Berthold Lasker, whom she followed in 1894 from her hometown of Elberfeld, in the Rhineland. These young people came from very different backgrounds. Jacobowski's father was a humble salesman, and the son never had enough money and consequently worked himself to death. Lasker-Schüler came from a very well-to-do family—her father was a banker and builder—and, at first, she lived with her physician husband in comfortable circumstances in Berlin. Immersing herself in the city's cultural life, she took painting lessons, went to the theater and opera, and visited art galleries. Peter Hille, a vagrant poet and the only mentor she ever had, introduced her to Die Neue Gemeinschaft (The New Community) of the brothers Heinrich (1855–1906) and Julius Hart (1859–1930), where Jewish and non-Jewish artists and intellectuals mingled freely (FIG. 53). The brothers propagated an anti-rationalist worldview and cult of nature and love. Here Lasker-Schüler met men like the Jewish philosopher Martin Buber (1878–1965), the poet and future revolutionary Erich Mühsam (1878–1934), and a young musician, Georg Lewin (1878–1941), to whom she would give the name Herwarth Walden (FIG. 54). Lasker-Schüler's bourgeois existence as the wife of a professional man became incompatible with a life committed to art. She divorced Berthold Lasker in 1903, and maintained that her son Paul, born four years earlier, was the son of a Greek prince.

Else Lasker-Schüler and the Berlin Avant-Garde

The break with bourgeois convention was typical for many of the young Jewish intellectuals who rose to prominence in the following years, especially during the "Expressionist decade," from 1910 to 1920. They fought against everything the earlier generation had considered desirable—upward mobility, social status, and prosperity.[8] As Hans Tramer pointed out, young Jews were especially attracted to the "new direction," that is, to Expressionism, for a number of reasons. Their fathers were members of the complacent bourgeoisie. Their families practiced a faith that had become superficial through assimilation, or they continued to adhere to a constricting religious orthodoxy. Both forms of religious observance were entirely unsatisfactory for a new generation that confronted daily the astonishing changes taking place in politics, the economy, and art. These changes strengthened their belief in progress for all humankind, including the Jewish people. Participation in modern culture promised an end to cultural and social marginalization and to the isolation inherent in religious orthodoxy. It meant not having to identify with the empire by assimilation or with the conservative, Romantic "organic" Judaism of Eastern Europe.[9] The best possible means of escape from the position of outsider in German society was found by many in the Expressionist movement, where "the German-Jewish symbiosis seemed to have come closest to being realized."[10] Indeed, the "cohabitation" and mutually beneficial collaboration among Jewish and non-Jewish artists, writers, critics, collectors, and promoters of modern art during this period could make one believe in this debated symbiosis.

The historian Steven M. Lowenstein warns us not to view the participation—he avoids the term "contribution"—of Jews in German culture as specifically "Jewish." It was always the act of an individual. In many cases, the individual was not even deeply rooted in Judaism. Instead of illustrating how Jews influenced (or dominated) German culture, as they were accused of doing long before 1933, Jewish participation can be viewed as a sign of the "acculturation of German-speaking Jews,"[11] the embracing of German culture without abandoning the Jewish faith or Jewish customs. The young Jewish writers and artists put their faith in the new because it held out the hope of renewal. It was the last time men and women—and none more than Else Lasker-Schüler—believed that art could save the world.

Peter Gay has repeatedly stressed the fact that not all Jewish writers in the Wilhelmine era were members of the avant-garde. This holds true especially for the early period, the last decade of the nineteenth century. Jacobowski and Lublinski wrote very much in the vein of nineteenth-century German literature. When Jewish poets joined the Expressionist avant-garde ten years later, they found, as Gay observes, "that the non-Jewish poets in their camp wrote, on the whole, much better than they did."[12]

When Gottfried Benn praised the Berlin Jewish artists, critics, and audiences for their "dead-certain" instinct for quality, he might have had in mind Else Lasker-Schüler, who demonstrated this *totsichere* instinct herself. When she read *Morgue*, Benn's cycle of poems, in 1913, she tried to persuade the publisher Kurt Wolff to reprint these masterpieces of early Expressionism. "These poems were written by a real tiger," she wrote. "Perhaps you know, Dr. Benn is a physician-surgeon and really powerful."[13] In a second letter she assured Wolff: "I am not romantically attached to Dr. Benn, I am doing this, word of honor, behind his back, out of my universal sense of values, not even for culture."[14] In a series of essays discussing Karl Kraus, Oskar Kokoschka, Max Brod, and Samuel Lublinski, among others, she characterized Benn's "horrifying art-miracles" in her unique nature and animal imagery.[15]

The artistic connection between Lasker-Schüler and Benn is but one, albeit a prime, example of the mutual recognition and inspiration typical among the avant-garde writers, both Jews and non-Jews, during the first decades of the century, and nowhere more than in Berlin. Another example was Der Neue Club (The New Club), an association of mostly Jewish students that began as a liberal fraternity and went on to organize "public evenings" in 1909. They invited contemporary poets and composers to give readings and performances, but they also read poetry by Friedrich Hölderlin and—

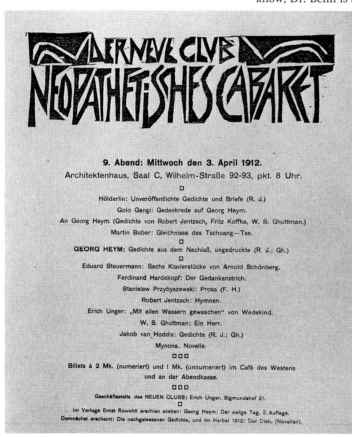

Figure 55
Karl Schmidt-Rottluff
**Der Neue Club,
Neopathetisches Cabaret**, 1911
Woodcut on thin laid paper,
1 7/8 x 6 5/8 in. (4.7 x 16.8 cm), 1911
Los Angeles County Museum of Art.
The Robert Gore Rifkind Center for
German Expressionist Studies.
Purchased with funds provided by
Anna Bing Arnold, Museum Associates
Acquisition Fund, and deaccession funds
(M.82.228.261)

at almost every meeting—texts by Friedrich Nietzsche. Nietzsche could be called the common denominator of German modernism. His "Umwertung aller Werte," a "revison of all values," had a major influence on Expressionism. Even Lasker-Schüler, who denied being influenced or even inspired by anyone, said to a friend: "Nietzsche created the language in which we all write."[16]

By 1910, Der Neue Club had changed its name to the Neopathetisches Cabaret (FIG. 55).[17] But its programs were a far cry from what is commonly understood today as Berlin cabaret. Besides recitations of poetry by Rilke, Stefan George, and Hugo von Hofmannsthal, or readings from plays by Frank Wedekind, the audience could hear piano music by Arnold Schönberg; once they even heard a lecture by Martin Buber. Most important, however, the Neopathetiker promoted their Berlin contemporaries. One of the most important Expressionist poets, Georg Heym

(1887–1912), was effectively discovered by members of the Neue Club. After his death, his work was salvaged and posthumously published by one of the club's founders, Erwin Loewenson. Heym is yet another of the many non-Jewish poets and artists who owed so much to their Jewish friends, publishers, editors, and art dealers. For example, Herwarth Walden gave a great number of artists and writers what was often their first chance to publish and to exhibit, among them Heinrich Campendonk (see PLATE 10), Oskar Kokoschka, Alfred Kubin, and the Expressionist poets Paul Scheerbart, August Stramm, and Paul Zech. Paul Cassirer and his successor, Walter Feilchenfeldt, paid yearly stipends to the sculptor Ernst Barlach, the painter Kokoschka, and the writer Heinrich Mann. The publisher Samuel Fischer discovered talents such as Thomas Mann and counted most of the great twentieth-century writers, from Gerhart Hauptmann to Hermann Hesse, among his authors; he also published lesser-known writers such as Annette Kolb.[18] Else Lasker-Schüler appeared at the Neopathetisches Cabaret with Georg Heym in December 1910 in a program of poetry and prose readings. Only five weeks later she was asked to read again, this time excerpts from her first play, *Die Wupper*. She had completed the work in 1909, but had to wait ten years to see it performed at Max Reinhardt's Deutsches Theater as part of a matinée series devoted to some of the playwrights known as "Young Germany" (FIG. 56). By then, in 1919, she was fifty, and ten to twenty years older than even the earliest Expressionists. But the younger generation admired her, she appeared in all the Expressionist anthologies—sometimes the only woman—and she, in turn, supported them.

Figure 56
Ernst Stern
Set design for **Die Wupper**
by Else Lasker-Schüler, 1919
Mixed-media and watercolor,
21¼ x 28⅜ in. (54 x 72 cm)
Theaterhistorische Sammlung
der Universität Köln

Figure 57
Else Lasker-Schüler
Die Wupper: Schauspiel in Fünf Akten (The Wupper: A Play in Five Acts)
Published by Paul Cassirer, Berlin, 1919
Private collection, United States

Die Wupper (FIG. 57), named for the river that flows through Lasker-Schüler's Rhineland hometown of Elberfeld with its dye factories, is a magic-realist play that explores a cross-section of society at the brink of the industrial age. She wrote it as an homage to the place and its colorful inhabitants, the old working-class women, religious sectarians, and outsiders who fascinated her as a child. Written in language that captures the dialect of the Wupper valley, the play juxtaposes working-class and capitalist families whose lives are intertwined. But *Die Wupper* is not a play about class struggle. It is neither a Naturalist nor Expressionist drama, although it is indebted to both artistic movements.

Figure 58
Emil Orlik
Paul Cassirer, ca. 1910
Pencil on paper, 5⅛ x 3⁹⁄₁₆ in. (13 x 9 cm)
Museum Ostdeutsche Galerie Regensburg

Promoters of Modernity

When Lasker-Schüler wrote *Die Wupper*, she was at the pinnacle of her productivity. She stood at the center of the modern movement in Berlin, which was most evident then in the newly established publishing houses and art galleries where primarily Jewish editors and gallery owners were turning Berlin into a capital of modernity.

Samuel Fischer (1859–1934) had founded his publishing company in 1886. Together with his editor, Moritz Heimann (1868–1925), who has often been compared to Lessing's Nathan the Wise,[19] he published a host of new writers, from Thomas Mann to Alfred Döblin and other early Expressionists.

Among those who furthered the rise of modern art and literature in Berlin, the Cassirers played a special role in disseminating modernism. (See Peter Paret's essay in this book.) In 1899, the cousins Paul (1871–1926) and Bruno Cassirer (1872–1941) opened a publishing house and art gallery in the Tiergarten district. Two years later, Bruno decided to devote himself solely to book publishing and Paul to the gallery, although Paul soon published such works as Alfred Lichtwark's *Aufruf zur Erneuerung des Lebens durch Kunst (Erziehung)* (Appeal for the Renewal of Life through Art [Education], 1905), counting among his authors Frank Wedekind, Georg Heym, Ernst Barlach, and Alfred Döblin. In 1919–20, he published the collected works of Else Lasker-Schüler in ten volumes, each with a cover designed by the poet (see FIG. 57). Paul Cassirer (FIG. 58) founded the Pan-Presse in 1908 for bibliophile editions, followed by the cultural and political journal *Pan* in 1910. And during the First World War he financed the magazine *Die weissen Blätter* (The White Pages), a dissident publication critical of the war, which had its editorial offices in Switzerland.

Figure 59
Herwarth Walden, 1918
Photograph: Nicola Perscheid

Paul Cassirer introduced Berlin to modern art as early as 1901, despite opposition from the highest ranks of Wilhelmine society. Modern art then was French Impressionism, the art of the enemy, and, according to Wilhelm II, it was "gutter art." The emperor had an opinion about everything, including modern painting. "Art that disregards the laws I have established is no art,"[20] he decreed. But an important segment of the Berlin art public seems not to have cared about the laws established by His Majesty. The Salon Cassirer, as the gallery was called, thrived and exhibited a wealth of modern art: Max Liebermann and the French Impressionists first, the Expressionists later.[21] The journal published by Bruno Cassirer, *Kunst und Künstler* (Art and Artist), was an important venue for promoting the Impressionists, among other modern artists.

If Paul Cassirer can be compared with any other impresario of modern art and literature in Berlin, it would be Herwarth Walden (see FIGS. 16, 59, 79, PLATES. 1, 2), whom Else Lasker-Schüler had met in the Neue Gemeinschaft, and whom she married after her divorce from Berthold Lasker in 1903. Walden was nine years younger, and son of the distinguished Berlin physician Victor Lewin, who had been awarded an honorary title by the state for his professional achievements. Walden was a pianist and composer. In 1897 he won a stipend from the Franz Liszt Foundation, which he used to study in Florence for a year. Upon his return to Berlin, he immersed himself in the city's cultural scene, as had Lasker-Schüler a few years earlier. Through his teacher, the pianist Conrad Ansorge, himself a student of Liszt, Walden met the most influential German poet of the day, Richard Dehmel (see FIG. 135), and through him a man who had fascinated young European intellectuals at the turn of the century, Stanislaw Przybyszewski (1868–1927). The Polish writer, strongly influenced by Nietzsche and the author of prose, drama, and poetry in German, was a leader of the Polish modernist movement. Like Walden, he was eager to discover new talent, to surround himself with like-minded companions, fight the bourgeois hierarchies, decry the mediocre, and acclaim originality in art, literature, and music.[22]

One of the first venues for presenting the "new" was Walden's Verein für Kunst, or Art Society, a more professionally organized group than Die Kommenden or the Neopathetiker. Here, each evening featured only one author, and everybody who was somebody in German literature was invited: Karl Kraus, the eminent critic and publisher of *Die Fackel* (The Torch) from Vienna, with whom Walden closely collaborated; Lasker-Schüler; Thomas Mann; Rilke; Wedekind. For a time, the Verein was also a publishing venture. It was there that Lasker-Schüler's second volume of poetry, *Der siebente Tag* (The Seventh Day), appeared in 1905. Alfred Döblin's short play, *Lydia und Mäxchen*, in which props play as big a role as actors, was produced that same year. Arnold Schönberg performed his compositions, as did Walden, who continued to set poems to music, among them works by Lasker-Schüler. His music pantomime *Die vier Toten der Fiametta*

Figure 60
Oskar Kokoschka
**Murderer, Hope of Women
(Mörder, Hoffnung der
Frauen)**, 1910
Ink on paper
From *Der Sturm* 1, no. 20 (1910)
Los Angeles County Museum of Art.
The Robert Rifkind Center for
German Expressionist Studies.
Gift of Robert Gore Rifkind
(AC1992.165.258)

(The Four Dead of Fiametta) had its first performance in Berlin in 1911.

Herwarth Walden and *Der Sturm*

Walden was a born publicist, and he began to edit one avant-garde magazine after another, with names like *Komet, Morgen* (Morning), and *Der neue Weg* (The New Way). These journals had a cosmopolitan quality. *Der Morgen* published Gogol, Gorky, and George Bernard Shaw. *Das Theater* included reports from abroad and dared to review variety shows and ballroom dancing. Nevertheless, Walden's tenure at each of these magazines was short; because of his refusal to support advertisers, it became clear that Walden would have to found his *own* journal.

The numerous journals that sprang up in Berlin between 1900 and 1920 deserve an essay of their own. Siegfried Jacobsohn's (1881–1926) *Schaubühne* (The Stage) was the most important theater journal in the Reich; after 1918, as *Die Weltbühne* (The World Stage), and during the Weimar Republic, it was where Kurt Tucholsky (1890–1935) published his incomparable satires under such pseudonyms as "Peter Panther" and "Theobald Tiger." Among the innumerable but short-lived little magazines abounding in Berlin was *Der arme Teufel* (The Poor Devil), founded by Erich Mühsam, poet and future revolutionary, who had also been one of Die Kommenden.

The most influential magazine for art and literature during the Expressionist decade was without question Herwarth Walden's *Der Sturm* (The Storm), which Else Lasker-Schüler is said to have

Figure 61
August Macke
Greeting (Begrüssung), 1912
Title page of *Der Sturm*
(December 1912)
Linoleum print, 19¼ x 14¼ in.
(48.8 x 36.2 cm)
The Metropolitan Museum of Art.
Bequest of Scofield Thayer, 1982
(1984.1203.191[8])

Figure 62
August Macke
The Storm (Der Sturm), 1911
Oil on canvas,
33⅛ x 44⅛ in. (84 x 112 cm)
Saarland-Museum, Saarbrücken

named. The first issue appeared on 3 March 1910, and Walden (see PLATES 1 and 2) continued to publish the magazine, first as a weekly, later in different formats, until 1932. In retrospect, and never modest, Walden summarized the journal's achievements as follows: "All the volumes of *Der Sturm* embrace the most significant period of German and European intellectual life. *Der Sturm* has published only those works of the young and innovative in the fields of poetry, literature, music, and graphic art that have engendered new horizons. For this reason the magazine had to reject those who could not reach new artistic goals."[23]

The importance of *Der Sturm* certainly was heightened through its reproduction of graphic art by the foremost modern European artists. During its first year of publication, in 1910, each issue contained a graphic work by Oskar Kokoschka (FIG. 60, PLATE 3). Kandinsky, Franz Marc (FIG. 66, PLATE 5), August Macke (FIG. 61), and Sonia and Robert Delaunay were represented in the journal, as were artists of the Dresden group Die Brücke (The Bridge)—Ernst Ludwig Kirchner (PLATE 4), Erich Heckel, and Karl Schmidt-Rottluff. Issues of the journal were planned to coincide with the exhibitions of the Sturm Galerie. Members of the Munich group Der Blaue Reiter (The Blue Rider), including Kandinsky (PLATE 6), Paul Klee, August Macke (FIG. 62), Franz Marc, Gabriele Münter, and Marianne von Werefkin, were represented in Walden's first exhibition at the Sturm Gallery in 1912. In 1913, thanks to the generosity of Macke's uncle, the industrialist Bernhard Koehler, Walden was able to present 366 works by 75 artists from twelve countries at the Erster Deutscher Herbstsalon, the First German Autumn Salon, which showed works by important European modernist artists, including Picasso, Léger (PLATE 13), the Italian Futurists (PLATES 15, 16, 18), Russian Cubo-Futurists, and Czech Cubists. Walden also published literary works by his artists, such as Kokoschka's play *Mörder, Hoffnung der Frauen* (Murderer, Hope of Women), as well as theoretical writings by Kandinsky and reports from the Paris art scene by Guillaume Apollinaire. Walden, who championed the Italian Futurists Filippo Marinetti and Umberto Boccioni (FIGS. 63, 120, PLATE 8), invited them to Berlin for an exhibition in 1912 that was advertised by sandwichmen in futurist attire on the streets of the city. Their "Futurist Manifesto" appeared in the *Der Sturm* catalogue.

Walden was a fervent polemicist. He went on the counterattack when some critics, mostly in provincial papers, demanded the removal of modern paintings—for example, Expressionist works by Franz Marc—from exhibition halls.[24] When a poem by Lasker-

Figure 63
Umberto Boccioni
Drawing After "States of Mind: Those Who Go," 1912
Pen and ink on paper,
12½ x 16¾ in. (31.8 x 42.5 cm)
The Metropolitan Museum of Art.
Bequest of Lydia Winston Malbin,
1989 (1990.38.27)

Figure 64
Oskar Kokoschka *(left)* and
Herwarth Walden in the office of
Der Sturm, 1916
Handschriftenabteilung, Staatsbibliothek
zu Berlin–Preussischer Kulturbesitz

Figure 65
Ernst Ludwig Kirchner
Portrait of Alfred Döblin, 1912
Oil on canvas,
20 x 16¼ in. (50.8 x 41.3 cm)
Courtesy of the Busch-Reisinger Museum,
Harvard University Art Museums,
Association Fund
©President and Fellows of Harvard College

Schüler was reprinted without royalties because it was cited as an example of the poet's "softening of the brain," Walden went to court. He lost, appealed, won, and wrote a brillant diatribe, "German Poets and German Judges,"[25] unmasking the bourgeois establishment that took the liberty of judging art in ignorance of the subject.

Alfred Döblin, a close friend of Walden and Lasker-Schüler's, and, along with Kokoschka (FIG. 64), Walden's most important collaborator in the early years of *Der Sturm*, was frequently represented in the magazine. He devoted himself, among other things, to music and published his ten "Conversations with Kalypso" in 1910. As music critic, Döblin was, in true Expresionist style, most irreverent. When *Der Rosenkavalier* by Richard Strauss was first introduced to the public by an admiring critic, it enraged Döblin. Whereas Wilhelm II (see FIG. 1) reacted to this new work with the comment, in Berlin dialect, "Det is keene Musik für mich [*sic*]" (this is no music for me)— "It was the first and the last Strauss opera the Kaiser ever heard," Allan Jefferson observed—it was already old hat for Döblin. The Berlin audience, however, disagreed both with Döblin and Wilhelm II, and requested that the opera be kept in the repertory of the Royal Opera House.[26]

Der Sturm proved to be the testing ground for the Expressionist elite of Berlin. It published Jakob van Hoddis (Hans Davidsohn) (see FIG. 124), who had been one of the founders of the Neue Club and whose poem "Weltende" (End of the World, 1912) would open the most representative anthology of Expressionist poetry, *Menschheitsdämmerung* (Twilight of Humanity), edited by Kurt Pinthus in 1919. Peter Gay fittingly characterized the poem as today sounding light-hearted and amusing, "but to its first hearers it captured the sense of impending doom that haunted so many in the late Wilhelmine days, which were so prosperous and seemed so hollow."[27]

Walden also published the grotesque texts by the learned and witty Mynona, or Salomo Friedlaender. He had studied philosophy and medicine, lived as an independent scholar in Berlin, and wrote philosophical works such as *Schöpferische Indifferenz* (Creative Indifference) in 1918. In Walden's magazine, he published gems such as "The Fatality of the Saxon Dialect," or "The Corpse in Love."

One of the longest lists of publications in *Der Sturm* belonged to Alfred Döblin (FIG. 65). His story "Die Ermordung einer Butterblume" (The Murder of a Buttercup) appeared in 1910, and its portrayal of a mind in disintegration became something of an Expressionist leitmotif, a foreboding of Döblin's 1928 masterpiece, *Berlin Alexanderplatz*. The novel juxtaposes a simple man and the metropolis, which is depicted in apocalyptic dimensions as the Great Whore Babylon. Released from prison and determined to remain "decent," the protagonist is swallowed up in an urban pandemonium and must pass through an underworld of crime, murder, and insanity before he is reborn to a new life.

Döblin also illustrates the political side of *Der Sturm*. Himself a physician for the working class in Berlin, he participated, for instance, in the debate about birth control that raged in the pages of the journal in 1911. The discussion was enlivened by Franziska Schultz, a social worker and founder of a Berlin home for unwed mothers and their infants. Schultz published a list of case histories of ill and exhausted working-class women with eight and more children to make her case in support of contraception and abortion.[28] Lasker-Schüler, in turn, published an article about Schultz in the magazine; in response to a poll several years later, Lasker-Schüler remarked that a judge who had not carried a child to term should not rule on the abortion issue.

Figure 66
Franz Marc
Atonement (Versöhnung), 1912
[for a poem by Else Lasker-Schüler]
Woodcut, 7⅞ x 10⅛ in. (20 x 25.7 cm)
Title page of *Der Sturm* (September 1912)
Courtesy of the Museum of Fine Arts, Boston. Horatio Greenough Curtis Fund

Der Sturm is usually characterized as less "activist," or less political, than its competitor, *Die Aktion*, founded in Berlin by Franz Pfemfert in 1911. But Pfemfert published many of the same writers that appeared in *Der Sturm*; and among the hundreds of articles written by Walden alone there are enough to justify the "activist" label. True, Walden's kind of activism was primarily aesthetic. He wanted to change the world, if at first mainly through art. This is why he expanded his publishing and gallery enterprises to include an art school in 1916 and a store specializing in reproductions of artworks as well as photographic portraits of his *Sturm* artists reproduced on postcards. A *Sturm* theater, comprising an acting school, opened in 1917. In 1920, a *Sturm* reading room made available newspapers from as far away as Egypt. Walden organized a lending gallery that loaned original works of art and further attempted to popularize the *Sturm* concept with a cabaret and costume balls.

Figure 67
Franz Marc
Yellow Seated Female Nude (Sitzender gelber Frauenakt), 1913
[Side of letter to Else Lasker-Schüler, dated 22 January 1913]
Watercolor and ink on paper, 5⅝ x 5¾ in. (14.3 x 14.7 cm)
Kupferstichkabinett, Staatliche Museen zu Berlin–Preussischer Kulturbesitz

Walden, not unlike Pfemfert, can be seen in the tradition of such early promoters of the modern as Ludwig Jacobowski, who had been active in the "Public Theater" movement to make modern plays accessible to the lower classes. He had also published penny-booklets with poetry and fairy tales for a mass audience illustrated by Art Nouveau artists such as Heinrich Vogeler. Walden subscribed to his collaborator Lothar Schreyer's concept of the *Bühnenkunstwerk*, the "art of the stage," as opposed to conventional theater. This new stage art did not focus on the details of producing a particular dramatic work, casting the play, or present-

Figure 68
Franz Marc
Dancer from the Court of King Jussuf [Tänzerin vom Hofe des Königs Jussuf], 1913
[Side of letter to Else Lasker-Schüler, dated 26 January 1913]
Watercolor and ink on paper,
8 13/16 x 6 15/16 in. (22.4 x 17.6 cm)
Kupferstichkabinett, Staatliche Museen zu Berlin–Preussischer Kulturbesitz

Figure 69
Else Lasker-Schüler, 1909–10
Photograph
Frontispiece from **Mein Herz: Ein Liebesroman mit Bildern und wirklich lebenden Menschen [My Heart: A Romance with Pictures and Real People]**, 1912

ing a specific reality. Rather, its aim was to represent a cohesive aesthetic vision by employing a diversity of artistic media and methods.[29] This idea is at the heart of Expressionism. Walden was able to realize it early on, publishing literature and art that complemented each other to an astonishing degree.

This complementary interaction between a work of visual art and poetry is represented by Franz Marc's woodcut *Versöhnung*, 1912 (FIG. 66), inspired by Else Lasker-Schüler's poem "Der Versöhnungstag," or "reconciliation"; "Der Versöhnungstag" is also the German word for Yom Kippur. Walden published the two works—but not next to each other—in the same issue of *Der Sturm*, volume 3, no. 125/126, in September 1912. When Lasker-Schüler saw Marc's woodcut—it was at the time of her divorce from Walden—she wrote to the artist, "Are you also as painfully lost as me, that I don't know the way anymore, only the abyss?"[30] Thus began a remarkable relationship between two artists that bore fruit in the series of watercolor postcards (FIGS. 67, 68) that Marc sent to Lasker-Schüler as "Messages to Prince Jussuf" and Jussuf's letters to his "half-brother" Ruben that appeared in *Die Aktion* and other periodicals, and later in the book *Der Malik*.

Orientalist Fantasies

During the first two years of *Der Sturm*, Lasker-Schüler published more than seventy poems and prose pieces in the magazine. These works demonstrate an astonishing development. Like many of her artist and poet friends, she had turned to other cultures for the inspiration that the cultural environment of Wilhelmine Germany could no longer provide. "I believe we gradually must understand what is involved if we want to call ourselves artists," Marc had written to Macke in 1911; and Lasker-Schüler would have supported that view wholeheartedly. "We have to courageously renounce everything that was dear to us good Central Europeans . . . to escape the tiredness of our European non-taste."[31] Those who were able traveled to exotic lands—for example, Paul Klee and August Macke, who journeyed to Tunisia in 1914, or Emil Nolde, who visited New Guinea at the same time. Others made pilgrimages to the newly established ethnological museums that displayed artifacts from remote and exotic cultures in Polynesia, Africa, and South America.[32]

This interest in displaying "primitive" cultures was represented in the construction of so-called native villages in the Berlin Lunapark, an amusement park where men and women from authentic African tribes could be observed performing their rituals and dances in a facsimile of a village setting. Lasker-Schüler was fascinated by her visits to these exhibitions; an "Egyptian exhibition" is mentioned repeatedly in her letters.

In her stories and poems, Lasker-Schüler created an Orientalist fantasy world of her own. Unlike the French poet Tristan Klingsor in his "Shéhérazade" poems, she does not express a longing for Asia or the cities of Persia. She is already there, in a self-

Figure 70
Karl Schmidt-Rottluff
The Reader (Die Lesende)
[Portrait of Else Lasker-Schüler], 1912
Oil on canvas, 40⅜ x 30⅛ in.
(102.7 x 76.5 cm)
Collection Hermann Gerlinger,
Würzburg, Germany

Figure 71
Else Lasker-Schüler
Sketch for **Thebes with Jussuf
[Theben mit Jussuf]**, 1922
From **Thebes [Theben]**, 1923
Colored ink drawing on telegram paper,
9¹³⁄₁₆ x 6⁵⁄₁₆ in. (25 x 16 cm)
Von der Heydt-Museum, Wuppertal.
On loan from the Else Lasker-Schüler-
Gesellschaft

Figure 72
Else Lasker-Schüler
**Snake Charmer in the Thebes
Marketplace [Der
Schlangenanbeter auf dem
Marktplatz in Theben]**, ca. 1912
Pen, colored pencil, collaged silverfoil,
11⅛ x 8⅞ in. (28.3 x 22.5 cm)
Franz Marc Museum, Kochel am See

created fantasy world of beauty, passion, and cruelty. The story "Ich tanze in der Moschee" (I Am Dancing in the Mosque) from the collection *Die Nächte Tino von Bagdads* (The Nights of Tino of Baghdad, 1907) is an Orientalist Art Nouveau dream, its language an attempt to imitate dance rhythms. Since the poet's native German cannot itself convey this poetic Orient, Lasker-Schüler resorts to Arabic language particles that are repeated rhythmically, such as *machmêde-machei*.

And she was not content simply to have her poems and stories appear in print. She had high-flying plans to give readings in a pseudo-Arab costume, a dagger stuck in her belt, with sound effects—she was looking for a bagpipe—and an Oriental boy as page handing her the manuscript sheets. These performances did not come about, but a photograph made for promotional purposes remains the most frequently reproduced picture of the poet (FIG. 69). Her drawings, however, are enduring testimony to her double talent as poet and artist, and of her conviction that word and image are mutually reinforcing. She produced watercolors, pastels, and collages throughout her life, and she illustrated several of her books. Beginning in the 1920s, when her son fell ill with tuberculosis— he died in 1927—her artwork provided most of her income.

Nowhere is this interconnection of word and image more evident than in Lasker-Schüler's letters, where hearts and stars are inserted in the midst of words and between lines, and little drawings of an oasis or the profiles of exotic faces adorn the page. The book *Theben* (Thebes), consisting of 10 poems and 10 lithographs, with 50 of the 250 copies hand-colored by the artist, is part of her artistic legacy (FIG. 71). Beginning in 1916, exhibitions of her graphic works were organized by art galleries in Berlin and by private collectors such as Karl Ernst Osthaus in Hagen. In 1920, twenty-three of her drawings were given by collector friends to the Berlin National Gallery.

Lasker-Schüler's poetry had undergone a most remarkable change by the time she published her "Oriental" prose. The collection *Meine Wunder* (My Miracles, 1911) contains these new works written in two-line stanzas replete with precious images in glowing colors and inimitable rhythms. The most famous poem, "Ein alter Tibetteppich" ("An Old Tibetan Rug") first appeared in *Der Sturm* in 1910, and was reprinted in *Die Fackel* by Karl Kraus, who praised it as a work "that like few after Goethe unites meaning and sound, word and image, language and soul."[33] This inter-

Figure 73
Else Lasker-Schüler
Title drawing from **Hebräische Balladen (Hebrew Ballads)**, 1912
Deutsche Schillergesellschaft, Marbach am Neckar

weaving of image, sound, and rhythm is evident in the first two lines of the poem:

Deine Seele, die die meine liebet
Ist verwirkt mit ihr im Teppichtibet.

Strahl in Strahl verliebte Farben,
Sterne, die sich himmellang umwarben.

Unsere Füsse ruhen auf der Kostbarkeit
Maschentausendabertausendweit.

Süsser Lamasohn auf Moschuspflanzenthron
Wie lange küsst deine Mund den meinen wohl
Und Wang die Wange buntgeknüpfte Zeiten schon?

Your dear soul that is in love with mine
Is twined in it in the Tibetan carpet.

Strand in strand the lovestruck colors,
Stars that wooed each other heaven-long.

Our feet rest on the precious treasure
Mesh for mesh a thousand-meshes-wide—

Sweet lama son upon sweet sultan throne,
How long will your mouth go on kissing mine
And cheek on cheek the color-knotted hours live on?[34]

Many of these poems are love poems, often arranged in cycles, such as the one addressed to "Giselheer the Tiger." Directed specifically to Gottfried Benn, it expresses Lasker-Schüler's attempt to convert the "heathen" and "barbarian" to her own and fundamentally different concept of art. Benn's poems were addressed to no one. He created an absolute work of art in the Nietzschean sense—self-sufficient and autonomous. Lasker-Schüler's poems were always addressed to someone in particular, an intimate "you." They had a mission, to bring love into the world, as she stated in all her poems, from the earliest to the last.

If one could identify a "source" of Lasker-Schüler's writings, it is the Bible. This becomes evident in her *Hebräische Balladen* (Hebrew Ballads), which appeared in a small booklet in 1913 (FIG. 73). They are devoted to the great figures of the Old Testament—Abraham to Ruth, Esther, David and Jonathan—and to her people, from whom she felt estranged but at the same time intimately bound. The *Hebrew Ballads* were meant to remind her bourgeois German Jewish contemporaries of the Jews' great history, of which she was so proud and which she conveyed in a powerful and poetic language. "Mein Volk," or "My

Figure 74
The "Moderns" at their regular table at the Café des Westens
From *Der Weltspiegel*, Illustrated Biweekly of the *Berliner Tageblatt*, no. 41, 21 May 1905
Berlinische Galerie, Landesmuseum für Moderne Kunst

People," a poem in this collection, evokes her situation as a modern poet of an ancient people that has lost touch with the life-giving energy of its great past:

Der Fels wird morsch,
Dem ich entspringe
Und meine Gotteslieder singe . . .
Jäh stürz ich vom Weg
Und riesele ganz in mir
Fernab, allein über Klagesgestein
Dem Meer zu.

Hab mich so abgeströmt
Von meines Blutes
Mostvergorenheit.
Und immer, immer noch der Wiederhall
In mir,
Wenn schauerlich gen Ost
Das morsche Felsgebein,
Mein Volk,
Zu Gott schreit.

The rock is crumbling
From which I spring
And sing my hymns to God. . . .
I hurl myself from the path
And skid all inward-coiled
Far off, alone over wailing stone
Down to the sea.

So far have I drifted
From my blood's
Wine-press.
And yet, the echo resonates
In me still,
When seized with dread
The crumbling rock,
My people,
Faces East
And cries to God.[35]

Lasker-Schüler's favorite biblical figure was Joseph, with whom she identified as an interpreter of dreams, that is, a poet, misunderstood by his own people for whom she cared and whom he rescued. After assuming the persona of Tino, the Oriental princess who appeared in the 1907 work *The Nights of Tino of Baghdad*, she created for herself the role of Jussuf, Prince of Thebes, around 1910. He personified the ideal in which art and power were finally united. Jussuf is a unique persona, neither Jewish nor Muslim, male nor female, and eternally young. The imaginary wealth of this poet-prince allowed her to provide in imagination for her friends what she could not do in reality.

She portrayed the reality of her Berlin existence in her final contributions to *Der Sturm*, the "Letters to Norway" that appeared in 1912 in a revised version with her drawings as *Mein Herz: Ein Liebesroman mit Bildern und wirklich lebenden Menschen* (My Heart: A Romance with Pictures and Real People). The fictitious letters were inspired by Herwarth Walden's brief trip, in 1911, with his friend Kurt Neimann to Sweden, where he met his second wife, Nell Roslund (see PLATE 20). They provide as precise a picture of modern Berlin as can be expected from a poet who knew the difference between truth and reality and which of the two is more important.

Café Culture in Berlin

Many of the letters, postcards, and telegrams that Lasker-Schüler included in *My Heart* begin with the sentence "I went to the café." They tell of the people she met there, the gossip, intrigue, arguments and reconciliations. There are reports of art exhibitions and theater performances, among them a devastating critique of Hugo von Hofmannsthal's adaptation of the English *Everyman* directed by Max Reinhardt. For a modern poet like Lasker-Schüler, the medieval play was an abominable anachronism. Despite its Rhenish humor and Berlin wit, *My Heart* is, above all, a sad story of a relationship that has come to an end, of disappointment and loneliness from which the writer tries to escape through her art. She assures Herwarth and "Kurtchen" repeatedly that she has fallen in love again with various people, presented as different personae such as "Minn the son of the Sultan of Morocco" and, of course, "Giselheer." The other escape route leads to the café, and *My Heart* is the most important literary document of the Berlin café culture.

The café under discussion is the famous Café des Westens at Kurfürstendamm and Joachimsthaler Strasse (FIG. 74). It had opened in 1893 and became, at first, a meeting place for painters.[36] It later inherited its nickname, "Café Grössenwahn" (Café Megalomania), from a 1902 event that had been staged in Munich, the "Costume Ball at the Café Megalomania," actually Café Stephanie in Schwabing, the artist quarter. In 1899, the Café des Westens became the headquarters for Walden's art club, the Verein für Kunst, and it soon attracted a circle of writers and artists who could be called the "Berlin moderns." It was not an elegant place and gave the impression of an apartment that had had its partitions removed. Cheap tapestries and fake rococo stucco, brown from nicotine fumes, adorned the walls and low ceilings. The air was stale and filled with smoke. In short, the Café des Westens was as homely as it was unhealthy.

Why were so many people attracted to the cafés in Berlin? The Café des Westens was by no means the only café that catered to a particular artistic clientele. Theater people frequented the Café Bauer on Unter den Linden. Journalists preferred the Café Jolicke on Kochstrasse. Kleine Scala was the place for circus and variety-show performers. And soon the Café König would become the meeting place for people working in film. It seemed as if cafés had replaced the medieval guilds.

In many cases, there was a practical reason for spending the better part of the day in a café. The young writers and artists who had come to Berlin to try their luck often had limited financial means. They were able to rent only a room (the studio apartment with kitchenette had not yet been invented) from one of the legendary Berlin landladies, mostly lower-middle-class widows who often had some heart for the fledgling geniuses in their care. Money was in such short supply that sometimes two renters had to share a room. Friends were put up, which could lead to a fracas, and the café was the only refuge.[37] The Café des Westens was well known for its Viennese cuisine, but prices were reasonable and waiters were willing to extend credit. Lasker-Schüler gives a precise account in one of her "Letters to Norway" of how much she owes the "waiter at noon" and the "waiter at midnight."[38]

The café provided amenities that one could not obtain from a landlady. The Café des Westens soon had a telephone booth, crowned by a bust of Wilhelm II, where guests could make calls—in full view of the entire clientele—and, according to Lasker-Schüler, within hearing distance of the nearest tables (303). Most important, the café sub-scribed to many newspapers, including the international press, an enormous advantage for the literati. The Café des Westens employed a special "newspaper waiter," "Red Richard" with his flaming red hair, who served papers (adorned with the stamp "Stolen from the Café des Westens") as well as the latest reprint information relating to his guests' publications. Cafés offered free chessboards and billiard tables, and in the ice-cold Berlin winters guests could save a small fortune by not having to pay heating costs at home.

The café, however, did much more than provide savings on living expenses. It was a place of communication like no other (FIG. 75). Here the most recent information about the publishing and art worlds was available (FIG. 76). What was in and what was out? Where was there a chance to have a new manuscript published? What sorts of contracts had been signed and with whom? "This is our stock exchange, that's where you have to go, where the deals are closed. There are all the playwrights, painters, poets."[39]

Figure 77
Adolf Loos, Karl Kraus, and Herwarth Walden, ca. 1919
Special Collections and Archives,
W. E. B. DuBois Library,
University of Massachusetts, Amherst

Figure 78
Else Lasker-Schüler, 1906
Deutsche Schillergesellschaft,
Marbach am Neckar

Finally, the café was a place for inspiration. Some needed the café in order to write, spending the quiet morning at their little marble "desk." Others, like Lasker-Schüler, went there after having "played a subjective role in literature" at home in the morning, since "there is nothing more objective than the café" (379). She was attracted by the "bazaarlike colorfulness" (390) of the guests, "ladies with gigantic hats, men with monocles, people sober and drunk, purple-powdered faces, also boys who put on powder," she writes to Jethro Bithell, Professor of Literature in Manchester and one of her first translators. But she also sees "many proletarians, who like to watch."[40]

Nearly all the people depicted by Else Lasker-Schüler in *Der Sturm* and *Die Aktion* appear in the literature surrounding this particular café, beginning with her guru Peter Hille, her fervent promoter Karl Kraus, the pioneer of sexual research Magnus Hirschfeld, the powerful theater critic Alfred Kerr (see FIG. 15), and the scholarly Samuel Lublinski. Table-hopping was a ritual that allowed the "Prince of Thebes" to hold court at the café. Newcomers to Berlin were taken by their friends to this gathering place to see and perhaps even meet celebrities. Karl Kraus took Kokoschka to the Café des Westens, where he met Walden (FIG. 77). The young Yiddish poet Abraham Stenzel described how his introduction to Else Lasker-Schüler came about in this way. She spotted Stenzel and asked the waiter to invite him to her table.[41] Thus began another of the many friendships that took root in the café, which was her artistic playground.

Lasker-Schüler's concept of art was closely related to play. Producing art was for her tantamount to child's play—free, creative, and innocent. One thinks of the biblical connotations of the word: "There I was, his beloved, playing before him all the time" (Prov. 8:30). Lasker-Schüler's language is rich in play metaphors, and her artist friends are presented as her playmates. In *Der Malik* (1919), several of them contributed drawings of crowns for the protagonist, the Prince of Thebes, now an emperor. Franz Marc drew the "play crown," Heinrich Campendonk the "hunting crown," and Egon Adler the "crown of the high priest"—six crowns altogether. Nearly all the artists were regulars at the Café des Westens. And they actually participated in Lasker-Schüler's artistic play. She used to sign letters to her friends with the signature of the Prince of Thebes, and they addressed her by that name. Someone even gave her calling cards engraved with the name "Prinz Jussuf von Theben."

However, the café was not an uncontested institution. In the early years, it was looked on with mistrust by the middle class as a place frequented by disorderly, if not outright dangerous, people with bushy beards and anarchy on their minds—and by lewd women. Walden wrote a forceful defense of the Café des Westens when a conservative paper compared it to a swamp. "Each time I enter this harmless place," he observed, "I look around in astonishment"; and he cited his friend Karl Kraus: "Megalomania does not mean thinking of oneself as more than one is but as what one really is." This rebuttal was followed by a witty satire of the café at midnight, when the rites of mutual adoration take place inside, unknown to the bourgeois passers-by.[42]

But even its inhabitants sometimes had second thoughts about the café, expressing feelings of boredom and distaste. "Secretly we all think of the café as the devil," Lasker-Schüler wrote. "But without the devil there is nothing" (298). She knew the café by heart, and she was tired of the "imitation poets," the "false word-jewels, the simili-thoughts" (313). But she could not live without it.

The time was up for the old Café des Westens in 1913, when the owner opened a new establishment a few houses down the Kurfürstendamm, raised prices, and credit became scarce. The old Café Megalomania closed in 1915. The regulars moved to Café Josty at Potsdamer Platz, and after 1917 to the Romanisches Café opposite the Kaiser Wilhelm Memorial Church on the Kurfürstendamm. The owner of the large and ugly interior, called a "waiting room for genius" by the writer Günther Birkenfeld, tried to imitate his colleague from the Café des Westens. He hired a newspaper waiter and was patient with guests who consumed little. However, if a guest spent twelve hours with one cup of coffee, according to Jürgen Scherbera, a small card was placed discreetly on his table, asking him to leave.

Lasker-Schüler wrote a piece on the closing of the Café des Westens that she called "Our Café."[43] Pretending to have received an article clipped by her sister from a Chicago paper—Lasker-Schüler really had a sister in Chicago—she explains why "our café is no longer our café." The owner had prohibited the poet Else Lasker-Schüler from coming to his premises because she did not "consume" enough. "Imagine! Is a poet who eats and drinks a lot still a poet?" Lasker-Schüler exclaims. Whereupon all her companions, "the chieftains," rallied around her in battle. Artists had made this café into the queen of all cafés, she lamented, and now it was a lost paradise.

The First World War dealt even a stronger blow to the Café des Westens. Many of those who had helped define it as a center of cultural life were killed in the war. Walden published obituaries in nearly every issue of *Der Sturm*. Following the death of Franz Marc, in 1916, he wrote: "Now an artist has fallen who cannot die."[44] Lasker-Schüler was devastated. Farsighted as she was, she had opposed this war from the beginning. She knew that it would destroy a world where the Prince of Thebes and his playmates gave proof of its redemption through art. *Der Malik*, Lasker-Schüler's swan song for an entire culture, echoes this lament. The Malik fails in all his endeavors, and after his half-brother, Ruben (Franz Marc)—who went to war voluntarily—is killed, he hangs himself. The book is a highly encoded work that parades a host of characters with fanciful names. Bestowing such names on her friends to adorn and honor them was one of the games that Lasker-Schüler loved to play. Behind each of these "chieftains," "wild Jews," "cardinals," and women with names like "Venus of Siam" hides a real person, many of whom "Jussuf" had met at his favorite playground.

Figure 79
Herwarth Walden, 1918

In the years prior to World War I, the café spawned a new generation that would carry the concept of modernity into the future. Walter Benjamin (1892–1940), who demonstrated his zeal for the new with his first publications in the journal *Der Anfang* (The Beginning) and who gave a reading of his essay "Jugend" (Youth) at one of the evenings organized by Franz Pfemfert's *Aktion*, knew the old Café des Westens. There, where Lasker-Schüler once "dragged" him to her table, he and his friends, in August 1914 fresh out of the Gymnasium, discussed how they could register for the draft so that they would stay together.[45] Later the café became a "daily necessity," although Benjamin did not develop this "vice" in Berlin. The city had "too strenuous an approach to pleasure," he observed. Nevertheless, Benjamin found the Prinzess Café to his liking precisely because it was not a meeting place of the literary world but rather of the "ladies of the night." Nestled in a booth, near a jazz band, the author whose name would become synonymous with modernity would write parts of his *Ursprung des deutschen Trauerspiels* (Origin of the German Mourning Play).

The café, from which Benjamin chose to withdraw without being able to give it up altogether, was first and foremost a democratic institution without class distinctions. Here the poor poet, the mighty critic, the powerful publisher gathered in this public place. They were open-minded about contemporary art forms and techniques, including film, the newest medium.[46] Although hardly aligned with particular parties, they were politically on the "left where the heart is," as Leonhard Frank, one of them, would later comment in the title of his autobiographical novel. These moderns championed women's rights, birth control, and the rights of homosexuals. Above all, they were opposed to nationalism, recognizing art as an endeavor that knows no national borders, requiring a free flow of creativity among artists and nations.

It was inevitable that the modern worldview would be attacked by National Socialism, its arch-enemy, which dealt a death blow also to what remained of the café culture in places like the Romanisches Café. Many of its patrons were suddenly dispersed throughout Europe and across the globe, and some would perish during the course of the Nazi genocide. Although they had been born in Germany, hardly any of the "Berlin moderns" died there. Alfred Döblin was a rare exception. Others lived out their lives in exile, like Else Lasker-Schüler, who died in Jerusalem, homesick and in despair of what had become of her world. Herwarth Walden's life ended in a prison in Saratow during a Stalinist purge in 1941. Abraham Stenzel died in London. Some were driven to suicide, such as Walter Benjamin in a Spanish border town after having fled France in 1940. Or they were murdered, like Erich Mühsam in the Oranienburg concentration camp near Berlin in 1934, or Jakob van Hoddis, who was taken from a Jewish mental hospital in 1942. All were victims of an ideology that negated and attempted to eradicate the values of modernity along with the Jews.

Notes

1. Quoted in Peter Gay, *Freud, Jews and Other Germans: Masters and Victims in Modernist Culture* (New York: Oxford University Press, 1978), p. 171.

2. Fred B. Stern, *Auftakt zur Literatur des 20. Jahrhunderts: Briefe aus dem Nachlass von Ludwig Jacobowski*, vol. 2 (Heidelberg: Lothar Stiehm, 1974), pp. 13–14.

3. Itta Shedletzky, "Ludwig Jacobowski (1868–1900) und Jakob Loewenberg (1856–1929): Literarisches Leben und Schaffen aus deutscher und jüdischer Seele," in *Juden in der deutschen Literatur. Ein deutsch-israelisches Symposium*, ed. Stéphane Moses and Albrecht Schöne (Frankfurt am Main: Suhrkamp, 1986), pp. 194–209.

4. "Weltflucht" is reprinted from Else Lasker-Schüler, *Werke und Briefe: Kritische Ausgabe*, vol. 1, no. 1, ed. Jürgen Skrodzki, with Norbert Oellers (Frankfurt am Main: Jüdischer Verlag and Suhrkamp, 1996), p. 34. The English version is reprinted from Else Lasker-Schüler, *Hebrew Ballads and Other Poems*, ed., trans., and with an introduction by Audrey Durchschlag and Jeanette Littman-Demestère (Philadelphia: The Jewish Publication Society of America, 1980), pp. 5–7.

5. Carl E. Schorske, *Thinking with History: Explorations in the Passage to Modernism* (Princeton, N.J.: Princeton University Press, 1998), p. 4.

6. Andreas Huyssen, *After the Great Divide: Modernism, Mass Culture, Postmodernism* (Bloomington: Indiana University Press, 1986), pp. 3–15.

7. Peter Gay, *Pleasure Wars: The Bourgeois Experience: Victoria to Freud* (New York: Norton, 1998), p. 26.

8. Hans Tramer, "Der Expressionismus: Bemerkungen zum Anteil der Juden an einer Kunstepoche," *Bulletin des Leo Baeck Instituts* 2, no. 5 (1958): 33–46.

9. Jon Milful, "Marginalität und Messianismus: Die Situation der deutsch-jüdischen Intellektuellen als Paradigma für die Kulturkrise 1910–1920," in *Expressionismus und Kulturkrise*, ed. Bernd Hüppauf (Heidelberg: Carl Winter, 1983), pp. 347–57.

10. Hanni Mittelmann, "Expressionismus und Judentum," in *Conditio Judaica: Judentum, Antisemitismus und deutschsprachige Literatur vom Ersten Weltkrieg bis 1933/38*, ed. Horst Denkler, part 2 (Tübingen: Niemeyer, 1993), pp. 251–59.

11. Steven M. Lowenstein, Paul Mendes-Flohr, Peter Pulzer, and Monika Richarz, *Deutsch-Jüdische Geschichte in der Neuzeit*, vol. 3: *1871–1918* (Munich: C. H. Beck, 1997), pp. 302–3.

12. Gay, *Freud, Jews and Other Germans*, p. 133.

13. *Lieber gestreifter Tiger: Briefe von Else Lasker-Schüler*, ed. Margaret Kupper (Munich: Kösel, 1969), p. 87.

14. Ibid., p. 88.

15. Else Lasker-Schüler, "Dr. Benn," in *Werke und Briefe: Kritische Ausgabe*, vol. 3, no. 1, *Prosa 1903–1920*, ed. Ricarda Dick (Frankfurt am Main: Jüdischer Verlag and Suhrkamp, 1998), p. 277.

16. Paul Goldscheider, "Wo ich bin ist es grün," in *Lasker-Schüler: Ein Buch zum 100. Geburtstag der Dichterin*, ed. Michael Schmid (Wuppertal: Peter Hammer, 1969), pp. 50–54.

17. For documentation and the extensive correspondence among organizers of Der Neue Club, see Richard Sheppard, ed., *Die Schriften des neuen Clubs 1908–1914*, vols. 1 and 2 (Hildesheim: Gerstenberg, 1980, 1983).

18. Kolb acknowledged her debt in a footnote to her novel *Die Schaukel*, which she completed in exile. She owed her discovery to the Berlin publisher Samuel Fischer and never forgot it. From the day that Jews became influential in intellectual life, she remarked, artists who always led an endangered existence felt they had a chance. Had this happened earlier, "a poet like Hölderlin would not have had to play the poor tutor and Schubert would not have had to die so young and as such a poor devil. Be that as it may, today in Germany there are a small group of Christians who are conscious of their debt of gratitude toward Jews." See *Die Schaukel* (Berlin: S. Fischer, 1934), p. 176. Concerning Barlach, see Konrad Feilchenfeldt and Rahel Feilchenfeldt, "Walter Feilchenfeldt als Verleger: Vorstudien zu einer Geschichte des Paul Cassirer Verlages," in *De Arte et Libris: Festschrift Erasmus 1934–1984* (Amsterdam: Erasmus Antiquariaat en Boekhandel, 1984), pp. 119–27.

19. Hans Tramer, "Der Beitrag der Juden zu Geist und Kultur," in *Deutsches Judentum in Krieg und Revolution 1916–1923*, ed. Werner E. Mosse with Arnold Pauker (Tübingen: J.C.B. Mohr, 1971), pp. 317–85. This extensive article provides a great deal of information on literary figures of the modern era in Berlin.

20. Cited by Christian Kennert, *Paul Cassirer und sein Kreis: Ein Wegbereiter der Moderne* (Frankfurt and Berlin: Peter Lang, 1996), p. 34.

21. See Peter Paret, *The Berlin Secession* (Cambridge, Mass.: Harvard University Press, 1980). Illustrations of the artworks are found in Georg Brühl, *Die Cassirers: Streiter für den Impressionismus* (Leipzig: Edition Leipzig, 1992).

22. See Georg Brühl, *Herwarth Walden und "Der Sturm"* (Cologne: Du Mont, 1983), p. 13. Brühl provides copious data and information about Berlin in the early twentieth century.

23. Ibid., p. 32.

24. See Herwarth Walden, "Von der Kunst," *Der Sturm* 3, no. 134 (1912): 198–99.

25. *Der Sturm* 3, no. 119–20 (1912): 102–4; vol. 3, no. 121–22 (1912): 114–15.

26. Allan Jefferson, *Richard Strauss "Der Rosenkavalier"* (Cambridge: Cambridge University Press, 1985), p. 90.

27. Gay, *Freud, Jews and Other Germans*, p. 134.

28. Franziska Schultz, "Mehr Kinder," *Der Sturm* 2, no. 56 (1911): 444.

29. See Brühl, *Herwarth Walden und "Der Sturm,"* p. 119.

30. Else Lasker-Schüler and Franz Marc, *Mein lieber, wundervoller blauer Reiter: Privater Briefwechsel*, ed. Ulrike Marquardt and Heinz Rölleke (Düsseldorf and Zürich: Artemis und Winkler, 1998), p. 28.

31. Hans Christoph von Tavel, ed., *Der blaue Reiter*, exhibition catalogue (Bern: Kunstmuseum Bern, 1986), p. 79.

32. This was by no means a phenomenon limited to Germany, as demonstrated by the exhibition *"Primitivism" in Twentieth-Century Art: Affinity of the Tribal and the Modern* held at the Museum of Modern Art in New York in 1984.

33. Quoted in full in Sigrid Bauschinger, *Else Lasker-Schüler: Ihr Werk und ihre Zeit* (Heidelberg: Lothar Stiehm, 1980), p. 11.

34. "Ein alter Tibetteppich" is reprinted from Else Lasker-Schüler, *Werke und Briefe: Kritische Ausgabe*, vol. 1, no. 1, ed. Jürgen Skrodzki, with Norbert Oellers, p. 130. The English translation is by Betty Falkenberg.

35. "Mein Volk" is reprinted from Else Lasker-Schüler, *Werke und Briefe: Kritische Ausgabe*, vol. 1, no. 1, ed. Jürgen Skrodzki, with Norbert Oellers, pp. 96–97. The English translation is by Betty Falkenberg.

36. Much information about the Berlin café scene can be found in Jürgen Scherbera, *"Damals im Romanischen Café . . .": Künstler und ihre Lokale im Berlin der zwanziger Jahre* (Leipzig: Edition Leipzig, n.d.).

37. The poet and future revolutionary Erich Mühsam, whose association with Lasker-Schüler stems from their mutual admiration of Peter Hille and Die Kommenden, gives a vivid description of this hand-to-mouth existence in *Namen und Menschen: Unpolitische Erinnerungen* (Leipzig: Volk und Buch, 1949).

38. Else Lasker-Schüler, *Prosa und Schauspiele* (Munich: Kösel, 1962), p. 304. Further page references to *Mein Herz* appear in the text in parentheses.

39. *Lieber gestreifter Tiger: Briefe von Else Lasker-Schüler*, ed. Margaret Kupper, vol. 1, p. 67.

40. Ibid., pp. 67–68.

41. See Heather Valencia, *Else Lasker-Schüler und Abraham Nochem Stenzel: Eine unbekannte Freundschaft* (Frankfurt am Main: Campus, 1995).

42. *Der Sturm* 2, no. 82 (1911): 651–52.

43. *Prosa 1903–1920*, pp. 291–92.

44. *Der Sturm* 6, no. 23–24 (1916): 1.

45. Walter Benjamin's reminiscences of Berlin café culture are found in "Berliner Chronik," in *Gesammelte Schriften*, vol. 4, ed. Rolf Tiedemann and Hermann Schweppenhäuser (Frankfurt am Main: Suhrkamp, 1985), pp. 480–84.

46. Several of the Café des Westens regulars, including Lasker-Schüler, are represented by their film outlines, or "film exposés," in Kurt Pinthus's *Kinobuch* of 1913.

Plate 1
Hans Richter
Portrait of Herwarth Walden, 1914
Gouache and pastel on cardboard,
19⅞ x 17½ in. (50.5 x 44.5 cm)
Berlinische Galerie, Museum für Moderne
Kunst, Photographie und Architektur

Plate 2
William Wauer
Portrait of Herwarth Walden, 1917
Bronze,
20½ x 12⅝ x 13¾ in. (52 x 32 x 35 cm)
© Indiana University Art Museum

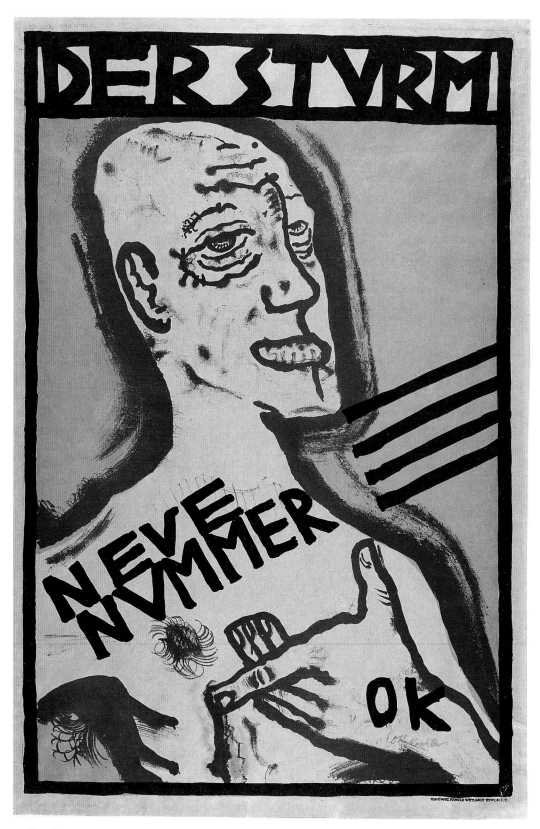

Plate 3
Oskar Kokoschka
Self-Portrait [Sturm Poster]
[Selbstbildnis [Sturmplakat]], 1910
Color lithograph,
26½ x 17⅝ in. (67.3 x 44.7 cm)
The Robert Gore Rifkind Collection,
Beverly Hills, California

Plate 4
Ernst Ludwig Kirchner
Three Nudes (Drei Akte), 1911
Published in *Der Sturm* (December 1911)
Woodcut,
18 1/16 x 10 5/16 in. (20.5 x 26.2 cm)
Print Collection, Miriam and Ira D. Wallach
Division of Art, Prints and Photographs.
The New York Public Library.
Astor, Lenox and Tilden Foundations

Plate 5
Franz Marc
**Sleeping Shepherdess
(Schlafende Hirtin)**, 1912
Woodcut,
7 13/16 x 9 7/16 in. (19.8 x 24 cm)
Print Collection, Miriam and Ira D. Wallach
Division of Art, Prints and Photographs.
The New York Public Library.
Astor, Lenox and Tilden Foundations

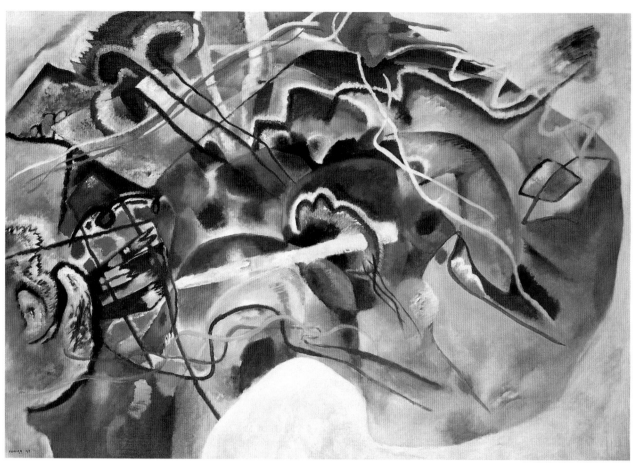

Plate 6
Vasily Kandinsky
Painting with White Border
[Bild mit weissem Rand],1913
Oil on canvas,
55¼ x 78⅞ in. (140.3 x 200.3 cm)
Solomon R. Guggenheim
Museum, New York.
Gift, Solomon R. Guggenheim, 1937
© The Solomon R. Guggenheim
Foundation, New York (FN 37.245)

Plate 7
Ludwig Meidner
Battle (Schlacht), 1914
Pen, brush, and ink on paper,
25⁹⁄₁₆ x 19¹³⁄₁₆ in. (64.9 x 50.6 cm)
The Marvin and Janet Fishman
Collection, Milwaukee

Plate 8
Umberto Boccioni
**Unique Forms of
Continuity in Space**, 1913
Bronze,
48 x 15½ x 36 in. (121.9 x 39.4 x 91.4 cm)
The Metropolitan Museum of Art.
Bequest of Lydia Winston Malbin,
1989 (1990.38.3)

Plate 9
Lyonel Feininger
The Bicycle Race
(Radrennen), 1912
Oil on canvas, 31½ x 39⅜ in.
(80 x 100 cm)
National Gallery of Art, Washington, D.C.
Collection of Mr. and Mrs. Paul Mellon
© 1999 Board of Trustees

Plate 10
Heinrich Campendonk
The Balcony (Der Balkon), 1913
Oil on canvas,
34 7/16 x 29 15/16 in. (87.5 x 76 cm)
Private Collection, Switzerland

Plate 11
Robert Delaunay
Windows in Three Parts, 1912
Oil on canvas,
13⅞ x 36⅛ in. (35.2 x 91.8 cm)
Philadelphia Museum of Art.
A. E. Gallatin Collection

Plate 12
Franz Marc
Stables (Stallungen), 1913
Oil on canvas,
29 x 62 in. (73.6 x 157.5 cm)
Solomon R. Guggenheim Museum,
New York
© The Solomon R. Guggenheim
Foundation, New York (FN 46.1037)

Plate 13
Fernand Léger
Nude Model in the Studio, 1912–13
Oil on burlap,
50⅜ x 37⅝ in. (127.8 x 95.7 cm)
Solomon R. Guggenheim Museum,
New York.
© The Solomon R. Guggenheim
Foundation, New York (FN 49.1193)

Plate 14
Alexander Archipenko
Collage: Two Figures, 1913
Gouache and pasted paper,
18¾ x 12⅜ in. (47.5 x 31.5 cm)
Moderna Museet, Stockholm

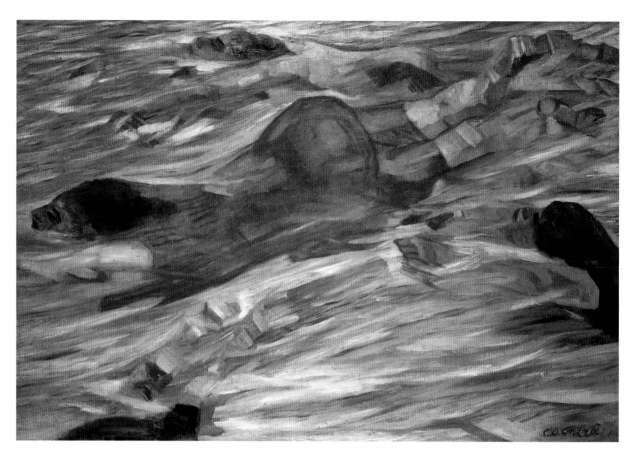

Plate 15
Carlo Carrà
The Swimmers, 1910–12
Oil on canvas,
41 7/16 x 61 1/4 in. (105.3 x 155.6 cm)
The Carnegie Museum of Art,
Pittsburgh.
Gift of G. David Thompson, 1955

Plate 16
Giacomo Balla
Dynamism of a Dog on a Leash,
1912
Oil on canvas,
35¾ x 43⅜ in. (91 x 110 cm)
Albright-Knox Art Gallery,
Buffalo, New York.
Bequest of A. Conger Goodyear and
Gift of George F. Goodyear, 1964

Plate 17
Natalia Goncharova
River Landscape, ca. 1909–11
Oil on canvas,
39 x 34¼ in. (99 x 87 cm)
Private Collection, Switzerland

Plate 18
Gino Severini
Festival at Montmartre, 1913
Oil on canvas,
35 x 45¾ in. (88.9 x 116.2 cm)
Richard S. Zeisler Collection, New York

Plate 19
Marc Chagall
The Flying Carriage, 1913
Oil on canvas,
42 x 47¼ in. (106.7 x 120.1 cm)
Solomon R. Guggenheim Museum,
New York
© The Solomon R. Guggenheim
Foundation, New York (FN 49.1212)

Plate 20
Photo of Herwarth Walden and
Nell Walden at home in front of
two paintings by Marc Chagall—
The Poet, 1911 (*left*), and
The Flying Carriage, 1913

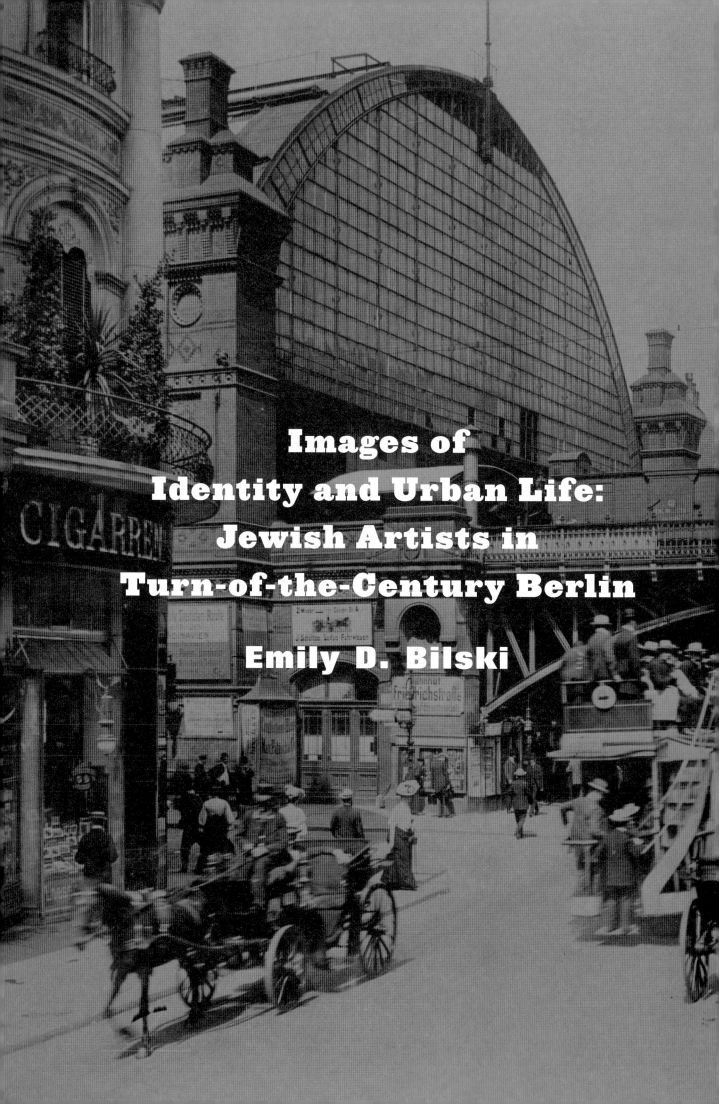

Images of
Identity and Urban Life:
Jewish Artists in
Turn-of-the-Century Berlin

Emily D. Bilski

No major city in Europe grew as quickly as Berlin in the late nineteenth century. At century's end, it was one of the three largest European cities, the capital of a great military and industrial power, and the center of an innovative modern culture. Because Jews moved to the urban centers nearly a generation before most other Germans, they played a major role in defining the modern metropolis. Jews were especially active in many areas that came to be associated with the notion of urban life: journalism, the department store, theater, cabaret, and the new medium of film. Indeed, the nexus between Jews and modern urban culture became the subject of comment and debate among Jews and non-Jews, those who supported and were opposed to modernism.

Given the intimate association of modern Jewry with the modern metropolis, how did issues of identity and urbanism manifest themselves in the work of Jewish artists in Berlin at the turn of the century? Did their images represent—in both style and subject—the dramatic transformations of the city, as well as the tension between Jewish assimilation and difference? And do these themes of urban life and Jewish identity interact in their artistic production? These questions are addressed in the work of four of the most prominent Jewish artists in Berlin at the time: Max Liebermann (1847–1935), Lesser Ury (1861–1931), Ludwig Meidner (1884–1966), and Jakob Steinhardt (1887–1968). As modernists, they turned to Impressionism,[1] Symbolism, and Expressionism, artistic currents that developed in response to the rapid changes in urban life. Yet the subject matter of their work—depiction of Jewish motifs and the choice of biblical themes—also demonstrates a yearning for continuity.

Max Liebermann

It has often been remarked how Max Liebermann, the product of a wealthy and distinguished Berlin Jewish family, who lived in the heart of Berlin on the Pariser Platz, eschewed urban imagery in his work. One of the very rare exceptions is the unusual pastel of 1900, *View of the Tiergarten from the Artist's Living-Room Window* (FIG. 80), which captures the gray atmosphere of the Charlottenburger Chaussee, with its dusting of snow, smattering of pedestrians proceeding carefully on the icy street, horse-drawn carriages, and yellow streetcar. Liebermann depicted this view from his window, it seems, only because he was unable to leave his home: he had broken his leg a few days earlier by slipping in the inclement weather. With his leg in a cast, he lay on a chaise longue in his apartment and rendered the scene below.[2]

In one group of works, however, he traveled quite a distance and negotiated a myriad of inconveniences in order to portray urban activity. This coincides with one of the rare instances of Jewish motifs in his work:[3] the series of works executed between 1905 and 1909 depicting the Jewish Quarter, or *Judengasse*, of Amsterdam (FIGS. 81–84, 134). These included numerous oil paintings, drawings, pastels, and prints.[4] During those years, Liebermann

Figure 80
Max Liebermann
**View of the Tiergarten from the
Artist's Living-Room Window (Blick
aus dem Wohnzimmerfenster des
Künstlers auf den Tiergarten)**, 1900
Pastel on paper,
24¹³⁄₁₆ x 32¼ in. (63 x 82 cm)
Firma Vera Eisenberger K.G.

returned to the Jewish Quarter, renting a room from which to observe the activities of the street, with its lively market and bustle of human activity. These works are thus anomalous in Liebermann's oeuvre for two reasons: they depict scenes of intense urban activity and they unfold in a Jewish milieu. Liebermann's involvement with this subject, despite the obstacles he endured to realize it, compels one to try and account for what can be described as a near-obsession.

During the 1870s and 1880s, Liebermann was concerned with themes of people engaged in physical labor: the simple life of a community in harmony with nature, the dignity of peasants plucking geese (see FIG. 24) or harvesting potatoes. Liebermann visited Holland nearly every year, and he admired the Dutch social-welfare institutions that cared for the poor and elderly in an exemplary way.[5] He depicted these communities as well in works like *Leisure Hour in the Amsterdam Orphanage*, 1882 (see FIG. 25). In the 1890s, however, there was a gradual shift away from these themes to representations of Liebermann's own class, the upper bourgeoisie, engaged in leisure activities (see FIG. 45): at the seashore, horseback riding, playing tennis, relaxing in parks and beer terraces. There are no signs of commerce, of work, of the bustle of the crowded urban environment.

Matthias Eberle has speculated that Liebermann's shift away from the imagery of the 1870s and '80s may have been a response to the reactionary Right's adoption of many of Liebermann's themes, particularly the appropriation of Rembrandt as the model for a Nordic Germanic renewal, exemplified by Julius Langbehn's

Rembrandt als Erzieher (Rembrandt as Educator).[6] Liebermann's obsession with depicting scenes from Amsterdam's Jewish Quarter would then seem to be related to reinstating a "Jewish" construction of Rembrandt—as the artist who lived in Amsterdam's Jewish Quarter and portrayed the Jews there with sympathy.[7] Liebermann's interest in representing people in motion was well-served by the scenes of the Jewish Quarter; yet that alone cannot

Figure 81
Max Liebermann
**Vegetable Market in Amsterdam
[Gemüsemarkt in Amsterdam]**, 1908
Oil on canvas,
29⅛ x 33¹¹/₁₆ in. (74 x 85.5 cm)
Staatliche Kunsthalle zu Karlsruhe

explain the obstacles he endured in pursuing this subject. In a letter to Hermann Struck of 27 August 1905, Liebermann recounted the difficulties he had in persuading his fellow Jews to allow him to depict them, where even bribery was to no avail; and two years later he worried that the Jewish holidays would prevent him from accomplishing his work in the quarter.[8] Yet in spite of all that, Liebermann persisted. If the model of Dutch community life had been spoiled for Liebermann due to its appropriation in the service of reactionary cultural politics, he may have recognized in the traditional Jewish community of the Jewish Quarter another paradigm of social welfare and responsibility. Here was an expression of community untainted by a nationalist *völkisch* ideology. Yet, lively scenes of poor Jewish markets were available to him close at home in Berlin's *Scheunenviertel*, which had become home to thousands of Jewish immigrants from Eastern Europe.

Why travel to Amsterdam? Apart from the close associations with Rembrandt, which were clearly important to Liebermann, other explanations suggest themselves. The scenes of Amsterdam's Jewish Quarter are decidedly unmodern. They present a view of urban life in the early modern period, before industrialization, whereas the *Scheunenviertel* was situated in the midst of a modern metropolis. Seventeenth-century Amsterdam was viewed as a second "Jerusalem," and its Jewish community was seen as living in a "golden age," because of the welcome Jews received from the Dutch Republic and the opportunities they enjoyed for economic prosperity and religious freedom.[9] During the years that Liebermann painted in the quarter, it still retained much of its seventeenth-century atmosphere, as Liebermann noted in a letter of 10 January 1925 to Franz Landsberger: "The Jewish Quarter has changed tremendously in the past twenty-five years, but earlier I myself experienced lighting exactly like that to be found in Rembrandt's etchings."[10] Thus, despite the dirt and squalor, Amsterdam's *Judengasse*, or Jews Alley, reflected an ideal of Jewish life, and of a moment in Jewish history, that the poor Jewish neighborhoods of Berlin could never hope to represent.[11]

Liebermann was hardly alone in locating his images of Jewish life at geographical arms' length. The distancing—through time,

Figure 82
Max Liebermann
**Jewish Quarter in Amsterdam
[Judengasse in Amsterdam]**, 1905
Oil on canvas, 17 x 21⅝ in. (44 x 55 cm)
© Krefelder Kunstmuseen

Figure 83
Max Liebermann
**Jewish Quarter in Amsterdam
[Judengasse in Amsterdam]**, 1905
Oil on canvas,
23¼ x 28¾ in. (59 x 73 cm)
Wallraf-Richartz-Museum, Cologne

Figure 84
Max Liebermann
**Jewish Quarter in Amsterdam
[Judengasse in Amsterdam]**,
ca. 1910
Etching, 7 x 9⅛ in. (17.8 x 23 cm)
The Jewish Museum, New York

space, or their combination—of Jewish subjects from the contemporary milieu of the artist is a phenomenon of modern Western Jewish art, beginning with the scenes of Jewish family and religious life by Moritz Daniel Oppenheim (1800–1882). Oppenheim did not depict Jewish life in the nineteenth-century Frankfurt that he inhabited; rather, he set his scenes in the old Frankfurt ghetto and peopled them with figures in eighteenth-century dress, focusing on the cohesiveness of the family and the community (see FIG. 147).[12] Contemporaries of Liebermann, like Lesser Ury (FIGS. 90, 92, 96), Hermann Struck (see FIGS. 152, 153), and E. M. Lilien (FIG. 148), situated their Jewish works in the biblical past, in the shtetls of Eastern Europe, or in Palestine. Yet Liebermann was too much of a "realist" and painter from life to engage in this kind of imaginative manipulation. He found his ideal subject in the Holland that he loved. His paintings of the Amsterdam Jewish Quarter are among the freest and most dynamic in his oeuvre, where he rendered the rich coloristic impressions of his in situ observations, the swirling human activity and daily encounters.

If Berlin views were rare in Liebermann's oeuvre, night scenes were even more so; yet *Evening at the Brandenburg Gate*, 1916 (FIG. 85), combines both these elements. Employing an exquisitely controlled palette of browns, grays, and deep teal blue with touches of white and yellow, Liebermann contrasts the dark trees and darkly clad pedestrians with the white of the stone wall and the few glimmers of brilliant light emanating from the electric illumination. Despite the loose brushwork, there is an overriding sedateness to this painting; the pedestrians, streetcar, and horse-drawn cab are placed parallel to the picture plane and to the stone wall, trees, and building facade in the left background. Unlike Ury's bustling night scenes (see FIGS. 99, 105) or the jaunty freneticism of Steinhardt's nocturnal Berlin (see FIG. 121), there is an elegiac mood that reigns here, as if the crowd were moving in a funeral procession. The uniformed man as well as the 1916 date situate this work in the middle of the war years; and the Prussian eagles that adorn the stone wall are reminders of the context of the conflict. Liebermann's powers of observation did not fail him; yet the mood expressed in this work transcends what he was able to see in order to evoke an attitude of war weariness.

Lesser Ury

Lesser Ury (FIG. 86) has been credited with being the first artist in Germany to depict the modern metropolis.[13] At the same time

Figure 85
Max Liebermann
**Evening at the Brandenburg
Gate (Abend am
Brandenburger Tor)**, 1916
Oil on canvas,
21⅝ x 33⁷⁄₁₆ in. (55 x 85 cm)
Deutsche Bank AG, Frankfurt am Main

that he was exploring the appropriate strategies for portraying
the urban experience, he was evolving a new visual language for
expressing the Jewish experience from the vantage point of turn-
of-the-century Berlin. Despite the seeming disparity of these two
artistic projects, an analysis of Ury's major statements of these
two themes reveals an underlying cohesiveness or unifying
Weltanschauung.

Even during his lifetime, Ury's biography was subject to
romanticization. He was portrayed as an isolated figure, born into
poverty, and as a struggling artist, who endured hunger in order
to pursue his artistic calling.[14] The critic Franz Servaes, in the
introduction to Ury's Memorial Exhibition held at the National
Gallery in Berlin in 1931 shortly after the artist's death, wrote of
Ury's "lifelong martyrdom,"[15] and described him as "the born outsider who remained thus his whole life, more due to his nervous
temperament, which often impeded his relations with people,
than due to his artistic qualities, which enabled him to take his
place among the leading artists."[16] Though Ury enjoyed good
critical reviews and a healthy market for his art, he fell out with
a number of influential friends he had made in the 1890s, most
notably Max Liebermann (see the essay by Peter Paret) and Walther
Rathenau, whom Ury portrayed in a pastel of 1896 (see FIG. 14).

Ury himself actively contributed to this outcast image. In an
autobiographical sketch published in 1898, he summarized his
life as follows:

> After the death of my father, I came to Berlin with my
> mother and brothers, where I attended the Luisenstädt-
> ische Realschule. . . . Due to my precarious financial
> position, I was obliged and compelled to become a
> tradesman, but I soon abandoned this profession, in
> order to devote myself to painting. I stayed for longer or
> shorter periods of time in Düsseldorf, Brussels, Antwerp,

Figure 86
Lesser Ury
Self-Portrait (Selbstbildnis), 1898
Pastel on paper,
19¼ x 14⅛ in. (49 x 36 cm)
Courtesy of the Leo Baeck Institute,
New York

Paris, Munich, and Stuttgart. For the last seventeen years I have been occupied with painting; for eleven years I have been in Berlin. I was awarded the Michael-Beer Prize in 1890; I am a member of the Munich Secession; I have many enemies and few friends.[17]

Moreover, the portion of his oeuvre that Ury himself most clearly prized—the monumental interpretations of subjects derived from the Hebrew Bible and Jewish history—were the least well-received, both during his lifetime and posthumously. Although many of these works were indeed flawed in their realization, their conception represented a new approach to Jewish subject matter—a Jewish Symbolism—and remained unique among Ury's contemporaries.

Ury was born in 1861 in the town of Birnbaum in the eastern province of Posen. Recent scholarship has indicated that he was born into a family of the middle class. After the death of his father, when Ury was eleven, the family did experience some financial hardship. Yet following the relocation of his widowed mother with her two sons to Berlin, Ury received a good general education before being apprenticed to a merchant. He showed an early interest in art, however, and decided to abandon a commercial career in order to devote himself to painting.[18]

Ury left Berlin in 1879 for Düsseldorf to study at the famous art academy there. En route he stopped in Kassel to view the many paintings by Rembrandt in that city's museum. Rembrandt's work, particularly his depictions of biblical subjects, would provide a source and inspiration for Ury throughout his career. At the Düsseldorf academy, Ury came into contact with the history painter Hermann Wislicenus (1825–1899). After a year in Düsseldorf, he resumed his travels, remaining for a time in Antwerp and Brussels, before arriving in Paris in 1881. Ury's fascination with urban experience as a subject for his art seems to have originated during this Parisian sojourn. In particular, he was drawn to the effects of nocturnal illumination, which he may well have admired in pastels and monotypes of Degas.[19]

In 1882, Ury entered the Royal Academy of Fine Arts in Brussels, where he found a supportive teacher in Jean-François Portaels[20] and was awarded the first prize in his class for life drawing.[21] Ury's fellow students in the Academy's painting class included the future Belgian Symbolist painter Jan Toorop (1858–1928) and Charles Meunier (1864–1910), son of the artist Constantin Meunier.[22] Indeed, certain characteristics of Ury's art in the following years would demonstrate affinities with the art of the Belgian Symbolists. In 1883 he continued his studies in Paris with Jules Joseph Lefèbvre, before returning to Belgium in 1884 and settling in the village of Volluvet on the outskirts of Brussels. Ury's depiction of the rural landscape and inhabitants of Volluvet reveals affinities with the art of many of his contemporaries who were drawn to the life of the peasantry for its perceived simplicity and elemental human values of hard work, religious faith, and community.[23] Like many of these artists, Ury attributed an innate dignity to people who worked the land. However, Ury's treatment of these subjects differed from the scenes of communal work or man in harmony with nature that characterized much of the depiction of rural life in the European art of the 1880s. Not only were Ury's scenes devoid of all sentimentality, but he tended to present his peasants in a kind of hieratic isolation both from the surrounding landscape and from one another. In *Volluvet* of 1884 (FIG. 87), the woman in the foreground is presented in strict profile, her form pushed right up to the edge of the picture plane. Her head and body slightly bowed, she seems oblivious to the man with hoe standing in the right middle-ground, just as he seems totally absorbed in his own thoughts.[24] The spindly trees, whose pointed branches pierce the sky, are the most animated elements in the composition. Ury creates an airless, stifling atmosphere reminiscent of works by some of the Post-Impressionist painters, particularly Seurat.[25]

Figure 87
Lesser Ury
Volluvet, 1884
Location unknown

The *gravitas* and dignity with which Ury depicted the inhabitants of Volluvet would be carried over into his depictions of figures from the Hebrew Bible. Ury would locate paradigms for Jewish authenticity and heroism in the biblical past, as other Jewish artists would find their models in the shtetls of Eastern Europe or the Jewish inhabitants of Palestine. This search for a primal authenticity is not limited to Jewish artists, but can be linked to many other artistic projects of the late nineteenth century, from the Arcadian landscapes of Puvis de Chavannes and Hans von Marées to the interest in Breton peasant life by the members of the Pont-Aven school, as well as Gauguin's complex interpretations of Tahitian culture.

Ury's Jewish Themes

Whereas Ury considered his works based on subject matter drawn from Jewish texts and history the most significant part of his oeuvre, these works have received a decidedly mixed reception, both during his lifetime and posthumously. The philosopher Martin Buber praised Ury's Jewish works, and contributed many valuable insights to our understanding of them. Franz Servaes devoted an enthusiastic article to his monumental painting after seeing Ury's *Jerusalem* exhibited in 1896.[26] Yet in the introduction to the Ury memorial exhibition, Servaes addressed Ury's shortcomings as a monumental painter:

> A powerful artistic ambition is articulated therein [that is, in the religious paintings], at the same time as a profound and heartfelt feeling drawn from the

mysteries of the race. No one will fail to recognize the painterly passion that is expressed in these colossal compositions. Nevertheless, Ury's compositional and graphic abilities were not strong enough to allow the artistic solutions to triumph over the literary impulse in all cases.[27]

In an article published in 1974, the art historian Alfred Werner took up and expanded upon Servaes' criticism of this portion of Ury's oeuvre:

> Perhaps the least important of Ury's works are his monumental compositions on Jewish biblical or philosophical subjects. . . . The young Martin Buber, in his understandable enthusiasm for "Jewish" elements in contemporary art, overrated Ury's ambitious compositions on biblical and Jewish scenes. In the first place Ury . . . did not have the compositional power demanded by the monumental proportions. He also lacked the calm perseverance and strict discipline required for the orderly and careful execution of these large works, which he approached with his quasi-impressionistic technique.[28]

Werner describes an encounter between Ury and the critic Arthur Galliner, who commented on a huge canvas, its face turned to the wall, which Ury turned around for his visitor to see: "It was an unfinished work, *Jacob Blessing Benjamin*. 'It is madness to paint such a subject today, in this inhuman, irreligious period,' the artist said."[29]

This subject, in fact, constituted Ury's earliest grappling with Jewish subjects: a pastel dated 1884, *Jacob Blessing Benjamin*

Figure 88
Lesser Ury
Jacob Blessing Benjamin
[Jakob segnet Benjamin], 1884
Pastel on paper,
8½ x 10½ in. (22 x 26 cm)
Location unknown

(FIG. 88).[30] As with many of his compositions, Ury returned to this scene over the course of many years.[31] Ury depicts the young Benjamin kneeling in profile before his aged father, his shoulders hunched, as if seeking protection beneath his father's hands, which hover above the boy's head. It is a strikingly intimate scene, devoid of any details of setting or costume to distract us from the emotional content of the moment. Ury's generalized treatment of the figures and their simple drapery diverges from many biblical depictions of his time that aimed at historical accuracy by including details of dress or physical surroundings gleaned from contemporary archaeological excavations.[32]

This work is always referred to as *Jacob Blessing Benjamin*, although this phrase usually refers to the patriarch's blessing his youngest son, along with all his sons, before his death; yet in this episode Benjamin is already a grown man, not the young boy in Ury's composition.[33] The only incident that could account for this scene, with Benjamin depicted as a boy, is recounted in chapter 43 of Genesis. Jacob must send his beloved youngest son, Benjamin, along with his brothers to Egypt in order to secure food for the family in a time of famine. Unbeknownst to Jacob, it is Joseph—who years before had been sold into slavery by his jealous brothers— who has insisted that Benjamin journey to Egypt. The midrashic texts describe Jacob's anguish at having to send Benjamin, as well as the older sons' arguments to convince their father that he has no other choice. But neither biblical nor midrashic texts refer specifically to Jacob's bidding Benjamin farewell or to his bestowing upon him a blessing.

Ury has imagined what might have transpired between the aged patriarch as he sends his beloved son to an unknown fate, in effect "sacrificing" him to save the family from starvation. Ury's treatment reveals the poignancy of the scene expressing deep love, but also fear and ambivalence. In a charcoal drawing of 1908,[34] Ury retained the central group of Jacob and Benjamin, but expanded the scene to depict Benjamin's older brothers standing in an outer room, visible in the left background, perhaps to help identify the scene. This composition was later executed as a lithograph, ca. 1920 (FIG. 89).

How did Ury come to depict this scene? It obviously held a profound attraction for him, since he repeated it with modifications over many years in a variety of media.[35] A father bidding his son farewell might have had a personal resonance for Ury, whose own father died while the painter was a boy of the age depicted here. His study of Rembrandt may have provided another impetus for this work. The similarity of the poses of the two figures in Ury's composition to those of the father and son in Rembrandt's engraving of 1636, *The Return of the Prodigal Son*, is noteworthy.[36] Rembrandt's depiction of biblical subjects had a profound influence on Ury, as on many of his contemporaries.[37] Ury may have been moved by Rembrandt's engraving to imagine a similar scene taken from the Hebrew Bible. The emotional shift from a scene of return and reconciliation to one of parting may reflect Ury's personal concerns. Finally, *Jacob Blessing Benjamin* is unusual in Ury's oeuvre as it depicts an intimate emotional encounter between two human beings.

Ury depicted scenes from the Bible, which he called "simply the most beautiful book ever written,"[38] throughout his career. Many were depictions of characters from the Bible: "For me the biblical figures are just so great that I can never forget that they continually awaken in me new feelings of edification and inspiration."[39] Ury tended to emphasize the individual qualities of the biblical characters rather than the stories in which they were

Figure 89
Lesser Ury
**Jacob Blessing Benjamin
(Jakob segnet Benjamin)**, ca.1920
Lithograph, 12 x 14½ in. (30.5 x 36.8 cm)
The Jewish Museum, New York.
Anonymous Gift

Figure 90
Lesser Ury
Rebecca at the Well [Rebekkah am Brunnen], ca. 1908
Oil on canvas,
27½ x 18⅛ in. (70 x 46 cm)
Stiftung Jüdisches Museum, Berlin

Figure 91
J. James Tissot
Abraham's Servant Meeteth Rebecca, ca. 1896–1902
Gouache,
10⁵/₁₆ x 7¹³/₁₆ in. (26.2 x 19.8 cm)
The Jewish Museum, New York. Gift of the heirs of Jacob Schiff, x1952.107

embedded. *Rebecca at the Well*, ca. 1908 (FIG. 90) is an excellent example of Ury's general approach.[40] Rebecca stands at the edge of a well of water, her left hand holding a pitcher she has rested on the rim. The scene refers to the episode in the twenty-fourth chapter of Genesis where Abraham has sent his servant to find a wife for his son Isaac. The servant will know he has found the right woman if she not only gives water to Abraham's servant, but also offers refreshment to the camels. Ury eliminates the narrative elements from the composition; only the suggestion of the well and the pitcher resting on its ledge allude to the biblical episode. Instead, Ury has concentrated on the overall mood of the scene, the rich glow of the yellow sky, and its brilliant reflection in the water. The suggestion of sunset does not accord with the time of day in the biblical narrative, but is used for expressive purposes: the warm glow seems to refer to the warmth and kindness of Rebecca's character. To contemporary critics, Ury was known above all for his unique and passionate use of color as the key to his expressive artistic language.[41]

Ury also depicted physically robust figures in his biblical characters, perhaps to counter the prevailing image of the Jew as physically weak.[42] Rebecca's strong bare arms and ample figure suggest a biblical "Brünnhilde" far removed from the more fragile and feminine, or slightly eroticized, depictions of other artists, such as Tissot (FIG. 91); and the wispy trees serve to emphasize the monumentality of her figure.

Jerusalem **and** *Jeremiah*

Adolph Donath claimed that Ury began to work on several of his monumental works of the 1880s, specifically *Jerusalem*, 1896 (FIG. 92) and *Jeremiah*, 1897 (FIG. 96), while still at the Brussels Academy, in the large studio sprovided by Portaels.[43] The monumental versions of these works are lost, but are known to us from photographs. As was Ury's custom, he also executed smaller versions of his compositions; a number of these have survived, along with studies for the monumental canvases. *Jerusalem* and *Jeremiah* are the most successful of Ury's works on Jewish subjects and give the clearest indication of his contribution to creating a new "Jewish" visual idiom.

Martin Buber relates that as early as 1881, in Brussels, Ury had the idea to depict the destruction of Jerusalem as "an historical moment in a tragic landscape":

> And, to be sure, [to do so] in his manner: not by means of the theatrical pathos of "heroes," but rather through the more profound, stiller, and more refined pathos of a group of nameless people, from whose unpretentious and unclichéd demeanor, precisely because it is so simple and without cliché, illuminates for us the solemn power of a great fate.[44]

Figure 92
Lesser Ury
Jerusalem, 1896
Destroyed

Buber describes two sketches for *Jerusalem* dating from 1881, enabling us to trace the evolution of this work. The first study depicts the destroyed Temple on the left, its broad steps littered with the corpses of the defeated defenders, broken vessels for the Temple offerings, and torn priestly vestments. On these same steps sit mourning Jewish women and children. The ruins of the city, with its fallen fighters, appear on the right; in the distance, a group of women and children with packs on their backs begin their wandering. Buber refers to a traditional depiction of Jerusalem's destruction, known from many works of art, among them Eduard Bendemann's *The Exile of the Jews into Babylonian Captivity*, 1872 (FIG. 93).

Buber describes a second sketch, which, though similar in many respects, presented the scene in a more condensed manner. A stairway strewn with corpses remained the main element in the foreground; in the background, the ruins of a hall with pillars inhabited by motionless old men. In this second sketch, Ury introduced a new element: in the middle of the composition, between the corpses, a long, thin bench with seated women. This bench would become the dominant element in Ury's painting of 1896, both in terms of the compositional structure and construction of meaning. Since the two sketches of 1881 are known only from Buber's description, it is hard to tell how closely the early bench resembles its final realization. I would suggest, however, that the bench owes a debt to another work of art, which may have inspired Ury to transform the bench into the vehicle for conveying the symbolic content of the painting.

Ferdinand Hodler's *The Disappointed Souls*, 1891–92 (FIG. 94), depicts five old men seated next to one another on a long white bench. Dressed in similar black robes, each is presented in a different attitude or gesture; yet all express the same resigned despair. Though seated next to one another and united by virtue

of their attire, expressive demeanor, and the frieze-like arrangement of their figures, there is no interaction between them. As Sharon L. Hirsh notes in her study of Hodler's symbolist works: "Having lost all hope of life, they await death together, but without communication."[45] Ury employed many of the same compositional devices as Hodler in his progression from depicting a particular historic moment to representing the very idea of exile: the elongated bench, the frieze-like arrangement of figures, the commonalities of dress, the vertical figures forming a grid with the horizontals of bench and horizon, the generalized landscape setting.

The *Jerusalem* of 1896 no longer represents the destruction of the city, but rather the ontological reality of living with the results of that destruction. The title of the painting has evolved from being descriptive of the action depicted to connoting an absence responsible for an existential state. Having lost Jerusalem, the Jews were relegated to the situation of exile; that existential experience is the subject of *Jerusalem*. Rather than depicting the destruction of Jerusalem, the painting addresses the issues presented in Psalm 137:

> By the rivers of Babylon,/ There we sat down, yea,
> we wept,/ When we remembered Zion./Upon the willows
> in the midst thereof/ We hanged up our harps.

The presence of water and the two trees make reference to the imagery of the biblical text; but the meaning of the painting lies in the dilemma articulated by the Psalmist: "How shall we sing the Lord's song in a foreign land?" This foreign land symbolizes all the foreign lands that Jews have lived in since the destruction of the Second Temple. The combination of men and women of different ages, along with a young boy, as well as the generalized nature of their clothing allow these figures to represent Jews from many times and places. The abnormally elongated bench, without a visible beginning or end, becomes a kind of timeline extending infinitely in both directions, into both the past and the future. Ury may have been moved to take up this subject by the plight of refugees from the pogroms that had terrorized Jews in Russia beginning in the 1880s.[46] A number of other Jewish artists turned

to this subject in works that represented the desperate situation of Jews in Eastern Europe,[47] but those works were marked by a specificity of location, dress, or gesture that linked them to a particular historic moment, as, for example, Maurycy Minkowski's *After the Pogrom*, 1905 (FIG. 95). In Minkowski's work, the diversity of facial expressions and clothing of the foreground figures, the specificity of the village setting, and the line of figures continuing their wandering in the distance create the impression of reportage. Ury's approach is more in keeping with Yosef Yerushalmi's analysis of a particular model of Jewish historical understanding, whereby new historical experiences are assimilated by means of "established conceptual frameworks. Persecution and suffering are, after all, the result of the condition of being in exile."[48] Thus, a representation of the plight of Ury's coreligionists in Russia could best be articulated in terms of the archetypical experience of Jewish exile. Ury's elongated bench symbolizes this basic continuity in Jewish historical experience.

Figure 95
Maurycy Minkowski
After the Pogrom, 1905
Oil on canvas mounted on board,
39¼ x 60½ in. (100 x 153.7 cm)
The Jewish Museum, New York.
Gift of Lester S. Klein, 1986–80

Buber seized on this fundamental aspect of Ury's painting when he wrote:

> It is an evening among many evenings and Jews among many Jews. But these people are the entire Jewish people, and this evening is its entire history. This is Ury's long, blessed road of struggle from the sketch to the final work: he set out to paint the Jewish past and he discovered the Jewish eternity.[49]

Ury's artistic project during the last years of the nineteenth century was the creation of a Jewish symbolic art, drawing on the innovations of international Symbolism and infusing these with a profound sensitivity to the Jewish historical and literary idiom. Despite the imperfect realization of these goals, Ury's work influenced many of his contemporaries. That they became icons for the burgeoning Zionist movement—lauded by Buber, reproduced as postcards and in Jewish periodicals—is not surprising. (See the essay by Inka Bertz in this book.) Their symbolism also bore a more universalist interpretation, as noted in the article by Franz Servaes mentioned previously. For Servaes, the image of sorrowing Jews had significance beyond Jewish suffering, and had become a universal symbol for all downtrodden people:

> Like the Jew, so the proletariat, the suffering hero of the fourth estate.... The demeaned and insulted of all humanity stand here before us in venerable representatives.[50]

Servaes used Ury's painting to arrive at a definition of monumentality within the modern idiom. Every historical period creates its own monumentality, Servaes maintained, and he located the monumental of his own time in the "personal":

It is to be demanded from a modern-monumental work of art that it reflects our own era at the same time that it carries the stamp of the personal. The one is as important as the other, and both must be presented in a state of equilibrium.[51]

In the *Jeremiah* of 1897, Ury took this process of reduction and symbolization one step further. In contrast to nineteenth-century German depictions of the prophet lamenting the destruction of Jerusalem amid the ruins of the Temple and victims of the Roman onslaught, Ury presents a radical image of the solitary prophet lying on the ground beneath a vast expanse of starry sky, as if he were the last inhabitant on earth. (Compare Ury's painting [FIG. 96] with Eduard Bendemann's *The Exile of the Jews into Babylonian Captivity*, 1872 [FIG. 93], which was in the collection of the National Gallery in Berlin before it was destroyed during the Second World War.)[52]

Contemporaries were aware of Ury's radical departure from the usual depiction of this subject; Martin Buber contrasted Ury's conception of the prophet with these traditional interpretations:

The stylistic corruption of our time has accustomed us to think of a strikingly draped old man, who with a pathetically mournful mien is enthroned upon stage-set-like ruins, when mention is made of a painting of Jeremiah. Now we approach this Jeremiah. A broad night sky imparting a shudder of the infinite over a small and desolate piece of earth.[53]

Jeremiah's monumental scale invited the viewer to enter the space of the painting, which was dominated by the expanse of blue and purple sky with its twinkling stars reminiscent of a Whistler "Nocturne." Much of the work's expressive power is derived from this depiction of nature, which is endowed, as Buber noted, with a profound spiritual message. Ury became known for his landscapes of Italy and the region surrounding Berlin, all infused with an almost pantheistic fervor and characterized by an original and powerful harnessing of intense color (see FIGS. 103, 104).

Ury's Jeremiah is neither the lamenting prophet of Bendemann nor of Michelangelo. The closest artistic model is found in Rembrandt's *Jeremiah Lamenting the Destruction of Jerusalem*, 1630 (FIG. 97), where the prophet's pensive expression is heightened by the similar gesture of hand to ear.[54] In both canvases, Jeremiah's hand and face are illuminated to focus attention on his mental and spiritual activity. Indeed, Ury's canvas ultimately is about the nature of prophecy itself as seen from the perspective of the prophet. Jeremiah's fundamental isolation is the result of his prophetic vision, spiritual sensitivity, and experience of the divine. Rather than a lamenting figure, Ury's Jeremiah appears like a rocky outcropping of the earth, deeply rooted, like a force of nature.[55] The star-filled sky ultimately is a portent of hope: it brings to mind the verses in Genesis where God promises Abram (the future Abraham) that He will make his descendants as numerous as the stars in the heaven.[56] The stars are a reminder of the covenant and of the continuation of the Jewish people, despite their exile and tribulations; Jeremiah looks out to the right, as if into the future.[57] Jeremiah, who was humiliated and persecuted because of his prophecy, is also an alter ego for the artist himself. Ury's biographer, Adolph Donath, writing in 1921, drew a connection between the solitary Ury and Jeremiah when he saw in this painting "the inner echo of his [Ury's] own bitterness."[58]

Figure 97
Rembrandt van Rijn
Jeremiah Lamenting the Destruction of Jerusalem, 1630
Oil on panel, 22¹³⁄₁₆ x 18⅛ in. (58 x 46 cm)
Rijksmuseum, Amsterdam

The *Jeremiah* raises for us another important issue in Ury's religious pictures, namely, the claim that his drawing talents were not up to the task at hand. In the *Jeremiah*, the hand supporting his head is drawn in an indistinct way. The other hand appears clumsy, overly massive, uncouth. In *Transience* (*Vergänglichkeit*)

1898 (FIG. 98), the same issue of clumsy execution arises, particularly in the treatment of the columns and the way in which the brilliant orange pigment of the background interrupts their contour.[59] It seems clear, however, that Ury, the winner of the first-prize medal for life drawing while he was a student at the Brussels Academy, was capable of drawing a well-articulated hand or column. His drawing, as well as his use of often garish color combinations, was put at the service of a higher expressive goal. Buber described Jeremiah's hands as belonging to a prophet and a revolutionary, seizing upon their expressive power.[60] It is as if Ury felt the subjects of these works were too awe-inspiring to be served by a graceful drawing style; that they required something rawer, less refined, and ultimately more eloquent than the pleasing effects he was perfectly capable of achieving in his pastels or oil paintings of landscapes and city scenes.

In a 1905 interview, Ury articulated his conviction that art must be engaged with the fundamental ideas of society and humanity:

> The painter must also contribute to the elevation of humanity. It is ridiculous to say that a painter is only a painter and nothing more, and I confess that unfortunately I, too, when I was young, was of that opinion. At that time, twenty-five years ago, I was one of the first who believed that we could achieve greatness in art with mere naturalism, with the transcription of nature. . . . Art is spirit. But art is not about only reproducing external appearances. And today one snuffles around, whether a picture is drawn properly, whether it is painted naturalistically, and thereby one completely forgets that authentic art only begins once handicraft has been completely surmounted.[61]

Metropolitan Life

At the same time that Ury was constructing monumental compositions of Jewish history and memory, he was producing works that recorded ephemeral phenomena of light, weather, and the movement of traffic and pedestrians in contemporary Berlin. While Ury's treatment of Jewish subjects bears stylistic affinities to Symbolist works, for his renditions of contemporary urban life he looked to the French Impressionists for inspiration.

More than any other artist, Ury is associated with the depiction of the Berlin metropolis that emerged during the last decades of the nineteenth century. Whereas other artists produced picturesque views of "Old Berlin," Ury was the first to create images to express the experience of urban dwellers: the modern means of transportation, new modes of display and consumerism, electrical nocturnal illumination, and the particular blend of closeness and distance that characterizes human encounters in the public spaces of the street and the café. Ury was mesmerized by the perceptual phenomena of pedestrians and horse-drawn carriages reflected in

Figure 98
Lesser Ury
Transience (Vergänglichkeit), 1898
Oil on canvas,
41 x 30¹¹⁄₁₆ in. (104 x 78 cm)
Stiftung Jüdisches Museum, Berlin

the wet asphalt of rain-swept streets, of street lamps casting long beams of light onto the wet boulevards at night, of electric light refracted off the mirrors and large windows of the city's cafés.

Am Bahnhof Friedrichstrasse (At the Friedrichstrasse Station), 1888 (FIG. 99), depicts the bustling activity around the busy rail station in the center of Berlin at either 5:45 or 9:30 on a snowy evening. The newly completed (1882) glass and steel Friedrichstrasse station (FIG. 100) was a hub of the new "Stadtbahn," or municipal transit system, which linked the outlying areas of the newly bourgeoning city to its center, the area called "Berlin Mitte."[62] Friedrichstrasse was the main artery of a new commercial center of department stores, cafés, and places of entertainment; and the new transporation system made it accessible to Berlin's citizens from different neighborhoods and social and economic classes. Much of this social context is visible in Ury's painting: the elegant woman in the foreground is contrasted to the poor street vendor seen in profile in the middle distance, who has to eke out a living, standing outdoors in inclement weather, by selling wares from a tray hanging from her neck.

Even the affluent woman, despite her elegant and warm attire, hardly appears carefree; her tilted head and large wistful eyes betray a melancholy and self-absorption that isolates her from the surrounding urban bustle. In the large clock dominating the scene, the diversity of urban types, and the mutual indifference of pedestrians to one another, Ury's painting evokes a view of metropolitan life similar to that articulated by the great Berlin sociologist Georg Simmel.[63] (See FIG. 8 and essays by Paul Mendes-Flohr and Barbara Hahn in this book.)

Ury's delight in atmospheric effects of light, steam, and mist in the context of a train station clearly owe a debt to Claude Monet's paintings of the Gare Saint-Lazare in Paris (FIG. 101). Yet the differences are telling. Monet's rapid brushwork renders the people as dabs of paint; he is not interested in differentiating among the crowd, only in showing their movement. Ury's approach is at once more decorative—note how the white swirl of the woman's scarf and hat plume is echoed in the steam from the train, which seems almost to rise from behind her head—and less distanced from the theater of human activity. Monet leaves the foreground of his train station empty of people;[64] Ury confronts us head-on with Berlin's inhabitants. In many of his compositions, Ury chooses a perspective from the pavement, whereas the French Impressionists

Figure 99
Lesser Ury
**At the Friedrichstrasse Station
[Am Bahnhof Friedrichstrasse]**, 1888
Opaque watercolor on board,
25½ x 18¼ in. (65.5 x 46.8 cm)
Stiftung Stadtmuseum Berlin.
Purchased with funds from the
Museumsstiftung Dr. Otto
and Ilse Augustin

Figure 100
Bahnhof Friedrichstrasse, 1907
Photograph: Max Missmann

Figure 101
Claude Monet
**Arrival of the Normandy Train,
Gare Saint-Lazare**, 1877
Oil on canvas,
23½ x 31½ in. (59.6 x 80.2 cm)
The Art Institute of Chicago.
Mr. and Mrs. Martin A. Ryerson
Collection, 1933.1158
Photograph ©1999. All Rights Reserved.

Figure 102
Lesser Ury
**Night Impression
(Nachtimpression)**, ca. 1918
Etching on paper,
14 x 10¼ in. (35.6 x 26 cm)
The Jewish Museum, New York

tended to view the city from a window, as did Liebermann in his pastel of 1900 (see FIG. 80).[65]

In the etching *Night Impression*, ca. 1918 (FIG. 102),[66] Ury has condensed the experience of a Berlin night into this encounter with light, steam, and mist. The city's inhabitants are present only as the implied passengers and drivers of the elevated train and the horse-drawn carriage. Juxtaposing these two modes of transportation—the old and the new—as they move perpendicular to one another through the Berlin night, Ury conjures a mysterious world. Though it is constructed of the elements found in the cityscapes of the French Impressionists, it ultimately diverges from them in critical ways. The steam and mist of *Night Impression* are the result of Ury's extremely sensitive observations of the visual phenomena in his surroundings; yet in the final analysis, they transcend the ephemeral and enter the same symbolic realm as Ury's landscapes and monumental figural works, such as *Jerusalem*. By extracting the essences of his experiences, he subjectivizes and elevates them to a metaphysical level, so that Ury's Berlin night scenes are imbued with the same incandescent spirit as his magical landscapes (FIGS. 103, 104).

Another urban subject that Ury depicted with relentless interest was the café, an important scene of social, artistic, and intellectual exchange in turn-of-the-century Berlin. (See the essay by Sigrid Bauschinger in this book.) Certain hallmarks of Ury's approach to this subject are already evident in works that survive from his first Parisian sojourn. A small drawing dated 1882 (FIG. 106) depicts a café interior with a man seated in profile reading a newspaper in the middle ground of the composition. The foreground is occupied by the suggestion of an empty chair. By far the dominant element in the composition is the café table, which appears unnaturally large, an open white expanse in a dark interior. Ury used the white of the paper and then highlighted it further with white heightening. In the distance, another table and coffee cup are visible. Each table resembles a floating island of illumination within the composition, emphasizing the isolation of the café's inhabitants.

This essential view of the alienation of urban life epitomized by the café—not a site of convivial exchange, but rather a place where urban dwellers retreat to be alone among others—was no doubt influenced by the works of Degas and Manet from the same period, for example, Manet's *A Café in the Place du Théâtre-Français* of 1881 (FIG. 107).[67] Theodore Reff has described Manet's café as "a world of strangers adrift in a seemingly limitless space, who are cut off severely at its edges, reflected ambiguously in its mirrors, remote from each other even when seated together."[68] These words would apply as well to the many café

Figure 103
Lesser Ury
Untitled (Mountain Landscape), n.d.
Oil on canvas,
30¼ x 37⅝ in. (77 x 95.5 cm)
Courtesy of Bineth Gallery, Tel Aviv

Figure 104
Lesser Ury
Untitled (Landscape with Lake), n.d.
Oil on canvas,
28 x 39⅞ in. (71 x 101 cm)
Courtesy of Bineth Gallery, Tel Aviv

Figure 105
Lesser Ury
**Berlin Street Scene–Leipziger
Platz (Berliner Strassenszene–
Leipziger Platz)**, 1898
Oil on canvas, 42⅛ x 26¾ in. (107 x 68 cm)
Berlinische Galerie, Landesmuseum für
Moderne Kunst, Photographie
und Architektur

Figure 106
Lesser Ury
Man in Café, 1882
Ink on paper,
6⅜ x 4½ in. (17 x 12.3 om)
Collection of the Tel Aviv Museum of Art.
Gift of Dr. U. Eitingon, No. 7189

scenes produced by Ury once he returned to Berlin. *Café* of 1889 (FIG. 108), which also served as the basis for a print ca. 1920, is a more accomplished presentation of the elements visible in the Paris gouache. Ury constructs the composition as if the viewer were the café patron at the round table that dominates the foreground. A large white cup occupies the center of this table and is the focal point of the painting. A number of empty chairs are arranged around the table, whose polished surface shimmers with reflected light. Two gentlemen at separate tables occupy the middle ground; one smokes a cigar, the other reads a newspaper, partially cut off by the edge of the canvas, like the figure at the left of Manet's canvas.

Ury's café pictures interject yet another dimension of urban life: the interpenetration of interior and exterior public spaces, the ambiguities of observer and observed. The city beyond the confines of the café is visible through the huge glass window facing the street: a horse-drawn carriage, women with umbrellas, three trees. The gray atmosphere of a rainy day is echoed in the tonalities of café tables and coffee cups and in the drifting smoke, billowing like clouds from the cigar of the top-hatted gentleman. The curtain rod demarcates the border between the café and the street; yet it serves pictorially to accentuate the flatness of the picture plane, thus conflating the three spaces of the scene: viewer, café, and street. The drawn curtain calls attention to the performative aspects of city life, the entertainment value of watching the passing pedestrians. These pedestrians, in turn, can observe the denizens of the café. The city has become a theater, whose inhabitants are both actors and audience.

The next generation of Berlin Jewish artists, exemplified by Ludwig Meidner and Jakob Steinhardt, were also mesmerized by the metropolis and sought to convey their relationship to the city in their work. Influenced by the writings and work of the Italian Futurists and by the art of Robert Delaunay, however, they went beyond the depiction of visual phenomena in seeking the pictorial means of representing the way it *felt* to inhabit the metropolis and experience its dynamism and frenetic pace. Like Ury, they also turned to subjects related to their Jewish background: images of Jewish history and contemporary suffering and subjects drawn from the Bible. As in Ury's work, one senses the artist's identification with his Jewish subjects; but the works of the younger artists are executed in a style that moved beyond Ury's Symbolism to an Expressionist idiom.

Ludwig Meidner

Ludwig Meidner was born in Bernstadt, Silesia, in 1884; his parents owned a textile business. By the age of sixteen, his early

Figure 107
Edouard Manet
A Café in the Place du Théâtre-Français, 1881
Oil and pastel on canvas,
12¾ x 18 in. (32.4 x 45.7 cm)
The Burrell Collection, Glasgow
Museums and Art Galleries

Figure 108
Lesser Ury
Café, 1889
Oil on canvas,
23¼ x 19¹⁵⁄₁₆ in. (59 x 49 cm)
Location unknown

interest in art had already developed into a penchant for subjects both religious and macabre: ascetics, pillar saints, death figures and ghosts. Enthusiastic about the visionary art of neo-Romantics like Arnold Böcklin and Franz von Stuck, he sent examples of his work to Stuck, who encouraged Meidner in his artistic ambitions.[69] Many of Meidner's early works deal with religious themes, such as the pen-and-ink drawing of 1901 entitled *Jehuda ben Halevy* (FIG. 109). An old bearded man sits amid ruins, the fingers of his hand clenched in pain. Blood streams from a wound in his chest, dripping down the fallen pillar upon which he is seated. An inscription beneath the drawing contains the following verses:

> Ruhig floss das Blut des Rabbi
> Ruhig seinen Sang zu Ende
> Sang er und sein Sterbeletzter
> Seufzer war Jerusalem!

> (Quietly flowed the Rabbi's blood
> Quietly his song came to an end
> He sang and his last dying
> Sigh was Jerusalem!)

These lines are taken from the unfinished poem "Jehuda ben Halevy," written by Heinrich Heine during his final illness toward the end of his life.[70] In this poem, Heine explored his complex relationship to Judaism through the prism of the great medieval Hebrew poet, scholar, and doctor Yehuda Halevi (1075–1141), who lived in Spain during the Golden Age. Many of Halevi's poems express the pain of exile and his longing to return to the Land of Israel. Indeed, he left the comforts of Spain, his career, and family to travel as a pilgrim to Jerusalem, where, according to legend, he was murdered at the moment when he first glimpsed Jerusalem.[71] If the poet Heine, who converted from Judaism to Christianity, identified at the end of his life with the great dying poet Halevi,[72] Meidner's treatment of this subject points to an early interest in Jewish artistic expression and, in particular, to poetry.

In the poem, Heine makes reference to Jeremiah and the text of Psalm 137; Meidner's depiction of Halevi bears comparison with the lamenting exilic figures in Ury's paintings. Meidner's emphasis on Halevi's suffering, his placement in profile among ruins in a barren landscape, and his bowed head are reminiscent of the figures in Ury's *Transience* (FIG. 98). Yet, whereas the half-nude draped figure endows Halevy with a timeless quality, his facial features resemble caricatures of European Jews and introduce a note of contemporaneity.

Another early work reveals Meidner's predilection for expressions of ecstatic religious fervor, this time taken from the Christian tradition. *Mortify the Flesh* (*Töte das Fleisch*) of 1902 depicts monks in the act of self-flagellation beneath two large crucifixes of rough wood.[73] *Golus*, also of 1902, depicts a half-naked Jew leaning on a tombstone, to which he appears to be chained. Meidner places considerable emphasis on the man's exposed genitals, a provocative choice bearing no relation to the subject of the work, but revealing Meidner's penchant for creating disturbing images.[74] "Golus" refers to the exilic situation of the Jews, and was the subject of other works at this time that depicted groups of sorrowful Jews in their wanderings, compared to which Meidner's conception is striking in its originality, if not necessarily in its execution.[75]

In 1903, Meidner studied at the Art School in Breslau, moving to Berlin in 1905, where he supported himself as a fashion illustrator, work he later described as "artistic prostitution."[76] Studying etching with Hermann Struck, he met Jakob Steinhardt, another young Jewish artist from Silesia, with whom he embarked on a long and productive friendship; in 1912 they would together found the Pathetiker group.

In July 1906, Meidner went to Paris, financed by an aunt. He briefly attended the Cormon and Julien academies, which were popular with foreign students, but his primary education came from the art he saw at the Louvre and in the contemporary exhibitions. Meidner later recalled the impact of his encounters with the art of Manet, Van Gogh, Cézanne, and the Fauves, and his friendship with the Italian Jewish painter Amedeo Modigliani. Nevertheless, Meidner expressed disappointment with Paris in a letter of January 1907 written to his old school friend Franz Landsberger:[77]

Figure 109
Ludwig Meidner
Jehuda ben Halevy, 1901
Watercolor, pen, hand-colored on paper,
17 15/16 x 14 1/2 in. (45.6 x 36.8 cm)
Museum Ostdeutsche Galerie
Regensburg

> Paris means the monuments of the past. Today the French are no longer productive. . . . How different Berlin is! Berlin is pregnant! Berlin has become the intellectual and moral capital of the world.[78]

Returning to Berlin in the summer of 1907 for his compulsory military examination, Meidner eventually moved to Kattowitz, in Silesia, where he directed a school for painting and drawing. A letter written from there to Struck, 10 November 1908, reveals his attitude of "épater le bourgeois," and provides insights into his artistic personality. He complained that his social encounters were limited to the local Jewish bourgeoisie, with whom he had nothing in common:

> My way of life and point of view is unbourgeois, gypsy-like, rebellious. I have an instinctive and uneducated hatred for this entire satisfied social class. . . . The sufferings of a painter are horrible, especially when he must live in exile.[79]

Berlin had thus clearly become his home, from which he was now "in exile." He went on to relate his poverty, which he claimed did not make him unhappy; but it hindered his artistic development, since he was unable to afford materials and models. His solution was to engage in an intense artistic fantasy life, imagining the paintings he was unable to produce materially:

> In point of fact, I have never led a dream existence of such intensity as I have here. All afternoon I run around my room, smoke my pipe . . . and paint my imaginary pictures. These pictures are not naturalistic, for I renounced Naturalism once I became acquainted with the great new movement in Paris. They are well composed, my pictures, synthetic, full of rhythm, and they have a pronounced decorative style. I love blue very much, also lots of white and black. In general, I lean toward this simplified color scale of the Divisionists, without, however, adopting their technique. On the contrary, I apply the pigment in broad strokes, succinctly—*C'est mon oeuvre imaginaire!* [This is my imaginary oeuvre!][80]

This experience of painting as an imaginary act seems to have unleashed Meidner's already prodigious imaginative faculties.

The following years in Berlin were marked by continued physical deprivation and hunger, the result of Meidner's extreme poverty. His absorption in the city is evident in the works he executed depicting its physical transformation during the course of relentless urban expansion and development. In the drawing *Construction Site Between Houses*, 1911 (FIG. 110), Meidner depicts jagged layers of dislocated earth, suggesting the concomitant upheaval for the inhabitants of the neighborhood visible as ciphers moving about in the background. One recalls Meidner's statement "Berlin is pregnant!" for indeed the physical landscape of the city bulges with protrusions heralding the new buildings to come.

Building the Underground of 1911 (FIG. 111) has the pictorial structure of the *Apocalyptic Landscape* of 1913 (see FIG. 126). Great swathes have been cut into the sandy ochre earth of the Brandenburg to make way for the new subterranean transportation lines, linking the developing areas of the ever-expanding metropolis. Within this vast urban landscape, human figures appear ant-like as they carefully make their way through the ravine of disturbed earth. The city appears in the distance beneath an eerily lilac, Fauvist sky. The dynamic rhythm of the picture, moving from the left foreground into the middle back-

Figure 110
Ludwig Meidner
Construction Site Between Houses (Baustelle zwischen Häusern), 1911
Black chalk on paper,
18½ x 21⅛ in. (47 x 53.7 cm)
Museum Ostdeutsche Galerie
Regensburg

Figure 111
Ludwig Meidner
**Building the Underground
in Berlin-Wilmersdorf
(U-Bahn-Bau in Berlin-
Wilmersdorf)**, 1911
Oil on canvas,
27¾ x 34 in. (70 x 86 cm)
Stiftung Stadtmuseum Berlin.
Purchased with funds from
the Museumsstiftung Dr. Otto
and Ilse Augustin

ground; the dominant ochre tones of the foreground, interrupted by a large dark brown area in the right foreground; the tiny figures visible in the ravines—all are elements of the 1913 *Apocalyptic Landscape* prefigured in *Building the Underground*.

Die Pathetiker

In November 1912, the Eighth Exhibition held at Herwarth Walden's Der Sturm gallery was devoted to a group of Silesian artists who called themselves Die Pathetiker (Those filled with pathos): Ludwig Meidner, Jakob Steinhardt, and Richard Janthur.[81] The choice of the name *Pathetiker* related the group to the Neopathetisches Cabaret, the literary cabaret that was the public platform of Der Neue Club, with which Meidner had been associated and whose members he had portrayed. (See the essay by Sigrid Bauschinger in this book.) The term *Pathos* appeared in a number of writings during this period concerned with artistic regeneration as well as forging a more intimate relationship between artists (including writers) and their audience.[82] The phrase *neue Pathos* came from Stefan Zweig's 1909 book on the Belgian Symbolist poet and author Emile Verhaeren. In the chapter entitled "Das neue Pathos," Zweig described the "pathos" of ancient poetry before the advent of writing, "because it arose out of passion and wanted to generate passion in its listeners."[83] When printed texts replaced poetry that had been recited aloud before the group, poets lost "this intimate, fervent contact with the masses":

> Slowly the public became something imaginary for the poets. . . . The poet became accustomed to speaking only for himself. . . . But precisely in our day there appears to be a return to that original intimate contact between the poet and the listener, which is preparing the way for the re-emergence of a new pathos.[84]

The public reading of poetry in the Neopathetisches Cabaret was an attempt to forge this direct contact between poet and public. Zweig invoked Nietzsche in his discussion of the desired effect this new art would have on the people:

> Whoever wants to coerce the masses must have the rhythm of its new and agitated life within himself; whoever speaks to them must be animated by the new pathos. And this new pathos, the "affirming pathos par excellence" in Nietzsche's sense, is above all the desire, power, and will to engender ecstasy.[85]

Meidner contributed fifteen works to the Pathetiker exhibition, including an *Apocalyptic Landscape*, and others with titles such as *Cosmic Landscape with Comet, Landscape with Burned-Out House*, and a number of portraits. Steinhardt's works had, for the most part, biblical titles, and also included an *Apocalyptic Landscape*. Years later, Steinhardt recalled the genesis of the Pathetiker and their goals:

> My friend Meidner and I often debated through the night on the new way that art would now have to take. The Gothic and El Greco, at the time popularized in Germany by Meier-Graefe, made an extraordinary impression on us. Under this impression we painted with burning vigor; themes like Job—apocalypses—the end of the world, which in their contortions went beyond even El Greco. Our joint work and discussions resulted in the foundation of a new movement, which called itself Pathetiker. . . . What did the Pathetiker want? They wanted to give the pictures content, great exciting content. They wanted to create an art that would enthrall the people and humanity, and not only serve the aesthetic needs of a small social stratum. Our painted and unpainted pictures inspired and excited us, and we were convinced that with these works we were inaugurating a new era in art.[86]

Jakob Steinhardt

Jakob Steinhardt was born in 1887 in Zerkow, a small town in Posen, which is today part of Poland. At the age of nine, his parents sent him to Berlin to study. By this time he had already developed a love of drawing; he spent his time in Berlin visiting

Figure 112
Jakob Steinhardt
Two Jews [Zwei Juden], 1904
Pastel on paper,
6¾ x 5⅞ in. (17 x 15 cm)
Collection The Israel Museum,
Jerusalem

museums, where, like Meidner, he discovered the art of Böcklin. Each year, during school vacation, Steinhardt returned to Zerkow where he drew his family and the local inhabitants; thus these early works often portray Jewish subjects. Whereas Meidner's early works on Jewish themes were the product of his fantasy, Steinhardt's resulted from his close observation of life in Zerkow and possess none of Meidner's violent imagery. In *Two Jews*, a pastel of 1904 (FIG. 112), Steinhardt depicts his two elderly subjects with sympathy and delicacy, bathing them in the warm glow from the fire in the center of the room. After a family friend showed several of Steinhardt's pastels to the director of the museum in Posen, who was impressed with the young artist's talents, a number of wealthy Posen Jews provided Steinhardt with a stipend that enabled him to pursue his art; he continued receiving these funds until the beginning of the war in 1914.

At the age of eighteen, Steinhardt became a student of Lovis Corinth; he subsequently studied etching with Struck, in whose studio he began his friendship with Meidner. During a yearlong sojourn in Paris (1909–10), Steinhardt attended the Julien Academy, Matisse's art school, and the Colarossi Academy, where he studied with Théophile Steinlen.

Like all recollections after the fact, Steinhardt's about the founding of the Pathetiker must be read with a healthy skepticism; yet the *Pathetiker* period does indeed seem to have been a remarkably productive one of cross-fertilization between the two artists.[87] In noting El Greco and the Gothic, Steinhardt pinpointed important formal influences on his work of this period. El Greco was practically rediscovered during these years: paintings were exhibited at the Paul Cassirer Gallery in September/October 1907; and Meier-Graefe published the journal of his 1908 Spanish trip in 1910, describing his encounter with El Greco's art as "probably the greatest experience that could occur to any of us."[88] For similar reasons, the enthusiastic reception of Matthias Grünewald's *Isenheim Altar* in Germany at this time had a significant impact on many artists of the Expressionist generation, including Steinhardt.[89]

Cain, 1912 (FIG. 114), reflects both of these influences on the development of Steinhardt's artistic idiom, particularly in the elongated figure and expressive hand gesture of Cain. The figure of Cain bears a striking resemblance to the left-most figure in El Greco's *Laocoön*, ca. 1610–14 (FIG. 115); and the treatment of the pulsating landscape and prismatic application of color reveal Steinhardt's debt to El Greco.[90]

Steinhardt chose not to depict the physical struggle between Cain and Abel, but rather the psychological anguish of Cain in the aftermath of the murder. The entire landscape reverberates with this emotion—

Figure 113
Jakob Steinhardt
**Apocalyptic Landscape
(Apokalyptische Landschaft)**, 1912
Oil on canvas, 31 ⅞ x 22 ¹³⁄₁₆ in. (81 x 58 cm)
Collection The Israel Museum, Jerusalem.
On loan from Josefa and Eli Bar-On

Figure 114
Jakob Steinhardt
Cain (Kain), 1912
Oil on canvas, 37 ⅜ x 29 ½ in. (95 x 75 cm)
Jüdisches Museum, Frankfurt am Main

not the tragedy of the victim, who is relegated to the background like a boulder amidst the scenery, but rather the pathos of the killer. Cain, the outcast and wanderer, is presented as a figure eliciting our empathy. In the premodern period, Cain was seen as the embodiment of evil and a symbol of the unrepentant Jew and of the "other"; with the advent of Romanticism, however, Cain was transformed into a questioning and seeking figure who challenged and violated the existing order, becoming an agent of regeneration.[91] Cain was thus poised to become a natural symbol for the Expressionists.[92] In 1911, the Jewish anarchist and socialist Erich Mühsam had started to publish a cultural, political, and literary journal in Munich entitled *Kain: Zeitschrift für Menschlichkeit* (Cain: Journal for Humanity), which he described as a "totally personal organ for whatever the editor as poet, as citizen of the world, and as fellow human being has in his heart."[93] Cain's plight—"I shall be a fugitive and a wanderer in the earth" (Gen. 4:14)—had become an object of empathetic self-identification rather than condemnation. In addition, Cain as the founder of the first city (Gen. 4:17) was a particularly apt figure for those artists and writers engaged in the life of the metropolis.

In other works with biblical subjects from the Pathetiker period, Steinhardt represents figures in emotionally charged landscapes. Steinhardt later described these paintings as exemplifying the expressionism of the Pathetiker:

> How did these pictures look? Let us take Jeremiah, which I painted in 1912. He was not some handsome sad prophet sitting on well-arranged ruins, declaiming his laments with a well-rounded gesture. No, the picture is intended to represent the expression of pain by means of form and color. A gray, wrinkled, shattered ancient in ragged red clothes sits on cold-blue sharp-edged rubble with a yellow sky glowing above in glaring contrast. This was already what was later called Expressionism.[94]

This description fits a painting that has alternatively been called *Jeremiah* and *Job Amidst the Mountains*, bearing the date 1913 (FIG. 116). The fact that it is difficult to determine which afflicted old man is portrayed is itself telling; Steinhardt is interested in representing anguish and suffering *per se*, independent of any specific narrative context. A pastel of *Job*, 1912, is differentiated by the depiction of a nearly futuristic city in the background.[95] Similarly *The Prophet*, 1913 (see FIG. 117), Steinhardt's most ambitious and monumental work (see FIG. 154), which was exhibited at the landmark Erster Deutscher Herbstsalon (First German Autumn Salon) at Walden's Der Sturm Gallery in 1913, presents a generic prophet admonishing the people, while in the background the city seems headed for destruction. Other images of devastation that Steinhardt produced at this time include *Apocalyptic Landscape*, 1912 (see FIG. 113), where the jagged rock formations, rendered in paint thickly applied with a palette knife, echo the bent forms of the corpses; in the background, the ruins of a burned-out city are all that remain beneath a smoldering sky of yellow and pink.

The Artist and the Metropolis: A New Pathetic Fallacy

In two declaratory works, Steinhardt's drawing for a Pathetiker exhibition poster, 1912 (FIG. 118),[96] and Meidner's cover illustration for the first issue of *Das neue Pathos*, 1913 (FIG. 119), each artist presents a self-portrait within an urban context. In Steinhardt's drawing, the buildings sway and buckle, echoing the pose of the artist's inclined, slightly melancholy head. The vertical structure of skyscrapers and portrait head, emphasized by Steinhardt's elongated neck, is pulled downward. The movement in Meidner's work, in contrast, is centrifugal. Meidner's open mouth emits a cry that seems to find its echo in the buildings that quiver and swoon, the rushing streetcar visible at lower left, the small dark figures hurrying up a white expanse that denotes both a road and Meidner's chest, and the energetic rays of light (or sound?) that detonate in the background. In both works, the environment reverberates with the artist's emotions. This is an urban reworking of the pathetic fallacy of the Romantics; in place of reading human emotions into nature, the urban environment seems to reflect the passions and anxieties of its inhabitants.

Both graphic works reflect Meidner and Steinhardt's encounter with the art of the Italian Futurists, exhibited at Der Sturm in the spring of 1912 and well represented in the Erster Deutscher Herbstsalon: works by Umberto Boccioni (see FIG. 120, PLATE 8), Carlo Carrà (see PLATE 15), Gino Severini (see PLATE 18), and Giacomo Balla (see PLATE 16). The tottering buildings in the Pathetiker works closely resemble those of Boccioni's *The Street Enters the House*, 1911 (FIG. 120), while Steinhardt's *The City*, 1913 (FIG. 121), with its powerful diagonals and bluish tonalities, reveals a debt to the Italian artist's *The Strengths of a Street*, 1911; both Futurist paintings were exhibited at Der Sturm. But if Steinhardt adopted from Boccioni the jagged rhythms and dynamic rays emitted by street lights, his evocation of nocturnal city life differs from Boccioni's in significant ways. Steinhardt's focus remains the human experience in the city—in the teeming throngs moving

Figure 117
Jakob Steinhardt
Study for **The Prophet**, 1913
Watercolor and ink on paper,
18⅛ x 13⅜ in. (46 x 34 cm)
Courtesy of Bineth Gallery, Tel Aviv

Figure 118
Jakob Steinhardt
Self-Portrait (Drawing for an Exhibition Poster: Die Pathetiker) (Selbstporträt (Zeichnung für ein Ausstellungsplakat: Die Pathetiker)), 1912
Pen and ink over charcoal, pencil, with white highlighting, on paper,
17 x 11¾ in. (43 x 30 cm)
The Marvin and Janet Fishman Collection, Milwaukee

Figure 119
Ludwig Meidner
Self-Portrait from *Das neue
Pathos* 1, no.1 (1913)
Ink drawing, 9⅞ x 7¼ in. (25.1 x 18.4 cm)
Rare Books Division, The New York
Public Library. Astor, Lenox, and
Tilden Foundations

Figure 120
Umberto Boccioni
The Street Enters the House, 1911
Oil on canvas,
39⅜ x 41¾ in. (100 x 100.6 cm)
Sprengel Museum, Hannover

through the street and the diverse scenes glimpsed through the windows of buildings that seem like flimsy stage sets: a nude woman in a state of reverie alone at her window; a group of figures seen through the window above. At lower left, an inclined head with closed eyes—echoing the inclining buildings—seems to have conjured the whole scene; most likely it represents Steinhardt himself. We have come a long way from Ury's night-time view of the Friedrichstrasse train station (see FIG. 99), which appears elegiac in comparison, despite its subtle references to urban ennui and social inequalities. Steinhardt also goes beyond Ury's play of observer and observed in the "people-watching" of pedestrians and café patrons; the nudity of the woman in the apartment building—perhaps a prostitute—turns us into voyeurs.

Meidner's urban scenes underwent a transformation around 1912. The views of urban construction, where the population is reduced to miniscule figures, gave way to depictions of busy streets with rushing pedestrians and animated cafés. If we compare Ury's bourgeois café scenes of isolated patrons (FIGS. 106, 108) with Meidner's and Steinhardt's views of the café as the site of intense interaction and feverish debate (FIGS. 75, 76), we can gauge the involvement of the Pathetiker artists in the intellectual circles of writers around the Neue Club and Walden's Der Sturm. Indeed, it was the work of many of these writers as well as the art of the Italian Futurists and the Parisian artist Robert Delaunay, exhibited at Der Sturm Gallery (see PLATE 11), that served as catalysts for the developments in style and subject matter evident in Meidner's art around 1912. Delaunay's optimistic embrace of the city, particularly of themes reflecting its modernity, and his fragmentation of forms to evoke the effects of light hitting the buildings, were evident in works like *The City*, 1911 (FIG. 122), which was exhibited at Der Sturm.

Inspired by the Futurist Manifesto, which Walden had published in German translation on the occasion of the Futurist exhibition at Der Sturm, Meidner in 1914 penned "An Introduction to Painting Big Cities," which began: "The time has come at last to start painting our real homeland [*Heimat*], the big city which we all love so much. Our feverish hands should race across countless canvases, let them be as large as frescoes, sketching the glorious and the fantastic, the monstrous and dramatic—streets, railroad stations, factories, and towers."[97] His use of the term *Heimat* reminds us of Meidner's complaints about being in exile that he expressed in a letter to Struck written from Kattowitz.

Figure 121
Jakob Steinhardt
The City (Die Stadt), 1913
Oil on canvas,
24 x 15¾ in. (61 x 40 cm)
Nationalgalerie, Staatliche Museen
zu Berlin

In his treatise on painting the metropolis, Meidner criticizes the "sweetness and fluffiness" of the city scenes of the Impressionists like Pissarro and Monet, "these agrarian painters," and challenges himself and his fellow artists:

> But should you paint strange and grotesque structures as gently and transparently as you paint streams; boulevards like flower beds!? . . . We have to forget all earlier methods and devices and develop a completely new means of expression. . . . We can't simply carry our easel into the middle of a furiously busy street in order to read off blinking "tonal values." A street isn't made out of tonal values but is a bombardment of whizzing rows of windows, of screeching lights between vehicles of all kinds and a thousand jumping spheres, scraps of human beings, advertising signs, and shapeless colors. . . . The Futurists have already pointed this out in their manifestos—not in their shabby goods—and Robert Delaunay three years ago inaugurated our movement

with his grand visions of the "Tour Eiffel." In the same year, in several experimental paintings and in a few more successful drawings, I put into practice what I advocate here in theory.

Indeed, many of Meidner's urban subjects from 1912–13 illustrate these precepts. In the drawing *Südwestkorso, Berlin, Five O'Clock in the Morning*, 1913 (FIG. 123), the converging lines of the street-car tracks and the "whizzing rows of windows" impart a furious energy and sense of movement, despite the avenue being emptied of traffic and pedestrians at this early hour. The city itself, and the artist's subjective experience of his environment, are sufficient to generate this sense of oncoming rush.[98]

This early-morning scene of the avenue near Meidner's studio might have been experienced as the artist returned home after one of his long nocturnal walks through Berlin in the company of his friend the poet Jakob van Hoddis:

> I have fond memories of the hours-long treks that we often took across Berlin at night. This great metropolis was the major experience of those days, and not only for me, born and raised in a small city, but also for Hoddis, who was from Berlin. We left the Café des Westens after midnight and marched right off, smartly and somewhat briskly, through the streets, always following our noses. . . . We were 28 years old then and had a lot of endurance, which had not even run out by the time the sun came up. . . . We were so much in love with this city.[99]

Figure 123
Ludwig Meidner
Südwestkorso, Berlin, Five O'Clock in the Morning [Südwestkorso, Berlin, fünf Uhr früh], 1913
Carpenter's pencil, pencil on paper,
16 1/2 x 22 1/4 in. (42.1 x 56.6 cm)
The Marvin and Janet Fishman Collection, Milwaukee

"Apocalyptic Landscapes"

Meidner's friendship with van Hoddis, whom he portrayed a number of times (FIG. 124), and his close involvement with many of the young Expressionist writers placed him within a creative circle whose work during those years included pessimistic visions of a violent impending apocalypse. Their literary works—especially van Hoddis's "Weltende" (1911) and Georg Heym's "Umbra Vitae" (1912)—have frequently been cited in connection with a series of paintings referred to as the "apocalyptic landscapes." These paintings actually encompass somewhat diverse subjects, varying from specific Berlin locations, such as *Apocalyptic Landscape (At the Halensee Railroad Station)*, 1913 (FIG. 125), to more generalized views of the city beset by the destructive forces of man-made and natural disaster. A massive literature has been devoted to these works during the past decade, and this is not the place to revisit all the arguments and interpretations.[100] These works are overdetermined, reflecting the zeitgeist and myriad artistic and cultural influences, but ultimately shaped by Meidner's own idiosyncrasies.[101]

It is important to note, however, that only one of the paintings in question was originally entitled *Apocalyptic Landscape*; Meidner seems to have retitled the works sometime after World War I, once much of the art and literature of the prewar period had acquired an aura of prescient foreboding. Charles W. Haxthausen offers a convincing argument for understanding many of the so-called apocalyptic landscapes as expressions of Meidner's enthusiasm for the city, and the fractured forms as reflecting his attempts to paint the qualities of light in the metropolis.[102] The power of these works derives from their complexity and multiple layers of meaning. They reflect simultaneously a number of apparently conflicting attitudes toward the city: intoxication, fear, enthusiasm, alienation, ironic amusement. Yet, all these emotions can be experienced during the course of a single day by a city dweller.

In *Apocalyptic Landscape (At the Halensee Railroad Station)*, 1913 (FIG. 125), the vigorous brushwork outlining chevron forms in the ochre ground and Prussian blue sky imparts a sense of disquiet; but this is no more apocalyptic than the images of agitated earth in Meidner's earlier paintings and drawings that reveal the massive construction taking place in Berlin (see FIGS. 110, 111). The black-clad figures seem no more perturbed than most urban commuters anxious to catch a train; the agitated brushwork creates a sense of their jerky movements, much like those of figures in a flip-book of images, where a primitive cartoon is simulated by flipping quickly through the pages.[103]

A number of the paintings, however, are tours de force of the imagination, constructed modern fables with biblical overtones. *Apocalyptic Landscape*, 1913 (FIG. 126), revisits the pictorial structure of *Building the Underground*, 1911 (see FIG. 111); but here the sky has truly turned apocalyptic, with a blaze of white heat, like a volcanic eruption, illuminating the dark sky. The blood-red sun shares the heavens with huge gold stars, indicating that something

Figure 124
Ludwig Meidner
Portrait of Jakob van Hoddis, 1914
Reed pen and brush with
black ink over graphite,
18 x 16⅜ in. (45.8 x 41.5 cm)
The Art Institute of Chicago, 1987.286r
Photograph © 1999.

Figure 125
Ludwig Meidner
Apocalyptic Landscape
[At the Halensee Railroad Station]
[Apokalyptische Landschaft
[Beim Bahnhof Halensee]], 1913
Oil on canvas,
32¹⁄₁₆ x 38³⁄₁₆ in. (81.5 x 97 cm)
Los Angeles County Museum of Art. Gift
of Clifford Odets

Figure 126
Ludwig Meidner
Apocalyptic Landscape
[Apokalyptische Landschaft], 1913
Oil on canvas,
26½ x 31½ in. (67.3 x 80 cm)
The Marvin and Janet Fishman Collection,
Milwaukee

Figure 127
Ludwig Meidner
Study, 1912
Brush and ink on paper,
11 x 15⅛ in. (27.9 x 38.4 cm)
Collection The Israel Museum, Jerusalem

is dramatically amiss in the natural world; and the huge leg-like tree branch looming in the foreground has ominous overtones. Themes of human suffering and displacement had concerned Meidner for years. *Study*, 1912 (FIG. 127), depicting a group of refugees in a desolate landscape—with compositional allusions to Théodore Géricault's monumental painting *The Raft of Medusa*, 1818–19— is only one example of Meidner's images of people displaced, wounded, or burned out of their homes as a result of war, natural disaster, or perhaps pogrom. Many artists at this time produced images of catastrophe, as in Max Beckmann's view of the victims of the sinking *Titanic* or Steinhardt's images of pogroms (FIG. 155) and apocalyptic landscapes (see FIG. 113).[104]

But *Apocalyptic Landscape*, 1913, is a far richer and more complex work, combining elements of drama, fantasy, terror, and black humor. The latter is suggested by the caricatured image of Meidner fleeing the scene, as if escaping the destructive fury of his own golem. The center of the canvas is occupied by a reclining figure gazing toward the heavens; though dwarfed by the upheavals all around him, he dominates the canvas, his small dark form accentuated by the contrasting areas of ochre and white ground. His pose is reminiscent of Ury's *Jeremiah*, as if surrounded here by the realization of his feverish prophecy of destruction.[105] As we have seen, the prophet is a stand-in for the artist; and Meidner was soon to turn his attention to figures of prophets dwarfing the surrounding landscape—often as self-portraits—as in *Self-Portrait as Prophet*, 1915 (see FIG. 132).

In the final analysis, the depictions in *Apocalyptic Landscape* are the product of Meidner's prodigious imaginative faculties. He experiences the thrill of the "negative epiphany,"[106] the excitement and dread of actualizing the images in his mind. Meidner has succeeded in realizing his "oeuvre imaginaire." It is telling that many

Figure 128
Ludwig Meidner
Explosion, 1913
Wash and ink on paper,
18½ x 19¼ in. (48 x 49 cm)
Collection Arnold Rosner,
Tel Aviv Museum of Art, No. 12,332

Figure 129
Ludwig Meidner
**Apocalyptic Landscape
[Apokalyptische Landschaft]**, 1916
Oil on canvas,
31½ x 39⅜ in. (80 x 100 cm)
Museum Ostdeutsche Galerie Regensburg

of the "apocalyptic" scenes contain Meidner's self-portrait, as if to remind us from whose imagination these images have sprung. In the drawing *Explosion*, 1913 (FIG. 128), we see a man's head and gesticulating hands raised above his head facing scenes of tottering buildings and whizzing comets; it is as if the foreground figure with his back to us, like a conductor leading his orchestra, is conjuring the scene into existence. In the *Apocalyptic Landscape* of 1916 (FIG. 129), a turbulent and terrifyingly beautiful scene with black and yellow sky, three red-faced figures move trance-like in the foreground. Only the man on the left has distinguishable features, and he clearly resembles Meidner. With his eyes unnaturally widened, he engages us with a demonic look, as if to say, "Look what I have created, something so hideous and yet so beautiful."

Meidner later described the genesis of his first "apocalyptic landscape" in a frenzy of nocturnal creativity during the stiflingly hot summer of 1912, when, afflicted by a skin ailment, he sweated, suffered, and painted.[107] A self-portrait drawing, dated 12 July 1912, 8:45 a.m., of a nude Meidner at his easel represents the exhausted artist, stripped because of the heat, after a night of painting (see FIG. 131). Soon thereafter, he began to have mystical experiences, the first occurring on 4 December 1912:

> Quite suddenly, while I was painting one evening,
> I noticed that nothing was going right. I couldn't paint.

Figure 130
Ludwig Meidner
**My Nocturnal Visage
[Mein Nachtgesicht]**, 1913
Oil on canvas,
26¼ x 19¼ in. (66.7 x 48.9 cm)
The Marvin and Janet Fishman
Collection, Milwaukee

Then all at once, things began to happen so quickly that I simply began to watch myself paint. My arm was moving of its own accord and I was astounded. Then something came over me: It was the Holy Spirit. What was really surprising was—I did not believe in God! I can't describe the presence of the Holy Spirit. It was extraordinarily eruptive. It lasted only two or three minutes, but it left an after-effect. I observed that the feeling was what could be called "ecstasy."[108]

These episodes recurred, and the paintings that Meidner created in their aftermath are attempts to transform something of their power and intensity through the medium of paint. Meidner's work thus represents a fusion of the two strands we have been tracing—the religious and the urban. His visions took place in Berlin and seem indeed to have been stimulated, if not inspired, by the city: in his art he re-created something of those experiences and visions, and represented them within the urban context.

In 1916 Meidner would paint the last of these imaginative scenes set in the city (see FIG. 129); and he had begun to depict prophets and sibyls in dramatic poses. *Self-Portrait as Prophet* of 1916 (FIG. 132) is still characterized by an angular faceting that derived from Meidner's interest in artists such as Boccioni (see FIG. 120) and Delaunay (see FIG. 122); but soon this style would give way to rounded forms clad in voluminous robes rendered in flowing lines.

Conclusion: A Contemporary Perspective

One of the few reviews devoted to the exhibition of the Pathetiker at Der Sturm appeared in *Die Aktion* in 1912. Written by Kurt Hiller, it singled out Meidner as the most gifted of the three exhibiting artists; and while admiring Steinhardt's talents, Hiller voiced the following reservation in connection with his work:

> The true fully Jewish artist would not be Jewish in subject matter, but rather Jewish in modality; he would scarcely paint something biblical, educational, or episodes from the past, but rather he would paint something contemporary with a Jewish spirit (by which I mean: with spirit). A glaringly Jewish noble spirit in the kingdom of Prussia (1912) does not look like a naive celebrant of national memories, but rather seems intellectual, future-oriented, and conflicted. I remember a thesis of Jakob van Hoddis: "Zionism is the hysterical form of assimilation."[109]

Hiller formulated a challenge to modern Jewish artists that was difficult to meet, and that continues to resonate even in our own time. Liebermann did, indeed, depict scenes of a contemporary Jewish milieu in an animated manner, but they were hardly forward-looking; they referred back to a seventeenth-century community, to the origins of Jewish modernity. Steinhardt, in works

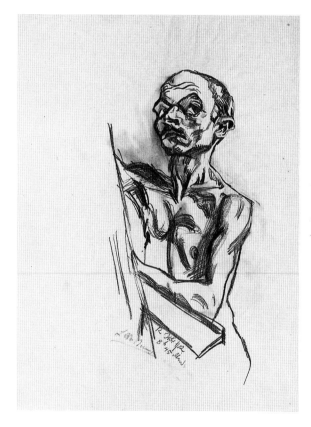

Figure 131
Ludwig Meidner
Nude Self-Portrait at the Easel, 1912
Pencil on paper, 18⅞ x 14⅛ in. (48 x 36 cm)
Collection The Israel Museum, Jerusalem

Figure 132
Ludwig Meidner
Self-Portrait as Prophet, 1916
Reed pen, brush, and india ink on
brown cardboard,
39½ x 28 in. (100.3 x 71.1 cm)
The Robert Gore Rifkind Collection,
Beverly Hills, California

like *Cain*, 1912, found symbols for contemporary identification in
traditional Jewish texts. Meidner created a unique synthesis from
a variety of literary and pictorial—including Jewish—sources.
From the vantage point of the end of the twentieth century, however, Ury may have the greatest resonance; he appears to be a
postmodern, rather than modern, artist. Viewed from a contemporary perspective, the apparent disjunction between Ury's urban
scenes and Jewish subjects is hardly disconcerting, given the way
contemporary artists adopt and appropriate diverse artistic styles
for a variety of expressive purposes. In its transformation of traditional Jewish texts, spiritualization of landscape, and symbolic use
of figuration, Ury's work is a forerunner of many late-twentieth-
century expressions of Jewish identity.

Notes

1. In his choice of subjects drawn from the recreation of the bourgeoisie, his penchant for painting out-of-doors, and his loose brushwork, Liebermann demonstrated many affinities with French Impressionism, of which he was a passionate defender and collector. Yet, as Gert Schiff has pointed out, German Impressionism differed from the French movement in significant ways: "The Germans adopted none of the most radical French innovations: the division of color into its spectral constituents, the organization of space by means of color alone, and the dissolution of color into light"; see Gert Schiff, "An Epoch of Longing: An Introduction to German Painting of the Nineteenth Century," in *German Masters of the Nineteenth Century: Paintings and Drawings from the Federal Republic of Germany*, exh. cat. (New York: The Metropolitan Museum of Art, 1981), p. 34. There is an extensive literature on the subject of Liebermann and French Impressionism; see, for example *Max Liebermann und die französischen Impressionisten*, ed. G. Tobias Natter and Julius H. Schoeps, exh. cat. (Vienna: Jüdisches Museum Wien, 1997); Thomas Gaehtgens, "Liebermann und der Impressionismus," in *Max Liebermann—Jahrhundertwende*, ed. Angelika Wesenberger, exh. cat. (Berlin: Nationalgalerie, 1997), pp. 141–52; Karl Heinz Janda and Annegret Janda, "Max Liebermann als Kunstsammler," *Forschungen und Berichte der Staatlichen Museen zu Berlin*, 15 (1973): 105–48; and Peter Krieger, "Max Liebermanns Impressionisten-Sammlung und ihre Bedeutung für sein Werk," in *Max Liebermann in seiner Zeit*, exh. cat. (Berlin: Nationalgalerie, 1979), pp. 60–71.

2. See *Max Liebermann und die französischen Impressionisten*, ed. Natter and Schoeps, p. 108.

3. Liebermann depicted the biblical subjects of Samson and Delilah and scenes from the apocryphal Book of Tobit on a number of occasions; see Matthias Eberle, *Max Liebermann 1847–1935: Werkverzeichnis der Gemälde und Ölstudien*, 2 vols. (Munich: Hirmer, 1995–96), nos. 1894/16–17, 1902/1, 1907/25–28, 1910/1 (Samson and Delilah); and nos. 1934/4–5 (The Return of the Young Tobias). A *Haman Before Ahasuerus and Esther* was painted in 1930 (Eberle 1930/6). Liebermann depicted the interior of the "scuola levantina" synagogue in Venice; see Eberle no. 1878/22 and *Was vom Leben übrig bleibt, sind Bilder und Geschichten: Max Liebermann zum 150. Geburtstag: Rekonstruktion der Gedächtnisausstellung des Berliner Jüdischen Museums von 1936*, exh. cat. (Berlin: Stiftung "Neue Synagoge Berlin—Centrum Judaicum," 1997), cat. no. 12, pp. 190–91; see also cat. no. 6, pp. 180–81. The Venetian synagogue served as the setting for *The Twelve-Year-Old Jesus in the Temple*, 1879. (See the essay by Chana Schütz in this book [figs. 140, 141].) Liebermann also painted the interior of the Amsterdam Synagogue in 1876; see Eberle, *Werkverzeichnis*, no. 1876/32.

4. See Eberle, *Max Liebermann 1847–1935: Werkverzeichnis der Gemälde und Ölstudien*, vol. 2, 1900–1935, pp. 638–45 (nos. 1905/6–12) and nos. 1907/5–11; 1908/7–11; 1909/1.

5. For Liebermann's relationship to Holland, see Barbara Gaehtgens, "Holland als Vorbild," in *Max Liebermann—Jahrhundertwende*, ed. Wesenberg, pp. 83–92. This model of a community that assumed responsibility for the social and financial needs of all its members closely resembles the organization of a traditional Jewish community. See also Irit Rogoff, "Max Liebermann and the Painting of the Public Sphere," in *Studies in Contemporary Jewry*, vol. 6, *Art and Its Uses: The Visual Image and Modern Jewish Society* (New York: Oxford University Press, 1990), pp. 105–7.

6. Matthias Eberle, "Max Liebermann zwischen Tradition und Opposition," in *Max Liebermann in seiner Zeit*, pp. 36–37. For Langbehn, *Rembrandt als Erzieher*, and its impact, see Fritz Stern, *The Politics of Cultural Despair: A Study in the Rise of the Germanic Ideology* (Berkeley: University of California Press, 1961).

7. See Emily D. Bilski, "Reclaiming Rembrandt: Jewish Artists in Germany at the Turn of the Century" (Paper delivered at the conference "Rembrandt as Battlefield: The Dutch, German, and Jewish Receptions, 1850–1950," Jerusalem, February 1999 [proceedings forthcoming]).

8. Max Liebermann, *Siebzig Briefe*, ed. Franz Landsberger (Berlin: Schocken/Jüdischer Buchverlag, 1937), pp. 35, 40–41.

9. See Simon Schama, "A Different Jerusalem: The Jews in Rembrandt's Amsterdam," in *The Jews in the Age of Rembrandt*, ed. Susan W. Morgenstern and Ruth E. Levine, exh. cat. (Washington, D.C.: The Judaic Museum of the Jewish Community Center of Greater Washington, 1981). This view was also expressed during Liebermann's time; see a lecture by Erwin Panofsky held in Berlin (dated 28 December 1920), for which Liebermann was in attendance: E. Panofsky, "Rembrandt und das Judentum," *Jahrbuch der Hamburger Kunstsammlungen* 18 (1973): 75–108. Panofsky's lecture before a Jewish audience is replete with language and allusions that imply a parallel between the relationship of Jews to the Dutch in seventeenth-century Amsterdam and the so-called German-Jewish symbiosis of Liebermann's and Panofsky's time. For a discussion, see Bilski, "Reclaiming Rembrandt."

10. Liebermann, *Siebzig Briefe*, p. 71. All translations are by the author unless otherwise noted.

11. Furthermore, the native German Jewish community viewed their coreligionists from the East with decided ambivalence, and often open hostility. See Steven E. Aschheim, *Brothers and Strangers: The East European Jew in German and German Jewish Consciousness, 1800–1923* (Madison: University of Wisconsin Press, 1982).

12. For Oppenheim's life and work, see Elisheva Cohen, *Moritz Oppenheim: The First Jewish Painter*, exh. cat. (Jerusalem: The Israel Museum, 1983).

13. Rolf Bothe, "Stadtbilder zwischen Menzel und Liebermann: Von der Reichsgründungsepoche zur wilhelminischen Grossstadt," in *Stadtbilder: Berlin in der Malerei vom 17. Jahrhundert bis zur Gegenwart*, exh. cat. (Berlin: Berlin Museum, 1987), pp. 220–22.

14. See, for example, Karl Schwarz, *Lesser Ury* (Berlin: Verlag für Jüdische Kunst und Kultur Fritz Gurlitt, 1922).

15. Franz Servaes in *Lesser Ury: Gedenk-Ausstellung* (Berlin: Nationalgalerie Berlin, 1931), p. 7.

16. Ibid., p. 5.

17. Lesser Ury in *Das geistige Deutschland am Ende des XIX. Jahrhunderts*, vol. 1, *Die bildenden Künstler* (Berlin, 1898); cited in Werner Doede, *Die Berliner Secession: Berlin als Zentrum der deutschen Kunst von der Jahrhundertwende bis zum Ersten Weltkrieg* (Frankfurt am Main/Berlin/Vienna: Ullstein, 1977), p. 131.

18. Hermann A. Schlögl, *Lesser Ury: Zauber des Lichts* (Berlin: Käthe-Kollwitz-Museum and Gebr. Mann Verlag, 1995), pp. 13–16. For a detailed account of Ury's early career, see pp. 16–20.

19. See, for example, Degas's *Women before a Café in the Evening*, pastel over monotype, in the collection of the Musée d'Orsay, Paris, reproduced in Theodore

Reff, *Manet and Modern Paris*, exh. cat. (Washington, D.C.: National Gallery of Art, 1982), p. 88, fig. 46. Degas depicted prostitutes sitting at café tables in front of a large glass window facing onto the street, which is illuminated by street lights. Ury would also favor compositions of café interiors with views out onto the urban street at night.

20. Adolph Donath, *Lesser Ury: Seine Stellung in der modernen deutschen Malerei* (Berlin: Verlag Max Perl, 1921), pp. 9–10.

21. Donath, *Ury*, pp. 9, 44; and Schlögl, *Ury*, p. 18. This is interesting in light of the criticism of Ury's rendering of the human figure in his paintings with Jewish themes, a subject addressed in this essay.

22. Schögl, *Ury*, p. 18.

23. See Linda Nochlin, *Realism* (New York and Baltimore: Penguin, 1971), pp. 111ff.; and Gabriel P. Weisberg, *The Realist Tradition: French Painting and Drawing, 1830–1900*, exh. cat. (Cleveland: The Cleveland Museum of Art, 1980), especially pp. 63–93, 201–36.

24. When Ury turned his attention to scenes of women in bourgeois interiors, he retained many of these elements. The women are seen in profile or with their backs to the spectator, engaged in solitary activities like sewing, letter writing, or reading. (See, for example, *Woman at a Writing Desk*, 1898, reproduced in Schlögl, *Ury*, p. 123.)

25. Seurat's works were to become very influential among avant-garde artists in Belgium in the late 1880s. Many of the French artist's works were shown in the exhibitions of Les XX in Brussels beginning in 1887. See Sarah Faunce, "Seurat and the Soul of Things," in *Belgian Art 1880–1914*, exh. cat. (Brooklyn: The Brooklyn Museum, 1980), pp. 41–55. There is no question of Ury's work in the early 1880s being influenced by Seurat, but rather of locating Ury's sensibility within a broader artistic climate of the times.

26. Franz Servaes, "Moderne Monumentalmalerei," *Neue deutsche Rundschau* 7 (1896): 281–86. An abbreviated version can be found in *Die Berliner Moderne 1885–1914*, ed. Jürgen Schutte and Peter Sprengel (Stuttgart: Philipp Reclam Jun., 1987), pp. 541–46. For more on *Jerusalem* and Servaes's discussion of this painting, see below.

27. Servaes in the introduction to the *Ury Gedenk-Ausstellung*, p. 10. Servaes goes on to agree with the verdict of Ury's biographer Adolph Donath about the achievement of the painter's *Jeremiah*.

28. Alfred Werner, "The Strange Tale of Lesser Ury," *Leo Baeck Institute Year Book*, 19 (1974): 206.

29. Ibid.

30. A study for this work from Ury's sketchbook is reproduced (undated) in Schlögl, *Ury*, p. 18. According to Donath (*Ury*, p. 10), Ury's first large painting was entitled *Benjamin*, and was painted in the studio made available to him by Portaels. Donath reports that Ury later had to destroy this monumental canvas (measuring 3 meters square) because he did not have the place to keep it in his small Berlin studio. To the best of my knowledge, no illustration of this destroyed work has survived.

31. Ury produced several versions of many of his biblical subjects; it is for this reason that we still have versions of many of Ury's works that were destroyed, either by the artist himself or during the Second World War. The *Jeremiah* (figs. 96, 149) exists in several smaller versions of the monumental canvas that can be seen in an installation photograph of Berlin's Jewish Museum, which opened in 1933

(see fig. 150). Moreover, it was generally Ury's practice to repeat as etchings and lithographs earlier compositions executed originally as paintings or drawings. See Lothar Brieger, *Lesser Ury*, vol. 9, *Graphiker der Gegenwart* (Berlin: Verlag Neue Kunsthandlung, 1921), pp. 15–16.

32. See Gert Schiff, "Tissot's Illustrations for the Hebrew Bible," in *J. James Tissot: Biblical Paintings*, exh. cat. (New York: The Jewish Museum, 1982), pp. 25ff.; and Malcolm Warner, "The Question of Faith: Orientalism, Christianity and Islam," in *The Orientalists: Delacroix to Matisse: The Allure of North Africa and the Near East*, exh. cat. (Washington, D.C.: National Gallery of Art, 1984), pp. 32–39.

33. For a depiction of Jacob blessing his grown sons, see Jakob Steinhardt, *Jacob Blessing His Sons*, 1925, oil on canvas, reproduced in *Jacob and Israel: Homeland and Identity in the Work of Jakob Steinhardt*, exh. cat. (Industrial Park, Tefen [Israel]: The Open Museum, 1998), fig. 188.

34. Reproduced and dated in Lothar Brieger, *Lesser Ury*, p. 25.

35. Adolph Donath (1921) mentions a *Benjamin* as Ury's first large painting, measuring 3 meters, which the artist was forced to destroy in Berlin because he had no place to keep it (*Ury*, p. 10). Martin Buber refers to a painting of 1883, *Jakob, seinen Sohn Benjamin segnend*, which "was later destroyed"; see "Lesser Ury," in *Jüdische Künstler*, ed. Martin Buber (Berlin: Jüdischer Verlag, 1903), p. 50. Ury also painted this subject in 1926 (oil on canvas, 181 x 191 cm). See Joachim Seyppel, *Lesser Ury: Der Maler der alten City; Leben—Kunst—Wirkung: Eine Monographie* (Berlin: Gebr. Mann Verlag, 1987), no. 359. This last work was exhibited in the Ury Memorial Exhibition at the Nationalgalerie in Berlin in 1931; see *Ury Gedenk-Ausstellung*, no. 124, as Collection Georg Kareski, Berlin. The same exhibition catalogue listed a pastel as the first study for the 1926 painting as ca. 1880/90 (cat. no. 119; 35 x 50 cm), but it is unlikely that this is identical with the 1884 pastel, especially since the dimensions of the two pastels are different.

36. A sketch in Ury's notebook, reproduced in Schlögl, *Ury*, p. 18, as a study for *Benjamin*, is even closer to Rembrandt's engraving than Ury's pastel of 1884 and his subsequent reiterations of this subject. In the sketchbook study, there are indications of the window in the middle ground and of the architectural framework found in Rembrandt's engraving. Perhaps the sketch began as a study after Rembrandt's engraving, and Ury subsequently found a Jewish subject for which he could utilize this composition.

Another Rembrandt engraving has been convincingly identified as *Jacob Caressing His Son Benjamin*; see Christian Tümpel, with Astrid Tümpel, *Rembrandt legt die Bibel aus: Zeichnungen und Radierungen aus dem Kupferstichkabinett der Staatlichen Museen Preussischer Kulturbesitz*, exh. cat. (Berlin: Bruno Hessling, 1970), cat. no. 20. However, here father and son are not presented in profile facing each other, the scene is less dramatically charged, and Benjamin is presented as a younger child. For a group of drawings by Rembrandt that actually relate to the episode of Jacob's sons journeying to Egypt, and whether Benjamin would accompany them, see Holm Bevers et al., *Rembrandt: The Master and His Workshop: Drawings and Etchings*, exh. cat. (New Haven and London: Yale University Press and The National Gallery, 1991), cat. no. 16, pp. 64–66. It is unlikely that Ury would have known any of these drawings, and compositionally they are not related to his *Benjamin*.

37. See the discussion of Ury's *Jeremiah* and *Rebecca at the Well* below. Other works by Ury reveal his study of Rembrandt's biblical subjects. For example, an undated oil painting, *Moses* (39¾ x 28¾ in.; 101 x 73 cm), is indebted to Rembrandt's *Moses with the Tablets of the Law*, 1659, which was already in the collection of the Berlin Nationalgalerie in Ury's time. Rembrandt's Moses lifts the tablets above his head, with one tablet placed in front of the other, elements that are repeated by Ury. For a reproduction of the Ury *Moses*, see Sotheby's Tel Aviv, *Nineteenth- and Twentieth-Century Paintings, Drawings and Sculpture*, sale cat. 22 April 1995, lot no. 41. For Rembrandt's *Moses*, see Staatliche Museen Preussischer Kulturbesitz Berlin, *Catalogue of Paintings: Thirteenth–Eighteenth Century*, 2d rev. ed., trans. Linda B. Parshall (Berlin: Gebr. Mann Verlag, 1978), cat. no. 811. For Rembrandt as a model for religious art in Germany in the late nineteenth and early twentieth centuries, see Johannes Stückelberger, *Rembrandt und die Moderne: Der Dialog mit Rembrandt in der deutschen Kunst um 1900* (Munich: Wilhelm Fink, 1996).

38. From an interview of 1905 with Adolph Donath, "Bei Lesser Ury," *Berliner Zeitung*, 16 March 1905, cited in Donath, *Ury*, p. 42.

39. Ibid., p. 43.

40. The date of ca. 1908 is based on another, larger (40⅛ x 27⅛ in.) version of the same subject, dated 1908. See Schlögl, *Ury*, p. 202, no. 87. The work Schlögl refers to is almost certainly identical with a *Rebecca* offered for sale in 1990: see Sotheby's, Israel, *Important Judaica: Books, Manuscripts, Works of Art and Paintings*, 19 April 1990, lot. no. 184 (ill). It is interesting to note that Rembrandt's painting *Christ and the Woman of Samaria*, 1659, entered the collection of the Berlin Nationalgalerie in 1907. (See Berlin Nationalgalerie, *Catalogue of Paintings*, no. 811B). Apart from both paintings depicting a woman at a well, the luminosity of Rembrandt's palette of red and gold suggests that Ury might have been inspired by the Berlin Museum's new acquisition; as with Rembrandt's *Return of the Prodigal Son*, Ury found a subject taken from the Hebrew Bible in place of the New Testament scene by Rembrandt. One of the wall paintings for the Lodge House of the Berlin B'nai B'rith entitled *Rebecca and Eliezer* (destroyed) is far less spare, depicting Rebecca handing Eliezer the pitcher of water, with her friends around the well at the left and two men with camels in the right background. For an illustration, see *Ost und West* 12, no. 4 (April 1912): 354.

41. For example, see Buber, "Lesser Ury," in *Jüdische Künstler*, p. 45; Servaes, *Gedenk-Ausstellung*, p. 6.

42. For a classic exposition of the position of the Jews' inherent physical inferiority, see Otto Weininger, *Geschlecht und Character: Eine prinzipielle Untersuchung* (Vienna and Leipzig: Wilhelm Braumüller, 1903). On Weininger, see Jacques Le Rider, *Modernity and Crises of Identity: Culture and Society in Fin-de-Siècle Vienna*, trans. Rosemary Morris (New York: Continuum, 1993). The need to develop a "muscle Jewry" to counteract this negative image was articulated by Max Nordau; see Max Nordau, "Muskel Judentum," *Jüdische Turnzeitung* 8 (1903): 137–38; and Nordau, "Jewry of Muscle," in *The Jew in the Modern World: A Documentary History*, ed. Paul Mendes-Flohr and Jehuda Reinharz (New York and Oxford: Oxford University Press, 1995), 2d ed., pp. 547–48. Nordau wrote, "Two years ago . . . I said: 'We must think of creating once again a Jewry of muscles.' Once again! For history is our witness that such a Jewry had once existed."

43. Donath, *Ury*, p. 10.

44. Buber, "Lesser Ury," in *Jüdische Künstler*, pp. 50–51.

45. Sharon L. Hirsh, *Hodler's Symbolist Themes* (Ann Arbor, Mich.: UMI Research Press, 1983), p. 21. See Hirsh's chapter "Theme of *The Disillusioned*: Culminations in 1891–1892," pp. 21–33. The canvas was exhibited in the Rose + Croix exhibition in Paris in 1892, where it received considerable attention. The painting's pendant, *The Disillusioned*, 1892, in the collection of the Neue Pinakothek, Munich, also presents five men seated on an extended bench; however, the attitudes of the men and the white robes in the Munich work suggest that the Bern painting, *The Disappointed Souls*, rather than the Munich canvas, served as a catalyst for Ury's 1896 version of *Jerusalem*. For a second version of *The Disillusioned* (Foundation for Art, Culture, and History, Küsnacht), see *Ferdinand Hodler 1853–1918*, exh. cat. (Paris: Musée du Petit Palais, 1983), cat. no. 35, ill. p. 35. For Hodler's symbolism, see also, in the same volume, Alexander Dückers, "Le symbolisme de Ferdinand Hodler," pp. 134–40. Dückers remarks that Hodler's practice of combining realism and idealism within the same image, a quality Hodler shared with Klinger, can appear disconcerting to us today; this observation also applies to Ury.

46. See Werner, *The Strange Tale of Lesser Ury*, pp. 206–7.

47. For a discussion of these "images of Jewish fate," and examples by artists such as Samuel Hirszenberg, Leopold Pilichowski, and Maurycy Minkowski, see Richard I. Cohen, *Jewish Icons: Art and Society in Modern Europe* (Berkeley: University of California Press, 1998), chap. 6. Many of the works discussed by Cohen were created in response to the new wave of pogroms in czarist Russia that began in 1903 with the Kishinev pogrom.

48. Yosef Hayim Yerushalmi, *Zakhor: Jewish History and Jewish Memory* (Seattle and London: University of Washington Press, 1982), p. 36.

49. Buber, "Lesser Ury," in *Jüdische Künstler*, p. 55.

50. Servaes, "Moderne Monumentalmalerei," in *Die Berliner Moderne*, p. 542.

51. Ibid., p. 546.

52. Bendemann, a Jewish convert to Christianity, also painted other versions of this subject: *By the Waters of Babylon*, 1832, oil on canvas, in the collection of the Wallraf-Richartz-Museum in Cologne, depicts Jeremiah sitting beneath a tree with a lyre hanging from his wrist, surrounded by mourning women; *Jeremiah on the Ruins of Jerusalem*, 1836, destroyed, was a work reproduced on German *mizrahs*, decorative prints marking the western wall of a home or synagogue and indicating the direction of Jerusalem and thus of prayer. See Inka Bertz, "Propheten und Ostjuden: Zur Verarbeitung von Zeiterfahrung im Werk Jakob Steinhardts vor und nach dem Ersten Weltkrieg," in *Jakob Steinhardt: Der Prophet*, exh. cat. (Berlin: Jüdisches Museum in Berlin Museum, 1995), pp. 66–71, for a discussion of these works as precursors of Ury and Steinhardt and for reproductions of the works in question. See also Inka Bertz, "The Prophets' Pathos and the Community of the Shtetl: Jakob Steinhardt's Work Before and After World War I," in *Jacob and Israel: Homeland and Identity in the Work of Jakob Steinhardt*, pp. 242–43.

53. Buber, "Lesser Ury," in *Jüdische Künstler*, p. 65.

54. The subject of Rembrandt's canvas had only recently been identified by Wilhelm von Bode. (See Christopher Brown et al., *Rembrandt: The Master and His Workshop: Paintings*, exh. cat. [New Haven and London: Yale University Press and The National Gallery, 1991], cat. no. 8, pp. 144–46.) In Rembrandt's canvas, the scene of Jerusalem's destruction is relegated to the left background, and the emphasis is on the expressive figure of the prophet. In the late nineteenth century, Rembrandt was prized as the artist of individualism and as something of a social outcast, who followed his own path. For the evolving images of Rembrandt, both as man and artist, see Jeroen Boomgaard and Robert W. Scheller, "A Delicate Balance: A Brief Survey of Rembrandt Criticism," in Brown et al., *Rembrandt*, pp. 106–23.

55. In the apocryphal text "The Paraleipomena of Jeremiah," a stone is transformed to resemble Jeremiah in order to fool the people who want to stone the prophet: "Light of the ages, make this stone become like me. And the stone assumed the likeness of Jeremiah. And they stoned the stone, thinking it was Jeremiah" (*The Apocryphal Old Testament*, ed. H. F. D. Sparks [Oxford: Clarendon Press, 1984, 1987], pp. 820, 833). This text was published in German translation in the 1870s. However, any relationship between the text and Jeremiah's "stony" appearance in Ury's painting is purely speculative.

56. Genesis 15:5. "And He brought him forth abroad, and said: 'Look now toward heaven, and count the stars, if thou be able to count them'; and He said unto him: 'So shall thy seed be.'" The luminous blue star-filled sky contrasts with the many references to black heavens in the prophecy of destruction found in the book of Jeremiah, for example, Jer. 4:23, 28. Jeremiah's prophecy includes reminding the wayward Children of Israel of the covenant (Jer. 11).

57. This belief in the future is also contained in the biblical book of Jeremiah. Jeremiah foretold the ongoing relationship between God and the Jewish people despite the loss of Jerusalem, and he articulated a strategy for Jewish survival in the Diaspora when he counseled the Jews taken captive to Babylonia: "Build ye houses, and dwell in them, and plant gardens. . . . take ye wives and beget sons and daughters . . . and multiply ye there, and be not diminished. And seek the peace of the city whither I have caused you to be carried away captive, and pray unto the Lord for it; for in the peace thereof shall ye have peace" (Jer. 29: 5–7).

58. Donath, *Ury*, p. 47. The identification of the prophet with the artist, and vice versa, became an important topos for the artists of the Expressionist generation. Both Ludwig Meidner and Jakob Steinhardt executed numerous works with the "prophet" as its subject, sometimes referring to a specific prophet, sometimes to a generic one. Other artists, such as Emil Nolde, also took up this theme, which was clearly influenced by the writings of Nietzsche and also had parallels in the literature of the period, as, for example, the poems by Rainer Maria Rilke, "Ein Prophet" and "Jeremias"; Rainer Maria Rilke, *Gedichte, Erster Teil*, vol. 1, *Sämtliche Werke* (Frankfurt am Main: Insel, 1987), pp. 566–68. For the prophet theme in the work of Steinhardt, see Bertz in *Jakob Steinhardt: Der Prophet*; for this theme in Meidner's work, see Thomas Grochowiak, *Ludwig Meidner* (Recklinghausen: Aurel Bongers, 1966), pp. 119–27, and Renate Ulmer, "'Bin voller heiliger Stimmungen und trage mit mir heroische, bewegte Bibelgestalten herum . . .': Religiöse Kompositionen im Werk Ludwig Meidners," in *Ludwig Meidner: Zeichner, Maler, Literat 1884–1966*, ed. Gerda Breuer and Ines Wagemann, exh. cat. (Stuttgart: Institut Mathildenhöhe Darmstadt, 1991), vol. 1, pp. 112–14.

59. *Transience* is a reworking of the themes in *Jerusalem*; the three columns mirror the three adult figures, representing different phases of life (man, old man, woman with baby), and also bring to mind the columns of the destroyed Temple. The title, however, gives the painting a more general meaning as a type of *memento mori* image.

60. Buber, "Lesser Ury," in *Jüdische Künstler*, p. 65.

61. Donath, "Bei Lesser Ury," cited in Donath, *Ury*, p. 43.

62. See *Berlin, Berlin: Die Ausstellung zur Geschichte der Stadt*, ed. Gottfried Korff and Reinhard Rürup, exh. cat. (Berlin: Berliner Festspiele and Nicolai, 1987), p. 190.

63. Simmel's essay "Die Grossstädte und das Geistesleben" was first published in 1903. Simmel's discussion of the reserve of urban dwellers and the importance of clocks and punctuality in regulating social and commercial discourse within the metropolis, particularly given the large distances it encompasses, are points alluded to in Ury's work of 1888. See Georg Simmel, "The Metropolis and Mental Life," in *Simmel on Culture: Selected Writings*, ed. David Frisby and Mike Featherstone (London: Sage Publications, 1997), pp. 177, 180.

64. In Monet's painting of the Gare Saint-Lazare of 1877 in the collection of the Fogg Art Museum, Cambridge, Massachusetts, a railworker occupies the foreground, but he is a generalized figure seen from the back; for an illustration, see *The New Painting: Impressionism 1874–1886*, exh. cat. (San Francisco: The Fine Arts Museum of San Francisco, 1986), p. 191, fig. 2.

65. Linda Nochlin has characterized the Impressionist city view as remote: "Yet the most typical . . . city view is the *distant* view, more properly the 'cityscape' or 'urban vista,' in which the very height and range of the artist's vantage point tends to distance the spectator from either involvement in dramatic anecdote or absorption in minute descriptive detail" (*Realism*, pp. 168–69). Ury's choice of vantage point and pictorial subject was opposite in its approach.

66. Donath reproduced a charcoal drawing of this motif dated 1914, with the title *Night Mood* (*Nachtstimmung*); see Donath, *Ury*, p. 50, fig. 23. The same composition, entitled *Night Impression* (*Nachtimpression*), was also executed in oil; for a color reproduction, see Siegfried Wichmann, *Realismus und Impressionismus in Deutschland* (Stuttgart: Schuler Verlagsgesellschaft, 1964), p. 137 (in a Munich private collection). Wichmann dates the painting as ca. 1906, whereas Schlögl (*Ury*, p. 97, no. 361) dates this painting to 1918.

67. For the influence of Degas, see n. 19 above.

68. Reff, *Manet and Modern Paris*, p. 27.

69. Ludwig Meidner, "Mein Leben," in Lothar Brieger, *Ludwig Meidner*, vol. 4, *Junge Kunst* (Leipzig: Klinkhardt & Biermann, 1919), p. 11. The Swiss-born Arnold Böcklin (1827–1901) painted mythological subjects such as nymphs, centaurs, satyrs, and sea gods that represented the forces of nature. His works, particularly the five versions of his best-known image, *Island of the Dead*, painted in the 1880s, had an impact on Surrealist artists. Franz von Stuck (1863–1928), one of the founders of the Munich Secession in 1892, was a leading proponent of Jugendstil in a variety of media: he was active in painting, architecture, sculpture, and the applied arts. Many of his most famous works, for example, *Sin*, 1893, developed the mythological and neoclassical themes found in Böcklin.

70. Heinrich Heine, "Jehuda ben Halevy (Fragment)" in *Historisch-kritische Gesamtausgabe der Werke*, ed. Manfred Windfuhr, vol. 3, no. 1, (Hamburg: Hoffmann und Campe, 1992), pp. 130ff.

71. For Halevi, see Raymond P. Scheindlin, *The Gazelle: Medieval Hebrew Poems on God, Israel, and the Soul* (Philadelphia and New York: The Jewish Publication Society, 1991).

72. See Klaus Briegleb, *Bei den Wassern Babels: Heinrich Heine, jüdischer Schriftsteller in der Moderne* (Munich: Deutscher Taschenbuch Verlag, 1997), pp. 246ff.

73. Illustrated in Grochowiak, *Ludwig Meidner*, p. 19, fig. 2.

74. Some commentators have seen, in this and other works, evidence of homoerotic leanings in Meidner during this period of his life. See Gerda Breuer, "Biographie," in *Ludwig Meidner: Zeichner, Maler, Literat 1884–1966*, ed. Breuer and Wagemann, vol. 2, p. 14; and Gerhard Leistner, "Figur und Landschaft im Frühwerk von Ludwig Meidner als Prolog zu seinem Verständnis von Expressionismus," in *Ludwig Meidner: Zeichner, Maler, Literat*, vol. 1, p. 18, where *Golus* is reproduced as fig. 7.

75. See, for example, Samuel Hirszenberg's *Exile* or *Golus* of 1904, reproduced in Cohen, *Jewish Icons*, p. 230.

76. Cited in Breuer, "Biographie," in *Ludwig Meidner: Zeichner, Maler, Literat*, ed. Breuer and Wagemann, vol. 2, p. 15.

77. Franz Landsberger (1883–1964) was born in Kattowitz in Upper Silesia. He studied art history, philosophy, and literature at the universities of Berlin, Geneva, Munich, and Breslau. After receiving his doctorate in 1907, he went to Berlin to continue his studies with Heinrich Wölfflin. From 1918 to 1933, he was Professor of Art History at the university in Breslau, and also lectured at the Art Academy there. After his dismissal with the ascent to power of the National Socialists, Landsberger took over the directorship of the Berlin Jewish Museum in 1934. Despite his incarceration in Sachsenhausen, he was able to emigrate in 1939. Following a brief stay in London, he received an offer from the Hebrew Union College in Cincinnati, where he taught the history of Jewish art and directed the museum. For Max Liebermann's correspondence with Landsberger, see n. 10 above.

78. Meidner-Landsberger correspondence, Leo Baeck Institute, New York; cited in Breuer, "Biographie," in *Ludwig Meidner: Zeichner, Maler, Literat*, ed. Breuer and Wagemann, vol. 2, p. 16.

79. Cited in *Ludwig Meidner: Zeichner, Maler, Literat*, ed. Breuer and Wagemann, vol. 1, p. 459.

80. Ibid.

81. Richard Janthur (Zerbst 1883—Berlin 1956) studied at the art school in Breslau. He came to Berlin in 1908 and exhibited at the Secession in 1911. Janthur published drawings in *Die Aktion*, and between 1919 and 1924 produced book illustrations for numerous works such as *The Jungle Book* and *Gulliver's Travels*. He was a founding member of the Novembergruppe in 1918.

82. For Der Neue Club and the concept of *neue Pathos*, see Roy F. Allen, *Literary Life in German Expressionism and the Berlin Circles* (Ann Arbor: UMI Research Press, 1983), pp. 75–92. See also Inka Bertz, "The Prophets' Pathos and the Community of the Shtetl: Jakob Steinhardt's Work Before and After World War I," in *Jacob and Israel: Homeland and Identity in the Work of Jakob Steinhardt*, pp. 238–41; and the essay by Inka Bertz in this book.

83. Stefan Zweig, *Emile Verhaeren* (Frankfurt am Main: S. Fischer, 1984), p. 131.

84. Ibid., pp. 132–33.

85. Ibid., p. 135. The influence of Nietzsche on the intellectual, literary, and artistic circles of Germany during this period was enormous; see Steven E. Aschheim, *The Nietzsche Legacy in Germany, 1890–1990* (Berkeley and Los Angeles: University of California Press, 1992), especially chap. 3. Meidner was an avid reader of Nietzsche, and some of his works have been given a pronounced Nietzschean interpretation by scholars; see Carol E. Eliel, *The Apocalyptic Landscapes of Ludwig Meidner*, exh. cat. (Los Angeles: Los Angeles County Museum of Art, 1989), especially pp. 17ff.

86. Jakob Steinhardt, "Erinnerungen," in *Jakob Steinhardt: Der Prophet*, p. 18.

87. A number of artworks attest to the close relationship between the two artists. Steinhardt executed several portraits of Meidner (for example: 1912, black chalk, pencil, and wash, Tel Aviv Museum of Art, 7982). Meidner portrayed Steinhardt's mother during a visit to Zerkow in the summer of 1911 (*Portrait of Jakob Steinhardt's Mother*, 1911, pencil, The Israel Museum; the work is inscribed to Steinhardt by Meidner). Other works in both artists' estates were given and inscribed to one another.

88. Julius Meier-Graefe, *Die spanische Reise*, cited in Jonathan Brown, "El Greco: The Man and the Myths," in *El Greco of Toledo*, exh. cat. (Boston: Little, Brown, 1982), p. 27. This essay is an excellent summary of the history of El Greco's reception, and includes other examples of German interest in his art at the turn of the century. For Meier-Graefe on El Greco, see Kenworth Moffet, *Meier-Graefe as Art Critic* (Munich: Prestel, 1973), pp. 103–13. Meier-Graefe's description of El Greco—"This Greek . . . who came from Italy and painted in Spain, without becoming a Spaniard, is wholly European in effect" (cited in Brown, p. 28)—transforms the seventeenth-century artist into a cosmopolitan contemporary. In the article "Spiritual Treasures," in *The Blue Rider Almanac*, originally published in 1912, Kandinsky and Marc expressed their enthusiasm for El Greco: "We like to emphasize the El Greco case, because the glorification of this great master is very closely connected with the flourishing of our new ideas in art. Cézanne and El Greco are spiritual brothers despite the centuries that separate them . . . Today the works of both mark the beginning of a new epoch of painting." See Vasily Kandinsky and Franz Marc, *The Blaue Reiter Almanac*, ed. Klaus Lankheit (New York: Viking, 1974), p. 59.

89. Cassirer Gallery exhibited a copy of the *Isenheim Altar* in October 1909; see Ingrid Schulze, *Die Erschütterung der Moderne: Grünewald im 20. Jahrhundert* (Leipzig: E. A. Seemann, 1991), p. 22.

90. Meier-Graefe published a reproduction of this painting in the second edition of *Entwicklungsgeschichte der modernen Kunst*, vol. 1 (Munich: Piper, 1914), fig. 32, cited this as in the collection of Eduard Arnhold, Berlin, on loan to the Alte Pinakothek in Munich. It had already been illustrated in an article by R. Förster, "Laokoon im Mittelalter und in der Renaissance," in *Jahrbuch der Kgl. Preussischen Kunstsammlungen* 27 (1906): 174, fig. 17.

91. For a history of the evolving interpretations of the Cain figure in literature from antiquity through the twentieth century, see Ricardo J. Quinones, *The Changes of Cain: Violence and the Lost Brother in Cain and Abel Literature* (Princeton: Princeton University Press, 1991). For medieval depictions of Cain, including the association of Cain with the Jews, see Ruth Mellinkoff, *The Mark of Cain* (Berkeley: University of California Press, 1981).

92. See, for example, the drama *Kain* by Friedrich Koffka (Berlin: Erich Reiss, 1918) and Gottfried Benn's poem, "Das Späte Ich," of 1922; see Gottfried Benn, *Prose, Essays, Poems*, ed. Volkman Sander (New York: Continuum, 1987), pp. 199–203.

93. Paul Raabe, *Die Zeitschriften und Sammlungen des Literarischen Expressionismus: Repertorium der Zeitschriften, Jahrbücher, Anthologien, Sammelwerke, Schriftenreihen und Almanache 1910–1921* (Stuttgart: J. B. Metzlersche Verlagsbuchhandlung, 1964), no. 5, pp. 38–39.

94. Steinhardt, "Erinnerungen," in *Jakob Steinhardt: Der Prophet*, p. 18. Steinhardt's contrasting of his own work with traditional depictions is strongly reminiscent of Buber's article on Lesser Ury, cited above, differentiating Ury's *Jeremiah* from its predecessors.

95. The pastel of *Job* is reproduced in *Jacob and Israel: Homeland and Identity in the Work of Jakob Steinhardt*, p. 23. Job and Jeremiah become important themes for German Jewish writers after the First World War, a phenomenon anticipated by more than a decade in the visual arts. For Job and Jeremiah as literary motifs, see Sigrid Bauschinger, "Hiob und Jeremias: Biblische Themen in der deutschen Literatur des 20. Jahrhunderts," in *Akten des VI. Internationalen Germanisten-Kongresses, Basel, 1980* in *Jahrbuch für Internationale Germanistik, Kongressberichte*, 8, no. 3 (Bern and Frankfurt am Main: Peter Lang, 1980), pp. 466–72.

96. For another sketch for this poster, executed in charcoal, see Rudolf Pfefferkorn, *Jakob Steinhardt* (Berlin: Stapp Verlag, 1967), fig. 7.

97. Ludwig Meidner, "Anleitung zum Malen von Grossstadtbildern," originally published in *Kunst und Künstler* 12 (1914): 299 ff., quoted here and below from the translation in Victor Meisel, *Ludwig Meidner: An Expressionist Master*, exh. cat. (Ann Arbor: The University of Michigan Art Museum, 1978), pp. 30–31.

98. For a perceptive analysis of this drawing and of its relationship to Meidner's theoretical writing, see Reinhold Heller, *Art in Germany, 1909–1936: From Expressionism to Resistance—The Marvin and Janet Fishman Collection*, exh. cat. (Munich and Milwaukee: Prestel and the Milwaukee Art Museum, 1990), p. 206, cat. no. 104.

99. Ludwig Meidner, "Erinnerungen an Jakob van Hoddis," in Jakob van Hoddis, *Weltende: Gesammelte Dichtungen*, ed. Paul Pörtner (Zurich, 1958); cited in Allen, *Literary Life*, pp. 206–7.

100. For discussions of the "apocalyptic landscapes," see Grochowiak, *Ludwig Meidner*, pp. 63–77; Meisel, *Ludwig Meidner*, pp. 4ff.; G. Leistner, *Idee und Wirklichkeit: Gehalt und Bedeutung des urbanen Expressionismus in Deutschland, dargestellt am Werk Ludwig Meidners* (Frankfurt am Main/Bern/New York: Peter Lang, 1986); Eliel, *The Apocalyptic Landscapes of Ludwig Meidner*; Michael Becker, "Ludwig Meidner und die frühexpressionistische Grossstadtlyrik," in *Ludwig Meidner: Zeichner, Maler, Literat*, ed. Breuer and Wagemann, vol. 2, pp. 57–69; see also Angelika Schmid, "Die sogenannten 'Apokalyptischen Landschaften' (1912–1916): 'Mahnende Rufer' des Künstlers Ludwig Meidner," in ibid., pp. 84–95. Reinhold Heller cites examples of contemporary poetry in relation to Meidner's work; see Heller, *Art in Germany*, pp. 205, 209. Much of the contemporary interest in the apocalypse was related to the idea of massive destruction as the necessary prelude to a future utopia.

101. For example, to take just one element found in these works, one will probably never be able to ascertain whether the blazing comets that appear in a number of Meidner's works are meant as portents of doom, references to the appearance of Halley's Comet (1910), or allusions to the poetry of Walt Whitman. On Halley's Comet, see Reinhold Heller, "Kandinsky and Traditions Apocalyptic," *Art Journal* (Spring 1983): 19–26. Heller describes the mood around the appearance of the comets in 1910 as the "high point of popular eschatological mania" (p. 25). For Meidner's affinity with Whitman, see Meisel, *Ludwig Meidner*, p. 20 n. 23.

102. Charles W. Haxthausen, "Images of Berlin in the Art of the Secession and Expressionism," in *Art in Berlin, 1815–1989*, exh. cat. (Atlanta: High Museum of Art, 1989), pp. 68–73.

103. On this painting, see also Meisel, *Ludwig Meidner*, p. 8; and Haxthausen, "Images of Berlin," pp. 69f.

104. Other works by Meidner include *The Stranded Ones*, 1911; *Horrors of War*, 1911; and *The Burned-Out (Homeless) Ones*, 1912. These are illustrated in Eliel, *The Apocalyptic Landscapes*, figs. 30–31 and 77. Eliel (pp. 50ff.) and Eberhard Roters, "The Painter's Nights" (pp. 67f.), discuss Beckmann's scenes of contemporary catastrophe (see figs. 53 and 65) as influencing Meidner.

105. Indeed, the scene depicted here is reminiscent of much of the imagery in the Book of Jeremiah, as, for example, in these verses from chap. 4 (20; 23–4; 26): "Destruction followeth upon destruction,/ For the whole land is spoiled: I beheld the earth,/ And, lo, it was waste and void;/ And the heavens, and they had no light./ I beheld the mountains, and, lo, they trembled,/ And all the hills moved to and fro. . . ./I beheld, and, lo, the fruitful field was a wilderness,/ And all the cities thereof were broken down/ At the presence of the Lord,/ and before His fierce anger." The small fire and group of tents in the foreground of the *Apocalyptic Landscape*, ca. 1913, in the Nationalgalerie in Berlin, might allude to verses in Jeremiah as well: for example, Jer. 6:20: "Your burnt-offerings are not acceptable, nor your sacrifices pleasing unto Me"; and Jer. 4:20: "Suddenly are my tents spoiled." For an illustration of the Berlin painting, see Eliel, *The Apocalyptic Landscapes*, fig. 34.

106. The phrase "negative epiphany" is taken from Tim Parks, "A Prisoner's Dream: Eugenio Montale in Translation," *The New York Review of Books*, 4 Feb. 1999, p. 36.

107. See Eberhard Roters, "The Painter's Nights," in Eliel, *The Apocalyptic Landscapes*, pp. 63ff., for a vivid evocation of this process, and for an English translation of Meidner's reminiscences.

108. Grochowiak, *Ludwig Meidner*, p. 119, translated in Meisel, *Ludwig Meidner*, p. 5. There was an intense interest in ecstatic experience and mysticism during this period; in particular, Martin Buber's book *Ekstatische Konfessionen (Ecstatic Confessions)*, published in 1909, exerted an enormous influence on the Expressionist generation. (See Paul Mendes-Flohr's essay in this book.) See Martin Buber, *Ecstatic Confessions*, collected and introduced by Martin Buber, ed. Paul Mendes-Flohr, trans. Esther Cameron (Harper & Row: San Francisco, 1985). In contemplating Meidner's experience, one is reminded of Buber's statement in the book's Foreword (p. xxxi): "I am not concerned with finding a conceptual 'pigeonhole' for ecstasy. It is the unclassifiable aspect of ecstasy that interests me. The ecstatic individual may be explained in terms of psychology, physiology, pathology; what is important to us is that which remains beyond explanation: the individual's experience."

109. Kurt Hiller, "Ausstellung der Pathetiker," *Die Aktion* 2, no. 48 (27 Nov. 1912): col. 1515.

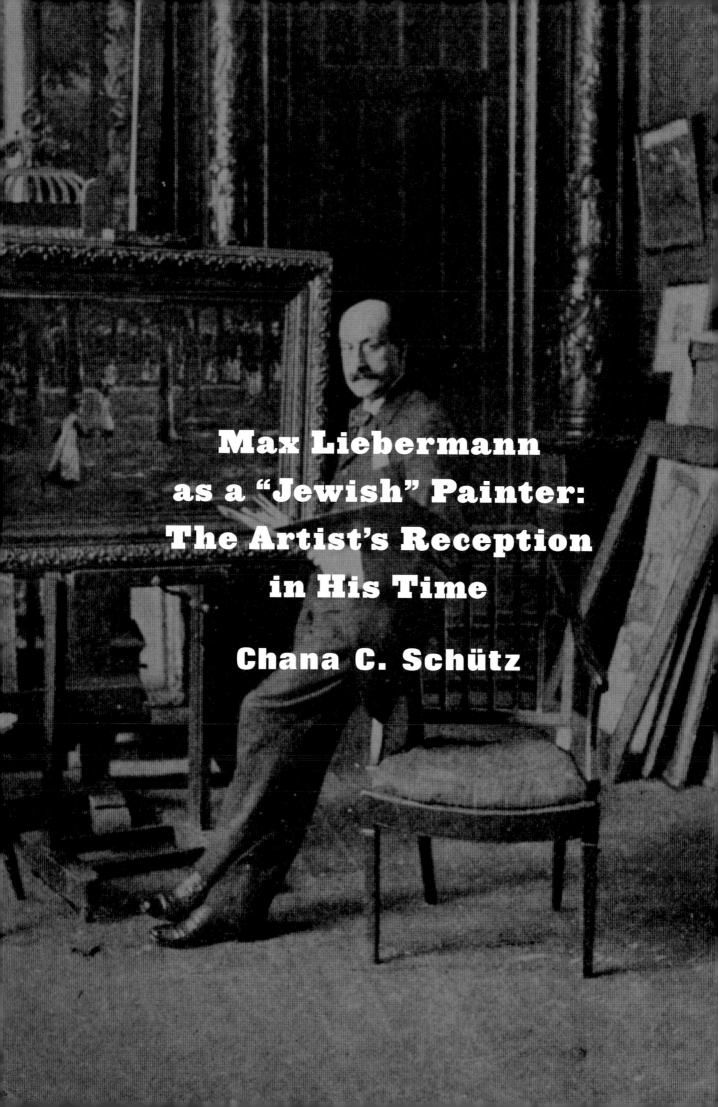

Max Liebermann
as a "Jewish" Painter:
The Artist's Reception
in His Time

Chana C. Schütz

The painter Max Liebermann (1847–1935) was a central figure in the art of the Wilhelmine era. A leading representative of the Naturalist movement in Germany, he was later instrumental in advancing the breakthrough of Impressionism. He was one of the founders in 1898 of the Berlin Secession, a movement of artists and gallery owners who broke with the established art associations at the end of the nineteenth century, signaling their protest against the official academic art. From 1920 to 1932, Max Liebermann was president of the Prussian Academy of Arts. In 1927 he was made an honorary citizen of Berlin. And he was a Jew.

Given the catastrophic fate of German Jewry, it is curious that the role of Liebermann's Jewishness is rarely considered in art-historical writing.[1] Yet the issues of the artist's national identity—German, Jewish, or some hybrid of the two—and whether he was a "Jewish artist" are at the core of Liebermann's reception as an artist during his lifetime. Does the painter's Jewishness refer to ethnic, "racial," or religious identity alone, or to the expression of Jewish experience, subject matter, or a particular style in his art? In the case of Liebermann, it involves the attitudes of German society and the art world toward the artist's Jewish identity as well as the artist's own complex relationship toward that identity. The tension between Liebermann's art and his Jewish identity also provides a context for considering the possibilities and limitations of assimilation in Wilhelmine society.

For the art historian Paul Westheim (1886–1963), longtime editor of the periodical *Das Kunstblatt* (The Art Journal), it was the distinctively Prussian and Berlin qualities that gave Liebermann's painting its particular character; and, as he emphasized in his 1935 eulogy for the painter published in the exile magazine *Das Neue Tagebuch* (The New Diary), "these traits were so strong that the Jewishness vanished completely." Of course, the question of whether his work was essentially Jewish art cannot be answered as simply "as it usually was by philo-Semites and anti-Semites" for more than a hundred years. To make his point, Westheim contrasts Marc Chagall (see PLATE 19) and Max Liebermann: "Chagall is without question, in his manner, in his form of expression, in his inborn kabbalistic mysticism, a specifically Jewish artist. If one compares Chagall and Liebermann, one can only conclude that Liebermann is a Berlin Realist, a student and successor of Schadow and Menzel."[2]

Figure 133
Unter den Linden and Pariser Platz, ca. 1890

Max Liebermann was born in Berlin on 20 July 1847. Although his family was wealthy and distinguished, their standing among the "established patrician"[3] families of Berlin was relatively recent. The artist's grandfather Joseph Liebermann had arrived in Berlin in 1823 from Märkisch-Friedland, a small town in the province of West Prussia, and he had prospered in the cotton

(opposite)
(Detail) Max Liebermann in his studio on the Kaiserin-Augusta-Strasse, 1898
Photograph: Max von Rüdiger

trade. His uncle Benjamin and his father, Louis, expanded the business. Their great economic success made it possible for them to rise into the upper-bourgeois elite of Berlin, a city that itself did not achieve economic and cultural significance until the first half of the nineteenth century. Benjamin Liebermann had lived since the 1840s at 6 Unter den Linden. In 1859, Louis Liebermann purchased the house at 7 Pariser Platz, in the same vicinity, right next to the Brandenburg Gate. After his mother died, in 1892, the artist moved to this house with his wife and daughter. It became his lifelong home.[4] The Liebermann family was actively engaged in the Jewish community of Berlin. For several years, members of the family sat on the community board of directors, and they supported Jewish welfare organizations. It can be assumed that a conversion to Christianity was not an option for the Liebermann family at any time.

Max Liebermann was proud of his family's commercial enterprises in Berlin. Yet, of his three brothers, only his eldest brother, Georg, would pursue a business career. Felix, four years younger, lived as an independent scholar in Berlin. A distinguished historian, he held honorary doctorates from Oxford and Cambridge.

During the first phase of Liebermann's artistic career, around 1870, he painted mainly naturalistic scenes, often presenting people engaged in physical labor. In the 1890s his work became more impressionistic, although he rejected the radical focus of Impressionist painting on the transitory effects of light on objects and color. The representation of people in motion—riders at the shore (FIG. 45) or pulsating market scenes in Amsterdam's *Judengasse*, or Jewish Quarter (FIG. 134, FIGS. 81–84)—was at the forefront of his work since the turn of the century.

Figure 134
Max Liebermann
**Jewish Quarter in Amsterdam
[Judengasse in Amsterdam]**, 1905
Oil on canvas, 16 x 21 in. (40.6 x 53.3 cm)
Collection of Alan and Ruth Barnett

The many portraits he made of public figures became of central importance around 1900. They are psychologically impressive pictures. One of the most important portraits, painted in 1909, is of Richard Dehmel (FIG. 135). Along with Detlev von Liliencron, Richard Dehmel (1863–1920) was one of the most prominent poets in Germany at the time. Beginning in the late nineteenth century, Liebermann and Dehmel had shared in a close exchange of ideas. Dehmel, who was sixteen years younger, had attracted attention for his radical thinking even as a high school student: the director of the Sophiengymnasium in Berlin prevented Dehmel from graduating because he had founded a student group dedicated to Darwinian ideas. After Dehmel obtained his doctorate in insurance law, he settled in Berlin.

Richard Dehmel was not Jewish, but he believed that intermarriage between Jews and Germans was fundamentally desirable. Dehmel's first wife was born Paula Oppenheimer. Her father, Julius Oppenheimer, was rabbi at the synagogue of the Reform Jewish Congregation in Berlin, and her brother was the economist and sociologist Franz Oppenheimer (1864–1943). After his divorce from Paula, Dehmel married Ida Coblentz, who came from a family of Jewish winegrowers in Bingen on the Rhine.[5]

In 1894, Richard Dehmel helped found the art association Pan. He participated in a roundtable of artists and literary figures who met regularly in the Schwarzes Ferkel, a Berlin restaurant on Schadowstrasse, where he met Edvard Munch and August Strindberg, both of whom impressed him deeply. In 1901, Dehmel moved to Blankenese, near Hamburg. Strongly influenced by Friedrich Nietzsche, he renounced the Classical-Romantic tradition in poetry in favor of a socially oriented and impressionistic Naturalism. Later he would become a forerunner and pioneer of Expressionism. His poems were characterized by free rhythms, rhymed or unrhymed, and striking imagery. A major theme was the power of Eros, and on several occasions it brought him into conflict with official censors.

In May 1908, Dehmel published a widely acclaimed essay entitled "Talent and Race" that took the form of an imaginary conversation between a German writer and a Jewish painter.[6] The model for the German writer was obviously Richard Dehmel himself, and the Jewish painter was surely Max Liebermann. The German writer, in this essay, speaks very firmly against a conception of art that is linked to racial characteristics and similarly against an evaluation of art based on the racial or ethnic background of the artist. Ironically, his praise of Liebermann as "one of the purest German artists who was ever shown in the

Figure 135
Max Liebermann
Portrait of the Poet Richard Dehmel [Bildnis des Dichters Richard Dehmel], 1909
Oil on canvas,
45¼ x 36³⁄₁₆ in. (115 x 92 cm)
Hamburger Kunsthalle

National Gallery" makes use of the racial thinking and language of the time.

Dehmel's conversation between a "Jewish painter" and a "German poet" focuses on a fictitious painting entitled *Judith and Holofernes*. Presumably, the painting refers to Liebermann's *Samson and Delilah* of 1902 (FIGS. 136, 137), which was shown in the same year at the fifth exhibition of the Berlin Secession. Dehmel's Jewish painter comments: "So it's very beautiful. But don't you see, the thing has race written all over it." The German poet replies: "If indeed you want to speak about it, then I must openly confess to you that I'd rather see something universally human." Whereupon the Jewish painter answers: "You are universally crazy. Something like that can be made only by someone who is Jewish."

Dehmel's dialogue represents a conflict between a universal art and a particularly Jewish style and subject matter that "has race written all over it" and is thus expressive only of a Jewish artist. Liebermann's attitude toward his Jewishness, however, was more complex and ambivalent. Although he did not deny his Jewish identity, he saw himself as fully integrated into German culture, free to ignore his Jewish background or to express it in some

Figure 136
Max Liebermann
Samson and Delilah (Simson und Delila), 1902
Oil on canvas,
157½ x 83½ in. (147 x 213 cm)
Städtische Galerie im Städelschen
Kunstinstitut, Frankfurt am Main

form. Even before the publication of this fictional conversation, in a letter to Dehmel of 24 February 1908, Max Liebermann described as "extremely flattering" the fact that he was made the model "of a type that became a portrait . . . of the Jewish painter." But at the same time, he distanced himself from the ethnic dialect or jargon commonly ascribed to German Jews. He made it clear that he did not want to be portrayed speaking German incorrectly: "Do not allow me to confuse the words *mich* and *mir* [accusative and dative of "me," used incorrectly in Berlin dialect]. *De la langue verte* as much as you like but no accu-dative and no Jewish German. . . . Let me use Berlin expressions, as much as you like, but neither incorrect German nor Jewish German. . . . Since I'm a dyed-in-the-wool Jew, Jewish words in the German language make me angry; at most I may allow *nebbish* and *meshugge* because there are no German words for them." Liebermann closed the letter with greetings to Dehmel's wife, "who will certainly be of the same opinion concerning the Jewish expressions."[7]

Like the majority of Berlin's Jewish upper bourgeoisie, Liebermann was highly assimilated. In a letter to Liebermann written in December 1911, Dehmel described his pleasure in seeing the artist's Dutch sketchbook that his wife had placed under the Christmas tree for him, "for we are not only German and Jewish, but also Christian. It seems as though you feel the same way."[8] And in a letter from Liebermann to Alfred Lichtwark,

Figure 137
Max Liebermann
**Samson and Delilah [Simson
und Delila]**, 1893
Oil on canvas,
15³/₁₆ x 21⁵/₈ in. (38.5 x 55 cm)
Stiftung Jüdisches Museum, Berlin

the director of the Hamburger Kunsthalle, we learn that in 1909, Liebermann had given his wife, Martha, the *Otter Fountain* by August Gaul (see FIG. 138) "as a Christmas present,"[9] actually the same sculpture that had been shown previously at the eighteenth exhibition of the Berlin Secession.[10] All this does not mean that Max Liebermann considered himself a Christian. It was much rather in keeping with the view widely held among assimilated Jews in Berlin that the celebration of Christmas was a German, not only a Christian, custom. A similar view is expressed by Gershom Scholem in his memoirs *From Berlin to Jerusalem*: "It was claimed that this was a German national festival that we celebrate not as Jews, but as fellow Germans."[11]

That Liebermann was very familiar with the German Jewish jargon and that he also enjoyed its use—especially for humorous effects—is evident from his letter of 1902 to Dehmel. Dehmel had suggested the title *Die Kunstschau* (The Art Show) for a new art journal to be issued by the publishing house of Bruno Cassirer. Liebermann replied in his letter that he had immediately sent this suggestion "to the publisher of the still-unchristened periodical— publisher and editor alike are in the same unchristened state. *Kunstschau* is a very good name, it just sounds too much like *Kunstschaute*, which your wife can perhaps translate for you."[12] The term *Schaute*, or *Schote*, stems from the Hebrew *shoteh*, meaning "fool" or "blockhead." The periodical, incidentally, ended up with the title *Kunst und Künstler* (Art and Artist). Under its first

Figure 138
August Gaul
**Otter with Fish [Fischotter
mit Fisch]**, 1903
Bronze,
7½ x 3¾ x 5⅛ in. (19 x 9.5 x 13 cm)
Museum der bildenden Künste Leipzig

Figure 139
August Gaul
Cat [Kater], 1901
Bronze with gilt eyes, 5½ in. (14.5 cm)
Georg Kolbe Museum, Berlin

editor-in-chief, Emil Heilbut (1861–1921), known by the pseudonym Hermann Helferich, the magazine from 1902 to 1906 became an important literary forum for modern art in Berlin.

Following the publication of "Talent and Race," Liebermann decisively reduced the role assigned to him as a "Jewish artist." In a letter to Dehmel of 22 June 1908, he described himself as a Jew for whom religion was a private matter and who, in all else, feels himself a German: "A Zionist perhaps thinks like your 'Jewish painter,'" he wrote, "but I do not wish in my old age to become a painter in Jerusalem, not even a court painter to His future Jewish Majesty."[13] Liebermann was quoted frequently, by Hans Ostwald in 1930 and later by many others, as denying any relationship between his identity as a Jew and his work as an artist: "Recently, a Hitler paper—it was sent to me—wrote that it was outrageous that a Jew should paint the Reichspräsident. Something like this only makes me laugh. I am convinced that Hindenburg, if he hears this, is also going to laugh about it. After all, I'm only a painter, and what has painting to do with Judaism?"[14] This quotation is inaccurate, as shown by Liebermann's actual remarks in a conversation with Lise Leibholz cited in the *C.-V.-Zeitung* of 15 July 1927: "After all, I am only a painter, and a Jew can surely be that, too."[15]

So much for Max Liebermann himself. He was a Jew; he was an artist; and he was both at the same time. But Jewish birth does not necessarily create a Jewish artist. Although cosmopolitan artists wanted to be free to express, or not express, their Jewishness in their art and life, the fact is that their ethnic identity was often ascribed to them by others. The extent to which Liebermann's Jewish origins and identity influenced his art has been debated from many viewpoints. The following discussion explores three very different perspectives: first, that of the anti-Semites; second, the view of cultural Zionists, who had their eyes on creating a Jewish cultural renaissance and a national art; and third, the views of German art critics of the period.

A multitude of anti-Semitic opinions were expressed about Jews in the arts in general and about Max Liebermann in particular throughout the course of his career. The attacks were directed almost exclusively toward Liebermann's artistic influence, and especially his support of modern art. He was, above all, criticized for introducing Germany to modernism, which then referred to French art, specifically Impressionism. The notorious *Sigilla Veri* (1929), also known as Philipp Stauff's *Semi-Kürschner* (see FIG. 17), an anti-Semitic lexicon of prominent Jews (see the essay by Peter Paret in this book) does not criticize Liebermann's ideas per se but rather the man for being a cosmopolitan, a Jew, and thus "corrupting" German culture: "For many people he seems a parasite on the body of German character and art, one of the birds of doom of the German spirit, international in outlook, and a servant of the Talmud." A related comment that "others have let themselves be corrupted by him and by people like him"[16] seems to be directed against Wilhelm von Bode, managing director of the Kaiser-Friedrich Museum in Berlin, who in 1907 referred to Liebermann as one of "the most German painters among living artists" to whom "the glory of being Germany's leading painter can no longer be denied."[17]

It is significant that German anti-Semites at this time had nothing original to say about Liebermann as an artist or about his paintings. Instead they relied on the opinion of a well-known critic, Lothar Brieger-Wasservogel (1879–1949), who was Jewish and had described himself as "a Jew and, in fact, a Jew by conviction" as well as "fully a supporter of modern art."[18] He was actually the author of a 1922 monograph published by Benjamin Harz on the graphic artist Ephraim Mose Lilien (1874–1925), a well-known Zionist who unequivocally considered himself a Jewish artist (see FIGS. 145, 146, 148). But in his book *Der Fall Liebermann: Über das Virtuosentum in der bildenden Kunst* (The Case of Liebermann: On Virtuosity in the Visual Arts), Brieger-Wasservogel maintains the view that Liebermann's work was nothing new but rather a continuation of the academic tradition, reproaching the painter for "his damnable and outdated model painting that simply relies on different models and a modern shine." Employing the imagery of organic corruption and unnatural hybridization, Brieger-Wasservogel found Liebermann to be "the most destructive parasite of modern art," who had drained its own life energy from a healthy tree in order to implant alien seeds and thus to impede rather than further its development. For this reason, wrote Brieger-Wasservogel, "German art must ignore him!" The Berlin Secession, with which Liebermann was strongly identified, is similarly described as "not an artistic but a purely commercial venture, hiding behind big words about art, . . . headed by a businessman painter and a very sharp art dealer."[19]

These and many other criticisms barely refer to Liebermann's paintings or to their themes. The one exception is the painting *The Twelve-Year-Old Jesus in the Temple* (FIG. 140), which caused a sensation in 1879 at the International Art Show in Munich. The painting has an interesting history.[20] The work depicted the twelve-year-old Jesus in the temple surrounded by stereotypical Jewish figures in traditional and modern dress. The artwork aroused great anger: the Crown Prince of Bavaria was outraged, the picture was debated in the Bavarian Parliament, and eventually it was removed from the exhibition. Court Chaplain Adolf Stoecker, who enjoyed the special support of Kaiser Wilhelm II and was the most vociferous anti-Semite of his time, is said to have later declared that this painting had caused him to become an anti-Semite.

Figure 140
Max Liebermann
The Twelve-Year-Old Jesus in the Temple (Der zwölfjährige Jesus im Tempel), 1879
Oil on canvas,
159¼ x 51 in. (151 x 131 cm)
Hamburger Kunsthalle

In a letter to Alfred Lichtwark of 5 July 1911, Liebermann wrote: "The nastiest newspaper feuds ensued. Nauseated by all the clamor that now, in view of the painting, is incomprehensible, I made the decision never again to paint a biblical subject. In the meantime, *Jesus* gave rise to the new style of religious painting."[21] In "Judaism and German Art (On the Max Liebermann Problem)," the art historian Heinrich Strauss observed that, at the time of this letter, Liebermann obviously had still not understood that the German public would grant liberties in painting New Testament themes to a non-Jew, such as Fritz von Uhde, that they would not grant to a Jew.[22]

As a matter of fact, Liebermann subsequently changed the Jewish look of his Jesus in the painting. In her *Studien zum Frühwerk von Max Liebermann* (Studies on the Early Work of Max Liebermann), Katrin Boskamp discovered an early version of the image in Richard Muther's *Geschichte der Malerei des XIX. Jahrhunderts* (History of Nineteenth-Century Painting, 1894), and was able to find two preliminary sketches (FIG. 141).[23] The scene is the same as in the well-known painting in the Hamburger Kunsthalle (FIG. 140). But in the sketch, Jesus is not depicted as a modestly dressed boy with blond hair, surrounded by scriptural scholars. Instead, he has prominent features, and

Figure 141
Max Liebermann
Sketch for **The Twelve-Year-Old Jesus in the Temple (Der zwölfjährige Jesus im Tempel)**, 1879
Crayon over pencil,
17 x 11 9/16 in. (43.4 x 30.4 cm)
Kupferstichkabinett, Staatliche Museen zu Berlin–Preussischer Kulturbesitz

his dark unruly hair falls in disarray over his temples; barefoot and disheveled, he confronts the men in the temple. Liebermann's original depiction of Jesus was thus more "Jewish" in appearance; only later, perhaps in response to the intense criticism, would the artist rework the painting. One could imagine that the debate over his painting would also have made it clear to Liebermann that those who disapproved of his image of Jesus, and with such fury, were not in fact objecting to the so-called modern style of the painting. They simply believed that a Jew should not paint "their" Jesus—and especially not as a Jew.

With the rise of the Jewish national movement under Theodor Herzl at the end of the nineteenth century, others emerged who were advocating Jewish cultural self-determination. A leading spokesman was Martin Buber (1878–1965) (see FIG. 11), who, with his associates, worked to bring about a resurgence of Judaism's spiritual and intellectual values. (See the essay by Inka Bertz in this book.) But Martin Buber wanted to achieve even more. He not only aimed to revitalize the spirit of Jewishness that seemed to be slipping away in Germany, but he was also convinced that a contemporary Jewish culture could be created in the present and among Jewish artists.

In connection with an exhibition that he organized in Basel with E. M. Lilien on the occasion of the Fifth Zionist Congress in 1901, Buber published a book entitled *Jüdische Künstler* (Jewish Artists). An attempt to explore the distinctively Jewish aspects in the art of several painters, this book sought the formation "of a conscious Jewish public for art that knows and loves its artists."[24] Included in this collection was an essay by Georg Hermann (1871–1943) on Max Liebermann that for the most part has little to do with the Jewish aspects of Liebermann's art.[25] Yet, in the essay, Hermann clearly felt compelled to comment in some way on Liebermann's Jewishness. He was convinced of Liebermann's "German essence" and claimed that this quality "in all its racial components could only be perceived by the full-blooded Jew Liebermann."[26] It is important to note that even a Jewish writer such as Georg Hermann employed the concept of race in discussing cultural issues. Encountering these terms in the post-Holocaust era is unsettling, but it must be kept in mind that they belonged to the general discourse of that time in Germany. Since Jews, anti-Semites, and philo-Semites often used the same language, a writer's political orientation cannot necessarily be ascertained by a consideration of his or her terminology.

On 24 July 1902, Martin Buber wrote to Theodor Herzl about the importance, for propaganda purposes, of establishing a modern cultural program for Zionism.[27] Buber also mentioned his conversations with Liebermann about *Jüdische Künstler*, in which he was struck by the artist's strong "racial pride" as well as his newfound appreciation of Zionism. In support of this view, Buber cited a letter from E. M. Lilien, who was at the forefront of the cultural-Zionist efforts to promote a distinctive Jewish national art. Lilien wrote:

When I spoke to him [Liebermann] of Zionism and told
him that "On to Palestine" is not a turning back but a
going forward, and when I told him that I am a convinced
Zionist but not religious—*which he hardly believed*—
he decided that he could see nothing but beautiful and
ideal elements in Zionism. At the beginning he called our
ultimate goal utopian, but an "ennobling" of utopianism.
Later, however, when Cassirer[28] joined us and spoke in
much the same way that Liebermann had spoken to me
earlier, Liebermann became excited and talked much as
the best Zionists would have done. I have only been
strengthened in my conviction that Liebermann will
become a Zionist by and by. He declared that if Zionism
imposes no barriers to his art, he will do all in his power
as an individual to counter such misunderstandings as
that every Zionist be a conservative Jew. He knew Struck,[29]
who eats only kosher food and wears tzitzis,[30] and so he
felt a strong resistance to professing conscious Judaism,
for he thought that then he would have to eat kosher also
and wear tzitzis. It might be possible eventually to convert
Israels[31] to that, he said, but not him. I talked a great deal
about Zionism, and especially about cultural Zionism,
with him. And since he himself already knew a great deal,
he now understands many things that were previously
incomprehensible to him.[32]

But Liebermann did not become a Zionist after all, although
the art historian Karl Scheffler (1869–1951), one of his biogra-
phers, noted that he increasingly stressed his Judaism.[33] In the
end, Liebermann did not consider the idea of "national art" a
valid concept. As he wrote to Wilhelm von Bode on 27 August
1905: "Since Dürer was a genius and just happened to be born
in Nürnberg, should we call the way he worked German?" Similarly, "Couldn't Millet much rather be a German and Menzel a
Frenchman, based on their work?"[34]

The *Jüdisches Lexikon*, the leading reference to Jewish topics
in Germany before Hitler's rise to power in 1933, also dismissed
the concept of a Jewish national art. One could speak of "art
made by Jews" or "art created for Jews," it stated, "but not in
the sense of inherently Jewish art." There is no "distinctive Jewish quality," because throughout the centuries Jewish artists
employed forms and motifs typical of their "host countries."
Perhaps with Liebermann in mind, the *Lexikon* observes: "Even
in recent times when Jewish artists have created important work,
their accomplishments belong more to the art history of the
people of the countries where they live than to the Jewish
people."[35] Karl Schwarz (1885–1962) wrote the article on Max
Liebermann in the *Jüdisches Lexikon*. He was the first director
of the Berlin Jewish Museum, and in the summer of 1933 became
director of the Tel Aviv Museum. Schwarz viewed Liebermann
as "the most important representative of Impressionism in

Germany: his penetrating intellect and his typically Jewish instinct for the psychological contributed to his extraordinary talent as a portrait painter."[36] Doubtless, Liebermann did not see his art as being at the forefront of a Jewish renaissance. And he expressed no great longing for a Jewish art based on ethnic or national traits. Early on, however, Liebermann supported the activities of Jewish artists in Palestine. Since its founding in 1906, he was a member of an action committee formed in Berlin "to promote home industry and crafts in Palestine." To the Bezalel School of Arts and Crafts, newly established in Jerusalem, he donated one of his pictures, the study of a Dutch peasant woman, probably from the year 1896.[37]

Influential art critics in Germany also addressed the Jewish element in Liebermann's art. In particular, Julius Meier-Graefe and Karl Scheffler, along with museum director Ludwig Justi, established themselves as authorities on the artist's life and work. These three men were not Jewish, but all of them distinguished themselves as opponents of National Socialism. Meier-Graefe left Germany after Hitler came to power, and both Scheffler and Justi could not continue their careers. Their critical judgments and prejudices, however, can be viewed as typical of their time and culture; notably, these critics did not consider the Jewishness of Liebermann's art in terms of its content, iconography, style, or function, but rather as expressing a Jewish "spirit," or, in a national or racial sense, reflecting distinctively Jewish, and not German, traits or character. Julius Meier-Graefe (1867–1935), for example, was one of the most important art critics of his time, an authority on French painting of the nineteenth century, and a champion of Impressionism. Together with Otto Julius Bierbaum (1865–1910) and Richard Dehmel (see FIG. 135), he founded the art magazine *Pan* in 1895. His major work, the *Entwicklungs-geschichte der modernen Kunst* (History of the Development of Modern Art), a comparative study of the visual arts as contributing to a new aesthetic, was first published in 1904.[38] In his revised and enlarged edition of 1920, he devoted a chapter to Liebermann, where he discussed the artist as representative of the *Weltgefühl*, or "feeling about the world," prevalent at the end of the nineteenth century: "Our improvised vision of the world recognized in him a realm beyond the blue jagged mountains of Romanticism, a realism that could confront our age with open eyes, the appropriate forms, and disciplined feeling that for reasons of taste alone would not be embraced by every viewer. His refusal to use windy rhetoric was in itself an asset."[39]

Meier-Graefe relies on broad generalizations about collective Jewish psychology and culture to convey the significance of Liebermann's Jewishness for his art. "A Jew feels at home both in a turbulent new world and a disintegrating old world," he observes. "Improvisation in life, in thought, in creativity, is for him a necessity by virtue of the history of his people." Furthermore, writes Meier-Graefe, "a Jew is a realist from self-defense. He has given us this defensive realism, an attitude perfectly

Figure 142
Max Liebermann
**Self-Portrait with Kitchen
Still-Life (Selbstbildnis mit
Küchenstilleben)**, 1873
Oil on canvas,
33½ x 54⅜ in. (85.3 x 139 cm)
Städtisches Museum Gelsenkirchen

suited to coping with turbulent new worlds and collapsing old worlds: take what lies before you; do it on your own; you know your own worth; you cannot rely on others." The Jew, however, is also a "sharer for reasons of self-defense: while others lament their downfall and therefore perish, he sets out to help himself. He is a brilliant pragmatist, who always perceives the world from the place where he is standing."⁴⁰

Along with Meier-Graefe, Karl Scheffler was one of the era's leading critics of the fine arts in Germany. For Scheffler, the long-time editor of the influential art journal *Kunst und Künstler* (see FIG. 35), Liebermann was one of those artists who could be better understood in the context of his origins: "He is not among those surprising phenomena who surface unexpectedly from the depth of the folk, as products of unruly blood mixtures, giving no explanation for the source of their talent." In this view, Liebermann was an artist who could "clearly be seen as a product of a family whose energy and culture has been passed on through the ages." The artist's Jewish background could not be disregarded, Scheffler implies, "although its slightest overemphasis would easily result in a distorted view of his art."⁴¹

Scheffler viewed this Jewish ancestry as the source of distinctively Jewish artistic gifts—for example, Liebermann's facility, mastery, and early maturity as an artist: "His talent for painting developed surely, quickly, without wavering, as if according to plan, and has attained a level of calm mastery that the specifically Germanic talent attains only after having borne the brunt of mistakes and crises." Other characteristic Jewish gifts, according to Scheffler, are "insight, energetic vitality, intelligent adaptation, persistence, tirelessness, and a revolutionary sense of reality."

But these same Jewish traits, for Scheffler, could take an artist only so far: "Jewish talent can almost always reach a respectable middle level. . . . As a result, the summits and valleys are lacking, the demonic is missing. Figures such as Moses Mendelssohn, Heine, Börne, Mendelssohn-Bartholdy, Meyerbeer, and Liebermann represent in Germany the summit of a collective racial power [*Rassenkraft*] that appears to be genius because it is indestructible; in the individual, artistic realm, however, it does not go beyond a certain point."[42]

Art historian Ludwig Justi (1876–1957) was director of the Berlin National Gallery from 1909 until July 1933, when the National Socialists forced his retirement. He knew Liebermann, particularly during the time when he was secretary of the Prussian Academy of Arts and Liebermann was its president. For Justi, Liebermann was an embodiment of the cosmopolitan culture of Berlin, expressed in his sharp intellect, pointed wit, gift of observation, and rejection of pomposity. Liebermann was also a typical Berliner in his appreciation of meticulous craftsmanship and, as a Berliner might put it, "the ever watchful readiness for combat, no allowances and no surrender, but instead the sharpened— but never poisoned—arrow always in the quiver and a quickness with the bow."[43] Some of what Justi characterizes as "berlinisch" might also be perceived as the Jewish strand in Liebermann's nature. And indeed, Max Liebermann was something of a representative of those Jews who made history as German Jews, and among whom were first and foremost the Jews of Berlin.

The world of these German Jews is explored in *Jüdisches Leben und Antisemitismus im 19. und 20. Jahrhundert* (Jewish Life and Anti-Semitism in the Nineteenth and Twentieth Centuries) by the Israeli historian Shulamit Volkov. Except for a small Orthodox group, she points out, traditional Judaism in Germany had practically disappeared before World War I: "In its place a new and modern Jewish community grew up. Its demographic, professional, and social distinctiveness reinforced the community's cohesiveness and its social and cultural identity, not in the traditional sense, but in a new way."[44]

Nor should we ignore the fact that these developments took place in the metropolis of Berlin, a melting pot in which many different groups in society—be they Silesians, Pomeranians, proletarians, small-business owners, Catholics, women, or Jews— lived through similar experiences. To be a Berliner meant something special. There were many Jews in Berlin who shared that something special with other Berliners. Max Liebermann was— in his unique way—one of them. It is important to point this out, especially in light of the view that German Jews had formed their own subculture in the midst of modern German society.

One of Liebermann's paintings may shed some light on the artist's connection to this intimate Jewish subculture and private Jewish identity, celebrated apart from his public life as a cosmopolitan Berliner. In this context, *Self-Portrait with Kitchen*

Still-Life, which Lieberman painted in 1873 (FIG. 142), has its own intimate family history.

In the *Kitchen Still-Life*, a happy Max Liebermann, wearing a cook's hat, looks out from behind a table spread with the makings of a bountiful meal, perhaps a soup—a cooking pot, cabbages, and an array of vegetables. There is also a chicken that reveals an interesting detail. From its neck hangs a slip of paper with a red tag, a sign of kosher slaughter. In the article "Max Liebermann as a Painter of His Family," published in the *Allgemeine Zeitung des Judentums* in 1917, Ludwig Geiger first pointed out this detail, which "one could perhaps designate as a delightful act of regard toward the customs observed at home."[45] Perhaps Liebermann was commemorating a Jewish observance that had been practiced in his mother's home. As with other assimilated Jewish artists of the period, Liebermann's references to Jewish themes in his art are oblique, even hidden. On the surface, the painting portrays a bourgeois domestic scene, but those familiar with Jewish customs may perceive other meanings and contexts.

Liebermann never intended this picture to be sold; it was painted exclusively for his own family. And it was part of the distinctive Jewish atmosphere of family life—limited exclusively to the private realm—characteristic of German Jews in the Kaiserreich.

Epilogue

The *Kitchen Still-Life* has its own history closely bound to the fate of the Liebermann family. It was probably painted on the occasion of the wedding of Georg Liebermann, the painter's elder brother, to Elsbeth Marckwald. Eleven years later, in September 1884, Max Liebermann married her younger sister Martha. After the death of Liebermann's father, the painting was inherited by his brother Felix. Felix's widow, born Cäcilie Lachmann, died on 27 January 1943, in the Jewish Hospital in Berlin, ten years after Hitler came to power. On 10 March of the same year, this is also where the widow of Max Liebermann would die in the aftermath of a suicide attempt made in the face of approaching deportation to the Theresienstadt concentration camp. Martha Liebermann had been forced to vacate the Liebermann home near the Brandenburg Gate in December 1938 because of a Nazi order banning Jews from living in the immediate vicinity of the seat of government. Following the deaths of Martha and Cäcilie Liebermann and the presumed confiscation of all of Liebermann's works that had remained with them in Germany, the picture was thought to be lost until 1956, when it surfaced at an auction in Switzerland. Today it is in the collection of the Städtisches Museum in Gelsenkirchen.

Max Liebermann died on 8 February 1935. The former president of the Prussian Academy of Arts, officially still an honorary citizen of Berlin—the capital of the Third Reich—he had been fully ostracized from public life. As a Jew he was an enemy. His paintings vanished from public and private galleries throughout Germany.

Only Berlin's Jewish Museum continued to exhibit Liebermann's work after 1935. It may well have been the widow of Felix Liebermann who made the *Kitchen Still-Life* available to the Liebermann memorial exhibition organized by the remaining Jewish community of Berlin for the Berlin Jewish Museum in 1936.[46] This exhibition was the only honor that Liebermann received at that time in his home city. What a contrast it was to the grand festivities occasioning his eighty-fifth birthday only a few years earlier, on 20 July 1932.

On 11 February 1935, Max Liebermann was buried in the Jewish cemetery on Schönhauser Allee in Berlin's Prenzlauer Berg.[47] The funeral was attended by very few non-Jews, among them Käthe Kollwitz (FIGS. 32, 170, 171), Georg Kolbe (FIGS. 18, 43), and Karl Scheffler. It was Scheffler who spoke of Liebermann as having been "a beacon by which German art determined its course anew and corrected itself again and again."[48] He ended his eulogy with a word to the deceased: "Max Liebermann, long-honored master, it was a good cause to fight for your art, it was an honor to struggle at your side for what is genuine, and it will represent no merit of mine to remain true to you in gratitude."

Notes

Translated by Almut Fitzgerald and Robert Kramer

1. In the catalogue of the 1979 Liebermann retrospective mounted at the Berlin National Gallery, Matthias Eberle states, "For the racists, he was a Jew." See Eberle, "Max Liebermann zwischen Tradition und Opposition," in *Max Liebermann in seiner Zeit* (Berlin: Nationalgalerie Berlin, 1979), p. 12.

2. Paul Westheim, "Liebermann," in *Paul Westheim, Karton mit Säulen: Antifaschistische Kunstkritik*, ed. Tanja Frank (Leipzig/Weimar: Gustav Kiepenheuer Verlag, 1985), pp. 186–90. Johann Gottfried Schadow (1764–1850) was a graphic artist and the most important German classical sculptor. In 1789 he designed the famous *Quadriga* on the Brandenburg Gate. From 1815 until his death, he served as director of the Prussian Academy of Arts in Berlin. Adolph Menzel (1815–1905) was a leading German painter and graphic artist. In the mid-nineteenth century, his paintings were often narrative in content, depicting scenes from the history of Prussia. Under the influence of French realism, much of his work focused on less elevated themes from everyday life. His free naturalistic style prepared the ground for the development of German Impressionism (see fig. 19).

3. Ludwig Justi, *Deutsche Malkunst im neunzehnten Jahrhundert: Ein Führer durch die Nationalgalerie* (Berlin, 1920), p. 299.

4. Within a few years of Liebermann's death in 1935, his widow, Martha, was forced to leave their home, since Jews were no longer allowed to live in the immediate vicinity of the National Socialist government headquarters.

5. Julius Bab, *Richard Dehmel: Die Geschichte eines Lebens-Werkes* (Leipzig: Haessel, 1926), p. 181.

6. Richard Dehmel, "Talent und Rasse: Ein Gespräch zwischen Künstlern," in *Der Tag*, 21 and 23 May 1908; Dehmel, "Kultur und Rasse: Ein Gespräch zwischen Künstlern," in *Gesammelte Werke*, vol. 8 (Berlin: S. Fischer, 1909), pp. 162–92, especially pp. 163, 191.

7. Max Liebermann, letter to Richard Dehmel, 24 February 1908, Carl von Ossietzky State and University Library, Hamburg, Dehmel Archive DA:Br:L332.

8. Richard Dehmel, letter to Max Liebermann, 25 December 1911 (postmark), Carl von Ossietzky State and University Library, Hamburg, Dehmel Archive DA:Br:D:4080.

9. August Gaul (1869–1921), German sculptor, was a founding member of the Berlin Secession. His primarily small sculptures of animals, which depict them in their diversity and independence rather than as subordinates to humans, distinguished Gaul from the generation of his teachers. Paul Cassirer became his sole dealer. In 1919, Cassirer organized a large retrospective for Gaul's fiftieth birthday.

10. Hermann Simon, "Liebermann und das Judentum," in *Max Liebermann: Der Realist und die Phantasie*, ed. Hamburger Kunsthalle (Hamburg: Dölling und Galitz, 1997), p. 46.

11. Gershom Scholem, *Von Berlin nach Jerusalem* (Frankfurt am Main: Suhrkamp, 1977), p. 41.

12. Max Liebermann, letter to Richard Dehmel, 10 July 1902, Carl von Ossietzky State and University Library, Hamburg, Dehmel Archive DA:Br:325. I thank Hermann Simon for his translation of the word *Kunstschaute*.

13. Max Liebermann, letter to Richard Dehmel, 22 June 1908, Carl von Ossietzky State and University Library, Hamburg, Dehmel Archive DA:Br:L334.

14. Hans Ostwald, *Liebermann-Buch* (Berlin: Franke, 1930), p. 304.

15. Lise Leibholz, "Besuch bei Max Liebermann," in *C.-V.-Zeitung*, 15 July 1927, p. 339; Katrin Boskamp, *Studien zum Frühwerk von Max Liebermann: Mit einem Katalog der Gemälde und Ölstudien von 1866–1889* (Hildesheim/Zürich/New York: Georg Olms Verlag, 1994), p. 53.

16. E. Ekkehard, ed., *Sigilla Veri (Ph. Stauff's Semi-Kürschner)*, 2d ed., vol. 3 (Erfurt: U. Bodung-Verlag, 1929), p. 1137.

17. Wilhelm von Bode, "Max Liebermann," *Kunst und Künstler* 5 (1907): 382.

18. Lothar Brieger-Wasservogel, *Der Fall Liebermann: Über das Virtuosentum in der bildenden Kunst* (Stuttgart: Verlag von Strecker und Schröder, 1906), p. 10.

19. Ibid., pp. 25, 52, 55.

20. Boskamp, *Studien zum Frühwerk von Max Liebermann*, pp. 75–115.

21. Else Cassirer, ed., *Künstlerbriefe aus dem 19. Jahrhundert* (Berlin: Verlag Bruno Cassirer, 1919), p. 407.

22. Heinrich Strauss, "Judentum und deutsche Kunst: (Zum Problem Max Liebermann)," in *Deutsches Judentum, Aufstieg und Krise*, ed. Robert Weltsch (Stuttgart: Deutsche Verlagsanstalt, 1963), p. 301.

23. Boskamp, *Studien zum Frühwerk von Max Liebermann*, pp. 78–85.

24. Martin Buber, "Vorwort," in *Jüdische Künstler*, ed. Martin Buber (Berlin: Jüdischer Verlag, 1903).

25. Georg Hermann was the pen name of Georg Borchardt, Berlin novelist and art historian, and author of the well-known novel *Jettchen Gebert*, a description of Jewish bourgeois life in Berlin during the 1840s. Hermann also worked as city editor of Berlin's most important liberal newspaper, *Berliner Tageblatt*. He was an active supporter of the "Centralverein deutscher Staatsbürger jüdischen Glaubens" (Central Union of German Citizens of Jewish Faith), abbreviated CV, which was Germany's largest Jewish organization, founded in 1893 to safeguard Jewish civil rights and social equality against anti-Semitic attacks. Hermann lived in Berlin until 1933, when he emigrated to Holland. After the German invasion he was deported to Auschwitz, where he died.

26. Georg Hermann, "Max Liebermann," in *Jüdische Künstler*, ed. Martin Buber, pp. 105–35.

27. Martin Buber, letter to Theodor Herzl, 24 July 1902, Central Zionist Archives, Jerusalem, Archive Bezalel, L 42, Z 1/337, letter No. 1672.

28. Supposedly Paul Cassirer (1871–1926), art dealer. (See the essay by Peter Paret in this book.)

29. Hermann Struck (1876–1944), a graphic artist, emigrated to Palestine in 1922 (figs. 48, 152, 153).

30. *Tzitzis* (or *zizit*) refers to the fringed garment worn by observant Jewish men to fulfill the commandments in Num. 15:37–41 and Deut. 22:12.

31. Jozef Israels (1824–1911), Dutch painter, started out as a history painter and became famous for his depictions of the lives of Dutch fishermen and peasants. He was the leading artist of the Hague School, influenced by the Barbizon School in France, which established a new landscape art based on seventeenth-century Dutch masters. He developed a friendship with Max Liebermann, whom he met in the Hague in 1881.

32. Cited in a letter from Martin Buber to Theodor Herzl, 24 July 1902; see n. 27. Reprinted in English in *The Letters of Martin Buber: A Life of Dialogue*, ed. Nahum N. Glatzer and Paul Mendes-Flohr, trans. Richard and Clara Winston and Harry Zohn (New York: Schocken, 1991), pp. 82–83.

33. Karl Scheffler, *Max Liebermann* (Berlin, 1922), p. 19.

34. Max Liebermann, letter to Wilhelm von Bode, 27 August 1905, in *Künstlerbriefe aus dem 19. Jahrhundert*, ed. Else Cassirer, p. 405.

35. Georg Herlitz and Bruno Kirschner, eds., *Jüdisches Lexikon*, vol. 3 (Berlin: Jüdischer Verlag, 1929), col. 934.

36. Ibid., col. 1107.

37. Matthias Eberle, *Max Liebermann: Werkverzeichnis der Gemälde und Ölstudien*, vol. 1: 1865–1899 (Munich: Hirmer, 1995), p. 455.

38. Julius Meier-Graefe, *Entwicklungsgeschichte der modernen Kunst*, 1st ed., vol. 2 (Stuttgart: Verlag Julius Hoffmann, 1904).

39. Meier-Graefe, *Entwicklungsgeschichte der modernen Kunst*, 2d ed., vol. 2 (Munich: Piper, 1920), pp. 324–25.

40. Ibid.

41. Scheffler, *Max Liebermann*, pp. 13–22.

42. Ibid.

43. Ludwig Justi, *Max Liebermann. Bemerkungen zu den Gemälden Liebermanns in der Nationalgalerie* (Berlin, 1921), p. 299.

44. Shulamit Volkov, "Selbstgefälligkeit und Selbsthass," in *Jüdisches Leben und Antisemitismus im 19. und 20. Jahrhundert*, ed. Shulamit Volkov (Munich: C. H. Beck, 1990), p. 185.

45. Ludwig Geiger, "Max Liebermann als Maler der Seinigen," *Allgemeine Zeitung des Judentums* 81 (1917): 452.

46. Anja Galinat, "Die Bilder der Max-Liebermann-Gedächtnisausstellung 1936," in *"Was vom Leben übrig bleibt, sind Bilder und Geschichten." Max Liebermann zum 150. Geburtstag: Rekonstruktion der Gedächtnisausstellung des Berliner Jüdischen Museums von 1936*, ed. Hermann Simon (Berlin: Stiftung Neue Synagoge Berlin—Centrum Judaicum, 1997), pp. 178–79.

47. Ernst Braun, "Die Beisetzung Max Liebermanns am 11. Februar 1935: Umstände, Personen, Überlieferungen, Pressereaktionen," *Jahrbuch der Staatlichen Kunstsammlungen Dresden* 17 (1985): 167–86.

48. Karl Scheffler, *Die fetten und die mageren Jahre: Ein Arbeits- und Lebensbericht* (Leipzig/Munich: List, 1946), pp. 354–56.

JUEDISCHER ALMANACH

Jewish Renaissance– Jewish Modernism

5663

Inka Bertz

The "Jewish Renaissance," proclaimed by Martin Buber in 1901,[1] was a German-Jewish cultural movement that sought to create a synthesis between Zionism, Jewish tradition, and modernity.

It was a child of the turn of the century, born from the encounter with the crisis of liberalism, anti-liberal cultural criticism, and modern anti-Semitism. In no small measure, it was also an expression of the broader movement of Jewish cultural and artistic renewal taking place in the late nineteenth and early twentieth centuries, which involved an exchange of ideas between Jews in Germany and Eastern Europe. The emergence of a "Jewish modernism" was connected politically to Zionism and aesthetically to modernist circles in Berlin and Vienna. The movement's program aimed therefore to create a Jewish national culture that was simultaneously part of a broader culture of modernism. This program was reflected in works of literature and art, the founding of journals and publishing houses, and the presentation of important exhibitions. These activities laid the cornerstone for a broader renaissance of Jewish culture in the Weimar Republic, as well as the establishment of many institutions still active in the State of Israel today.

The Crisis of Liberalism

Following the unification of Germany in 1871 and the subsequent ebullient years, Germany entered a deep crisis that was not only economic, but also political and cultural. In speaking of the "extirpation of the German spirit in favor of the 'German Reich,'"[2] Nietzsche was referring to the defeat of the liberal ideas of the 1848 revolution: its nationalism was turned into populist chauvinism by the prevailing military caste; liberalism was reduced to a principle of economic laissez-faire and unhampered free trade, and was held responsible for the social costs of unfettered capitalism. The anti-Semitic movement gained its momentum from the association of Jews with liberalism and capitalism. Where the 1870s and 1880s had marked the crisis of liberalism's political and economic concepts, the 1890s saw a questioning of its cultural and philosophical foundations: the ideas of positivism in the sciences, historicism in the humanities, and, in general, progress in all fields of culture, politics, and economics.

In this context, anti-Semitism turned into something approaching a cultural norm in Germany, a situation to which German Jews reacted in two principal ways. The vast majority, mainly well-established members of the prosperous middle class, organized themselves into the Central Organization of German Citizens of the Jewish Faith, known as the Centralverein or CV, which was dedicated to maintaining the ideals of liberalism and the Enlightenment, understood as a bulwark against the anti-Semitic menace. A small minority, from a younger generation— mostly students and free-floating intellectuals—had lost their trust in this kind of enlightened amelioration. Their stance was similar to that of the many non-Jewish intellectuals whose radical

(opposite)
E. M. Lilien
(Detail) Cover of **Jüdischer Almanach (The Jewish Almanac)**, 1902
Published by Jüdischer Verlag, Berlin, 1902

cultural pessimism and hopes for a reform of all areas of social and cultural life were reflected in calls for a "new beginning," a "return to nature," and a rejection of bourgeois values. The sensibilities of these young German Jews coincided with those of their counterparts in Eastern Europe, whose own cultural critique was directed against the world of their fathers, either bourgeois or traditionally religious. For Russian Jewish students, in particular, a Jewish national home seemed to offer a way past the political dead end of czarism. The emergence in Eastern Europe of a modern, secular Jewish cultural life was in harmony with their broader political aspirations as well as their vision of a unified and thriving Jewish nation.

The Jewish Renaissance and the Zionist Movement

"The Jewish Renaissance unfolds above all under the banner of Zionism," wrote Berthold Feiwel, one of the movement's champions.[3] For his part, Martin Buber saw the Renaissance as the broader, comprehensive movement, and Zionism as one of its "functions," what he referred to as "its conscious will." As Buber explained it, the movement "was created neither by so-called political Zionism, a more or less justified term, nor by the far older modern Zionism as such. But the reverse is certainly true, namely that the Jewish Renaissance gave rise to modern Zionism."[4] Buber conceived the Jewish Renaissance as one aspect of an international "renaisssance of humanity," a great "modern national-international cultural movement" carried forward by "the souls of nations engaged in self-contemplation."[5] In any event, from today's perspective it appears that, at least in its initial stages, the Renaissance was indeed an offshoot of the Zionist movement.

Forming close personal, artistic, and ideological connections with both the circles of cultural modernism in Vienna and Berlin and Hebrew-language writers from Eastern Europe, the "cultural Zionists," as they were soon called, reinvented and reshaped Jewish traditions according to contemporary needs and sensibilities. The hope was to create a new, cohesive Jewish tradition, based on selected cultural elements, as part of a larger process of national and cultural revival. Younger artists and writers began to view themselves as working within this new tradition, while continuing to rely on the artistic vocabularies furnished by the broader European cultural milieu into which they had been born.

Within the Zionist movement, the Jewish Renaissance was by no means as uncontroversial as Buber and Feiwel seemed to suggest. For one thing, the cultural Zionists ran into resistance from Zionism's political wing, led by Theodor Herzl, whose paramount concern was not "cultural rebirth," but the political and diplomatic struggle for the establishment of a "legally secured homeland in Palestine," as declared in the Basel Manifesto.[6] But the strongest opposition came from the religious Zionists: the idea of a modern national, hence secular, Jewish culture clashed with their conviction that culture and religion were inseparable. The relationship between the political and cultural Zionists was shaped by the fact that Herzl was politically dependent on the religious faction and consequently unwilling to yield to the demand for an active cultural program supported by the Zionist Organization.

Just prior to the Fifth Zionist Congress in 1901, the cultural Zionists formed themselves into the Demokratische Fraktion, or the Democratic Zionist Faction (Democratic Faction). Its founding members included Buber; Berthold Feiwel, editor of *Die Welt* (The World) and other Zionist publications; the graphic artist Ephraim Mose Lilien; Davis Trietsch, who would help guide settlement projects in Cyprus and elsewhere in the Mediterranean region; Chaim Weizmann (later the first president of the State of Israel), who had come to Berlin to study chemistry and became active in the project to create a Jewish university; and Leo Motzkin (then a mathematics student), who would become a leading Zionist Organization figure, active in the campaign to secure the rights of Jewish minorities after the First World War. The Democratic Zionist Faction itself emerged from the Russisch-jüdischer wissenschaftlicher Verein (Russian-Jewish Scientific Society), a group of Russian Jewish students living in Berlin that was ideologically influenced by Ahad Ha'am, as well as by ideas upheld by the *Narodniki*—Russian populist reformers—and competing socialist groups. The Verein also maintained close contacts with former members of Berlin's Jewish nationalist student circles from the 1890s, most of whom came from Germany's eastern regions.

The ideas of the cultural Zionists also were oriented toward the writings of Nathan Birnbaum—later to be a leading figure in the Orthodox Agudath Israel, but at the time still a secular Zionist with close connections to the socialist movement. With regard to cultural activism, the most notable members of this wing of the Zionist movement included Buber; Heinrich Loewe, who would become a prolific writer on Jewish ethnography; Max Jungmann, editor of the satirical magazine *Schlemiehl*; and the physician and author Theodor Zlocisti (FIG. 143). It is important to keep in mind that not only were these figures separated from Theodor Herzl and other Zionist political leaders through internal political and ideological differences; but for the most part, the cultural Zionists were ten to fifteen years younger than their political counterparts, and the gap between their experience and that of

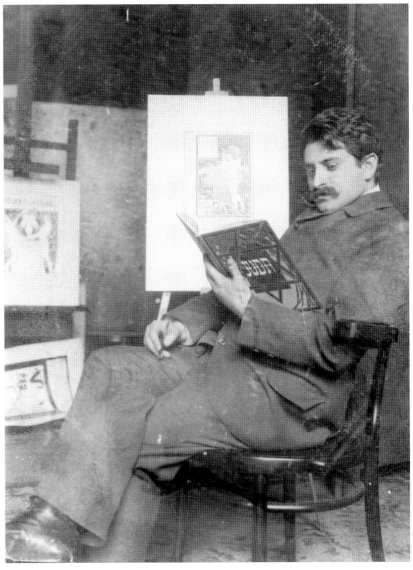

Figure 143
Theodor Zlocisti reading a copy of *Juda* in E. M. Lilien's studio, ca. 1901
Central Zionist Archives, Jerusalem

Herzl was as wide as the gap between their respective visions of culture and politics.

To Herzl, politics meant two things: sessions of the Zionist Congress—the movement's "parliament"—and confidential closed-door negotiations. Politics transpired primarily on the stage of international diplomacy, where Herzl tried to extract a legal guarantee for the Jewish settlement in Palestine from the Ottoman sultan. On the other hand, as revealed in Herzl's utopian novel *Altneuland* (Old–New Land), "culture" meant the Ringstrasse, the State Opera, department stores, and electricity. Herzl did not try to outline the elements of a specifically Jewish culture, or to define its form and essence. In his view, such a culture would develop gradually, in the distant future, and its indispensable precondition was an independent national state. On the whole, his vision remained firmly grounded in basic principles of bourgeois liberalism: representative parliamentarianism, a nation-state under the rule of law, and the equation of culture with modern Europe and the West.

In contrast, the cultural Zionists wished to supplement the political project of Zionism with a cultural program in order to create a comprehensive model of Jewish nationality. Politics to them was not secret diplomacy but *Kulturpolitik*—for which they coined the term *Gegenwartsarbeit*, "work in the present." What they meant was that the spiritual and cultural basis for Jewish nationhood had to be created now, in the Diaspora, and that the distinctive Jewish culture had to be renewed before the Jewish state could be created. Unlike Herzl, the cultural Zionists invoked a Jewish culture rooted in particular traditions; their dissenting position became open in the bitter debate over *Altneuland*, which Ahad Ha'am criticized for offering a universal ideal of modernization, devoid of a particular Jewish character.[7]

Zionism and Bohème

Cultural endeavor had been a part of Germany's liberal-reform Judaism before the rise of Zionism and the Jewish Renaissance: examples are the Societies for Jewish History and Literature and the circles around the *Allgemeine Zeitung des Judentums*, an influential German Jewish weekly. However, the project of the Jewish Renaissance needs to be distinguished from such institutions and activities in a number of crucial ways: it was linked to the Zionist movement; it rejected assimilation as its cultural reference point and liberalism as its political ideal; it turned its back on a historicist aesthetics; and finally, it had the character of a youth revolt, assuming an anti-bourgeois stance.

The boundaries between cultural-Zionist and bohemian circles were, in fact, fluid. Apart from casual encounters in artists' cafés, figures like the artist E. M. Lilien and, apparently, Berthold Feiwel met with Börries von Münchhausen (whose ballads Lilien illustrated) and Stefan Zweig (who published a monograph on the Jugendstil artist Lilien) in the Nollendorf Casino, a venue for the circle known as Die Kommenden (the Up-and-Coming), centered on the personality and ideas of Rudolf Steiner. (See the essay by Sigrid Bauschinger in this book.) Many representatives of the *Lebensreform*, or "life-reform" movement,[8] were associated with the Kommenden (FIG. 144), among them the popular draftsman Fidus; the sex researcher Magnus Hirschfeld; Adolf Brand, publisher of the homosexual magazine *Der Eigene*; and Karl Vanselow, publisher of the magazine *Schönheit* (Beauty). Mention also should be made of Franz Oppenheimer, who was planning projects for housing communes such as the Eden colony.

We know about Martin Buber's (FIG. 11) contacts with the Neue Gemeinschaft (New Community) circle around the brothers Heinrich and Julius Hart; under its auspices, Buber lectured on the mystic writings of Jakob Böhme. Buber also met Herwarth Walden (FIG. 54) in the Neue Gemeinschaft (FIG. 53), along with Else Lasker-Schüler (FIG. 51), Gustav Landauer (FIG. 168), Henry van de Velde, Felix Holländer, Ludwig von Hofmann, Walter Leistikow, Wilhelm Boelsche, and, once again, Fidus—a medley of artists, intellectuals, bohemians, and propagandists for the *Lebensreform* movement very similar to the sort of people one would find among the Kommenden.

The headings on a Neue Gemeinschaft program announcement included catchwords and phrases that would appear in similar or identical form in the writings of the Jewish Renaissance. We read, of course, of a "new community," and of an "order of the true life," and slogans calling for "the new person," "the overcoming of differences," "segregation into community," and "a celebratory way of living." Borrowing from Michael Georg Conrad, who has spoken of the mixture of "salon culture and socialism" typical of Munich around 1895, we might speak of a juncture of "salon culture and Zionism" in Berlin around 1900. This connection enabled the cultural Zionists to establish contacts with writers, artists, and critics who otherwise would have tended toward skepticism regarding Zionism as a national movement. When in 1902, a group of cultural Zionists founded the Jüdischer Verlag and published their first volume, the *Jüdischer Almanach* (see page 164), they included numerous works by writers and graphic artists ordinarily not known as doctrinaire Zionists—Karl Wolfskehl, for instance, as well as Georg Hirschfeld, Stefan Zweig, Ephraim Frisch, Issak Lewitan, and Jozef Israels; even Max Liebermann (FIG. 20) contributed a few illustrations. What linked these individuals was a vaguely formulated idea of Jewish culture and a "modern national-international cultural movement."

Figure 144
E. M. Lilien
Invitation postcard for **Die Kommenden (The Up-and-Coming)**, 1899–1900
Stiftung Jüdisches Museum, Berlin

In many respects, the Jewish Renaissance was a Jewish embodiment of the reform movement sweeping the German-speaking world at the turn of the century, and it shared the movement's social circles, aesthetics, and political slogans. Like many other reformist currents, the Renaissance was not so much a firmly established movement in its own right, or a cogent ideology, as a "sensibility,"[9] describing itself in organic metaphors of growth and development. In a 1902 article in *Ost und West* (East and West), Nathan Birnbaum spoke of a movement of "language creation, cultural becoming, a process of searching for and finding oneself":

> None of the parties and individuals active in this movement dictate its path. . . . Instead, the movement itself, aroused in the Jewish soul by the general process of economic and intellectual development, whirls the individual out of the mass, fuses the parties together and leads them, every which way, toward its own goals— goals that for the time being are not very clear. All parties are still essentially premature babies with large embryo heads and scrawny bodies. The nation still needs to be nursed along, a thousand path-ends still need to be tracked, so that at a thousand path-ends its spirit and body are continually replenished—so that its expressive powers grow, its innate spirituality blossoms, its urge to unite grows ever stronger, and all these gifts are adapted to the modern times in which we live and in which it is a joy to live.[10]

Since it was Birnbaum who first made use of the slogan "Jewish Modernism," in *Die jüdische Moderne*, a book published in Leipzig in 1896 under his pen name, Matthias Acher,[11] his remarks raise the question of the actual difference between the ideas of "Jewish Renaissance" and "Jewish Modernism."[12] The year 1896 also saw the publication of a very small and short-lived magazine also entitled *Die jüdische Moderne*, in which the publisher Max Jungmann presented examples of Berlin's literary modernism alongside the most recent Yiddish and Hebrew literature. The magazine's regular contributors included Samuel Lublinski, who would later offer reassessments of both the literary movement and the general concept of modernism.[13] (See the essay by Sigrid Bauschinger in this book.) Indebted to the then popular Jugendstil aesthetic, the agenda of the "Jewish Renaissance" was more radical than that of "Jewish Modernism," and was formulated with greater consistency; nevertheless, there is too little difference between the concepts to explain why the cultural Zionists would come to prefer the term *Renaissance* to *Moderne*. After all, Buber himself considered the Jewish Renaissance a part of the "modern cultural movement." And the journal *Ost und West*, for a number of years the most important mouthpiece of the cultural

Zionists, had the subtitle *Illustrierte Zeitschrift für modernes Judentum* (Illustrated Journal of Modern Judaism). Similarly, Herzl's pioneering tract *Der Judenstaat* (The Jewish State), published in the same year as Birnbaum's booklet *Die jüdische Moderne* was subtitled *Versuch einer modernen Lösung der Judenfrage* (An Attempt at a Modern Solution to the Jewish Question).

To be sure, Herzl and Buber entertained different notions of *Moderne*, reflecting their different conceptions of culture and politics. Although Herzl was as familiar as Buber with Vienna's literary and artistic life, in *Der Judenstaat* (The Jewish State) as in *Altneuland*, he uses the term *Moderne* in the sense of political and ideological modernization, social modernity rather than literary modernism. Buber, on the other hand, always identified the Jewish Renaissance with modernity's expression in literature and the graphic arts. In other words, while Herzl subscribed to the bourgeois and liberal notion that art and politics were separate spheres, Buber did not accept that distinction; in line with the cultural criticism of his time, he was striving to merge "art" and "life."

One reason for favoring the term *Renaissance* over *Moderne* may have been the inherent ambiguity of the latter option; a more important, yet related, reason may have been the essential ahistoricism of the notion of modernity: its stress on the fleeting and the transitory, central to its aesthetic theory.[14] This emphasis clashed with the need, at the dawn of the twentieth century, to supply the project of a national Jewish culture with historical legitimacy. In this historicist period, the idea of a national culture demanded historical precedents in traditions that had experienced cultural rebirth;[15] in contrast to the term *Moderne*, the term *Renaissance* implicitly signified historical legitimacy. Its use suggests how strongly the historicist thinking of the nineteenth century was still at play.

In fact, this was the time in which the cult of the Renaissance flourished, a cult with which Buber and his colleagues were very much in tune. Since the appearance of Jacob Burckhardt's masterpiece *The Culture of the Renaissance in Italy* (1860)—and particularly for Nietzsche, as for the heroic vitalist Gabriele d'Annunzio and the notorious pioneer of racist theory, the Comte de Gobineau—the Renaissance was regarded as the epoch of the "birth of the individual," of the autonomous, active, universally educated, and creative personality; for all the ironies that now seem manifest in the situation, this notion was important to the cultural Zionists as well. The "new Jew" they upheld as their ideal very much resembled the Nietzschean Renaissance man, or *Renaissancemensch*.[17]

About a decade later, there is a shift in emphasis on the part of Buber and other writers, from the image of the Jew as a "new," renascent individual to an emphasis on *Erlebnis*, the inner, essential experience of the individual Jew.[18] Buber and a new generation of Zionist intellectuals had now taken up the concept of *Lebensphilosophie* (vitalism), which found its most sophisticated expression in the work of Wilhelm Dilthey. Conflicts within the

Figure 145
Founders of the Jüdischer Verlag, 1902
(*Seated*: Berthold Feiwel, Martin Buber;
Standing: E. M. Lilien, Chaim Weizmann,
Davis Trietsch)
Stiftung Jüdisches Museum, Berlin

Zionist movement, and cultural disparities between Eastern and Western Jews, had demonstrated that Herzl's slogan "the Jews are a single people, a single people" would be difficult to realize. The mystique of *Erlebnis*, or "lived experience," provided a common denominator more grounded in individual experience than in shared communal traditions. This "essentialist turn" also offered a solution to the problem of historicism, the contradiction between the ahistorical character of modernist aesthetics and the need to base the new national culture on historical precedents. The notion of *Erlebnis* served, in fact, to bring together modernism's emphasis on the individual and transitory with the idea of an essential Jewish identity that could be expressed through artistic creativity.

The Artist as Educator

The young cultural Zionists did not simply move in artistic circles and adopt artistic slogans; they also regarded themselves as artists and pursued artistic endeavors: Martin Buber wrote poetry as well as philosophical essays, as did Nathan Birnbaum, Theodor Zlocisti, and Berthold Feiwel. Among the visual artists were the graphic artist E. M. Lilien and the sculptors Alfred Nossig and Boris Schatz: the latter founded Jerusalem's Bezalel School of Arts and Crafts in 1906. Many cultural Zionists were thus already responding to Buber's appeal not to be Zionist "the way one is conservative and liberal, but the way one is a human being or an artist."[19] Feiwel's description of the role of the *Schaffenden*, the "creative person," in the Jewish Renaissance can also be read as reflecting the identity and self-perception of its advocates: "But out of the wealth that will be created and offered by the alliance of men of spirit, the nation will gain new trust in its value and future destiny."[20] The task of the "creative person" was no less than "leading the nation to its true self," the artist thus taking on the role of "educator."[21]

It was in order to fulfill such a role that four members of the Democratic Faction—Buber, Feiwel, Trietsch, and Lilien—founded the Jüdischer Verlag in Berlin in 1902 (FIG. 145). "All publications," their program announced, "even the simplest and cheapest, will be designed and printed in a manner never before attempted by a Jewish publishing house. Thus they will have an educational effect through their appearance alone."[22] "We wish to create a Jewish cultural work," they added, "and even more so, to help pass it on, since we have called into being a center for the promotion of Jewish literature, art, and scholarship."[23] Their publishing house was not meant to serve as a mere business venture, but as a kind of cultural center.[24]

Whereas the cultural Zionists' use of the concepts of renaissance and modernity reflected the aesthetic debates of their time, their notion of a cultural center is indebted to the Russian Jewish thinker Ahad Ha'am (in Hebrew, "One of the People," the pen name of Asher Ginsberg), illustrating the ambivalent impact of the East European Jewish intelligentsia on the Jewish Renaissance movement in Berlin.[25] As early as 1892, Ahad Ha'am had criticized the settlement projects in Palestine, calling instead for a *merkaz ruhani*, or "spiritual national center" in the Holy Land, "a place that would be a refuge, not for the Jews but for Judaism, for our national spirit."[26]

This elitist notion of a center from which the new culture would radiate and be diffused had already been propounded by the *Narodniki* as well as by contemporary reform movements in Germany[27]—facts that facilitated its adoption by the cultural Zionists. But as with other ideas of Ahad Ha'am, his notion of a *merkaz ruhani* was adopted in a rather eclectic manner. For the most part, the cultural Zionists embraced his anti-assimilationist polemics; but selected essays of his were translated into German only after the Jüdischer Verlag was founded, when direct contact between Ahad Ha'am and Buber was also established. Although members of the Democratic Faction such as Chaim Weizmann and Leo Motzkin had been introduced into Ahad Ha'am's secret society of the Bnei Moshe, they were very young and had little direct contact with Ahad Ha'am himself, living as they did outside its central circles in Warsaw and Odessa. Although the Berlin cultural Zionists would contend otherwise later, the figure of Ahad Ha'am—as a renowned unassimilated Jew who supported and sustained the post-assimilationist attitude of the Western cultural Zionists—was more a symbol than a central philosophical source for their activities. Their references to Ahad Ha'am can be seen as a way of granting a Judaic essence to a cultural politics shaped primarily by influences outside the Jewish camp.[28]

The Cultural Sphere

Even if the ambitious goal of creating a cultural center was
scarcely feasible, the ideal of a Jewish Renaissance took on reality
through the gradual emergence of a Jewish cultural sphere. During the period between the turn of the century and World War I,
initially small reading circles and similar groups gave rise to a
network of publishers, writers, and artists who launched journals
and publishing houses through which they promulgated their
artistic work and program. Along with organizing lectures, readings, recitals, and art exhibitions, they initiated more permanent
projects—some not to be realized until after the Great War—such
as the Bezalel art school and a national university and national
library in Jerusalem. There were also a number of activities reflecting the emergence of a new physical culture (as well as the practical side of the turn toward *Lebensphilosophie*)—for example, the
gymnastics practiced in the Bar Kochba sports club, founded in
1898, and the hiking tours of the Jewish Youth Movement, which
developed during the years before the war. Alongside these activities were efforts to establish Jewish garden cities and settlements
in Palestine and to realize political autonomy for the Jewish
minorities in Eastern Europe.

The medium through which these various activities were most
effectively amalgamated and publicized was the journal, which
accurately reflected the Jewish cultural movement's strongly
intellectual character as well as its broad geographic base. The
existence of a prewar lingua franca—German—facilitated communication and allowed these journals to circulate throughout
Central and Eastern Europe. In Berlin, short-lived literary magazines such as *Die jüdische Moderne* and *Zion* emerged in Jewish
student circles in the 1890s. These magazines included essays
on cultural themes, as did, to a lesser extent, the official Zionist
party papers, *Die Welt*—the journal of the World Zionist Organization, launched in 1897—and the *Jüdische Rundschau* (The Jewish Review), first published in 1902 as the organ of the German
Zionist Organization.

The journal that eventually developed into the most important and lasting pre–World War I organ of the Jewish Renaissance
was *Ost und West* (FIG. 146), established in 1901 by Leo Winz,
Davis Trietsch, and a large circle of co-editors. In its conception
and design, it resembled other illustrated cultural reviews of
the time such as *Der Kunstwart* (The Guardian of Art) and *Die
Jugend* (Youth). It offered an assortment of political, historical,
and literary essays, as well as briefer pieces, fiction, poetry, and
fine arts. Although its board of editors included Zionists and
others, it was the young cultural Zionists who essentially shaped
its contents. The journal's title underscored one of the important
goals of the Jewish Renaissance: overcoming the divisions
between Jews in Eastern and Western Europe, and fusing the
groups into a new Jewish culture. The East was to contribute
a Jewish tradition that had remained authentic and vital, and

the West would respond with its vibrant and modern mores and values.

Aesthetics as a Communicative System

For most of the reform movements in the German cultural sphere around 1900, modern style was a way of staking the claim for a renewal that went far beyond aesthetics. Both the *Lebensreform* and the labor movement designed their pamphlets and magazines in the new Jugendstil; the free flow of its ornament became the visual equivalent of their demand for freedom and vision of a better future. At the same time, movements of aesthetic renewal such as the Deutscher Werkbund (German Association of Crafts-men) combined a call for aesthetic renewal with far-ranging social and political ideas. The Werkbund did not promote the new art for its own sake, but with the goal of educating the taste of the masses, as well as cultivating the national pride in solid material and design and—no less important—the possibility of increasing exports.

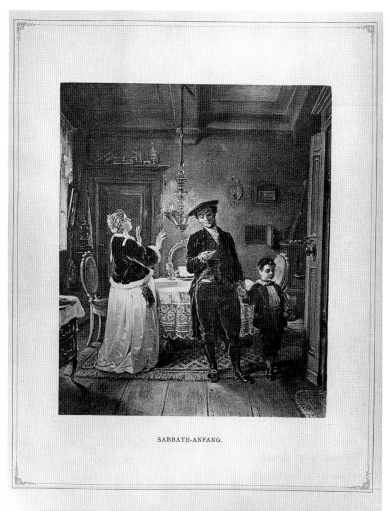

SABBATH-ANFANG.

In a society where, from the perspective of aesthetic reform movements, art had descended to the level of mere decoration, the hope of merging the aesthetic and the political was part of a broader effort at radical social criticism. The desire to break down the division between "art" and "life" challenged one of the key premises of liberal-bourgeois society and culture: the autonomy of the aesthetic sphere. With this challenge, art took on a crucial political and aesthetic role—also present in Zionism, where aesthetics became a system for negotiating issues of Jewish identity and consciousness. Art provided role models in the struggle to define what it meant to be a Jew and to shape a Jewish self-image. Works by Jewish artists were thus introduced as integral elements of both the Jewish communal sphere and Zionist culture. To be sure, the discourse about Jewish art was based not so much on coherent theories or philosophical concepts as on this "new sensibility," with the concept of renaissance—signifying *the* era of the "sense of beauty"—contributing its share.

In formulating their own aesthetic project, spokesmen of the Jewish Renaissance took up the motif of "refinement" through beauty so common in social and political reformist movements of the time. Thus we find the founders of the Jüdischer Verlag declaring: "Alongside the Jewish ethical ideal, which once again will give the Jewish people unity and resolve, a national and personal self-confidence, the goal is to build up the Jewish aesthetic ideal." Unity, resolve, and self-confidence are here linked to the ethical ideals of Judaism, while its aesthetic dimension is associated with the emotions: "Something deeply internal and soulful, a new power, a new beauty, would flow into a new Jewish concept of life."[29]

In both literature and music, forms of specifically "Jewish" artistic creation had long since been acknowledged—for instance, Jewish folk music, Yiddish and Hebrew literature. By contrast, in the visual arts, especially painting, no tradition of "Jewish art" had been established—a fact unaltered by the presence of a few figures such as Moritz Daniel Oppenheim, the popular nineteenth-century painter of eighteenth-century Jewish family life (FIG. 147). At the turn of the century, the journals and almanacs reflecting the ideals of the Jewish Renaissance provided a forum for the earliest theoretical debates about the nature of Jewish visual arts. In those debates, we can discern a number of recurring arguments. One was that Jewish art served to counter the anti-Semitic prejudice that Jews were incapable of true creative achievement, in general, and achievement in the visual arts, in particular. Another argument was that Jewish art itself constituted visible proof that a Jewish Renaissance was indeed taking place. Finally, the discourse on Jewish art provided a way of distinguishing the Zionist ideal of the "new" Jew from the "old" Jew of the Diaspora. Life in the Diaspora—notably oppression in the ghetto—so the Zionist thesis ran, caused Jews to lose their sense of beauty, along with their national pride. It was regarded as essential to regain that aesthetic sensibility, not least as preparation for life in a Jewish country.

Although he later was to claim that "noise and motion, not shape and color, are the forms of artistic expression most appropriate to the Jews,"[30] it was Martin Buber who first formulated a theory of Jewish art in the Jewish Renaissance context. In light of Buber's later role in making Hasidic mysticism popular and shaping a romantic image of East European Jewry and the shtetl,[31] the position he took around the turn of the century may seem surprising:

> For thousands and thousands of years, we were an unfruitful people. During the exile, the surplus of spiritual power we *always* had expressed itself only in an indescribably one-sided intellectual activity, making our eyes blind to all the beauty of nature and of life. . . . Whenever the longing for beauty rose up with shy and tender limbs, it was suppressed with an invisible and pitiless hand. . . . It was the entrance of the Jews into Western civilization that made possible the great shift whose first fruits we are seeing in our present age. I wish to emphasize this because recently a peculiar ghetto sentimentality has taken hold in many Zionist circles. In thus focusing on the strange beauty of the

closed-off folk-life we led in Europe into the eighteenth century, an important fact has been forgotten: that the modern Jewish national movement—that Zionism—could not have emerged without the remarkable stage in our people's development wrongly termed "emancipation". . . . But when in Europe's life, a healthy national self-consciousness replaced a bloodless ideal of humanity—when the view prevailed that just as every human being, every people best serves the universal by engaging its own gifts in fruitful creation—when the national recognition of what *is* had began to fuse with the social recognition of what *should be*—then again, it was our marriage with Western civilization that now allowed us to unfold our primeval urge for vital national expression, which made itself manifest over the centuries either as sultry-ardent lament or wild, messianic ecstasy, in the modern form that we have come to name Zionism.[32]

Buber thus saw the Zionist movement as part of the European national movements that emerged at the start of the nineteenth century. Articulating the importance of a national art in his keynote address at the Fifth Zionist Congress in 1901, Buber rejected the idea of art's "internationality," since "in artistic creation, the nation's specific qualities express themselves most purely; everything belonging to this people alone, the unique and incomparable of its individuality, discovers its palpable living shape in its art. In this way our art represents the most beautiful path of our people to itself." Buber consequently assigned art a threefold role: it was, first of all, "a great educator," offering people a sense of their identity; second, a "strong herald," helping to sway individual hearts to the Zionist cause; and third, a "cultural document," proof of the new, developing Jewish self-identity—"we will observe and recognize ourselves."

Figure 148
E. M. Lilien
Postcard commemorating the Fifth
Zionist Congress, ca. 1901
Stiftung Jüdisches Museum, Berlin

Nevertheless, Buber openly admitted that authentic Jewish art could be created by Jews only in their own homeland:

What we call Jewish art is no *being* but a *becoming*, no fulfillment but a beautiful possibility, just as today's Zionism is a becoming and a beautiful possibility. . . . A national Jewish art needs a unified human community from which it springs and for which it exists. We have only fragments of a community. . . . A whole and completed Jewish art will only be possible on Jewish soil, just as a whole and completed Jewish culture in general. But what we now have are cultural buds, art-buds; these must be nurtured here on strange shores with a tender, loving hand, until we can plant them in their home soil—the only soil within which they will be able to fully blossom.

In December 1901, Buber and Lilien presented some of these vitalist fin-de-siècle "seeds" to the public and delegates to the Fifth Zionist Congress in the first exhibition of modern Jewish art. The venue was the Stadtkasino in Basel, where the Zionist Congress was taking place. The exhibition showed work by Lesser Ury, Lilien, Hermann Struck, Alfred Nossig, Jozef Israels, and—interestingly—Eduard Bendemann, a baptized nineteenth-century artist of Jewish origin.[33] During the following years, a canon of what was regarded as Jewish art gradually emerged with the help of illustrations in *Ost und West,* the *Jüdischer Almanach,* and the anthology *Jüdische Künstler.* In addition to the artists already mentioned, the canon would embrace the work of Solomon J. Solomon, Jehudo Epstein, Mark Antokolski, Henryk Glicenstein, Maurycy Gottlieb, and Samuel Hirszenberg, along with Max Liebermann—the most prominent of Berlin's painters—Leonid Pasternak, and even Camille Pissarro. This canon was thus characterized by a multitude of styles, ranging from academic history painting to Naturalism, Impressionism, and Jugendstil. Expressionism would join the ranks in the years following the Great War.

What qualified a work of art as Jewish was primarily its themes, as well as the artist's evident sympathy with the experiences and characters the work portrayed. Sometimes this was accompanied by a quasi-psychological or ethnic argument—for instance, Buber's attributing the preference for glowing colors in Ury's landscapes (see FIGS. 103, 104) to the artist's "Oriental" heritage. The "Jewish sensibility" of an artist replaced subject matter as a vague but crucial category in Jewish art criticism.[34]

Figure 149
Lesser Ury
Jeremiah (Jeremias), ca. 1897
Charcoal on board, 16⁷⁄₁₆ x 17³⁄₄ in.
(41.8 x 45.1 cm)
Stiftung Jüdisches Museum, Berlin

Figure 150
Entrance hall of the Jewish Museum, Berlin
Opening date, 24 January 1933
On the left wall: Jakob Steinhardt's *The Prophet* (fig. 154); on the back wall: Lesser Ury's *Jeremiah* (fig. 96).

Images of Judaism

In the realm of design and style, praxis was more successful than theory, and frequently more to the point. For example, during the few years in which he was active, E. M. Lilien's graphic art succeeded in leaving a lasting imprint on the appearance of not only cultural-Zionist publications, but also those of the broader Zionist movement. Lilien designed the book jackets, title pages, and endpapers of the *Jüdischer Almanach* as well as *Ost und West* (see FIG. 146); and his decorative elements and vignettes appeared on program sheets and other printed material put out by the Zionist movement, including his design of a postcard commemorating the Fifth Zionist Congress (see FIG. 148). Influenced by the Munich Jugendstil and the English Arts and Crafts movement, he introduced into Zionism an aestheticism similar to that popular in the labor and *Lebensreform* movements. Lilien's work celebrated the

Figure 151
Lesser Ury
Study for **Moses on Mount Nebo**
(Moses auf dem Berg Nebo),
1927–28
Pastel, 26¾ x 20½ in. (68 x 52 cm)
Stiftung Jüdisches Museum, Berlin

image of the "new Jew" in a bare, muscular body, clad in severe, Egyptianizing ornamentation; the godparents of such images were the vitalist ideal of physical beauty and an Orientalism especially fashionable in the French decorative arts.

A different vision of the Orient is manifest in Lesser Ury's biblical heroes. While Lilien's Jugendstil imagery soon fell out of fashion in the Zionist movement, and Lilien himself eventually turned his back on this pictorial vocabulary, Ury's monumental biblical scenes represented—until the end of his creative activity in 1931—a striking contrast to his sketchy, airy depictions of street life in Berlin. (See the essay by Emily Bilski in this book.) In a letter to Buber, Ury claimed that the impressionistic pieces were merely the work that paid the bills, enabling him to create his monumental biblical paintings.[35] Doubtless, it was the sheer size of the biblical paintings that made them hard to sell. They required a public space, and, in fact, some of them were placed in Jewish public spaces: both a *Rebecca* and *David and Jonathan* by Lesser Ury hung in the large meeting hall of the B'nai B'rith Lodge; *Jeremiah*, 1897 (FIGS. 96, 149), found its place in the entrance hall of the Jewish Museum in Berlin (FIG. 150), although not until after Ury's death. *Moses on Mount Nebo* (FIG. 151) formed the centerpiece of the middle hall in the Jewish pavilion at the Pressa exhibition in Cologne in 1928.

In these works, Ury offered modern historical painting suitable for Jewish communal exhibition. The paintings do not contain the sort of luminous figures, drawn with beautiful lines, that we find in Lilien's work, but instead massive, superhuman forms. Their archaic coarseness was an entirely intentional stylistic device. Ury's scenes are located in an atemporal mythical realm; unmistakably defined as the ancient Near East, it is a setting from which the architectural and pictorial "new monumentalism" of the period also took its cue.[36]

Yet another image of Judaism, different from that presented through Lilien's Jugendstil and Orientalism and Ury's historical monumentalism, was offered by Hermann Struck in his portraits of anonymous, mostly elderly men (FIG. 152); frequently reproduced in Jewish publications of the turn of the century, these portraits bore a clear-cut debt to Rembrandt.[37] Rembrandt was especially popular in Jewish circles; his oeuvre offers one of the rare examples in art history of a highly sympathetic depiction of Jewish life and culture. Employing darkish, moody coloring, the Dutch painter Jozef Israels (1824–1911) would serve as a mediator between Rembrandt's tradition and modern Jewish art. Struck, in turn, was indebted to Rembrandt's pictorial language in presenting an image of the Jew imbued with the deep "inner" values of Rembrandt's art.

As one of the very few observant Jews close to cultural-Zionist circles, and as a member of Mizrahi, the modern Orthodox Zionist movement, Struck's concern was to furnish the image of the religious Jew with dignity and emotional depth (FIGS. 152, 153). His personal relations with the cultural Zionists, and with his colleague Lilien in particular, were hardly close, and seem to have been sometimes troubled.[38] His role within Berlin's Jewish art world can nonetheless hardly be overestimated, his studio becoming *the* meeting place for young Jewish artists arriving in Berlin, whom he was always ready to help through his many contacts.[39] Struck was, in fact, the teacher of almost all these artists—Jakob Steinhardt, Ludwig Meidner, Joseph Budko, Regina Mundlak, Abraham Palukst. It is well known that Chagall learned etching from Struck, a result being the portfolio *Mein Leben*; Else Lasker-Schüler also regarded him as her teacher.[40]

The Avant-Garde and Jewish Culture

The first decade of the Jewish Renaissance was a period of theoretical planning and of large-scale projects that often could not be realized until after World War I. Around 1910, a second generation stepped forward within the Zionist movement; it was in part allied with the original cultural Zionists, some of whom were now well established within the Zionist Organization. This new generation championed a radical, decision-oriented idealism of "action," again typical of its time. This development, along with the sharpening conflict with the Centralverein, led to a broad radicalization of ideological positions, an atmosphere leaving little room for

Figure 152
Hermann Struck
**Old Jew from Jaffa
[Alter Jude aus Jaffe]**, 1905
Etching, 8 3/16 x 5 13/16 in. (20.6 x 14.9 cm)
The Jewish Museum, New York. Gift of Mr. and Mrs. Peter Addelston in honor of the memory of Mrs. Tillie E. Hyman and Dr. and Mrs. Harold K. Addelston

Figure 153
Hermann Struck
Everyone Who Mourns Jerusalem Reaps Its Joy [At the Wailing Wall], ca. 1905
Lithograph, 13 x 10¾ in. (33 x 27.3 cm)
The Jewish Museum, New York.
Gift of Dr. and Mrs. George Wechsler

art and literature to flourish. There was, however, considerable intellectual debate, particularly when, after an absence of several years, Buber returned to the Zionist pulpit, delivering his *Drei Reden über das Judentum* (Three Talks on Judaism) in Prague in 1909–10. A new intellectual group had emerged in Prague's Bar Kochba student organization; it included Robert Weltsch, later the editor, for many years, of the *Jüdische Rundschau*; Shmuel Hugo Bergmann, future director of the National Library in Jerusalem; the historian Hans Kohn; the novelist Max Brod; and, only loosely connected with this group, Brod's friend Franz Kafka.

World War I forced a general clarification of perspectives among Jewish intellectuals. For many, the war marked a turning point in their lives. First sharing the patriotic emotions that were sweeping Germany, welcoming the struggle against a Russian empire so oppressive toward the Jews, they would discover that, once the fortunes of war turned against the fatherland, the "truce" at home could quickly succumb to anti-Semitic passion. A major step in this direction was the humiliating "Jew count" at the front, ordered by the War Ministry in 1916 and initiated by anti-Semitic

Figure 154
Jakob Steinhardt
The Prophet (Der Prophet), 1913
Oil on canvas,
90½ x 70⅞ in. (230 x 180 cm)
Jüdische Gemeinde, Berlin.
© Stiftung "Neue Synagoge Berlin–
Centrum Judaicum"

members of the Reichstag. The sense of alienation from one's com-
rades-in-arms clashed with feelings of solidarity experienced by soldiers encountering Lithuanian Jews near the
Eastern Front, and led many Jewish soldiers
to a new awareness of their Jewish identity.
As in 1900, new Jewish journals such as *Der
Jude* and *Neue jüdische Monatshefte* (New Jewish Monthly) were launched during the war.
This "second" Jewish Renaissance, however,
did not seek the official support of the Zionist movement and its institutions.

Figure 155
Jakob Steinhardt
Pogrom, 1913
Etching on paper,
5⅛ x 7½ in. (13.4 x 19.3 cm)
Stiftung Jüdisches Museum, Berlin

In the wake of the surge in bibliophilic
book production around 1920, a large number of new—sometimes short-lived—publishing houses also emerged, producing
graphic works or illustrated books on Jewish
themes; in contrast to the prewar period, a
number of general publishers were involved, including Georg
Müller in Munich and Erich Reiss in Berlin. In the sphere of
graphic art, the most important new publishing house was the
Verlag für jüdische Kunst und Kultur Fritz Gurlitt (see FIG. 156).
Under the direction of Karl Schwarz, later director of the first
Jewish Museum in Berlin, it was a branch of the well-established
art gallery of Wolfgang Gurlitt (himself a non-Jew).

The visual language of Expressionism now also found its way,
belatedly, into the Jewish cultural sphere; Fritz Gurlitt's press
published books and albums containing original works by Ludwig
Meidner, Joseph Budko, and, especially, Jakob Steinhardt. When
in 1912—in their roles as Pathetiker—both Meidner and Steinhardt had exhibited in Herwarth Walden's gallery Der Sturm, the
Zionist press made no mention of their work, despite the inclu-
sion of many paintings of biblical subjects (FIG. 154). We should
note the obvious lack of interest in Zionism on the part of these
artists: inevitably, the Pathetiker had contacts with many Jewish
writers and painters, but members of the group saw themselves as
affiliated, above all, with a broad avant-garde movement.

Rooted in the Greek term for suffering, the name these artists
chose for their group, *Die Pathetiker*, sheds light on a self-perception
at work in both Jewish and non-Jewish circles. *Pathos* was a key
term for Buber in his *Three Talks on Judaism*, denoting a particularly
Jewish "sensibility": the situation of being torn between two worlds,
the capacity for deep spiritual experience, and for suffering and
compassion—all of this prefigured in the "pathos of the prophets."
As Buber states, "whoever confronts the pathos of his inner struggles will discover that something continues to live within him
having its great, primeval national image in the struggle of the
prophets against the diverging multitude of the people's drives."[41]

Leaving aside Buber's evocation of the biblical prophets, a
similar notion of pathos was at work in the art criticism of the
period. Wilhelm Hausenstein, for example, distinguished among
various artistic states of mind: "Some encounter nature with a

Figure 156
Jakob Steinhardt
**Red and Glowing Is the Eye
of the Jew (Rot und glühend ist
das Auge des Juden)**
Woodcut, cover for book
Published by Verlag für jüdische Kunst
und Kultur Fritz Gurlitt, Berlin, 1920
Stiftung Jüdisches Museum, Berlin

certain inner tranquillity, others nervously, yet others with great pathos."[42] The ecstatic-pathetic character was given the highest value in this typology; we thus find a valorizing both of deep spiritual experience and heroic posture—the "pathetic" artist portrayed as tragic seer or prophet without honor.

It is perhaps not surprising that this self-image of the artist, not a little presumptuous, was thrown into radical question by the experience of the Great War. After his own encounter with the Jews of Poland and Lithuania, Steinhardt regarded the prophetic pathos of his prewar work as a mere pose. He now turned chiefly to themes from East European Jewish life. The spiritual remained an important dimension in his work, but his perspective had changed: his interest was no longer focused on the individual, the prophet, the almost "superhuman," but on the community, the family, the shtetl (see FIGS. 155, 156).

For the former Pathetiker, this connection to the Jewish cultural sphere was sought only after some distance had been taken from the avant-garde, when Expressionism had been declared passé by many of those who had championed it a decade earlier.[43] Strikingly, this state of affairs allowed Jewish artists to address a broader audience, for whom images of the shtetl served as a form of contact with a largely assimilated Jewish identity. In any event, it is important to take account of a particular reason for the increased separation of the avant-garde from the Jewish cultural sphere around 1910: the new character of the emerging modernist movements, of their social views and artistic preoccupations. In 1900, groups like Die Neue Gemeinschaft still had a critical or reformist approach to social questions, and the artist saw his role as largely pedagogic; in 1910, this perception had shifted to the role of "prophet without honor."

Social isolation and the artist's alienation from the public now became a dominant theme—for example, in the journal *Das neue Pathos* (see FIG. 119). Artists sought to overcome their anomie through mysticism, theosophy, and a religion of art. Later, in the revolutionary period that immediately followed the war, we find efforts to bridge the gulf between society and artist: in both the Novembergruppe and the Arbeitsrat für Kunst (Workers Council for Art)—a group in which Ludwig Meidner played a leading role—artists constructed utopian visions with the aim of building a "cathedral of socialism." With the crumbling of the revolution, those dreams also crumbled. The gap between the avant-garde and society-at-large was to remain a basic theme in twentieth-century art.[44]

Like the exhilaration of Jugendstil before it, the vigor of Expressionism could not last long: by the latter half of the 1920s, the utopian
energy of many projects conceived in the earlier, revolutionary
period had dissipated. The war experience had become remote.
Der Jude ceased publication in 1924; *Ost und West* had declined in
importance even before the war. The Jewish journals treating the
visual arts during the second half of the Weimar Republic, *Menorah*
and *Das Zelt* (The Tent), were not published in Berlin but in
Vienna. They were no longer forums for heated intellectual debate,
but respectable, somewhat tame, family-oriented magazines.

Still, an active Jewish cultural life continued to exist in Germany,
as did Jewish artists who worked with Jewish themes. But among
many of them, we can observe a certain detachment, a new sobriety,
even a tone of resignation. Jakob Steinhardt returned to the pictorial
vocabulary of his teacher Lovis Corinth, devoting himself to his
immediate surroundings, the urban landscape of Berlin. Joseph
Budko engaged in melancholic variations on the motif of the "old"
and "young" Jew. Hermann Struck had settled in Haifa, and Lesser
Ury finally received official recognition in being accepted as a member of the Berlin Secession.

The growing trend toward bourgeois solidity in the second half of
the 1920s is probably most directly expressed in the emergence of
the Soncino Society of Friends of the Jewish Book. Founded in 1924,
this association had many cultural Zionists among its members. Its
guiding ethos was as firmly bourgeois as any of the non-Jewish bibliophilic associations: the books published under the society's auspices
were partly reprints of German Jewish "classics," partly modern literature. Occasionally illustrated, they were always tastefully produced
in leather binding—and far from the avant-garde in spirit.

Whatever complacency may be revealed by this embourgeoisement, it is also clear that, following the Great War, key ideas of the Jewish Renaissance had spread beyond the small circles of Zionist Jewish
intellectuals to reach a wider Jewish middle-class audience, which now
considered *Jewish* culture part of its personal and cultural identity.[45]
Conversely, as a result of the resurgence of Jewish consciousness in
broader Jewish (including non-Zionist) circles, the Jewish Renaissance
gradually detached itself from organized Zionism as a point of reference in order to emerge as an autonomous cultural movement.

This development must be understood, of course, against the
backdrop of an unmistakable shift in Germany's political parame-
ters after the Great War. Perhaps nothing demonstrates this more
clearly than the subsequent careers of many figures with whom the
cultural Zionists had cultivated friendly relationships around the
turn of the century: Börries von Münchhausen, for instance, Fidus,
Arthur Moeller van den Bruck, Hanns Heinz Ewers. They now
belonged to the camp of the anti-democrats, mystics of the German
Reich, and anti-Semites. The earlier gatherings of the Kommenden
and festivities of the Neue Gemeinschaft would now split along the
critical issue of whether to support or reject the Weimar Republic.

Notes

Translated by Thomas Dunlap

I thank Joel Golb for his editorial suggestions.

1. Martin Buber, "Jüdische Renaissance," in Buber, *Die jüdische Bewegung: Gesammelte Aufsätze und Ansprachen 1900–1915*, 2d ed., revised and expanded (Berlin: Jüdischer Verlag, 1920), pp. 7–16. First published in *Ost und West* 1, no. 1 (January 1901): cols. 7–10.

2. Friedrich Nietzsche, *Unzeitgemässe Betrachtungen: Erstes Stück: David Strauss, der Bekenner und Schriftsteller*, in *Kritische Studienausgabe in 15 Bänden*, vol. 1 (Munich: Deutscher Taschenbuch Verlag, 1988), p. 160.

3. Berthold Feiwel, Preface to the 1st ed., *Jüdischer Almanach*, new ed. (Berlin: Jüdischer Verlag, 1904), p. 14.

4. Martin Buber, "Renaissance: Eine Feststellung," handwritten manuscript, Martin Buber Archive MS Var. 6/21, Jewish National and University Library, Jerusalem. Published in Hungarian in *Magyar Zsidó Alamanach* (Budapest: Évfolyam, 1911). An abridged German version was published in Buber's *Die jüdische Bewegung*, pp. 95–108.

5. Buber, "Jüdische Renaissance," p. 8.

6. Formulated and passed by the First Zionist Congress in 1897, the manifesto was a unifying guidepost for the entire Zionist movement. Different wings of the movement gave different emphases to the following goals mentioned in the manifesto: "(1) the efficacious settlement of Palestine with Jewish farmers, craftsmen, and tradesmen; (2) the organization and assembling of Jewry everywhere through appropriate local and commonly held assembly events, in accordance with national laws; (3) the strengthening of Jewish national feeling and awareness; (4) preparatory steps for bringing about governmental policies necessary for achieving the goals of Zionism." Cited in Adolph Boehm, *Die zionistische Bewegung*, vol. 1: *Die zionistische Bewegung bis zum Ende des Weltkrieges* (Tel Aviv: Hotzaah Ivrit, 1935), pp. 181f.

7. See Alex Bein, *Theodor Herzl: Biographie* (Frankfurt am Main/Berlin/Wien: Ullstein, 1983), pp. 267–78; Steven J. Zipperstein, *Elusive Prophet: Ahad Ha'am and the Origins of Zionism* (London: Peter Halban, 1993), pp. 194ff.

8. On the notion of *Lebensreform*, the various groups in this movement and their ideas, see Diethard Kerbs and Jürgen Reulecke, eds., *Handbuch der Reformbewegungen* (Wuppertal: Peter Hammer, 1998); Gottfried Küenzelen, *Der neue Mensch: Zur säkularen Religionsgeschichte der Moderne* (München: C. H. Beck, 1994); Christoph Conti, *Abschied vom Bürgertum: Alternative Bewegungen in Deutschland von 1890 bis heute* (Reinbek: Rowohlt, 1984); Corona Hepp, *Avantgarde: Moderne Kunst, Kulturkritik und Reformbewegungen nach der Jahrhundertwende* (Munich: Deutscher Taschenbuch Verlag, 1987); Janos Frecot, "Lebensreformbewegung," in *Das wilhelminische Bildungsbürgertum: Zur Sozialgeschichte seiner Ideen*, ed. Klaus Vondung (Göttingen: Vandenhoeck & Ruprecht, 1976), pp. 138–52.

9. See Susan Sontag's essays "Notes on 'Camp'" and "One Culture and the New Sensibility," in *Against Interpretation* (New York: Farrar, Straus & Giroux, 1966).

10. Matthias Acher (pseudonym of Nathan Birnbaum), "Die jüdische Renaissance-Bewegung," *Ost und West* 2, no. 9 (1902): col. 580. It was quite common in Jewish Renaissance circles to use Hebraizing pseudonyms. Birnbaum's allusion to Ulrich von Hutten's famous quotation from a letter to Pirckheimer of 1518, "O seculum! O literae! Iuvat vivere," constitutes one of the rare references in this context to Europe's historical Renaissance.

11. The book was published by the Literarische Anstalt August Schulze.

12. It is important to keep in mind that the German term *Moderne* signifies both modernism and modernity.

13. Samuel Lublinski, *Die Bilanz der Moderne* (Berlin: Cronbach, 1904); *Der Ausgang der Moderne* (Berlin: Cronbach, 1909).

14. See Baudelaire's key observation concerning the aesthetic of modernism: "the transitory, the fugitive, and the contingent are one half of art, of which the other half is the eternal and immutable"; *Le peintre de la vie moderne* (1859).

15. See Erwin Panofsky, *Renaissance and Renascences in Western Art* (Stockholm: Almquist & Wiksell, 1960); Sixten Ringboom, "Renaissance und nationales Bewusstsein. Über ein Denkmodell der Romantik," in *Die Renaissance im Blick der Nationen Europas*, ed. Georg Kaufmann, Wolfenbütteler Abhandlungen zur Renaissance-Forschung, vol. 9 (Wiesbaden: Fink, 1991); Eric J. Hobsbawm and Terence Ranger, eds., *The Invention of Tradition* (Cambridge: Cambridge University Press, 1983).

16. See August Buck, ed., *Renaissance und Renaissancismus von Jacob Burckhardt bis Thomas Mann* (Tübingen: Niemeyer, 1990); Walter Rehm, "Der Renaissancekult um 1900 und seine Überwindung," in Rehm, *Der Dichter und die neue Einsamkeit: Aufsätze zur Literatur um 1900*, ed. Reinhardt Habel (Göttingen: Vandenhoeck & Ruprecht, 1969).

17. It should also be mentioned, with regard to the demotion of the term *Moderne*, that modernity did not have an unambivalently positive connotation at the turn of the century. This ambivalence lurks within the title of Adolf Stoecker's anti-Semitic tract "Modern Judaism in Germany, Particularly in Berlin: Two Talks Presented to the Christian Social Workers' Party," 2d ed. (Berlin, 1880); it is also manifest in the writings of Georg Simmel, Werner Sombart, and, later, Max Weber; see Detlev Peukert, *Max Webers Diagnose der Moderne* (Göttingen: Vandenhoeck & Ruprecht, 1989).

18. See Paul Mendes-Flohr, *Von der Mystik zum Dialog: Martin Bubers geistige Entwicklung bis hin zum "Ich und Du"* (Königstein/Ts.: Jüdischer Verlag, 1979).

19. Stenographic minutes of the proceedings of the Third Zionist Congress, Basel, 15–18 August 1899 (Vienna: Erez Israel, 1899), p. 191.

20. Berthold Feiwel, preface to *Jüdischer Almanach*, p. 14.

21. The book—extremely popular at the time—that best exemplifies this attitude is Julius Langbehn's *Rembrandt als Erzieher* (Leipzig: E. L. Hirschfeld, 1890); within the Jewish Renaissance context, see also Martin Buber, "Die Schaffenden, das Volk, und die Bewegung," in *Jüdischer Almanach*, pp. 19–24.

22. Jüdischer Verlag, "An die Mitglieder des V. Zionistencongresses zu Basel," pamphlet, Printed Material Collection, Germany, DD-1 2/1/5, Box 2, Central Zionist Archives, Jerusalem.

23. Berthold Feiwel, preface to *Jüdischer Almanach*, p. 14.

24. See Martin Buber, "Ein geistiges Zentrum," *Ost und West* 2, no. 10 (October 1902): cols. 663–72. A brief version is found in *Die jüdische Bewegung*, pp. 77–93.

25. See Jehuda Reinharz, "Achad Ha'am und der deutsche Zionismus," *Bulletin des Leo Baeck Instituts* 61 (1982): 3–27.

26. Ahad Ha'am, "Dr. Pinsker und seine Broschüre" (1892), in Ahad Ha'am, *Am Scheidewege: Gesammelte Aufsätze*, vol. 1 (Berlin: Jüdischer Verlag, 1923), p. 173.

27. See Edith Hanke, "Das 'spezifisch intellektualistische Erlösungsbedürfnis' oder: Warum Intellektuelle Tolstoi lesen," in *Intellektuelle im Deutschen Kaiserreich*, ed. Gangolf Hübinger and Wolfgang Mommsen (Frankfurt am Main: Fischer, 1993), pp. 158–71.

28. See Zipperstein, *Elusive Prophet*, p. 148; see also Reinharz, "Achad Ha'am und der deutsche Zionismus," pp. 144, 148.

29. Berthold Feiwel, preface to *Jüdischer Almanach*, p. 16.

30. Martin Buber, *Drei Reden über das Judentum* (Frankfurt am Main: Literarische Anstalt Rütten & Loening, 1911), p. 90.

31. See Paul Mendes-Flohr, "Fin-de-Siècle Orientalism, the Ostjuden, and the Aesthetics of Jewish Self-Affirmation," *Studies in Contemporary Jewry* 1 (1984): 96–139; Steven E. Aschheim, *Brothers and Strangers: The East European Jew in German and German Jewish Consciousness, 1800–1923* (Madison: University of Wisconsin Press, 1982).

32. This and the following quotations taken from Buber's keynote address at the Fifth Zionist Congress in Basel, 1901, in stenographic minutes of the proceedings of the Fifth Zionist Congress, Basel (Vienna: Erez Israel, 1901), pp. 151–69; abridged version in *Die jüdische Bewegung*, pp. 58–67. For Buber's notion of Jewish art, see also "Lesser Ury," *Ost und West*, 1 and 2 (1901): cols. 111–28; preface to Buber, ed., *Jüdische Künstler* (Berlin: Jüdischer Verlag, 1903), pp. 7–12.

33. Stenographic minutes of the proceedings of the Fifth Zionist Congress, Basel, "List of Artworks Exhibited in Room 3," p. 459. A total of 48 works of art were exhibited.

34. Particularly in the domain of literary criticism, this tendency became even more pronounced after World War I. See Gustav Krojanker, "Vorwort des Herausgebers," in *Juden in der deutschen Literatur: Essays über zeitgenössische Schriftsteller*, ed. Gustav Krojanker (Berlin: Welt-Verlag, 1922), pp. 7–16; see also Karl Schwarz, *Die Juden in der Kunst* (Berlin: Der Heine Bund, 1928).

35. See undated letter of Lesser Ury to Martin Buber (1902 or early 1903), JNUL Jerusalem, MS VAR 350, 837:1: "To tell the truth, I consider my landscapes not all that important, but after twenty years of work they have at least allowed me to paint what I had firmly planned on. C'est la vie! In my large paintings, my feelings are indeed sometimes expressed with more purity and inward significance, and are also fully executed. My landscapes express *some* of these feelings, perhaps more sweetly, hence they are more popular."

36. See Peter Hutter, *"Die feinste Barbarei": Das Völkerschlachtdenkmal bei Leipzig* (Mainz: v. Zabern, 1990); see also Richard Hamann and Jost Hermand, *Stilkunst um 1900* (Munich: Nymphenburger, 1973). For a panorama of various artistic trends of the age, many of which have fallen into oblivion, see Richard Hamann, *Die deutsche Malerei des 19. Jahrhunderts* (Leipzig/Berlin: B. G. Teubner, 1914), pp. 326–58. In painting, the "new monumentalism" is associated with Ferdinand Hodler, Fritz Erler, and Albin Egger-Lienz, along with Max Klinger, Ludwig von Hofmann, and Franz von Stuck. Its best-known architectural representatives were Peter Behrens and Bruno Schmitz, and both Hugo Lederer and Franz Metzner created notable monumental sculpture. The term was first coined by either Richard Muther or Franz Servaes; see Servaes's essay on Ury, "Moderne Monumentalmalerei," in *Neue deutsche Rundschau* 7 (1896): 281–86.

37. Around 1900, almost any reference to the great Dutch painter stood in the shadow of Julius Langbehn's extremely popular book *Rembrandt as Educator*. First published in 1890, the book soon became one of the key works of conservative cultural criticism, calling for a German national renewal steered by the "truly German" values Langbehn discovered in Rembrandt's art. On Langbehn, see Fritz Stern, *The Politics of Cultural Despair: A Study in the Rise of the German Ideology* (Berkeley and Los Angeles: University of California Press, 1961).

38. See E. M. Lilien, *Briefe an seine Frau 1905–1925*, ed. Otto M. Lilien and Eve Strauss (Königstein/Ts.: Jüdischer Verlag Athenaeum, 1985), pp. 93, 135.

39. Struck, for instance, approached Martin Buber to find a publisher for Budko's Haggadah illustrations; he asked Arnold Zweig to write poems for a series of Budko's etchings entitled *Das Jahr des Juden*; and he was instrumental in the appointment of Budko as director of the New Bezalel in 1933.

40. See correspondence between Else Lasker-Schüler and Hermann Struck, Central Zionist Archives, Jerusalem, A 124/36.

41. Buber, *Drei Reden über das Judentum*, p. 24; also pp. 70, 76.

42. Wilhelm Hausenstein, *Vom Künstler und seiner Seele: Vier Vorträge gehalten in der Akademie für Jedermann in Mannheim* (Heidelberg: Richard Weissbach, 1914), p. 15. Hausenstein sees a "naturalistic" concept of form in the work of Leibl, Courbet, Velásquez, Leonardo, and Dürer, in contrast to a "nervous" concept he finds in Watteau, Frans Hals, and the Impressionists. He associates the "pathetic" vision with Gothic art and the art of the ancient Orient, as well as with Giotto, El Greco, Michelangelo—and Rembrandt. Also notable in this context is Stefan Zweig's essay of 1909, "Das neue Pathos," which treats the lack of understanding between artist and public; the essay is reprinted in Paul Raabe, ed., *Expressionismus: Der Kampf um eine literarische Bewegung* (Munich: Deutscher Taschenbuch Verlag, 1965), pp. 15–22.

43. See, for example, Wilhelm Hausenstein, "Vom Expressionismus in bildender Kunst," *Die neue Rundschau* 19, no. 2 (1918): 913–30. The poet Walter Hasenclever is quoted in 1920: "Es gibt wenige, denen was einfällt und viele Expressionisten!"

44. See Wolfgang J. Mommsen, *Bürgerliche Kultur und künstlerische Avantgarde: Kultur und Politik im deutschen Kaiserreich, 1870–1918* (Berlin: Propyläen, 1994); Thomas Nipperdey, *Deutsche Geschichte, 1866–1918*, vol. 1: *Arbeitswelt und Bürgergeist* (Munich: C. H. Beck, 1990), esp. p. 690.

45. See Michael Brenner, *The Renaissance of Jewish Culture in Weimar Germany* (New Haven: Yale University Press, 1996).

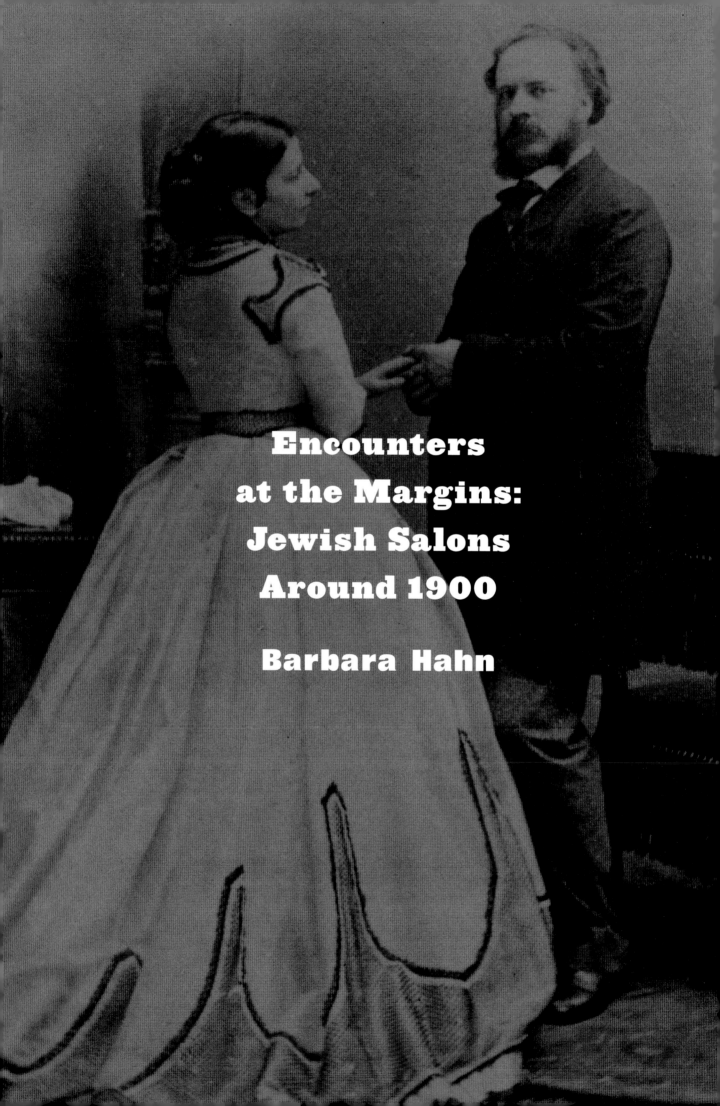

**Encounters
at the Margins:
Jewish Salons
Around 1900**

Barbara Hahn

Salons are ephemeral creatures. Conversation and laughter, hushed and loud voices alike, begin to fade the moment they emerge. Salons leave behind few traces—sometimes a billet or a letter with an invitation, sometimes a photograph of a room. But we cannot read in these signs what it is that aroused our interest. Photographs reveal empty rooms, not the afternoons or evenings of social activity. The letters and intimate notes reach us out of context, transcriptions of isolated moments spent writing. People do not write in a salon; they talk. Talk implies the presence of others, writing their absence. Salons resist being transmitted; written or photographic traces represent translations into other media. What, then, can we learn about these social and communicative experiments, for which there is no adequate mode of representation?

We do not know much about the salons that flourished around 1900. Compared with the lively salon culture that arose in Berlin around 1800, the fin-de-siècle salons have left considerably fewer traces. When, toward the end of the eighteenth century, the first generation of acculturated Jewish women opened their homes to visitors, the women themselves saw to it that their social experiment would not simply disappear after they were gone. Countless notes and letters have come down to us from the circle around Rahel Levin Varnhagen; and several autobiographical texts, including one by Henriette Herz, have been carefully collected and preserved.[1] The situation in 1900 was quite different. We still find many Jewish houses that were open to visitors, but the salonières seem to have paid little attention to the broader implications of their social activity. Obviously, their letters and billets had not been transferred to archives, but remained among their families, who were forced to leave Germany during the Third Reich. These signs of social life were mainly cast to the winds, and the search for published testimony remains largely futile. Instead, we find theoretical cultural studies, memoirs, and a few books of reminiscences, written almost exclusively by the non-Jewish guests, not their Jewish hosts. The image of salon life that has come down to us is therefore one-sided, and some texts reveal quite obvious anti-Jewish or anti-Semitic viewpoints.[2]

Reading these memoirs, one is struck by their melancholy associations. The salons seem to belong to the past, revealing a form of social life that has been lost. Even the term *salon* signifies something unreachable, a wish that cannot be fulfilled, a loss that cannot be replaced. At the turn of the century, many houses in Germany's capital were open to visitors. Most of them were the homes of wealthy, upper-bourgeois families, but there are traces of a diverse and interesting social life that took place in salons led by middle-class families as well. These turn-of-the-century salons were separated by social distinctions of class, wealth, and status. But among all these distinctions, Jewishness—even when a hostess had been baptized—was the crucial marker of exclusion in the social life of this period. Some salons were led by connoisseurs and art collectors; others displayed the high art of conversation or

"Old Berlin" *Gemütlichkeit*; and a few brought together a diverse group of people in an environment in which new ideas about art and society were introduced and disseminated. But what links the diverse salons presented in this essay is, above all, the fact that, in Wilhelmine society, they were perceived as "Jewish."

Sauces and Soups: Two Sketches of the Salon

Two scenes at table. One takes place in a large Berlin apartment on the Nollendorfplatz, in the immediate vicinity of Max Reinhardt's theater.[3] The other is a residence with garden in Berlin's West End, at that time still a rural area. In one we are presented to a lady who invites her guests to opulent dinners, in the other to a painter and a social philosopher who hold a private seminar in their home and who sometimes cook with their guests. In both instances, a social event takes place around the table. But this classic social site functions in opposite ways in the two scenes: one is a stage for self-display, the other for the high art of conversation.

Carl Ludwig von Schleich, writer and physician, presents in his memoirs the following sketch of the social activities at the home of Baroness Bertha von Arnswaldt (see FIG. 161), who welcomed her guests to a large residence in the center of the city:

> There we sat around a great round table, dominated by an immense platform piled high with the most commodious selection of silver tureens, jars, bowls with all sorts of spices, tasty condiments and ingredients for sauces, all surrounded by the appropriate bottles of wine. With a turn of this carousel of tiny delights, each person could reach out and take from a floral basket whatever his heart desired. . . . Whom did I get to know there, and in the spirit of uninhibited surrender of personality—in an atmosphere of enchantment, free of all discomfort, one truly had to show what lurked in one's heart— delve deep into his inner being.[4]

The table in this scene holds nothing to eat: no hors d'oeuvres, no main course, no dessert. There are only condiments—spices, ingredients, sauces—which do not satisfy the appetite. Instead of food, the guests place on this table their hearts, their most intimate selves, in full view of all. In conversation, they reveal an "uninhibited surrender of personality," which nonetheless seems to be just as insubstantial as condiments to a meal.

The second sketch is quite different: "Once again I see the long table, Simmel at the one end, his wife at the other, seven or eight listeners, no more. A symposium of a kind we can probably never hope to experience again. . . . On the table, in the center of the circle, a single object: a large photograph of a great work of art. Simmel's wisdom urged that reflection begin with a reliable object, recognized by the best connoisseurs and beyond any doubt sublime."[5] At the home shared by Gertrud and Georg Simmel the philosopher and sociologist (see FIG. 8),[6] the table has been transformed. As their son Hans observed in his memoirs, "We sat around the extended dining-room table, but beforehand we chatted for about twenty minutes in the living room, where the guests were served tea."[7]

In the transition from tea to conversation at the large table, all the eating utensils disappeared. Only an empty table could serve as a site for the intellectual activity that emerged from this unique form of social life. In the center stood an object that is typically found on museum walls or in the files of a library—a reproduction of a work of art. Drawn into the dining room, its role was to stimulate the imagination of the guests. The cultural theorist Margarete Susman has described what took place here: "The receptions at the Simmel house, the weekly 'jours,' were organized entirely in the spirit of the couple's culture. They were a sociological work in miniature, the product of a society that aimed to cultivate individuality in the extreme. Conversation took shape there such that no one could impose his idiosyncrasies, problems, or needs; it was a form that, liberated from all weightiness, floated in an atmosphere of spirituality, affection, and tact."[8]

The essence and movement of this mode of conversation are the opposite of what we observed in the first scene. Here the inner self is not on display, but rather obscured so that a real individuality may emerge. Only when those present ignore the personal do they become a community that, collectively, gives birth to something new. Such a group does not resemble the sauces and spices, to return to an image from the first scene; they are more like a dish prepared from a variety of ingredients. As the philosopher Ernst Bloch recounts, Gertrud and Georg Simmel would sometimes invite their guests to participate in creating a soup, a meal in which different "sauces and spices" are combined into a harmonious whole. The first scene presented an assembly of "well-known figures" whom even experts on this period no longer know; in the second, by contrast, are gathered young intellectuals who would leave their mark on Germany. The home of Gertrud and Georg Simmel hosted, among others, Margarete Susman, Gertrud Kantorowicz, Martin Buber (see FIG. 11), and Ernst Bloch.[9]

These two contrasting sketches span the spectrum of social life in Berlin's renowned Jewish salons around 1900. Unlike those of an earlier century, these diverse meeting places encompassed socially, culturally, and intellectually incompatible worlds. In fact, the guests and hosts at different salons barely knew one another. Only a few attended more than one salon; the guests at the Arnswaldt home, for instance, had nothing to do with those who visited the Simmels. A modern metropolis, Berlin reflected a social fragmentation that no single circle could overcome.

A Walk Through the Berlin Salons of 1900

The memoirs and letters that have come down to us provide traces of a variety of Jewish houses where guests were regularly received prior to 1914. Usually, a particular day of the week was established

Figure 157
Lesser Ury
**View of the Nollendorfplatz
[Blick über den
Nollendorfplatz]**, 1901–2
Oil on canvas,
16⅛ x 22¾ in. (41 x 58 cm)
Axel Springer Verlag, Berlin

on which those visitors who had already been introduced were expected without a special invitation. These people often brought new guests. Every sketch of the salon depicts an upper-bourgeois style of life that took place in the center of the city or in the old western section of Berlin. While gatherings for tea characterized the earlier period, the talk in 1900 was frequently of dinners staged in elaborately appointed residences. Often literary or musical compositions were presented in salon assemblies, and many artists made their debuts in these private spaces.

The oldest of the hostesses who established a salon between 1900 and 1914 was Babette Meyer (1835–1916), the daughter of a Berlin banking family. We know from the memoirs of Sabine Lepsius[10] that Meyer was educated by Lepsius's father, the painter Gustav Graef. She was "by far the most talented" of his pupils, described as "a beautiful, grand figure, dark, a star of society."[11] Unfortunately, no traces of Babette Meyer's work have been discovered—no picture that she painted, and no portrait for which she sat. Her residence in what is now the Berlin government district had achieved a certain fame among her guests, and was described by Marie von Bunsen, a chronicler of Berlin salon life around 1900: "All her life, Babette Kalckreuth [Meyer] lived in the house at the corner of Viktoria- and Bellevuestrasse. The house and its appointments stemmed from the fifties, and such authentically old-fashioned furnishings were perhaps found nowhere else in Germany . . . a red room, a green room, highly carved chairs standing stiffly in a row, a polysand[12] sofa table, banal oil paintings from that period. Nothing tasteful; everything stately and decorous."[13] Babette Meyer was the only unmarried Jewish woman who

hosted an open house. She had later been married, briefly, to the
painter Stanislaus von Kalckreuth, but to her contemporaries
the marriage was simply an episode: she is almost always referred
to as Babette Meyer.

We have no detailed knowledge of the life that was led in this
representative space. Richard Voss, a well-known writer of the
time, to whom Babette Meyer was introduced as "Berlin's most
intellectually accomplished woman," tells in his memoirs about
this "'green salon,' a thoroughly comfortable room, whose long
windowed wall looked out on the Tiergarten."[14] There he had
intimate conversations with the lady of the house, but we learn
nothing about their content. In a letter of Walther Rathenau (see
FIG. 14), the industrialist and writer who would become foreign
minister in the Weimar Republic, the hostess is referred to as
"my old friend"; but the other guests present that evening, who
were also introduced to Rathenau as close
friends of Babette Meyer, do not know him.
One of them, the poet Ernst von Wildenbruch, even asked Rathenau if he had been
long in Berlin. "For three generations" was
Rathenau's laconic answer.[15]

If Babette Meyer appears in the history
of Berlin salon life as a blank page—a
woman without a husband and without an
"important" father—visitors seem to have
known exactly where they were going when
they made their way to a hostess who for
years lived in the same vicinity. Cornelie
Richter (1842–1922), the youngest daughter
of Minna and Giacomo Meyerbeer, continued a tradition of two generations of social
life, for her grandmother Amalie Beer as
well as her mother had hosted musical
salons. Cornelie (FIG. 158) had been married to the painter Gustav
Richter (1823–1884) and was the mother of four sons. The social
events at her residence—which flourished primarily from 1890
through 1914—are quite well documented, since it was a gathering place for writers and painters, who recorded invitations to
breakfast or an evening party in their correspondence and memoirs. For example, Helene von Nostitz describes Cornelie's salon
as a tangible expression of "Old Berlin" that is nevertheless open
to new cultural ideas:

Figure 158
Cornelie Richter (born Meyerbeer) with
her husband, Gustav Richter, 1865

> One met at Cornelie Richter's house, first on the
> Bellevuestrasse, then on the Pariser Platz, where
> the paintings of the elder Gustav Richter hung between
> lovely old tapestries, and the harmonious family life
> between mother and sons created such a wonderful
> atmosphere. . . . Cornelie Richter herself, with her
> soft, large black eyes that shown with goodness and
> understanding, always sat with a comprehending

smile in the flat light of her great lamps. She showed a benevolent openness to all living things; and although she was entirely rooted in old Berlin, which still seemed to breathe the air of Schinkel and Rauch, and found its expression in her father Meyerbeer, in Menzel, Hertel, Meyerheim[16]—she was among the first to receive Henry van de Velde, and had him give a lecture in her house, where, in his fanatic enthusiasm, he condemned all the furniture and paintings among which he stood, and would have liked to toss them out the window. Cornelie Richter listened, as always, with deep understanding.[17]

Worlds collide in this scene, but without a trace of conflict. Henry van de Velde, architect and "designer," championed a

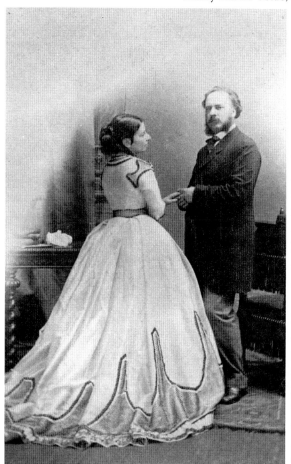

Figure 159
Cornelie Richter (born Meyerbeer) with
her husband, Gustav Richter, 1864

radical rejection of the Gründerzeit[18] style typical not only of Cornelie Richter's home at the time. His "enthusiasm" did not so much reflect a preference for this or that sort of furnishing, but was rather an attack on a concept of life that, especially in the eyes of youth, was embodied in this heavy, "powerful" furniture. They called their movement the "youth style," Jugendstil, or Art Nouveau. That this confrontation met no resistance, but was so sympathetically fended off, illustrates the dilemma in which Cornelie Richter found herself regarding her salon: far from being a neutral site for conversation, it had become charged with distinctive cultural connotations.

Whoever writes about Cornelie considers her in relation to her famous father, the composer Giacomo Meyerbeer, whose name is identified with the debate on "Jewishness in music" stirred up by Richard Wagner. In part because of the anti-Semitic attack in Wagner's text, Meyerbeer's musical career was centered in France and not in Germany; only after his death did his wife return to Berlin with the children. As the daughter of this family, Cornelie Richter, unlike Babette Meyer, was always referred to as a "Jewess," a mark of discrimination, in Berlin at the close of the nineteenth century. And as the widow of the painter Gustav Richter, she was likewise out of step with the times. For Richter's art had fallen from favor and become old-fashioned by the end of the Wilhelmine era. It seems that the hostess tried to counter her precarious situation with indifference. But it was precisely this attitude that irritated those visitors who knew their precise place in this society. One such guest was Hildegard von Spitzemberg, the wife of a Württemberg diplomat in Berlin, whose diary recorded the political and social life of the ruling

classes in Germany's capital. Referring to the circle around
Cornelie Richter as a "clan," she observed: "I can't warm to them,
and feel myself at heart alien, respected but not trusted, however
well I get along with each person individually, and however much
I recognize their talents. I find the mutual exaggeration and lack
of seriousness in so many of them unpleas-
ant, and not compensated by intimate personal relationships."[19]

Baroness von Spitzemberg specifies the
source of this feeling of alienation in another
diary entry. From the standpoint of a noble-
woman sympathetic to the Prussian court,
Cornelie Richter's house mixed together
elements that ought to be strictly separated.
In March 1908, for example, she was invited
to breakfast, where she met "a motley assembly: Director Reinhardt of the Deutsches
Theater (see FIG. 186), the poet Hofmannsthal and his wife, Mrs. Förster-Nietzsche,
Raoul [Richter] and wife, Count Hoyos,
Count Kessler, whom I haven't seen in ages,
looking cheerful and handsome, finally Mr.
Eyde."[20] Cornelie Richter brought together
people in her salon who, for whatever reason, were "important," particularly those
involved with poetry and theater. Since the
politics of Cornelie Richter's invitations had
no explicit criteria, her salon was perceived
as "typically Jewish."

How subtly this social boundary was
drawn is evident from remarks about
Cornelie Richter (FIGS. 158, 159) in the
memoirs of Marie von Bunsen: "More than all other women of
Jewish extraction who have gained social standing among us, she
was taken into our hearts. She was loved. She was refined, warm-
hearted, and feminine, she did not talk too much, was not important, but she had an instinctive understanding of people."[21]
However, with the phrase "among us," a line is drawn that places
Cornelie Richter on the other side. She is positioned in this social
context quite differently from Babette Meyer, who, with her old-
fashioned furnishings, seemed to represent something devoid of
obvious Jewish connotations, what was perceived as her unique
cultural identity. Others registered this fine difference in external
details. Helene von Nostitz remarked, for instance, that Cornelie
Richter "often assembles her friends for small dinners. The table
always glowed with luminous flowers amid the dazzling faience."[22]
This seems a bit overdone: "luminous" flowers that do not, say,
complement the white porcelain, but rather clash with the bril-
liantly colored faience. In a futile competition between "dazzling"
and "luminous" colors, the efforts of the hostess are neutralized.

Figure 160
Marie von Leyden

195

Figure 161 — Bertha von Arnswaldt (oval portrait, upper left)

Figure 161
Bertha von Arnswaldt

The salons led by these two Berlin women represent different social and cultural environments. Babette Meyer, who seems to have emerged *sui generis* from the void of history, as did Rahel Levin Varnhagen one hundred years before her, was more readily accepted into high society than Cornelie Richter, whose parents and grandparents had resisted conversion to Christianity. A glance at other salons reveals that those women who moved to Berlin unencumbered by the details of a particular family history had it easier.

Imports from the provinces brought new life to a frozen tradition, as illustrated by Marie von Leyden (1844–date unknown) (FIG. 160), who was born into the Oppenheim family in Königsberg. Together with her husband, Ernst Victor von Leyden, a professor of medicine, she moved to Berlin in 1876. From his autobiography we learn that his wife's parents had led an open house, a tradition that she brought with her to Berlin. Her salon in the capital is not mentioned in her husband's autobiography;[23] but a French journalist who lived in Berlin around 1900 talks about her "well-attended" gatherings.[24]

Leonie Schwabach's (1845–1930) social life reached to the upper levels of high society. Descended from the Kayzer family of Dutch merchants, she married the banker Julius Leopold Schwabach. Her salon in a former aristocratic palace on the Wilhelmsplatz was frequented by influential nobility. A diplomat who published memoirs of his years in Berlin under a pseudonym characterized the hostess as "extraordinarily intelligent, and at a time when it was not easy to find an intellectual salon in Berlin, hers was a place where one could talk of everything that was going on in the world of literature and art, with a sprinkling of politics now and then to give zest to the conversation."[25] Her son Paul, director of the Bleichröder banking house, like his father before him, was granted a hereditary peerage in 1907. Unfortunately, no other descriptions of this salon have survived.

This is not the case for the salon hosted by Bertha von Arnswaldt (1850–1919) (FIG. 161), which we encountered in an introductory sketch. Born Bertha Holland in London, she had lived for many years in Frankfurt am Main. During her marriage to the Berlin architect Hermann Giesenberg, she resided briefly in the German capital; but only after the death of her third husband, member of parliament Hermann Baron von Arnswaldt, did she, in 1910, settle permanently in Berlin. According to the memoirs of her granddaughter Ursula von Mangoldt, "she would sit until late at night in her lovely residence on the Nollendorfplatz, whose noise disturbed her not in the least, or on her balcony.

Figure 162
Felicie Bernstein
Courtesy of Harvard University Fine Arts
Library, Cambridge, Massachusetts

When passing friends saw her there, or the light burning in her room, however late it might be, they went up. And they were always received with enthusiasm and a small repast."[26]

In addition to its regular "jours," the Arnswaldt house seems always to have been open, which adds to its charm and at the same time points to a problem: there were no fixed criteria governing the selection of guests, for which the hostess attempted to compensate by promoting some of them to "favorites." The contradiction between a subtle favoritism and the openness of this salon is reflected in the remarks of one of her "anointed," Carl Ludwig von Schleich, a "genial doctor who had invented local anesthesia and was also a talented poet." He characterizes his hostess as "a woman who, with nothing more than a fundamentally good, merry, and pious heart—which are, nonetheless, the strongest magnets in the world—managed to bring together in her home an elite of the most significant and attractive men and bind them into a league such as Berlin had never possessed nor is likely to see again." He continues:

Figure 163
Max Liebermann
**Portrait of Professor
Dr. Carl Bernstein**, 1892
Oil on board, 17 5/16 x 13 3/4 in. (44 x 35 cm)
Private Collection, Zurich

> It was a salon in the best sense, a brilliant mixture of wit and art; perhaps the last German salon, since this sort of free, happy social interchange is likely gone for good. A house whose doors, when one was welcome, were open at any time of day—and, one could add, night. When her favorites appeared, among whom I could count myself, it was time for a celebration; she telephoned here and there, and with unmatched skill pulled together a meal . . . that almost always had the magic of a symposium. . . . And admittedly helped by a reckless dispensation of Bacchus's gifts, she soon had everyone feeling as if he wore roses in his hair and laurels on his temples.[27]

Schleich's remarks, referring both to a "league" and the masterfully blended conviviality with which the passage concludes, points up a contradiction. Numerous "leagues" and "circles" were founded at the time that brought together people who shared common goals and ideas. Each of these groups was committed to a particular program, however vaguely formulated. A salon, however, cannot be bound to a preconceived program. Salons flourish in their mingling of heterogeneous elements, when the forces of conflict and alliance are held in balance within the group. But the salons of the time were no longer the scenes of such free and diverse social interaction. Socially and culturally, they had become highly regulated and exclusionary meeting places. Yet the criteria for acceptance and exclusion could not be revealed without completely undermining the basis for the group's existence. Many salons maintained this tension between the illusion of open access and the hidden mechanisms by which a few participants were elevated to the elect.

Two Jewish women from Eastern Europe attempted to negotiate these tensions and contradictions. We are unusually well informed about both of them, since recollections of these houses were set down by others. In the case of Felicie Bernstein (FIG. 162), born Rosenthal (1850–1908), and Carl Bernstein (1842–1894) (FIG. 163), it was the archaeologist Georg Treu, a friend of the family, who, after Felicie's death, put together a *Gedenkbuch*,[28] or collection of reminiscences by her friends. The salon of Aniela Fürstenberg (1856–1915) was described after her death by her husband, the banker Carl Fürstenberg (1850–1933), who drew on her diary entries and guest books, which are now lost.

Felicie and Carl Bernstein emigrated from St. Petersburg, but had been educated in Germany. Carl Bernstein was "ausserordentlicher Professor" of Roman law at the university in Berlin, an unpaid and untenured position. The Bernsteins' thoroughly composed style of life, which required a certain social space for its presentation, is mirrored by the cleverly constructed book that their friends prepared to commemorate it: their Wednesday evenings during the 1880s took place in a suitably grandiose setting designed for, but never occupied by, the president of the Reichstag. "When we moved to Berlin, our house caused a sensation," Felicie Bernstein wrote in a letter.[29] As we can infer from surviving photographs and descriptions, this residence (FIGS. 164, 165) was conceived as a total work of art: a perfect composition of furniture, tapestries, carpets, and paintings, all brought to Berlin from foreign lands, primarily France and Italy. It was a residence that emphasized through representative "modern" objects the provinciality of the capital's ruling class. As shown in the *Gedenkbuch*, this cultural criticism was above all reflected in the Bernsteins' collection of paintings. Essays written by "experts" assessed the value of the objects they had assembled. Wilhelm von Bode (1845–1929), Director-General of the Berlin State Museums, described the sixteenth- to eighteenth-century paintings, among them one by Adriaen Brouwer and one by Jan van Goyen. Hugo von Tschudi (1851–1911), Director of the Berlin National Gallery, concentrated on the modern art, of which the Impressionist works aroused the greatest furor: the Bernsteins were the first in Berlin to show paintings by Manet, Monet, and Sisley (see FIG. 165).

In these reminiscences, the social activity at the Bernstein house recedes behind the art objects and interiors, which are themselves depicted as genre paintings. Felicie Bernstein is more discernible as a letter writer than as a hostess. Only Max Liebermann attempts in his essay to erect a monument to her, which gets him into unexpected difficulties. She appears only at the

Figure 164
Reception room in the home of Carl and Felicie Bernstein
Courtesy of Harvard University Fine Arts Library, Cambridge, Massachusetts

Figure 165
Music room in the Bernstein home,
showing some of their collection
of Impressionist art. On the left wall:
Edouard Manet, *White Lilacs in a
Glass Vase*, 1882, today in the
collection of the National Gallery of Art,
Berlin; to the left of the doorway,
above: Alfred Sisley, *The Seine at
Argenteuil*, 1875; to the right of the
doorway, *above*: Edouard Manet,
The Departure of the Folkestone Ferry,
1869, today in the collection of the
Philadelphia Museum of Art; and *below*:
Camille Pissarro, *Peasants Working
in the Fields, Pontoise*, 1881
Courtesy of Harvard University
Fine Arts Library,
Cambridge, Massachusetts

end—in contrast to her husband and nameless sister-in-law. Prior to that, she is swallowed up by references to the "Bernsteins": "Everyone met at the Bernsteins: besides Mommsen and Curtius . . . Frau Artôt de Padilla or another star of the stage, Georg Brandes and Max Klinger, Bode and Lippmann from the museum, in later years Tschudi, from Dresden Treu and Seidlitz, writers such as Karl Emil Franzos and all the others—who just had a work staged, politicians and diplomats from all quarters, and Russians currently staying in Berlin."[30]

Max Liebermann referred to Felice Bernstein's gatherings as the "reincarnated salon of Mrs. Henriette Herz," one of the first Jewish women to enter the world of high German culture one hundred years earlier. But Liebermann suggests that Felicie could not measure up in appearance to that celebrated beauty: "One would call Frau Bernstein ugly rather than attractive," he wrote:

> What mighty magnet drew her friends, even after
> her spouse's death, so powerfully to her? The magnet
> consisted in her heart's largeness and goodness. . . .
> She had helped countless poor artists, and indeed in
> such a manner that the recipient of the favor had no
> need for shame, not to mention the innumerable poor
> countrymen and coreligionists, none of whom ever
> left her door empty-handed.[31]

In his sketch of the hostess, drawn from the clichéd repertoire of the "beautiful Jewess," Liebermann implies that "ugly" women have only their hearts to bring to the field. We get a more nuanced picture of the exceptional social skills that were on display at Felicie Bernstein's salon in some pieces that Georg Treu chose not to include in his book. For example, Sabine Lepsius represents Felicie Bernstein as a woman who gained a place in society by raising conversation to the level of serious cultural criticism:

> [She] possessed that engaging quality that unites oppo-
> sites, encourages clever and amusing conversation—
> in short, that nourishes intellectual competence and
> flexibility. She was tolerant without being lax, recognizing
> strong personalities and praising them decisively. She
> paid respect to the famous without stooping to flattery,
> and provided the shy with a sense of security through

her consideration. Significant conversations about art or other intellectual domains were conducted in this salon.[32]

The salon of Emma Dohme (1854–1918) was often seen as a successor to that of Felicie Bernstein, who died in 1908. But the few descriptions that have come down to us give the impression that her salon could not measure up, intellectually or socially, to Felicie Bernstein's gatherings. The Tuesday evenings at her house were often so well attended that the conversation could no longer be steered by the hostess. Like Bertha von Arnswaldt, Emma Dohme had a telephone quite early, so that she could call guests together at a moment's notice. "At the home of Frau Geheimrat Emma Dohme, the widow of the late art historian and friend of Kaiser Friedrich, the topics for discussion, aside from art and the administrative bureaucracy, were in particular science and literature. Max Liebermann, Lovis Corinth, Hugo von Tschudi, Meier-Graefe, Valerian von Loga, Dora Hitz, Werner Sombart,[33] and many others were frequent guests on these famous Tuesdays, where the most exquisite cuisine, such as the oyster-stuffed 'chicken à la Liebermann,' the obliging housewife's pride, mitigated the often opposing viewponts of her guests."[34] In none of the surviving reports do we find any traces of conversations that overstepped the boundaries of polite discussion. Memories of particular delicacies of the Dohme kitchen seem to have been longer-lasting.

Whereas the Bernstein salon reconciled unstructured conversation and a programmatic purpose through its focus on art, particularly painting, the salon of Aniela Fürstenberg (FIG. 166), born Natanson in Warsaw, emphasized literature and intellectual debates. It was documented by the banker Carl Fürstenberg, Aniela's second husband, who observed that "Aniela successfully managed to imbue the social life of our own house with a particular texture. . . . My home was for twenty years one of the most social in Berlin" (FIG. 167). The uniqueness of this salon lay less in its decor than in its cultural setting: "She hosted scholarly lectures, let the occasional poet hold a reading in her salon, and set great store by her friendships with women who had intellectual interests and were masters of the art of conversation." These women included the writers Gabriele Reuter and Berta von Suttner;[35] and the hostess's philosophical interests tended toward Schopenhauer and Nietzsche. Her talent for creating the right mix of stimulating people and ideas, according to Fürstenberg, enabled his wife to "come as close to the founding of a salon as was possible at this time in Berlin."[36] Unfortunately, Aniela's diary, "an almost complete chronicle of Berlin social life in the last years before the war," as well as her guest books for "more intimate friends" appear to have been lost. Carl Fürstenberg, who was indebted to these lost texts for his memoir, briefly quotes one such guest book, documenting the years 1909–10, which included entries by the suffragette and salonière Hedwig Dohm as well as her daughters Hedwig Pringsheim and Else Rosenberg.[37] Walther Rathenau contributed "his own pencil drawing of an Arab crouching in the dust,"[38] and quotes aperçus by Maximilian Harden and Alfred Kerr (see FIG. 15).

Figure 167
Aniela Fürstenberg's residence
(exterior view), Viktoriastrasse 7

The salon of Auguste Hauschner (1850–1924), who had moved in the mid-1870s from Prague to Berlin, enjoyed a special status. She was the only wealthy salonière known to us who published her writings. She cultivated with particular ardor the intellectual tradition of the salon, attending private tutorials in philosophy and organizing lectures at her home. When, after her death, the Berlin lawyer and writer Martin Beradt assembled a volume of letters to her, he took special note of the social life of the Hauschner household: "In the best of her five rooms, at ground level on Karlsbad 25, a room not richly appointed but made lively by two facing grand pianos, up until the country's collapse and the end of Auguste Hauschner's prosperity, many writers of the last quarter of a century would meet, primarily to engage in intimate conversation. In the large winter parties that she hosted before the war, one could perceive a bit of the aura of the old salons in her apartment." Like Babette Meyer, Auguste Hauschner was remembered for nourishing the art of conversation. As Beradt observed, "pomp and publicity vanished behind the much more frequent and, in the end, personal conversations between two or three people; her gift for stimulating conversation was as great as her patience in listening."[39]

Another contributor to the book, the Swiss writer Jakob Schaffner, alludes to the particular diversity of Hauschner's circle, which included leading proponents of contemporary, even radical, ideas: "Who can count the long rows of men and women who passed through her salon in the Berlin that existed before the war? Women, men, people on the rise, those who had already reached the heights, controversial and notorious people, poseurs and people of substance. She was there for everyone, heard everything, saw everything, represented everything with an indefatigable freshness; and what she created were encounters, hours, evenings, conversations, communities, intimacies, stimulation, earnest interpretations and frivolous flashes of insight; and while she managed to be everywhere, she seemed to be nowhere."[40]

Schaffner provides no litany of famous names, but rather a hint of the flow of conversation and intellectual engagement that filled Auguste Hauschner's social gatherings; her salon seems not to have needed external legitimation. The letters collected in the remembrance book evoke a circle fundamentally different from the other salons: here are letters from Fritz Mauthner, Gustav Landauer, and Martin Buber; we also find Hedwig Lachmann, Hedwig Dohm, and Louise Dumont, who herself led a salon during her Berlin years.[41] We know that some of these people were

Figure 168
Gustav Landauer
Courtesy of the Leo Baeck
Institute, New York

not particularly sociable types; they likely attended the private lectures. Not only in her writing did Auguste Hauschner break through the upper-bourgeois framework that confined the more conventional salons of her time. The political spectrum in which she moved extended to the boundaries of socialist anarchism. She even sought out Clara Zetkin of the German Social Democratic Party; and she was friends with Gustav Landauer (FIG. 168) until his death, time and again supporting him financially. In comparison with that of other salon hostesses, Auguste Hauschner's circle of friends was extremely wide: Max Liebermann and Clara Zetkin mark two poles of a cultural field that in the early twentieth century was no longer cohesive. What were otherwise incompatible worlds—social, political, and cultural—met at Auguste Hauschner's gatherings: on 1 January 1901, for example, she invited Fritz Mauthner and Gustav Landauer, as well as Max Liebermann (FIGS. 20, 22), the artist, wealthy art collector, and president of the Berlin Secession. (See the essays by Chana Schütz and Peter Paret in this book.)

A different type of salon was established by women who did not belong to Berlin's high society—middle-class women, often associated with the women's movement and working as writers. The most famous was Hedwig Dohm (1833–1919), born Schlesinger, who published a series of books on women's rights and male prejudice.[42] She invited her guests for tea on Monday afternoons at a "fairly modest apartment" where her four daughters "could enjoy intellectual stimulation rather than light and sun."[43] As Carl Fürstenberg recollects in his memoirs, hot sausages were all that guests could expect to eat when they stayed for the evening: "All the better usually was the intellectual 'food. . . ' We talked about the last premiere, about an exhibition that just had opened," and sometimes about politics.[44] It is not simply coincidence that we already have been introduced to Hedwig Dohm as a guest at the salons of Aniela Fürstenberg and Auguste Hauschner, who seem to have been especially interested in fostering close contacts with intellectual women and, in the process, bridging social and political gaps.

Decline of the Salon

In considering the range of Jewish salonières, one is struck by the fact that they are all at least fifty years of age in the period that interests us, and that almost all of them created their salons after they were widowed, if they were married at all. The next generation is markedly absent. Although younger women were hosting salons in Berlin prior to World War I, there are almost no Jewish women among them. With the First World War, the great tradition of Jewish salons in Berlin appears to have come to an end.

After 1918, only a few of the notable salon hostesses were still alive. Most likely it was not only their advanced age that prevented the few survivors from sustaining the social life they had led before the war. Revolution and civil war, hunger and inflation forced even the formerly rich to change their style of life. From letters written to Auguste Hauschner, we know that she had lost most of her money and could no longer afford to invite friends. But the Jewish salons did not flourish even when times stabilized in the mid-1920s. We know of some open houses, such as that of Edith Andreae (1883–1952) (FIG. 169), sister of Walther Rathenau (see FIG. 14) and daughter-in-law of Bertha von Arnswaldt. From the autobiography of Hans Fürstenberg, son of Aniela and Carl Fürstenberg and also a wealthy banker, we get the impression that a reason for the disappearance was growing anti-Semitism: "I think that our house would have become one of the most hospitable houses in the German capital if the first attempts were not stopped by the trend of the time,"[45] he wrote in looking back to the Weimar Republic.

The two principal chroniclers of salon life, Marie von Bunsen (1860–1941) and Sabine Lepsius (1864–1942), could not perceive the new political implications. Their reflections on this unique form of social life are melancholy recollections of a lost world. For von Bunsen, the salon's disappearance in the years after 1914 was the result, "aside from the catastrophes of war and inflation," of "the acceleration, the Americanization of our existence, the restless need for travel and variety, the increase in hotel hospitality, the clubs, the passion for sports."[46] What was the reason, though, that Jewish salons were particularly hard hit? For von Bunsen, there was in Berlin a "lack of women who could set the tone," and "the Jewish women as well had little to toss into the scale. . . . Mrs. Cornelie Richter, in her quiet way, was a personality; Frau von Leyden and Mrs. Leonie Schwabach were remarkably versatile, clever, and elegant, but rich in spirit [*geistreich*] they were not."[47]

One might ask why Jewish women in particular had to be *geistreich*. Is the term used primarily to connote difference? Jews were ethnically stereotyped in Berlin society, as reflected in Marie von Bunsen's remark: "But in Berlin one assumes that every intelligent, swarthy person is a priori of Semitic blood; and only my blue eyes contradicted this assumption."[48] This exclusionary gesture is noteworthy even in a positive context, for example, in a comment by Hermann Bahr that "the spirit of the great German tradition had again and again to be sheltered beneath the protection of noble Berlin Jewesses. There I found it, while otherwise all around me heads were turning toward the future, toward the new, toward industry. There I found calm, spirit, and grace, in a smiling disrespect for idiotic money."[49] In this context, both anti-Semitic and philo-Semitic tendencies come dangerously close to defining stereotypes of Jewish difference in Wilhelmine society.

As these remarks by Bahr and von Bunsen make clear, non-Jewish guests at the Berlin salons around 1900 were as little inclined to forget whom they were visiting as in 1800. The salons led by Jewish women were no doubt affected by this subtle form of discrimination, which in the long run destroyed the free flow of social and intellectual interaction. The labeling of Jews as "others" could only undermine the creative process of conversation that was perhaps the salon's most distinctive form of discourse.

Figure 169
Edith Andreae

Writing in 1913, Sabine Lepsius lamented a scarcity of the refined skills required for the "art of conversation," particularly of a hostess who could not only focus but also synthesize the disparate strands of a discussion. "It is a matter of talent," she wrote, "to be able to sense whether a circle includes a soloist for whom the interplay of questions and objections serve as stimulants that enable a precious construction of ideas to soar before our very eyes, or provide a dramatic account of his experiences. That speaker is rare who, free from vanity, has only the idea or the presentation in mind, and who can nonetheless commit his entire personality in conversation."[50]

Lepsius's definition of conversation as constructive intellectual activity is similar to what Margarete Susman observed in the Simmel household. Perhaps the intellectual salon was a final refuge for the art of conversation because it established a framework in which speakers could maneuver. No one could retreat into self-presentation and specialized interests without interrupting the flow of talk. Chatter as well as formal rules of discussion were also out of place, as Hans Simmel expressly recalls: "My father was indeed a master of conversation, but he had no interest in 'discussions' in the usual sense of the word. It for the most part did not matter to him whether or not one could find points of discrepancy or refute contrary opinions. Those words and interpretations of the other person that he could pick up in order to expand, to enrich, to deepen the conversation—that was for him the essential and interesting thing. He expected to be listened to carefully, and he, too, listened well; petty objections, even when they were true, made him impatient when they did not further the conversation as a whole. But, gladly and enthusiastically, he engaged those remarks that introduced a new constructive viewpoint, regardless if they accorded more with his perspective or the other person's."[51]

Simmel here outlines the risk in any conversation: all the participants are engaged in a mutual process toward finding a "truth" that can no more be fixed than each person's individual contribution. This process can work only when all of the participants manage to an extent to forget who they are. As long, however, as one group brands the other with exclusionary labels, as long as the word *Jew* is employed in this context, the attempt is futile.

From this perspective, the Simmel salon can also be seen as a response to inadequacies in the larger society's institutions of knowledge. In contrast to the situation in other countries, Prussian universities were largely closed to women during the Kaiserreich; and Jewish intellectuals were continually blocked from participation or advancement in their academic careers. For decades, Georg Simmel was able to work as a professor only in an unpaid position; he finally was granted a chair in 1914, at the age of fifty-six. None of his Jewish guests could become professors in Germany. His "jours" offered a free intellectual space to those in the society—women, Jews—who were deprived of an institutional site and recognition.

The Unknown Salon

In addition to the famous salons, which were primarily meeting places for high society, there were in Berlin at that time a plethora of more modest salon-like social arrangements that have disappeared along with their hosts. A few traces remain. In Berlin in 1913, there appeared a book with the provocative title *Die moderne Jüdin* (The Modern Jewess). Written by Else Croner (1878–1940), who was already known as an author of children's books, it portrays the salon as an intrinsic part of the social life of middle-class Jewish circles in the western section of the city: "The salon is the actual domain of the modern, elegant Jewish woman," she wrote. "When one speaks today of a 'salon' in Berlin, it is a Jewish salon. All of western Berlin is a single great salon."[52] These salons, she argues, are the spaces in which social mixing takes place. Large numbers of young Jewish families, particularly from the eastern provinces, had streamed into the German capital in search of greater social and economic opportunities. But social life in Berlin for the Jewish middle class was not as open as many wished to believe. Gershom Scholem, for instance, recalled that his parents tended to associate only with other Jewish families, without even being aware of it.[53] And Walter Benjamin describes how his family cultivated its own intimate society within the broader culture: "In my childhood I was a prisoner of the old and the new west. My clan resided then in both of these quarters, with an attitude that combined stubbornness and self-awareness, and that created a ghetto that it considered its life. I remained enclosed in this propertied quarter, and did not know any other."[54]

In the chapter entitled "Society" of Benjamin's *Berliner Kindheit um Neunzehnhundert* (Berlin Childhood around 1900), the author captures this self-imposed social insularity in an impressive metaphor: "The plain dress shirt that my father wore that evening seemed to me a suit of armor, and in the glance that but an hour before he had thrown across the vacant chairs, I discovered now his weapons."[55] The house's access to the world is undermined by defenses against the intrusion of the foreign and heterogeneous. The "salon," usually open only on social evenings, was a bastion; the merrily decorated table in the center a barricade.

It is not surprising that the restless intellectuals of the city searched for other social and intellectual forms of expression— and precisely in response to the increasing social, economic, and political pressures. They founded groups that attempted to confront and address the conflicts of modern Germany: Zionism or acculturation, socialism or liberalism, for example. And they organized themselves around newspapers, book series, and "leagues." In order to expand the boundaries of their social life, they moved from western Berlin to the suburbs that had recently been integrated by rail into the city. As a significant cultural space in the modern metropolis, the salon by 1914 was disappearing.

Notes

Translated by James McFarland

1. Rahel Levin Varnhagen (1771–1833) began to collect letters and billets from friends and family when she was young, and she continued to do so throughout her life. After her death, her husband, Karl August Varnhagen, published her correspondence in several volumes. Henriette Herz (1764–1847) wrote her autobiography, and she also told her story to a young man who published her memoirs after she died.

2. On the history of the Berlin salons, see Petra Wilhelmy, *Der Berliner Salon im 19. Jahrhundert (1780–1914)* (Berlin and New York: Walter de Gruyter, 1989); and Dolores L. Augustine, *Patricians and Patrons: Wealth and High Society in Wilhelmine Germany* (Oxford and Providence: Berg, 1994).

3. The theater, built in 1906–7, was originally named the Theater am Nollendorfplatz.

4. Carl Ludwig von Schleich, *Besonnte Vergangenheit: Lebenserinnerungen 1859–1919* (Berlin: Vier Falken Verlag, 1920), pp. 321–22.

5. Charles du Bos, "Widmungsbrief an Bernhard Groethuysen" (1949), in *Ästhetik und Soziologie um die Jahrhundertwende: Georg Simmel*, ed. Hannes Böhringer and Karlfried Gründer (Frankfurt am Main: Vittorio Klostermann, 1976), pp. 245–46.

6. Gertrud Simmel (1864–1938), born Kienel, studied painting and published several books on religion and issues of gender under the pseudonym Marie Louise Enckendorf. Georg Simmel (1858–1918) was one of the founders of the modern disciplines of sociology and cultural studies. His work has been translated widely into English. See *Georg Simmel on Individuality and Social Forms: Selected Writings* (Chicago: University of Chicago Press, 1972); *The Philosophy of Money* (London: Routledge, 1978); *Simmel on Culture: Selected Writings* (New York: Sage, 1997).

7. Hans Simmel, "Erinnerungen," in *Ästhetik und Soziologie*, ed. Böhringer and Gründer, p. 255.

8. Margarete Susman, *Ich habe viele Leben gelebt: Erinnerungen* (Stuttgart: Deutsche Verlags-Anstalt, 1964), pp. 52–53. Unfortunately, the work of Margarete Susman (1874–1966) has not yet been introduced to an English-speaking audience. Her books include studies on modern poetry, women in the Romantic period, the Book of Job as metaphor for the Holocaust, Goethe, and Charlotte von Stein.

9. Gertrud Kantorowicz (1876–1945) was an art historian; she died in Theresienstadt. Her posthumously published book on the art of antiquity has recently been translated into English as *The Inner Nature of Greek Art* (New Rochelle: Aristide Caratzas, 1993). Martin Buber (1878–1965) played a leading role in the Jewish Renaissance, and is well known for his *Tales of the Hasidim* (New York: Schocken, 1991) and *I and Thou*, among other works. Ernst Bloch (1885–1977), a philosopher, is the author of a number of books available in English; see *The Principle of Hope* (Oxford: Basil Blackwell, 1986) and *Heritage of Our Times* (Oxford: Polity, 1991).

10. Sabine Lepsius (1864–1942) was a painter and writer. Besides her autobiography (see n. 11), she published a memoir of her friendship with Stefan George: *Stefan George: Geschichte einer Freundschaft* (Berlin: Verlag die Runde, 1935).

11. Sabine Lepsius, *Ein Berliner Künstlerleben um die Jahrhundertwende: Erinnerungen* (Munich: Gotthold Müller Verlag, 1972), p. 29.

12. *Polysand* refers to the wood of the jacaranda tree, usually imported from Latin America and used for furniture.

13. Marie von Bunsen, *Zeitgenossen, die ich erlebte: 1900–1930* (Leipzig: Koehler und Amelang, 1932), pp. 51–52. Marie von Bunsen (1860–1941), who also ran a salon in Berlin, traveled the world by herself and wrote widely on her travels. After Babette Meyer's death, she asked the staff of the Berlin Museum to take photographs of Meyer's apartment. Unfortunately, that photographic document has disappeared.

14. Richard Voss, *Aus einem phantastischen Leben: Erinnerungen* (Stuttgart, 1920), pp. 170–71.

15. See Harry Graf Kessler, *Walther Rathenau: Sein Leben und sein Werk* (Frankfurt am Main: Fischer 1988), pp. 50–51.

16. Karl Friedrich Schinkel (1781–1841) was an architect and painter; Christian Daniel Rauch (1777–1857) was a sculptor; Adolph von Menzel (1815–1905), Albert Hertel (1843–1912), and Paul Meyerheim (1842–1915) were painters.

17. Helene von Nostitz, *Aus dem alten Europa: Menschen und Städte* (Reinbek: Rowohlt Verlag, 1964), pp. 35–36.

18. Gründerzeit refers to the period following the founding (*Gründung*) of the German Empire in 1871.

19. Rudolf Vierhaus, ed., *Am Hofe der Hohenzollern: Aus dem Tagebuch der Baronin Spitzemberg 1865–1914* (Munich: Deutscher Taschenbuch Verlag, 1965), pp. 126–27.

20. Ibid., pp. 233–34. The Baroness Spitzemberg refers to Max Reinhardt (1873–1943) (see fig. 186 and the essay by Peter Jelavich in this book); the Austrian poet Hugo von Hofmannsthal (1874–1929); Elisabeth Förster-Nietzsche (1846–1935), sister of Friedrich Nietzsche, who wrote a biography of her brother and published his work; Raoul Richter (1871–1913), son of Cornelie Richter and professor of philosophy in Leipzig; his wife, Lina Richter, born Oppenheim; Alexander Count Hoyos (1876–1937), an Austrian diplomat in Berlin; the Norwegian engineer Samuel Eyde (1866–date unknown); and Harry Count Kessler (1868–1937), diplomat and writer who published the first biography of Walther Rathenau in 1928.

21. Von Bunsen, *Zeitgenossen*, p. 63.

22. Von Nostitz, *Aus dem alten Europa*, p. 37.

23. Ernst von Leyden, *Lebenserinnerungen* (Stuttgart and Leipzig: Deutsche Verlags-Anstalt, 1910).

24. Jules Huret, *Berlin um Neunzehnhundert* (1909; reprint, Berlin: Verlag Elvira Tasbach, 1997), p. 352.

25. Count Axel von Schwering, *The Berlin Court under William II* (London: Cassell, 1915), p. 220.

26. Ursula von Mangoldt, *Auf der Schwelle zwischen gestern und morgen: Begegnungen und Erlebnisse* (Weilheim: Wilhelm Barth-Verlag, 1963), p. 47.

27. Von Schleich, *Besonnte Vergangenheit*, pp. 321–22.

28. *Carl und Felicie Bernstein: Erinnerungen ihrer Freunde*, ed. Georg Treu (Dresden, 1914).

29. Ibid., p. 37.

30. Max Liebermann, "Meine Erinnerungen an die Familie Bernstein" (1908), in Max Liebermann, *Gesammelte Schriften* (Berlin: Bruno Cassirer, 1922), pp. 125–26. Mentioned are Theodor Mommsen (1817–1903), professor of history; Ernst Curtius (1814–1896), professor of ancient history and archaeology; the singer Désirée Artôt de Padilla (1835–1907); Georg Brandes (1842–1927), the Danish writer and literary historian; Max Klinger (1857–1920), a painter, who also created a new form of etching; Friedrich Lippmann (1838–1903), director of the Berlin Graphics Museum; Woldemar von Seidlitz (1850–1922), an art historian; and Karl Emil Franzos (1848–1904), a novelist who portrayed the culture of East European Jews.

31. Liebermann, "Meine Erinnerungen an die Familie Bernstein," p. 127.

32. Sabine Lepsius, "Das Aussterben des Salons," *März* (1913): 226–27.

33. Lovis Corinth (1858–1925) was a painter associated with the Berlin Secession; Julius Meier-Graefe (1867–1935) was an art historian and writer. Dora Hitz (1856–1924) was a painter and member of the Secession; Werner Sombart (1863–1941) was a professor of economics. (See also the essays by Paret, Schütz, and Mendes-Flohr in this book.)

34. Oskar Schmitz, *Ergo sum: Jahre des Reifens* (Munich: Georg Müller Verlag, 1927), p. 78.

35. Gabriele Reuter (1859–1941) was a novelist; Berta von Suttner (1843–1914), a writer, was the first woman to win the Nobel Prize, in 1905; she was the author of a well-known pacifist novel that was translated into many languages; see *Disarm! Disarm!* (London: Hodder and Stoughton, 1913).

36. Hans Fürstenberg, *Carl Fürstenberg: Die Lebensgeschichte eines deutschen Bankiers 1970–1914* (Wiesbaden: Rheinische Verlags-Anstalt, 1961), pp. 397–99. In his autobiography (see n. 45), Hans Fürstenberg claims that he is the author of his father's memoirs.

37. Hedwig Pringsheim-Dohm was an actress married to Alfred Pringsheim, professor of mathematics in Munich. Their daughter Katia became the wife of Thomas Mann. Else Rosenberg was married to the banker Hermann Rosenberg.

38. Fürstenberg, *Carl Fürstenberg*, pp. 505–11.

39. Martin Beradt, "Introduction," in *Briefe an Auguste Hauschner*, ed. Martin Beradt (Berlin: Ernst Rowohlt, 1929), pp. 7–8. Hauschner was the author of novels and short stories, among them *Die Familie Lowositz*, 2 vols. (Berlin: Fleischel, 1908–10).

40. Jacob Schaffner, "Rede, gehalten bei der Gedächtnisfeier für Auguste Hauschner im Lyzeumklub," in *Briefe an Auguste Hauschner*, p. 246.

41. Fritz Mauthner (1849–1923) was the author of novels and, among other theoretical texts, a philosophy of language and a history of atheism; Gustav Landauer (1870–1919) wrote on revolution and socialism and also published literary criticism, notably essays on Shakespeare and Tolstoy; in 1919 he was murdered as a member of the *Münchner Räterepublik*, the socialist government established in Bavaria in 1919. Hedwig Lachmann (1865–1918) was a poet and translator; she married Gustav Landauer in 1899. Louise Dumont (1862–1932), was an actress, director, and adviser on the drama who lived in Berlin from 1896 to 1905.

42. See, for example, *Die wissenschaftliche Emanzipation der Frau* (Berlin: Wedekind und Schwieger, 1874); *Der Frauen Natur und Recht* (Berlin: Wedekind und Schwieger, 1876).

43. Fürstenberg, *Carl Fürstenberg*, p. 95.

44. Ibid., p. 221.

45. Hans Fürstenberg, *Erinnerungen: Mein Weg als Bankier und Carl Fürstenbergs Altersjahre* (Wiesbaden: Rheinische Verlags-Anstalt, 1965), p. 243.

46. Marie von Bunsen, "Unsere letzte gesellige Blüte," in *Frauengenerationen in Bildern*, ed. Emmy Wolff (Berlin: Herbig, 1928), pp. 99–103; see p. 102.

47. Marie von Bunsen, *Die Welt, in der ich lebte: Erinnerungen aus glücklichen Jahren, 1860–1912* (Leipzig: Koehler und Amelung, 1929), pp. 185–88.

48. Ibid., p. 189.

49. Hermann Bahr, *Selbstbildnis* (Berlin: S. Fischer, 1923), pp. 264–65.

50. Lepsius, "Das Aussterben des Salons," pp. 230–35.

51. Hans Simmel, "Erinnerungen," p. 254.

52. Else Croner, *Die moderne Jüdin* (Berlin: Axel Juncker Verlag, 1913), pp. 80–82.

53. Gershom Scholem, *Von Berlin nach Jerusalem*, revised and enlarged edition (Frankfurt am Main: Jüdischer Verlag, 1994), p. 30.

54. Walter Benjamin, *Berliner Kindheit um Neunzehnhundert*, in *Gesammelte Schriften*, vol. 4, no. 1 (Frankfurt am Main: Suhrkamp, 1972), p. 287.

55. Ibid., pp. 264–65.

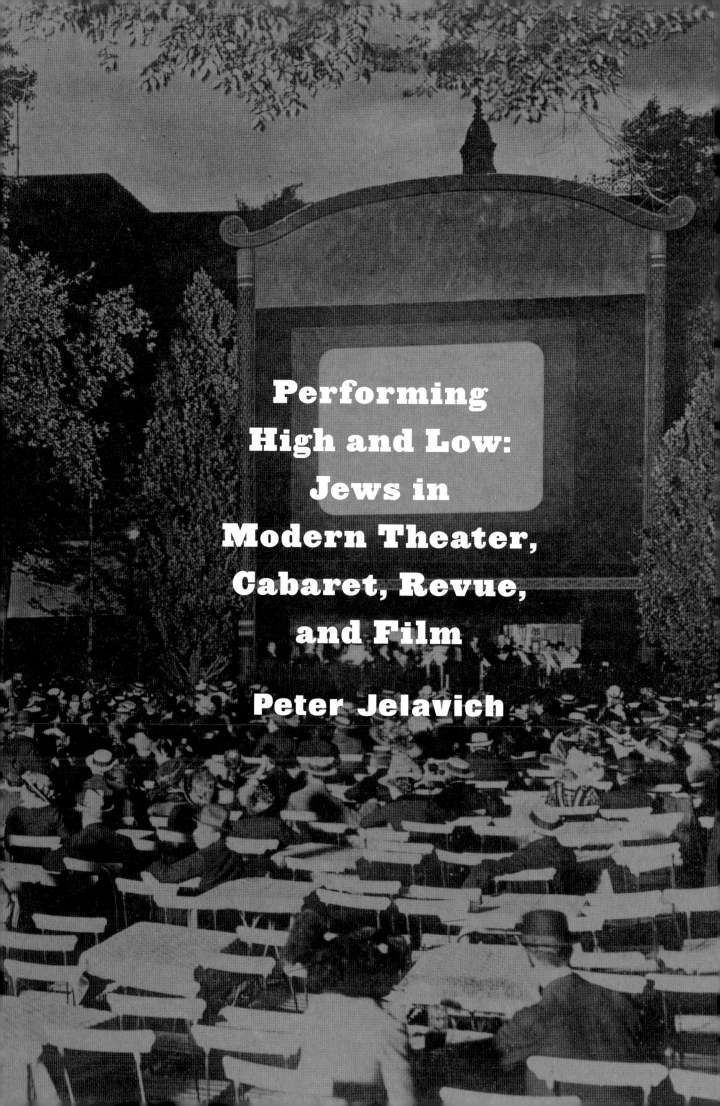

Performing High and Low: Jews in Modern Theater, Cabaret, Revue, and Film

Peter Jelavich

In Imperial Berlin, Jews played important and often decisive roles in the development of theater. Across the whole spectrum of acted performance—from "high" drama to more popular forms like cabaret and revues, and eventually film, the newest mass medium—Jewish artists could be found in the forefront of metropolitan entertainment. To be sure, their roles were not spread evenly across the field. In the realm of dramatic theater, the two most innovative directors and producers were Jewish, as were many actors, but Berlin had hardly any Jewish playwrights. In popular entertainment, by contrast, Jews were prevalent on all fronts, as composers, scriptwriters, producers, and performers. Film, too, had important Jewish producers, actors, and directors. Jews were also important as consumers; in particular, the audiences for Berlin's most innovative dramatic productions were disproportionately Jewish. This essay will not attempt to be encyclopedic, but rather focus on a few outstanding personalities who illustrate the variety of roles played by Jews on the stages and in the cinemas of Imperial Berlin: the theater directors Otto Brahm and Max Reinhardt; the cabaret composer Rudolf Nelson; the revue stalwarts Julius Freund and Viktor Hollaender; and the film comedian and director Ernst Lubitsch.

The Naturalist Theater of Otto Brahm

The beginnings of modernist theater in Berlin can be traced to the efforts of Otto Brahm (1856–1912), an indefatigable advocate of Naturalist drama. The son of a Hamburg merchant, Otto Abrahamsohn began as a bank clerk, but after three years decided to attend university and study literature. In 1877 he moved to Berlin, and the following February he saw a performance of Henrik Ibsen's *Pillars of Society* that changed his life. He started to write theater reviews, and under his assumed name, Otto Brahm, he soon became a regular critic for some of the most prestigious liberal newspapers in Germany, such as Berlin's *Vossische Zeitung* and the *Frankfurter Zeitung*. He favored the budding realist and socially critical tendencies of the day, which were being propagated by a number of foreign authors. In France, Emile Zola called for a thoroughgoing "naturalist" style of unflinching realism, which he exemplified in his numerous novels. As for drama, Brahm believed that similar tendencies were embodied most powerfully in the works of Ibsen. In the 1880s, the Norwegian's plays were considered so daring that they frequently were rewritten for production or banned outright. The ending of *A Doll's House* invariably was changed, so that Nora, rather than slamming the door as she departs, relents at the last minute and returns to her husband. Censorship kept *Ghosts*, with its themes of marital hypocrisy and hereditary syphilis, completely out of public sight for many years.

The only way to circumvent the German censors was to mount so-called closed performances, to which only invited guests were admitted. *Ghosts* received its Berlin premiere—a single

(opposite)
(Detail) Open-air movie theater on the Kurfürstendamm, 1913
Stiftung Deutsche Kinemathek, Berlin

performance—under those conditions in 1887. That event, along with the recent precedent set by André Antoine's *Théâtre libre* in Paris, inspired Brahm and several associates to found the Freie Bühne (Free Stage) in 1889. It was organized as a private association, and only dues-paying members were admitted to its productions. That policy served a dual purpose: not only did it obviate censorship, but it also provided a forum for staging innovative plays by authors whose works were not considered profitable by commercial theater directors. Predictably, the first performance, on 29 September 1889, was of *Ghosts*. But it was the second production, on 20 October, that caused a bona fide scandal. *Vor Sonnenaufgang* (*Before Sunrise*), written by the young, still unknown Gerhart Hauptmann (1862–1946), was a paradigmatically Naturalist work, replete with poverty, incest, hereditary disease, alcoholism, and other social and medical afflictions. The text had been circulated in advance, and some members of the audience came to the performance prepared to cause a rumpus. After an incestuous scene in the second act, a physician in the audience shouted: "Are we in a brothel here?" During the last act, when a woman struggles in a prolonged childbirth offstage, the same doctor waved a forceps over his head, causing the audience to erupt in shouts for and against the play. Hauptmann became an overnight celebrity, and in the ensuing years he was, next to Ibsen, the playwright whom Brahm promoted most. On 16 February 1893, the Freie Bühne hosted the "closed" premiere of his most famous play, *Die Weber* (*The Weavers*), a hard-hitting and relentlessly depressing work about a revolt by starving Silesian workers in 1844.

During its first season (1889–90), the Freie Bühne mounted nine performances and had a membership of several hundred subscribers. After that, however, it sponsored productions only sporadically, in part due to the high cost of staging works for a single evening, but also because commercial theaters began to perform modern dramas. Indeed, in 1894 Brahm himself took over a commercial venue, the Deutsches Theater. A Berlin police report noted that since Brahm did not possess enough capital to rent the theater, he received financial backing from twenty individuals, "among whom nineteen are Jews."[1] Not only were the investors Jewish, but so was much of the audience. Brahm appealed to the courts to overturn the censors' ban on *The Weavers* and won; hence he was able to mount public performances beginning on 2 October 1894. A police observer who attended opening night reported: "A very great majority of visitors to the sold-out house consisted of Jewish elements."[2] Examination of the membership lists of the Freie Bühne association likewise confirms a preponderance of Jews.[3]

Figure 170
Käthe Kollwitz
March of the Weavers
(Weberzug), 1898
From the cycle **Weavers'**
Uprising (Weberaufstand)
Etching,
8½ x 11⅝ in. (21.6 x 29.5 cm)
The Art Complex Museum,
Duxbury, Massachusetts

The fact that Brahm, his financiers, and his audience were largely Jewish underscores the importance of Jewish patronage for innovative theater in the German capital. But it is important to realize that patronage did not necessarily mean approval. The doctor who disrupted the premiere of *Before Sunrise* at the Freie Bühne society was named Isidor Kastan. Referring to the social radicalism of some of Brahm's productions, the Berlin police noted in an internal memorandum: "Even Jewish newspapers that stand close to the Deutsches Theater, like *Das Kleine Journal*, have publicly criticized the subversive tendencies of the current director."[4] Jewish audiences and critics actively patronized institutions that allowed newcomers to have a hearing; but that does not mean that they always liked what they heard, or that they responded as a united front. The Jewish audiences that let new playwrights speak were hardly willing to keep silent about their own opinions. And that was well and good, according to Brahm, who wrote in July 1891: "It is in no way a community of like-minded people who have gathered together here: nowhere are contrary opinions expressed more loudly, in no theater do the opinions clash more forcefully than in the performances of the Freie Bühne."[5] To be sure, there were limits to Brahm's tolerance for dissent, since he expelled Kastan from the Freie Bühne society for having caused the ruckus. But Kastan took the case to court and won, since the judges ruled that his behavior did not violate the regulations or the spirit of the association.[6]

Jewish patrons were hardly united in their support of Naturalism, or any other movement, but at least they gave it a chance to develop—against the wishes of some of Germany's highest authorities. Although there were significant tensions between the Naturalists (a group of "bourgeois" literati) and the Social Democrats (Germany's large working-class party that espoused Marxist doctrine), conservatives regarded both movements as one of a kind. A typical reaction was voiced by the future chancellor, Prince Chlodwig zu Hohenlohe-Schillingsfürst. In a diary entry of 11 December 1893, he noted that he had attended Brahm's production of Hauptmann's *Hanneles Himmelfahrt* (*Hannele Goes to Heaven*), about a poor girl who dies of tuberculosis: "This evening at *Hannele*. A frightful concoction, Social Democratic–realistic, at the same time full of sickly, sentimental mysticism, uncanny, nerve-rattling, altogether awful. Afterward we went to Borchardt, to put ourselves back into a human state of mind with champagne and caviar."[7] Official attitudes were summed up by Berlin's chief of police, who defended a ban on a Naturalist play with the argument (in Berlin dialect): "*Die janze Richtung passt uns nicht.*" (We find the entire movement disagreeable.)[8] Wilhelm II (see FIG. 1) himself accused the Naturalists of being unpatriotic: "When art, as is often now the case, does nothing more than depict poverty as being more dreadful than it already is, then it commits a sin against the German people." According to the Kaiser, art should provide inspiration and edification, goals that it could achieve only when "it is uplifting, not when it descends into the gutter."[9] He regarded Hauptmann's *Weavers* as the most egregious example of such "gutter art." After its public premiere, he permanently canceled his subscription to the stage box at the Deutsches Theater (an arrangement that the Imperial court routinely made with Berlin's major theaters). In 1896 and again in 1898, Wilhelm personally prevented the prestigious Schiller Prize from being awarded to Hauptmann; and in the latter year, he also blocked the jury of the Berlin salon from presenting a gold medal to Käthe Kollwitz for her graphic cycle inspired by *The Weavers* (FIGS. 170, 171).

Although anti-Semites liked to claim that Naturalism was "Jewish" art, neither Ibsen, nor Hauptmann, nor Kollwitz, nor any of its major creators was Jewish. Naturalism was, however, one of a number of currents that were sustained by a network of Jewish patronage that supported new movements, if necessary in the face of official hostility. The undeniable prevalence of Jews among audiences for innovative theater in Imperial Berlin—despite the fact that they made up only 3 percent of the city's population—is a puzzling phenomenon. Given the fact that theater had been considered the queen of the arts in Germany since the eighteenth century (when its importance was established and codified by Lessing, Schiller, and Goethe), it could be argued that Jewish attraction to theater expressed a desire to assimilate to the dominant culture. That might have been true to a certain extent, but the disproportionate numbers of Jews in the audience for unconventional works, many of which flew in the face of classical tradition and official taste, hardly attests to a desire to blend into the surrounding society. In his book on Jews in German theater (1928), Arnold Zweig suggested that the "unprejudiced attitude" (*Vorurteilslosigkeit*) and hunger for the new on the part of Berlin's Jewish public was to a large extent a metropolitan phenomenon, and no different from that of citizens of Paris, London, and Madrid, or even ancient Athens and Rome. But what made Berlin's Jews—as opposed to gentile Berliners—even more susceptible to the new, according to Zweig, was the fact that they did not have a long tradition of being socialized to the dominant aesthetic tradition.[10] Relatively few came from families that had belonged for many generations to the *Bildungsbürgertum*, Germany's prestigious class of educated bourgeois; indeed, almost all the notable figures of theater and film considered in this essay had fathers engaged in business or retail, most frequently in the textile trades. Lacking long-standing ties to German "high" culture, Jews could enter the cultural realm with open, unprejudiced eyes. Moreover, the fact that their advancement in traditional institutions of higher education and culture—universities, court

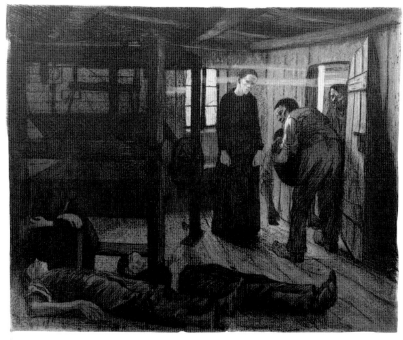

Figure 171
Käthe Kollwitz
The End [Ende], 1898
From the cycle **Weavers'**
Uprising [Weberaufstand]
Etching, aquatint, and mezzotint,
9⅝ x 12 in. (24.5 x 30.5 cm)
The Art Complex Museum,
Duxbury, Massachusetts

theaters, museums—was blocked, despite nominal civic equality, also must have encouraged them to look to new styles and new venues for their personal and professional development.[11] As producers of theatrical culture, Jews were most prevalent in the most recent and least traditional realms: revue, cabaret, and film. In the more established area of drama, Jewish directors were limited to private associations and commercial theaters (rather than court or state theaters), a competitive market in which novelty could pay off. And novelty was rewarded because there was a significant body of Jewish theatergoers who delighted in sponsoring, seeing, and occasionally shouting down innovative plays and productions, such as those of the Naturalists.

The New Theatricality of Max Reinhardt

In July 1891, Otto Brahm proclaimed that "modern theater will be naturalistic—or it will not be at all."[12] Greater or lesser degrees of realism did indeed dominate the modern stages of Berlin during the 1890s, but countertendencies began to develop as well. Ironically, it was Brahm himself who "discovered" the man who eventually would supplant both him personally and Naturalist theater more generally. The son of a Jewish small-businessman, Max Goldmann (1873–1943) grew up in Vienna, the city with what was arguably the richest theatrical tradition in Central Europe. After adopting the stage-name Reinhardt and performing on various stages in the suburbs of Vienna and the provinces of Austria, he joined Salzburg's municipal theater in 1893. It was there that he attracted the attention of Brahm, on the lookout for fresh talent to perform at the Deutsches Theater. Reinhardt was brought to Berlin in the fall of 1894, and soon after his arrival he wrote to a friend: "Berlin is veritably a magnificent city—Vienna multiplied by more than ten. Truly metropolitan character, immense traffic, a tendency to the grandiose throughout, and at the same time practical and upright."[13] The young actor enjoyed great respect as a member of Brahm's ensemble, but with each passing year he became more disenchanted with the ultrarealist style of the Deutsches Theater. By trying to copy slavishly everyday speech and gesture, Naturalism seemed to deny the expressive potential of the stage. According to Reinhardt, nature was natural enough; art was a realm that could and should transcend mundane existence. He stated in 1902: "What I envision is a theater that gives joy back to people. Which leads them past themselves, out of the gray misery of daily existence into the bright and clear air of beauty. I feel that people are fed up with encountering their own troubles in the theater, and that they long for brighter colors and a heightened sense of life."[14]

Reinhardt's vehicle for bursting the chains of Naturalism and liberating the playful elements of the stage was Schall und Rauch (Sound and Smoke), a cabaret that he cofounded in 1901 (FIG. 172). *Cabarets artistiques* had been launched in Paris in the 1880s, but it took more than a decade for the idea to cross into Germany.

Ernst von Wolzogen's Überbrettl, the first such venture in Berlin, opened on 18 January 1901. Reinhardt was attracted to cabaret because its mixture of music, song, dance, pantomime, and skits offered the exuberance and the variety of theatrical experiences that he missed on conventional stages of the day, which were dominated by spoken words and realistic acting. He began his theatrical experimentation at Sound and Smoke, which started as a small company by and for insiders of the theater. The first performance, on 23 January 1901—just five days after the opening of Wolzogen's Überbrettl—took place before invited guests consisting of luminaries of literature and the stage. The show, replete with parodies of the performing arts, was introduced by Reinhardt and the two other founders (Friedrich Kayssler and Martin Zickel, fellow actors at Brahm's Deutsches Theater) dressed in Pierrot outfits (FIG. 173). The high point of the evening was a parody of Schiller's *Don Carlos*, a profoundly idealistic and moving tragedy that was a mainstay of the German dramatic repertory. The work was presented in four radically abbreviated versions, each in a different theatrical style. The first, billed as "Old School, 1800–1890," made light of the traditional mannerisms of court theaters as well as provincial troupes. The second, entitled "Karle: A Comedy of Thieves," parodied the dramas of Hauptmann and the acting style of Brahm's troupe, to which the founders of Sound and Smoke belonged. The sketch was set among an impoverished Silesian family suffering from the usual afflictions of Naturalist theater: alcoholism, mental retardation, suicide, and incest. In Schiller's elevated drama, Carlos longed for his stepmother, Elisabeth of Valois; in the pseudo-Naturalist version, Karle lusted after his natural mother. The third version, representing "the Symbolist school, September 1900–January 1901," was entitled "Carleas und Elisande" and attributed to "Ysidore Mysterlinck." A work of total obfuscation, it replicated the incomprehension that greeted Maurice Maeterlinck's *Pelléas et Mélisande* and other Symbolist works that were just beginning to be performed. The final version, depicting "the Überbrettl school, 18–31 January 1901," was a takeoff on the latest fad to which Sound and Smoke itself belonged. Elisabeth was portrayed by a man singing variety-show tunes, and Carlos entered juggling oranges and uttered, in the broken, multilingual argot of clowns, "O God, O God, ich lieben meine Mutter!" [15]

The first appearance of Sound and Smoke was a great success. Kayssler wrote to a friend after the premiere: "The really beautiful thing about the evening was the fact that all these hard-bitten Berliners turned into children." [16] The troupe performed six more times in the ensuing four months, continuing its parodies of theatrical styles and dramatic literature. Needless to say, that did not mean that Reinhardt intended to damn the arts of the stage. Rather, he made light of a situation that he had criticized as early as 1895: "Formerly there were good and bad actors. Today there are pathetic, naturalistic, declamatory, modern, realistic, idealist, pathological, extrovert and introvert actors, evocative actors,

Zur Erinnerung an „Schall und Rauch"

Figure 173
The founders of **Schall und Rauch**
[Sound and Smoke]:
Left to right: Martin Zickel, Friedrich
Kayssler, and Max Reinhardt, 1901

emotive actors and rational actors, etc. etc. etc. etc. Earlier there were actors who portrayed humanity. Today there are Ibsen actors, Hauptmann actors, stylized actors, and so forth. This, too, is a sign of our times, which has the petty pedantic need to place everything, even art, into boxes, drawers, crates, or molds."[17] What Reinhardt opposed was not any particular style, but a mentality that claimed the monopoly of one style. Having felt constrained by Brahm's persistent and monotonous employment of Naturalism, Reinhardt advocated pluralism: he wanted to celebrate the arts of the stage in all their variety and diversity. Soon his own productions would adopt whatever style he deemed most appropriate to the given drama.

The Sound and Smoke parodies could focus on the performing arts because in its first months, the troupe performed for invited audiences drawn from the theatrical community. Moreover, it was not simply a case of actors performing for fellow actors; it also was a case of Jews performing for fellow Jews. The predominance of Jews among Reinhardt's audiences, like those of Brahm, can be gleaned from the lists of people invited to the "closed" performances of Sound and Smoke and its more serious successor, the Kleines Theater.[18] Since Reinhardt was well aware that he had a largely Jewish clientele, his skits included many jokes about Jews—some of which hardly would have been appropriate to perform in a public, non-Jewish context. For example, the "Karle" episode of the *Don Carlos* parody contained the figure of Markwitz, described in the published version of the text in terms of derogatory stereotypes of the Jewish body: "He is doubtlessly a Hebrew, but does not like to admit it. In addition he has had himself baptized several times, but not to any apparent advantage. His nose has the boldly curving line of the Chosen People. It is white and huge and sweats constantly. The moustache under this nose resists being forced to look like that of the Kaiser." Markwitz considered himself "the paradigm of a beautiful Teuton," despite the fact that he spoke in a "guttural" fashion and walked with a "Jewish" gait.[19] Obviously, this figure caricatures a Jew who so desperately wants to assimilate that he has converted to Christianity and even tries to look like Wilhelm. Berlin's Jewish community did, in fact, face the problem that many of its members turned to Christianity and German nationalism in order to adapt themselves to the dominant culture, and Reinhardt clearly was attempting to make merciless fun of such people. In the process, however, he employed some of the most offensive anti-Semitic stereotypes. The same can be said of the "Chorus of Investors" in another Sound and Smoke skit: "They are well-fed and well-dressed men with hats and frock coats and intensively Roman noses. They bow and bend, murmur and sigh, as if before the Wailing Wall in Jerusalem."[20]

While such caricatures do not seem to have caused any problems as long as Reinhardt and his colleagues performed for invited and predominantly Jewish audiences, they were less welcome after Sound and Smoke went public. The group took over a small theater in the very heart of Berlin, near the corner of Friedrichstrasse and Unter den Linden. It opened on 9 October 1901, but the public premiere was not a success: whereas parody of theater worked well for a select audience of stage connoisseurs, that was too narrow a focus for a general public, which was put off by the barrage of insiders' jokes. Later in the season, the telling of Jewish jokes led to actual disturbances in the audience. A Berlin police report records that on 20 and 21 March 1902, Emanuel Reicher—one of Brahm's best actors—was recounting a series of Jewish anecdotes, entitled the "Story of the Dead Rabbi," when some members of the audience tried to drown him out with shouting, whistling, and foot stomping. The police reported that "seven apparently Jewish students" were apprehended for causing a public nuisance.[21] Although the documents do not indicate the specific reasons for the protest, it seems likely that the students were decrying the public telling of ethnic jokes that reinforced stereotypes. Then, as now, such humor was a fraught issue. Jews like Reinhardt and Reicher obviously believed that the atmosphere of Imperial Berlin was safe and tolerant enough to allow ethnic jokes. Others—who probably had not forgotten the extensive anti-Semitic rhetoric of the 1880s and early 1890s, the heyday of racists like the historian Heinrich Treitschke and the court preacher Adolf Stoecker—were much more cautious. As we shall see, Ernst Lubitsch saw no reason to conceal his Jewishness, even in stereotyped form, in the films he made during World War I, despite a renewed and very pronounced rise in anti-Semitism. The issue finally exploded in 1926, when Jewish organizations held massive meetings to protest the telling of jokes about Jews by Jewish cabaret performers.[22]

After going public, the members of Sound and Smoke learned that they would have to modify their previous recipe of theatrical parody sprinkled with dashes of self-deprecating Jewish humor. Their new winning formula, very much in the spirit of cabaret, was political satire. That was embodied most overtly in the "Serenissimus and Kindermann" scenes. These figures were modeled after a series of caricatures in the satirical journals *Jugend* and *Simplicissimus* featuring Serenissimus, a fictitious potentate of a petty German principality. Politically and culturally benighted, Serenissimus had to have the world explained to him by Kindermann, his loyal adjutant. These popular caricatures had been brought to life by Sound and Smoke during a guest performance at the Deutsches

Theater on 22 May 1901. On that occasion, the troupe pretended to mount a special production of Hauptmann's *Weavers* rewritten to conform to the taste of His Highness. At the beginning of the skit, Serenissimus—played by the Jewish comic actor Victor Arnold—took a seat in the very box that the Kaiser had canceled (FIG. 174). Kindermann explained to him from the stage that he had "ground down the sharp edges of the work, eliminated the rude and repulsive aspects, and amplified and elaborated the few poetic and moral passages."[23] The curtain then opened to reveal, in place of a hovel of starving workers, a cozy bourgeois household, in the center of which stood a table laden with sausage, cake, and wine. The skit continued in that vein to the very end: whereas Hauptmann's play concluded with soldiers firing a volley into a crowd, the Sound and Smoke version had the populace cheer the soldiers marching in while singing "Deutschland über Alles." The success of that skit in the early days of Sound and Smoke encouraged the troupe to revive Serenissimus at the new venue on 15 November 1901. Thereafter he appeared at every performance, and his antics became the frame for the entire show. At the beginning of a program, Serenissimus would take a seat in the stage loge, introduced by an excruciatingly long fanfare. Throughout the evening, he would interrupt numbers with his dim-witted comments: after a pantomime, for example, he would complain about the bad acoustics, since he "could not hear a word." Often he would descend on stage to set the actors straight or flirt with good-looking actresses. Although monarchist newspapers railed against the Serenissimus scenes and the police censors kept a close watch on them, nothing could be done to prevent them because they did not explicitly impugn any particular monarch—even though everyone who attended the shows knew that the Kaiser was often the butt of the jokes. The censors also realized that any attempt to suppress the scenes would have produced a tremendous scandal, since they were so popular: indeed, they were the main reason that people attended Sound and Smoke during the 1901–2 season.

Figure 174
Kindermann (Gustav Beaurepaire) explains the world to Serenissimus (Victor Arnold) in Sound and Smoke's production, 1902.

Having hooked theatergoers with the bait of political satire, the members of Sound and Smoke gradually weaned them onto a more robust diet: modern drama. In the spring of 1902, Sound and Smoke began to shift from cabaret-style numbers to one-act plays—at first comic skits, but eventually also serious works, such as Strindberg's *The Stronger*. By the fall of 1902, the troupe dropped all satirical elements, renamed itself the *Kleines Theater* (Small Theater), and performed contemporary dramas. The performances displayed a strikingly new sense of vitality derived from cabaret: they were full of music and color and

Figure 175
Salome (Gertrud Eysoldt, *right*)
confronts Jochanaan in Reinhardt's
spectacular production of **Salome**,
1903.

motion, the elements of theatricality that Reinhardt found missing on the Naturalist stage.

One of the first full-length plays that he produced was Oscar
Wilde's *Salome*, which culminates in a seductive dance. Because
of censorship, the work initially could be presented only as a one-
time, "closed" performance (15 November 1902). Several months
later, after the play finally was approved for public viewing (29
September 1903), Reinhardt mounted a spectacular production,
whose opulent sets and costumes were designed by the sculptor
Max Kruse and the Impressionist painter Lovis Corinth (FIG. 175).
Reinhardt also sponsored the Berlin premiere of Frank Wedekind's first "Lulu" play, *Erdgeist* (*Earth Spirit*) (17 December 1902),
another sensuous drama full of vaudevillian and circus elements
that burst the bounds of theatrical as well as bourgeois convention.
After the opening of the play, directed by Reinhardt's associate
Richard Vallentin, Kayssler wrote the author: "So you know what
you have done today? You have strangled the naturalistic monster
of verisimilitude and brought the element of play to the stage."[24]
While Reinhardt became one of Wedekind's greatest champions
as both producer and director, his name became even more closely
linked with a fellow son of Vienna, Hugo von Hofmannsthal, who
likewise propounded a new, revitalized sense of theatricality.
Inspired by Gertrud Eysoldt's performances of Salome and Lulu,
Hofmannsthal penned a taut reworking of the Electra story, in
which the monomaniacal heroine releases her pent-up energy in
an ecstatic dance at the end of the play. The premiere (30 October
1903), once more designed by Corinth and Kruse and starring
Eysoldt, marked the beginning of a lengthy collaboration between
Reinhardt and Hofmannsthal (FIG. 176).

Reinhardt's productions of these and other contemporary
works—most notably, Gorky's *The Lower Depths* (23 January 1903,
directed by Vallentin) and Maeterlinck's *Pelléas et Mélisande* (3 April
1903, directed by Reinhardt)—achieved widespread acclaim.
Indeed, his success was so great that he took over a second theater,
the Neues Theater on the Schiffbauerdamm, which would gain

Figure 176
Clytemnestra (Rosa Bertens)
is challenged by Electra (Gertrud
Eysoldt) in Hofmannsthal's collaboration
with Reinhardt, 1903.

Scene aus „Ein Sommernachtstraum"

Figure 178
Rudolf Schildkraut as Shylock in
The Merchant of Venice, 1905

renewed fame after World War II as Bertolt Brecht's stage. In that larger venue, Reinhardt started to direct classics of world drama, suffusing them with a liveliness that had been absent from the staid, overly respectful productions of the nineteenth century. He began in 1904 with Greek and German classics (Euripides' *Medea*, Lessing's *Minna von Barnhelm*, Schiller's *Kabale und Liebe*), but he scored his biggest success with Shakespeare's *Midsummer Night's Dream* (31 January 1905). The play transpired on a revolving stage— a technological novelty, first employed in Munich in 1896. On it was constructed an ultrarealistic forest with mossy ground, thick underbrush, and three-dimensional trees— a striking contrast to the usual "flat" set design of the time. Unlike the conventional stage elves, who traditionally had appeared as cute pixies in tutus, the inhabitants of Reinhardt's forest were dark and mischievous creatures led by a very impish Gertrud Eysoldt as Puck. By all accounts, the forest was as much an actor as the humans (FIG. 177). The audience loved it and demanded hundreds of performances.

Riding a wave of artistic as well as commercial success, Reinhardt gave up the Kleines Theater in 1905 and took over the Deutsches Theater, which Brahm had vacated the previous year. That transition marked the displacement of Naturalism by an eclectic and pluralistic theatricality. Reinhardt's greatest triumph in his first season at the Deutsches Theater was Shakespeare's *Merchant of Venice* (9 November 1905), and once more he broke new ground. In the nineteenth century, the work had tended to be performed as a dark tragedy centered on Shylock; that focus had been reinforced by the practice of ending the play after Shylock's defeat and humiliation in the fourth act, and omitting the fifth act, where the various lovers are reunited. In Reinhardt's production of the entire play, however, Shylock was treated as a secondary role, and performed in a somewhat understated fashion by Rudolf Schildkraut (FIG. 178).

One reviewer observed that—in contrast to traditional performances that reinforced anti-Semitic stereotypes—"Schildkraut realized that Shylock's predominant characteristic is hatred, not greed or haggling." At the outset, Schildkraut acted as if the discrimination that Shylock faced was simply business as usual, which he had been socialized to meet with restraint. But when faced with the loss of his daughter Jessica, he snapped and unleashed the "hatred bottled up inside him due to the discrimination he had endured over many years." The accumulated hatred was so great that Shylock himself was taken aback: "Schildkraut's Jew is so overcome by hatred that he has to correct himself, for example, when he curses his daughter and then, startled, strikes himself on the mouth to exorcise his own words."[25] This sympathetic and psychologically complex portrayal of Shylock was novel, but just a sideshow in Reinhardt's production. It focused instead on the romance between Portia and Bassanio and the glitter of Venice, amid sets designed by the Art Nouveau artist Emil Orlik. In the words of the prominent critic Siegfried Jacobsohn, "Venetian zest for life is the dominant tone of the production, Hebraic suffering just a dissonant note."[26]

Why had Reinhardt chosen this perspective? One can only conjecture, but several explanations come to mind. For one, it probably conformed more to Shakespeare's own intentions; the play was, after all, classified as a comedy. Then there was Reinhardt's increasing propensity for theatrical showmanship, which the scenes of Venetian high society provided ample opportunity to display. But beyond that, there is the possibility that Reinhardt hesitated to confront directly the issue of anti-Semitism. Obviously, had he desired to avoid it entirely, he would not have chosen to produce that particular work. But by simultaneously selecting it and consigning Shylock to a secondary role, he seemed to be downplaying the seriousness of the issue—just as, in Sound and Smoke, he had made fun of overly enthusiastic assimilationists at the same time that he thoughtlessly employed derogatory stereotypes. Rather than faulting Reinhardt, one might perhaps regard such contradictions as evidence of the tension and ambivalence latent in the Jewish experience of fin-de-siècle Berlin. Indirect pressures to assimilate, as well as the rhetoric of anti-Semitism, constituted a constant background noise that one could belittle, but hardly deny—though some people tried to do so. For example, in 1912 Otto Brahm, at the time manager of the Lessing Theater, turned down the opportunity to perform Arthur Schnitzler's *Professor Bernhardi*, a drama about Catholic anti-Semitism set in Vienna's medical circles. Brahm claimed that the subject matter would be too "foreign" for Berlin's audiences, not only because the Prussian capital lacked a Catholic majority, but also because "Berlin's

Figure 179
Edvard Munch
Set Design for Ibsen's **Ghosts**
(Pastor Manders, Mrs. Alving, and Osvald), 1906
Tempera on canvas,
23 13/16 x 40 3/8 in. (60.5 x 102.5 cm)
Munch-museet, Oslo

Jewish doctors are not persecuted, they are predominant."[27] By using parochial—indeed, misleading—arguments to refrain from staging a major new play, Brahm very willfully avoided addressing the issue of anti-Semitism.

During the 1905–6 season, Reinhardt managed two large stages: the Deutsches Theater and the Neues Theater. Yet he seems to have regretted the absence of a smaller, more intimate venue. Thus in the fall of 1906 he gave up the Neues Theater, and he converted the property adjacent to the Deutsches Theater to a 300-seat chamber theater—the Kammerspiele. His first two productions there were knockouts. As if to hammer home his slaying of Naturalism, he chose for the theater's opening what had been the flagship realist drama of the 1880s and '90s—Ibsen's *Ghosts* (8 November 1906). Reinhardt commissioned the Norwegian painter Edvard Munch to design the sets (FIG. 179), and he wrote to the artist: "Interiors in Ibsen plays have until now been incredibly neglected and abused. I am of the opinion that they constitute an essential part of the *many* things that stand between and behind the words in Ibsen's works, and that they not only frame the plot,

but symbolize it."[28] Munch heeded this explicit call for a Symbolist interpretation by creating suggestive set designs, in which a black fauteuil in the middle of the room provided the dominant and disquieting motif. Munch also was commissioned to create a cycle of paintings entitled *Frieze of Life*, which was hung in an upstairs salon of the Kammerspiele.

Ghosts was followed by the world premiere of Frank Wedekind's *Frühlings Erwachen* (*Spring Awakening*) (20 November 1906). Though published fifteen years earlier, censors throughout Germany had kept this play about the turmoil of adolescent sexuality off the stage. By cutting the scenes dealing with masturbation and homosexuality, and by providing a packet of letters from prominent intellectuals and writers attesting to the value of the work, Reinhardt was able to persuade Berlin's censors to permit its performance.[29] The explosive subject matter guaranteed the play an extremely long run. Moreover, in stylistic terms it marked a turning point: the Expressionist movement that arose in the 1910s was prefigured by that play's theme of generational conflict, as well as by the fantastic final scene, in which Moritz, having committed suicide in a previous act, arises from his grave with his blown-off head under his arm (FIG. 180). Not surprisingly, Reinhardt later became one of the earliest patrons of the Expressionists; he directed the world premiere of Reinhard Sorge's *Der Bettler (The Beggar)* (23 December 1917) during the darkest days of World War I (FIG. 181).

Reinhardt's movement away from realistic acting and spoken drama to a more gestural and visual mode of theatricality reached its logical conclusion in 1910, when he abandoned words altogether to stage a pantomime, *Sumurun*. Based on a tale of passion, intrigue, adultery, and murder from *A Thousand and One Nights*, it was a true spectacle, featuring fast-paced acting as well as exotic costumes and colorful sets created by Ernst Stern, who had become the company's chief designer. But Reinhardt hardly abandoned the classics: indeed, the same year saw the premiere of *Oedipus Rex*, in a new translation by Hugo von Hofmannsthal. It was conceived as a theater-in-the-round production, to be staged before thousands of spectators. First performed in an exhibition hall in Munich for a summer theater festival, it was moved to a circus arena in Berlin during the fall. The outstanding cast was led by Paul Wegener as Oedipus and Tilla Durieux (FIG. 182) as Jocasta (FIG. 183); but many observers believed that the real stars of the production were the hundreds of supernumeraries whom Reinhardt transformed into an agitated crowd of Thebans. At various intervals, a barrage of spotlights cut through the darkness to highlight gestures of the masses, such as arms raised in defiance or supplication (FIG. 184). The shadowy lighting and the theater-in-the-round format were designed to erase the boundaries between the crowd and the audience, so that the public would succumb to the illusion of the performance and the intense emotions that it sought to evoke. *Oedipus* was the first major theater-in-the-round production (FIG. 185) in modern times that featured masses of actors performing for a mass audience.

Figure 182
Ernst Barlach
Tilla Durieux, 1912
Bronze, 7½ in. (19 cm)
Courtesy of the Busch-Reisinger Museum, Harvard University Art Museums.
Gift of Naomi Jackson Groves and Association Fund
© President and Fellows of Harvard College

Figure 183
Tilla Durieux as Jocasta in Reinhardt's production of **Oedipus Rex**, 1910

Figure 184
Theater by and for the masses: the crowd of Thebans in **Oedipus Rex**, 1910

Figure 185
Emil Orlik
"In Front of the Palace" [sketch of an impression of the performance],
Oedipus Rex, 1910
Mixed media and watercolor
Theaterhistorische Sammlung der Universität Köln

Metropolitan Entertainment: Cabaret and Revue

While Reinhardt took the performance of dramas in new directions, cabaret—the genre that had provided the springboard for his theatrical reforms—also was evolving. The founder of Berlin's first cabaret, Ernst von Wolzogen, was not Jewish—in fact, he later was outspokenly anti-Semitic—but the success of his venture was attributable largely to the works of his Jewish in-house composer, Oscar Straus. It was primarily as composers and writers of lyrics that Jews shaped and sustained the cabaret movement in both the Imperial and Weimar eras. The major composer and producer of cabaret in Berlin was Rudolf Nelson (1878–1960). Born Rudolf Lewysohn into an impecunious family, he demonstrated musical talent as a very young child, but for pragmatic reasons his parents steered him toward a career in the textile trade. After several miserable teenage years as an underling in that business, he began to perform as a pianist and composer for a number of cabarets. Soon he made his mark, and his fortune, with performances at private parties hosted by extremely wealthy individuals—not just bankers and industrialists, but also Prussian aristocrats. Indeed, in 1908 he was invited to perform for the Kaiser himself. This success enabled him to open a number of

Figure 187
Julius E. F. Gipkens
Poster for **Chat Noir**, ca. 1910
Lithograph,
27⅛ x 37⁹⁄₁₆ in. (69 x 95.4 cm)
© Krefelder Kunstmuseen

cabarets, beginning with the Roland von Berlin in 1903 (see FIG. 188), and followed by the Chat Noir (FIG. 187) in 1907. His venues invariably featured urbane entertainment for well-to-do audiences.

Nelson himself composed the music to all the songs performed in his cabarets. Although many of his extremely successful chansons were set in Berlin high society, some reflected back on the Jewish textile milieu of his youth. Such was the case with his hit *Jacques Manasse* (1912), which recounted how a pretty young woman showed up at her first job (FIG. 189). The refrain listed the people to whom she was introduced: "First the apprentice Jacques Manasse, the young man with the petty-cash box; then the severe managing clerk, the firm's token Christian [*Reklamechrist*]; and next the silent shareholder, over fifty and still a bachelor; and then in person, the head of the company, I. S. Cohn." The following stanzas described how she turned the heads of all these men, made assignations with each one of them, and finally—after a baby appeared on the scene—made the rounds to all of them to collect paternity payments. The song's carefree use of Jewish stereotypes, which were accentuated graphically on the cover of the sheet music (FIG. 189), indicated that Nelson, like Reinhardt, believed that Jews were so well integrated into Wilhelmine society that self-deprecatory humor would cause no problems. Nelson's feeling of security doubtlessly was reinforced by the fact that his audience included members not only of Berlin's haute bourgeoisie, but also the highest levels of the Prussian aristocracy. As we shall see, by 1915, with the rise of more overt anti-Semitism during the war, the use of humor based on stereotypes of Jewish difference began to be questioned by Jewish members of Nelson's audience. But just as Shylock was a sideshow in Reinhardt's production of *The Merchant of Venice*, the Jewish milieu provided merely background ambience for Nelson's *Jacques Manasse*. Prewar audiences would have considered it above all a typical "modern" song of its day, inasmuch as it focused on sexuality in general and

Figure 188
Rudolf Nelson (*center left*) among the performers at the cabaret Roland von Berlin, 1906

Figure 189
Carefree use of Jewish stereotypes: Rudolf Nelson's **Jacques Manasse**, 1912

Figure 190
A policeman prevents Monna Vanna
from disrobing in the Metropol
Theater's parody of Maeterlinck's
drama—and of censorship.

Fritzi Massary

Figure 191
Fritzi Massary, the star soprano
of the Metropol revues, shows
off *haute couture*. . .

the supposed perils of female employment in particular. It also showed Eros to be the great social leveler, one that collapsed a shop hierarchy ranging from poor Jacques Manasse to the wealthy I. S. Cohn. The song was witty, but not barbed; serious social criticism was not to be expected of Nelson, let alone his audience.

Somewhat more satirical punch could be found in the ten revues that were produced annually by the Metropol Theater between 1903 and 1913, under the management of the former actor Richard Schultz (who was not Jewish, unlike his major collaborators). The scripts of these revues, always written by Julius Freund (1862–1914) and usually composed by Viktor Hollaender (1866–1940), focused on the fashions and foibles of metropolitan Berlin. Annually updated "revues" of the year's events had been popular on Parisian stages like the Folies Bergère, so Schultz and Freund transplanted the format to the Prussian capital. In the process, they cribbed rather shamelessly from a variety of other sources; after all, the idea was to present and often parody everything noteworthy in the metropolis. The first show, entitled *Neuestes!! Allerneuestes!!!* (Get the Latest!! The Very Latest!!!), had a loose plot centered on a visit to Berlin by Serenissimus, of Sound and Smoke fame. The fourth act of the revue—again, inspired by Sound and Smoke—consisted of parodies of recent plays by Hauptmann, Maeterlinck, and Wedekind. A level of political satire was added insofar as a policeman kept interrupting the skits to censor dubious actions, as in the scene where Maeterlinck's Monna Vanna is about to throw off her clothes (FIG. 190).

Get the Latest!! did not, however, limit itself to satire and parody. Indeed, its main purpose was to tout Berlin, and in particular, its modernity. By giving Serenissimus a tour of the capital, the revue could promote and applaud the city's newest embellishments, like the Wertheim Department Store (see FIG. 195) and the elevated commuter train. At a time when reactionary, back-to-*Heimat* ideologues were lambasting Berlin as a "Chicago on the Spree," the revue encouraged the audience to take pride in the fact that their capital was so very up-to-date. That being the case, it came as no surprise that the main theme of the Metropol revues was fashion.

Couture was not only central to the economy of Berlin, but it also was an area of business clearly dominated by Jewish firms, in terms of both manufacture and retail. In turn-of-the-century Berlin, the garment trade was the largest occupational sector after the civil service. Moreover, much of the city's retailing—particularly that of the department stores—was geared to selling clothing and other fashionable commodities. Thus it was hardly surprising that the Metropol revues did their best to promote the latest trends

Figure 192
. . . while the chorus touts fashionable
undergarments, 1909

in outer- and underwear. The height of glamour in the Metropol
revues was embodied by Fritzi Massary (1882–1969), a dazzling
soprano from a Viennese Jewish family who was the star of the
shows. She not only displayed her great talents as a singer and
comedienne, but she also appeared in the latest *haute couture*
(FIG. 191). The performers of lesser parts likewise had a role to
play in the fashion show. A song like "What the Fashionable Lady
Needs" was not just a tentative striptease number that showed the
style of shoes, stockings, garters, chemises, and corsets that "a
woman of the world" and "a woman of today" were expected to
have (FIG. 192).[30] It also promoted the types of commodities that
were manufactured and retailed in the most "Jewish" sector of the
Berlin economy.

The Metropol revues were not, however, overtly Jewish shows.
Their main audience consisted of tourists from all over Germany,
and the revues fostered pride not only in the German capital, but
also in the German nation. Despite its use of the Serenissimus
figure and its satire of police censors, *Get the Latest!!* included a
production number in the style of a military parade as well as a
scene glorifying the recently deceased Otto von Bismarck. In 1907,
the revue even had a number praising German troops in Southwest
Africa—a fraught political issue, given the brutality of the German
colonial regime. That scene launched the song "Annemarie," which
became one of the most popular songs among German troops in
both World Wars (much to the embarrassment of the Nazis, who
eventually claimed that it had been written by a common soldier in
World War I, since they could not attribute it to Hollaender and
Freund, the song's Jewish creators).[31] In Imperial Berlin, there was
no necessary contradiction between being Jewish and being a German patriot. The crafters of the Metropol revues, like many of their
coreligionists, felt themselves to be simultaneously members of the
Jewish community, proud inhabitants of Berlin, and citizens of the
German Reich. But that was a juggling act that worked only in an

Figure 193
Fritzi Massary plays a bedridden
Wendla in a parody of Wedekind's
Spring Awakening, 1907

atmosphere of tolerance and pluralism, values that were, in fact, promoted by the Metropol revues. To the extent that they engaged in political satire, it was to chide officialdom for censorship and clinging to outmoded taste. If the revues had a message, it was: "Be open to the new." But they also implied that one should not accept uncritically everything that came along; hence the prevalence of parody. Freund's witty takeoff on Reinhardt's production of *Spring Awakening* certainly made light of Wedekind's play for its sexual themes and adolescent pathos (FIG. 193). But at the same time, the show implied that Reinhardt's production was one of the many sights that made Berlin so special—and thus, as the title of Freund's 1907 revue proclaimed, *Das muss man sehen*, (*You Gotta See It*).

That same production included a skit that summarized the combination of satire and appeals for toleration so typical of the Metropol revues. In a takeoff on debates about the roles of "nature" versus "nurture" in the formation of personality, the scene dramatized an experiment wherein two unrelated children spend six months with each other's families. One of the swapped children in the satirical skit was the son of Count Pückler, a rabid and outspoken anti-Semite. Beginning in 1899, Jewish organizations repeatedly brought Pückler to court—with varying success—on account of his public speeches in which he advocated physical violence against Jews; finally, in 1908, he was committed to a mental asylum. In the Metropol skit, the son of this mad count exchanged places with the daughter of one of the Hungarian-born Herrnfeld brothers, owners of a Berlin theater that specialized in Jewish dialect comedy. Anton and Donat Herrnfeld wrote and performed all their plays, which usually were set in the Habsburg borderlands, with Anton playing a Bohemian and Donat a Jew. Though looked down upon by many Jewish intellectuals and some Jewish organizations—because of the unsophisticated nature of the entertainment, as well as the generous use of ethnic stereotypes—the "Gebrüder Herrnfeld Theater" epitomized what was known as *Jargontheater* (Jargon Theater), and it was extremely popular with lower-middle-class Jewish audiences.[32]

In the Metropol skit, the son of the anti-Semitic count, having spent six months with a Herrnfeld, has turned into a big-city gamin spouting Yiddish words; conversely, the daughter of the Jewish entertainer, after half a year on a country estate, has become a snooty aristocrat voicing "Teutonic" and anti-urban slogans. The scene obviously was a slap at racial theorists, inasmuch as it implied that "nurture," not "blood," fashioned personality and identity. On the visual level as well, the joke was entirely on Pückler: whereas the Herrnfeld daughter was performed by the glamorous Fritzi Massary, the son of the racially obsessed count was portrayed by Guido Thielscher, a rotund, "doofy," and non-Jewish comic actor who was anything but the epitome of so-called Aryan beauty. What made the skit such a paradigm of the Metropol revues was the fact that it both parodied and touted a "competitor" in the entertainment field—in this case, the

Herrnfeld Theater—at the same time that it indirectly promoted an inclusive and tolerant view of German citizenship, by satirizing those who would exclude Jews from the nation.

The Emergence of Film: Early Comedies of Ernst Lubitsch

Jews played significant roles not only in forms of live entertainment like cabarets and revues, but also in film, the newest and most popular mass medium. Having been launched as the closing number in Berlin's Wintergarten variety theater in November 1895, film rapidly became an attraction in vaudeville houses throughout Germany. After a decade it began to take off, as small stores were converted into venues that specialized exclusively in screening films (the equivalent of nickelodeons in the United States). At first, the medium catered to the lower classes as well as children; given the technical crudeness of early films and the crowded and stifling atmosphere of early screening rooms, most members of the middle classes stayed away. To rectify that situation, Paul Davidson, a Jewish entrepreneur based in Frankfurt, founded a chain of upscale cinemas beginning in 1906; they had more comfortable chairs, better ventilation, and larger screens than the average nickelodeon. The first such cinema in Berlin was the Union Theater on the Alexanderplatz, which opened in 1909 and billed itself as "the largest and most elegant cinema in the world" (FIG. 194). Soon thereafter, Davidson moved his headquarters to Berlin, and he also founded a production company, known as PAGU (Projektions-Aktien-Gesellschaft "Union").

Viele Grüsse aus dem Union-Theater, Berlin, Alexanderplatz
Grösste und vornehmste Tonbild-Bühne der Welt

Figure 194
The Union Theater on the Alexanderplatz, Berlin's first upscale cinema, 1909

Just as he sought to attract a middle-class public by providing more elegant cinemas, Davidson also tried to lure the bourgeoisie with films that were more "elevated" than the common cinematic fare. As part of that policy, he was able to coax Max Reinhardt into directing two films in 1913. Unfortunately, the stage genius proved to be a mediocre film director. *Die Insel der Seligen* (*The Isle of the Blessed*, 1913) was certainly fanciful—it involved a group of tourists who land on an island inhabited by mermaids, nymphs, and satyrs —but the execution was simply too clunky to be effective. *Eine venezianische Nacht* (*A Venetian Night*, 1914), based on Reinhardt's stage production of Karl Vollmöller's pantomime of that name, was no more successful; audiences could not fail to compare it very unfavorably with the live performance. Nevertheless, Reinhardt's involvement with film was very significant, since in 1912 the association of theater directors, fearful of the growing competition from cinema, had ordered actors to boycott the film industry. By breaking ranks, Reinhardt effectively ended the boycott and ensured that film companies could draw on Germany's best acting and directing talent. Though Reinhardt himself did not benefit from his action, many of his actors did. One of them was Ernst Lubitsch.

Lubitsch (1892–1947) was born in Berlin, the son of (what else?) a Jewish owner of a women's clothing store. He started out as an apprentice at a textile retail firm, then became an accountant in his father's expanding business. But his real passion was theater, so in 1910 he began to take acting lessons from Victor Arnold, who had played Serenissimus at Sound and Smoke a decade earlier. A year later, Arnold arranged to have Lubitsch join Reinhardt's company at the Deutsches Theater, where he played small roles—*very* small roles—until 1918. Lubitsch was frustrated by his inability to land larger parts, but once again Arnold helped him out by giving him a foothold in the film industry. He began to appear on screen in 1913, and in January 1914 he was seen in his first major role. *Die Firma heiratet* (*The Firm Gets Married*), a PAGU production, was a comedy set in a fabric shop, whose owner was played by Victor Arnold. Lubitsch had the main supporting role: an apprentice named Moritz Abramovsky, who constantly disrupts the business but saves his job by finding a wife for his boss. The film was a great success, as was Lubitsch; indeed, within months he had the starring role in another PAGU production, *Der Stolz der Firma* (*The Pride of the Firm*). Here he played Siegfried Lachmann, whom we first see as an apprentice in a clothing store of a provincial East European town. After being fired for wrecking the shop through his clumsiness (he topples off a ladder and smashes the storefront window and display), he sets off for Berlin. There he gets a job in another clothing store and, after a series of comic misadventures, marries the daughter of the owner (again played by Arnold).

Figure 195
Wertheim Department Store,
Leipziger Strasse, 1906

From 1914 to 1918 Lubitsch would star in, and eventually direct, a number of very successful comedies (see FIG. 196), many of which were set in the Jewish retailing milieu. That would not have been surprising were it not for the fact that those years coincided with World War I. Indeed, *The Pride of the Firm*, which premiered to great acclaim on 30 July 1914, was pulled off the screen within days, as the German authorities banned all frivolous comedies for the duration of what they thought would be a short conflict. But as the war dragged on and the civilian population became increasingly desperate for distraction, the censors relented and allowed *The Pride of the Firm* to be re-released in January 1915. Lubitsch appeared in a number of other comedies, and in 1916 he served for the first time as director of a feature-length film, *Schuhpalast Pinkus* (*Pinkus's Shoe Palace*).

Here Lubitsch played Sally Pinkus, whom we encounter as a most un-model schoolboy: he is late to class, constantly flirts

Figure 196
Josef Fenneker
Poster for **Der Fall Rosentopf**
(A film directed by Ernst Lubitsch),
1918
Color lithograph,
37 7/16 x 55½ in. (95 x 141 cm)
Stiftung Deutsche Kinemathek, Berlin

with the girls, and cheats in gym class and on exams. After being expelled, he lands a job in a small shoe store, but is fired for making moves on the owner's daughter. He manages to be hired at a much more fashionable shoe salon, where he almost gets fired again: he not only flirts with the female staff, but caresses and tickles the feet of the female customers. Yet he saves his job by making a difficult sale. The dancer Melitta Hervé keeps rejecting the shoes brought out by the owner, insisting that the size is too large. Sally then brings out one of the very same pairs of shoes, after having written a smaller size on the box. Melitta's vanity having been assuaged, she is delighted that Sally found the "right" size and asks him to deliver the shoes to her apartment. A flirtation ensues, and Melitta offers to provide funds for Sally to open his own shop. He launches a large and elegant boutique that bills itself a "shoe palace." At first, business is slow, until Sally hits upon the right advertising ploy. He uses the occasion of one of Melitta's dance appearances to tell the assembled spectators that she wears shoes purchased in his store, and that soon he will host a show of the latest fashions. Customers flock to Sally's shop to see a spectacle that, under Lubitsch's direction, carried leg, foot, and shoe fetishism to new cinematic heights. In fact, the film censors of 1916 ordered cuts in "the close-ups of the feet of the salesgirls showing off boots."[33] At the end of the film, Sally and Melitta agree to marry.

The connections between entertainment and retailing, so marked in the Metropol revues, were also represented in *Pinkus's Shoe Palace*. Not only does the (fictional) Sally use his lady-friend's dance evenings as a forum for advertising his wares, but the film itself flashes texts that advertise the (real) stores in Berlin where the shoes can be purchased. This early example of "product placement" operates, in short, on both a fictional and an actual level—which means that the film simultaneously satirizes and participates in the conflation of commerce and entertainment.

The satire works as well at a more general level, inasmuch as the film shows vanity to be a powerful motivating force. Sally first attracts Melitta's attention by playing along with her vain belief that her feet are smaller than they are in reality. Once he has use of her capital, he opens a shop that is not content to be called a simple store, but has to proclaim itself a "palace." That was an indirect joke on the movie business: many of the people watching the film in 1916 would have been sitting in a venue that called itself a *Lichtspielpalast*—literally, "light-show palace"—the grandiose name that pretentious cinemas were given to distinguish them from simple nickelodeons.

There was an even more fundamental level of subversion (and humor) operating in the film, especially if we remember that it was premiered in the midst of World War I, a time when German culture was suffused with images of militarism and masculinity. Most films and plays glorified men who were honest, noble, brave, muscular, and blond; and such men, in such shows, invariably got the girl in the end. Lubitsch completely inverted that paradigm, first and foremost by emphasizing his stereotypical Jewishness: not only is the milieu Jewish, but the camera work often fixes on Lubitsch's short stature, dark features, and wholly non-"Teutonic" physiognomy. Reversals of "noble" ideals also pervade *Pinkus's Shoe Palace*: rather than being a model pupil, he cheats; being a weakling, he has to fake his prowess in gym; he dissembles to get a job or make a sale—but in the end, it is he who gets the girl. Indeed, to emphasize the fact that he is playing with ethnic and romantic stereotypes, Lubitsch—though himself visually typecast as Jewish—pointedly (and rather cruelly) rejects "Jewish-looking" women for blond, Germanic types in some of his early films. The fact that works like *Pinkus's Shoe Palace* were so successful in the midst of the war not only indicates that audiences were desperate for humorous distractions; it also suggests that many citizens were fed up with the constant barrage of militaristic, macho rhetoric. The popularity of Lubitsch's slyly subversive works seems to corroborate numerous police reports indicating that by 1916, civilian morale was extremely low.

Some later commentators have been troubled by the fact that in films like *Pinkus's Shoe Palace*, Lubitsch employed what might have been considered anti-Semitic stereotypes for humorous purposes.[34] As we saw in connection with Reinhardt, it was a sensitive issue in Imperial Berlin, and it became even more so during the Great War, a time that experienced a very noticeable rise in anti-Semitic agitation. Since tens of thousands of young Jewish men were fighting and dying at the front, it was particularly bitter for them and their families to hear diatribes claiming that Jews were evading the draft in large numbers. The most terrible blow came in October 1916, when the Imperial army ordered the *Judenzählung*, a tally of Jewish soldiers at the front. It was undertaken ostensibly to counter anti-Semitic accusations; in reality, the racists in the military wanted to collect evidence to feed anti-Semitic fires. That became most evident when army officials

Figure 197
Twofold Lubitsch: Siegfried Lachmann
confronts his past at the conclusion
of **The Pride of the Firm
(Der Stolz der Firma)**, 1914.

refused to publicize the results of the count, which indicated that
Jews were represented proportionately on the battlefields. The
Judenzählung was a monstrous insult to Germany's Jewish citizens, and did nothing to calm the domestic waters; it broke the
spirit of many patriotic Jews at the same time that it fanned the
flames of anti-Semitism.[35]

In such circumstances, it was understandable that many Jewish citizens bristled at skits by Jewish humorists that seemed to
emphasize Jewish differences from Germans more generally. For
example, in January 1915 the Berlin police received an anonymous
letter, signed only by "a decent Jewish woman" (*eine anständige
Jüdin*), complaining about a performance at Rudolf Nelson's
cabaret: "At a time when hundreds of Jewish soldiers are earn-
ing the Iron Cross, is it fitting that filthy Jewish tales [*jüdische
Unflätigkeiten*] are told—unfortunately by a person who is himself
Jewish?" The woman deplored in particular the use of the Yiddish
words *tineff, chutzpeh,* and *ponim.*[36] Though she obviously considered the Yiddish expressions vulgar, they were heard frequently in
Jewish dialect skits, like those of the Herrnfeld brothers. Even
during peacetime, employing such markers of Jewish difference
for comic effect had been somewhat controversial. But during
the Great War, a period of nationalistic fervor and growing racist
agitation, the fear that Jewish self-deprecating humor might play
into the hands of anti-Semites was especially acute.

Since film was a silent medium, Lubitsch's screen persona
was a visual and pantomimic equivalent of Jewish dialect theater.
His awareness of the controversies surrounding that genre was

indicated by his rather defensive reply in 1916 to an interviewer who asked him about his preference for "films set in a Jewish milieu." Lubitsch responded "in an excited manner" that "it has often been said that films set in a Jewish milieu are considered offensive. That's a completely unbelievable standpoint. Should it ever be the case that such a film incurs disapproval, then it is solely due to a type of performance that either does not correspond to the essence of Jewish humor, in which case the actor should steer clear of such roles; or it is excessively exaggerated, but that would harm any type of artistic performance and destroy its effect. Wherever it appears, Jewish humor is sympathetic and artistic, and it plays such a great role everywhere that it would be silly to forgo it on the screen."[37] The fact that Lubitsch's wartime films were so successful among Jewish and gentile audiences alike suggests that the mounting anti-Semitic agitation had not yet been able to poison the general public's positive enjoyment of a genre of ethnic humor that was an accepted form of entertainment in the Imperial era.

Lubitsch could not conceive of a cinema landscape devoid of Jewish characters; he could not imagine a silver screen where Jews could not be depicted. Even at the height of a nationalist war, when anti-Semitic voices were becoming ever more strident, he refused to obliterate his identity. Indeed, if there is an archetypal shot in Lubitsch's early films, it has to be the concluding scene of *The Pride of the Firm* (FIG. 197). On the left side of a split screen, we see Lubitsch as the poor, provincial Siegfried Lachmann whom we encountered at the beginning of the film. He looks directly at the audience with a smile on his face, and he gestures with his thumb to the right, where we see Lubitsch again; here he is the older, successful, well-dressed Lachmann, who looks left toward his alter ego, scowling and shaking his hand in a gesture of disapproval, as if to ward off his past. Lubitsch obviously was chiding the social parvenus in his audience for trying to hide their roots. He also might have been telling the audience that he, for one, would not deny his Jewishness. Lubitsch soon would become part of the Hollywood establishment, where one of the standard precepts for a successful production was expressed in the quip: "Write Yiddish—cast British." But in the last years of Imperial Berlin, Lubitsch could still create a hit by both writing and casting "Yiddish."

To be sure, the early films of Ernst Lubitsch were somewhat anomalous. Very few of the stage and film works produced by Jews in Imperial Berlin were overtly Jewish, let alone Yiddish. But at the same time, the theatrical culture of prewar Berlin would have been unimaginable without the participation of Jews. As directors they revolutionized theatrical practice, and as composers, writers, and performers, they revitalized popular entertainment. If Berlin's stages and screens were sites of innovation, excitement, open-mindedness, and, above all, *play*, it was to a great extent due to the efforts and inspiration of its Jewish citizens.

Notes

1. Police report of 26 March 1895, reprinted in Alfred Dreifuss, *Deutsches Theater Berlin* (Berlin: Henschelverlag, 1987), p. 118.

2. Police report of 2 October 1894, reprinted in Helmut Praschek, ed., *Gerhart Hauptmanns "Weber": Eine Dokumentation* (Berlin: Akademie-Verlag, 1981), p. 288.

3. See the membership lists of the Freie Bühne from June 1889 and January 1890, reproduced in *S. Fischer, Verlag: Von der Gründung bis zur Rückkehr aus dem Exil*, ed. Friedrich Pfäfflin and Ingrid Kussmaul (Marbach: Schiller-Nationalmuseum, 1985), pp. 34–44.

4. Police report of 26 March 1895, reprinted in Dreifuss, *Deutsches Theater Berlin*, p. 119.

5. Otto Brahm, *Theater, Dramatiker, Schauspieler*, ed. Hugo Fetting (Berlin: Henschelverlag, 1961), p. 409.

6. See "Der Naturalismus vor Gericht," *Freie Bühne für modernes Leben* 1 (1890): 132–34.

7. Chlodwig zu Hohenlohe-Schillingsfürst, *Denkwürdigkeiten* (Stuttgart: Deutsche Verlags-Anstalt, 1907), vol. 2, p. 507. Borchardt was (and still is) one of Berlin's most expensive and exclusive restaurants.

8. Oskar Blumenthal, *Verbotene Stücke* (Berlin: H. Steinitz, 1900), p. 16.

9. Ernst Johann, ed., *Reden des Kaisers: Ansprachen, Predigten und Trinksprüche Wilhelms II* (Munich: Deutscher Taschenbuch Verlag, 1966), p. 102.

10. Arnold Zweig, *Juden auf der deutsche Bühne* (Berlin: Welt-Verlag, 1928), pp. 101–2.

11. For a general discussion of possible reasons for novelty and creativity among Jewish artists and intellectuals in Imperial Germany, see Steven M. Lowenstein, "Explaining Jewish Cultural Creativity," in *German-Jewish History in Modern Times*, ed. Michael Meyer (New York: Columbia University Press, 1997), vol. 3, pp. 331–35.

12. Brahm, *Theater, Dramatiker, Schauspieler*, p. 413.

13. Max Reinhardt, letter to Berthold Held, fall 1894, in Max Reinhardt, *Ich bin nichts als ein Theatermann: Briefe, Reden, Aufsätze, Interviews, Gespräche, Auszüge aus Regiebüchern*, ed. Hugo Fettig (Berlin: Henschelverlag, 1989), p. 37.

14. Cited in Arthur Kahane, *Tagebuch eines Dramaturgen* (Berlin: Bruno Cassirer, 1928), p. 115.

15. The first three versions are published in Max Reinhardt, *Schall und Rauch* (Berlin: Schuster und Loeffler, 1901), pp. 27–125.

16. Friedrich Kayssler, letter to Christian Morgenstern, 27 January 1901, in Christian Morgenstern, *Ein Leben in Briefen* (Wiesbaden: Insel Verlag, 1952), p. 117.

17. Reinhardt, letter to Berthold Held, 9 March 1895, in Reinhardt, *Ich bin nichts als ein Theatermann*, p. 61.

18. For example, see the invitation list to the closed performance of *Salome* on 15 November 1902, in Brandenburgisches Landeshauptarchiv, Pr. Br. Rep. 30 Berlin C, Pol. Präs. Tit. 74, Th 804.

19. Reinhardt, *Schall und Rauch*, p. 79.

20. Ibid., p. 129.

21. Police report of 21 March 1902, in Brandenburgisches Landeshauptarchiv, Pr. Br. Rep. 30 Berlin C, Pol. Präs. Tit. 74, Th 804.

22. See Peter Jelavich, *Berlin Cabaret* (Cambridge, Mass.: Harvard University Press, 1993), pp. 201–2.

23. Friedrich Kayssler, "Die Weber: Soziales Drama: Auf Wunsch Sr. Durchlaucht von Serenissimus für eine Sondervorstellung bearbeitet von Freiherr von Kindermann," reprinted in *Schall und Rauch: Erlaubtes und Verbotenes: Spieltexte des ersten Max-Reinhardt-Kabaretts*, ed. Peter Sprengel (Berlin: Nicolai, 1991), p. 54.

24. Cited in Julius Bab, *Das Theater der Gegenwart* (Leipzig: J. J. Weber, 1928), p. 121.

25. Heinrich Stümcke, "Von den Berliner Theatern 1905/06," *Bühne und Welt*, 8 (1905–6): 210–11.

26. Siegfried Jacobsohn, *Max Reinhardt* (Berlin: Erich Reiss, 1910), p. 2.

27. Oskar Seidlin, ed., *Der Briefwechsel Arthur Schnitzler–Otto Brahm* (Tübingen: Max Niemeyer, 1975), p. 347.

28. Reinhardt, *Ich bin nichts als ein Theatermann*, p. 111.

29. The letters in support of the performance are reprinted in Reinhardt, *Ich bin nichts als ein Theatermann*, pp. 526–30.

30. Julius Freund, *Halloh!!! Die grosse Revue!!!* (Berlin: Bote & Bock, 1909), p. 15.

31. For the fate of "Annemarie," see Walter Freund, "Aus der Frühzeit des Berliner Metropoltheaters," *Kleine Schriften der Gesellschaft für Theatergeschichte* 19 (1962): 62–63.

32. On the Herrnfeld Theater and the discussions it provoked, see Peter Sprengel, *Populäres jüdisches Theater in Berlin von 1877 bis 1933* (Berlin: Haude & Spener, 1997), pp. 62–98.

33. Herbert Birett, ed., *Verzeichnis in Deutschland gelaufener Filme: Entscheidungen der Filmzensur 1911–1920* (Munich: Saur, 1980), p. 549. The censors also ordered the deletion of an earlier scene "in which the boss strokes the feet of a lady."

34. Such criticisms are summarized and discussed in Sabine Hake, *Passions and Deceptions: The Early Films of Ernst Lubitsch* (Princeton: Princeton University Press, 1992), pp. 30–31.

35. See Werner Angress, "The German Army's 'Judenzählung' of 1916: Genesis-Consequences-Significance," in *Leo Baeck Institute Year Book* 23 (1978): 117–37.

36. See the anonymous letter of 15 January and the police report of 29 January 1915, in Brandenburgisches Landeshauptarchiv, Pr. Br. Rep. 30 Berlin C, Pol. Präs. Tit. 74, Th 1514.

37. Julius Urgiss, "Künstlerprofile: Ernst Lubitsch," *Der Kinematograph*, 30 August 1916.

Chronology: 1890–1918

Mira Goldfarb Berkowitz and Alexandra Nocke

	World History and Politics	**Jewish History and Culture**
1890	German Chancellor Otto von Bismarck is succeeded by Leo von Caprivi. At the Erfurt Congress, German Social Democrats adopt a Marxist agenda. The American National Women's Suffrage Association is formed.	The "Odessa Committee" (Society for Agricultural Workers and Craftsmen in Syria and Palestine) is founded to assist Jewish settlement in Palestine. Baronne Charlotte de Rothschild purchases the Isaac Strauss Collection of Judaica for the Musée de Cluny in Paris.
1891	The Triple Alliance is renewed among Germany, Austria-Hungary, and Italy. France and Russia negotiate entente. The skeletal remains of *Pithecanthropus erectus*, or "Java Man," are discovered.	Jews are systematically expelled from Moscow. As persecution continues, Baron Maurice de Hirsch negotiates the transfer of 6,000 Jews to Argentina.
1892	A pan-Slav conference is held in Cracow. Henry Ford builds his first automobile. A cholera epidemic in Hamburg kills 9,000.	The American Jewish Historical Society is founded. B'nai B'rith establishes a national library in Jerusalem. Ludwig Jacobowski's novel *Werther der Jude* (Werther the Jew) is published. Israel Zangwill's *Children of the Ghetto* is published. In his first major role on the Yiddish stage in New York, Jacob P. Adler appears in the *Jewish King Lear* by Jacob Gordin. Adler plays Shylock in 1901.
1893	Economic crisis takes hold in Germany. England's Independent Labour Party is formed. New Zealand is the first country to grant women the right to vote.	In Berlin, the Centralverein (Central Organization of German Citizens of Jewish Faith, or CV) is founded to combat rising anti-Semitism in universities and society at large, and to promote full civil rights for Jews. The Anglo-Jewish Historical Society is formed in London. The Smithsonian Institution presents the first exhibition of Judaica in the United States at the World's Columbian Exposition.

Berlin Art and Culture	International Art and Culture	
Otto Brahm's Freie Bühne (Free Stage), a members-only theater exempt from censorship, has its first season (1889–90).	Vincent van Gogh dies by suicide. Georges Seurat paints *Le Cirque* (The Circus). Publication of *Hedda Gabler* by Henrik Ibsen. Publication of *The Principles of Psychology* by William James, in which he defines the "stream of consciousness."	
Leopold Ullstein starts to publish the *Berliner Illustrirte Zeitung*.	At Emile Zola's request, the French Writers' Association commissions Auguste Rodin to create a monument to Balzac. Paul Gauguin settles in Polynesia, where, inspired by local culture, he creates a large body of work. Monet exhibits his series of fifteen *Haystack* paintings. Peter Ilich Tchaikovsky completes the ballet *The Nutcracker*. Publication of Oscar Wilde's *Picture of Dorian Gray*. Seurat dies at age thirty-one.	**Naturalism/Realism 1848–80** Naturalism is identified with the mid-nineteenth-century Realist movement, which in France and Germany, as well as the United States, signified a dissatisfaction with artifice and the Romantic and idealist themes and styles that had dominated academic canons of art and literature at the time. In Europe, industrialization and the 1848 revolutionary fervor had created both an audience and new subject matter for the writer, dramatist, or painter of modern life. And the concurrent emergence of empirical science and photography engendered an appreciation for accurate and objective recording of the real world. The opponents of Realism and Naturalism criticized the focus on a pedestrian, often harsh reality, represented in art by images of rural peasants and urban factory workers (in the work of Jean-François Millet, Gustave Courbet, Adolph von Menzel, Wilhelm Leibl, and Max Liebermann) and in drama and literature by proletarian struggle or family dysfunction (in the writings of Emile Zola, Gustave Flaubert, Henrik Ibsen, and Gerhart Hauptmann). Menzel was a leading Realist artist in Berlin, with his unflinching commitment to accuracy of detail that he brought equally to his history painting and modest family scenes.
An exhibition of Edvard Munch at Verein Berliner Künstler (Association of Berlin Artists) provokes a scandal and is closed. "The Eleven" is founded by Walter Leistikow, Max Liebermann, and other members of the Association of Berlin Artists to hold exhibitions of modern art outside of the salon system. Birth of Ernst Lubitsch. Birth of Walter Benjamin	Symbolist artists exhibit in the first Salon de la Rose + Croix in Paris. Paul Cézanne paints *The Card Players*. The Munich Secession is launched with an exhibition dominated by Naturalist and Symbolist works. The Linked Ring photographic secession group is founded in London. It is later renamed the Royal Photographic Society.	
Fritz Gurlitt Gallery exhibits works by French Impressionists. The Free Theater premieres Gerhart Hauptmann's Naturalist drama *Die Weber* (The Weavers). Café des Westens opens, and becomes a meeting place for writers and artists.	Antonin Dvořák completes his Ninth Symphony, *From the New World*. Tchaikovsky completes his Sixth Symphony, *The Pathétique*; he dies of cholera.	

World History and Politics	Jewish History and Culture
1894 Nicholas II becomes Russia's last czar. Prince Hohenlohe becomes chancellor of Germany. A commercial treaty is signed between Germany and Russia.	French Captain Alfred Dreyfus is wrongly accused and found guilty of treason. He is sent to Devil's Island in French Guiana. "Bontshe Shvayg," a Yiddish short story by I. L. Peretz, is published.
1895 Kaiser Wilhelm Canal connects the North Sea and Baltic Sea. Japan wins its war with China and gains dominance in the region. Wilhelm Roentgen invents the X ray.	Gesellschaft für Sammlung und Konservierung von Kunst und historischen Denkmälern des Judentums (Society for the Collection and Conservation of Jewish Art and Historic Monuments) is established in Vienna. Six years after its founding on the Lower East Side of New York, the Educational Alliance provides art instruction to young immigrants and holds annual art exhibitions. Among its later students are Ben Shahn, Barnett Newman, and Mark Rothko.
1896 Athens holds the first modern-age Olympic Games.	Theodor Herzl publishes his pamphlet "Der Judenstaat: Versuch einer modernen Lösung der Judenfrage" (The Jewish State: An Attempt at a Modern Solution to the Jewish Question). In Germany, Nathan Birnbaum publishes *Die jüdische Moderne* under a pen name. A literary magazine under the same name featuring modern Hebrew and Yiddish literature is briefly introduced. Ahad Ha'am (pen name of Asher Ginsberg) becomes editor of the Odessa Hebrew monthly *Ha-Shiloach*, the major cultural forum for Zionist debate and Hebrew literature in Eastern Europe. Solomon Schechter retrieves text fragments from the rediscovered Cairo Genizah, where religious and secular texts were stored since medieval times.
1897 The electron is discovered by Scottish physicist Joseph J. Thompson. Guglielmo Marconi invents wireless telegraphy.	The first World Zionist Congress resolves in the Basel Manifesto to establish a "legally secured homeland in Palestine." The movement launches its journal *Die Welt*. The Bund, a Jewish socialist labor organization, is established in Vilna. Gesellschaft zur Erforschung jüdischer Kunstdenkmäler (Society for the Research of Jewish Art Monuments) is established in Frankfurt am Main. The American Yiddish daily *Forverts (Jewish Daily Forward)* is founded.

As director of the Deutsches Theater, Otto Brahm succeeds in his effort to repeal the censor's ban on *The Weavers*. Following its public premiere, Kaiser Wilhelm II cancels his subscription to the theater. Max Reinhardt joins the ensemble.

The Reichstag building, or German parliament, is inaugurated.

Else Lasker-Schüler arrives in Berlin from Elberfeld in the Rhineland.

The French state debates and rejects the bequest of Gustave Caillebotte's collection of Impressionist paintings, which are eventually accepted into the Musée du Luxembourg.

The Cinematograph is invented by Louis Lumière.

Thomas Edison opens his Kinetoscope ("peep show") parlor in New York.

Pan, a journal of avant-garde art and literature, is founded by Richard Dehmel, Otto Julius Bierbaum, and Julius Meier-Graefe.

Germany's first public screening of motion pictures takes place at the Berlin Wintergarten.

In Paris, Samuel Bing opens the Galerie de l'Art Nouveau, giving the movement its name.

The first Venice Biennale takes place.

Oscar Wilde is imprisoned for homosexual practices.

Louis Sullivan completes his early skyscraper, the Guaranty Trust Building, in Buffalo.

Publication of *Effi Briest* by Theodor Fontane.

Impressionism 1870–90

In 1874, a group including Claude Monet, Auguste Renoir, Camille Pissarro, Edgar Degas, Berthe Morisot, and Paul Cézanne staged the first exhibition of Les Indépendants—later known as the Impressionists—at the studio of the photographer Nadar. The term *Impressionism* was coined by critic Louis Leroy in reaction to Monet's painting *Impression, Sunrise*, 1873, which captures the effects of a shimmering sunrise in a seascape. Encouraged by Edouard Manet's introduction of painterly brushwork in his Realist paintings, the Impressionists sought to render the transitory effects of light and color in individual strokes, or *tâches*, which combine in the eye of the viewer to form a perceived object. The Impressionist subject matter remained in line with the Realist program of depicting scenes from everyday life; but with the rapid pace of industrialization and the growth of a bourgeoisie during the final decades of the nineteenth century, the Impressionists were soon portraying a different urban and suburban environment. Their exploration of the variable effects of time, weather, and light—transforming seascapes, haystacks, or a cathedral facade into changing perceptual phenomena—was radically new and enormously influential.

French Impressionism reached Germany via dealers and critics such as Paul Cassirer and Julius Meier-Graefe. Its primary German practitioners were Lovis Corinth, Max Slevogt, Lesser Ury, and Max Liebermann; the latter also amassed an important collection of Impressionist masterworks. Equally influential for modern German art were the movements spawned by Impressionism: Neo-Impressionism, which carried the theory of optical mixing to its ultimate consequence in Georges Seurat's Pointillism; and Post-Impressionism, a reaction against Impressionist objectivity that would take form in Fauvism, Symbolism, Art Nouveau, and Cézanne's proto-Cubism.

Kaiser Wilhem II intervenes to prevent the Berlin Salon jury from awarding the Gold Medal to Käthe Kollwitz for her graphic series *Weavers' Uprising*.

After compelling him to decline the previous year, the German government permits the painter Max Liebermann to accept the French Legion of Honor.

Rainer Maria Rilke invites Jewish writer Ludwig Jacobowski to join his Bund der Moderne (Modern Association).

Lesser Ury paints *Jerusalem*.

Hugo von Tschudi becomes director of the National Gallery.

Munich weekly satirical journals *Jugend* and *Simplicissimus* popularize the new Jugendstil.

James Jacques Tissot begins his series on the Hebrew Bible.

Giacomo Puccini's opera *La Bohème* premieres in Turin.

The Nobel Prize is established in five disciplines: physics, physiology and medicine, chemistry, literature, and peace.

Henri Bergson publishes *Matière et Mémoire* (Matter and Memory) on his philosophy of time, memory, and consciousness.

The Berlin National Gallery is the first museum to purchase a painting by Paul Cézanne.

The Salon celebrates Liebermann's fiftieth birthday with a retrospective.

The Vienna Secession is founded by Gustav Klimt and others.

Gustav Mahler converts to Christianity in order to accept appointment as director of the Vienna Hofoper (Imperial Opera House).

Opening of the Tate Gallery in London.

World History and Politics	Jewish History and Culture
1898 The Spanish-American War concludes with the American purchase of Cuba, Puerto Rico, Guam, and the Philippines for $20 million. Empress Elizabeth of Austria is assassinated by an Italian anarchist. German inventor Rudolph Diesel perfects his multi-purpose engine. Marie and Pierre Curie discover radium.	Emile Zola publishes his letter "J'Accuse," criticizing the French government's handling of the Dreyfus Affair. Many artists and writers take strong positions on the case. In a military retrial, Dreyfus is again found guilty, but he is issued a presidential pardon. Kaiser Wilhelm II visits Palestine, where he meets with Theodor Herzl.
1899 The Hague peace conference establishes the Permanent Court of International Justice and Arbitration. The Boer War breaks out between Great Britain and the Boers in South Africa; the war ends in 1902, with South Africa becoming a British colony.	
1900 King Umberto of Italy is assassinated by an anarchist. Bernhard von Bülow becomes the new chancellor of Germany. Ferdinand von Zeppelin makes his first flight. The Quantum Theory is formulated by German physicist Max Planck. The International Ladies Garment Workers Union (ILGWU) is founded in New York to fight for the rights of labor in the garment industry.	
1901 William McKinley is assassinated, and Theodore Roosevelt becomes the twenty-sixth president of the United States. Germany and Great Britain abandon negotiations for an alliance. Queen Victoria dies; Edward VII becomes King of England.	At the Fifth Zionist Congress in Basel, Martin Buber and E. M. Lilien present an exhibition of Jewish art. The Jewish National Fund for the settlement of the Land of Israel is established at the congress. Martin Buber coins the term *Jüdische Renaissance* (Jewish Renaissance) in the first edition of *Ost und West* (East and West: Illustrated Journal of Modern Judaism). Hilfsverein der deutschen Juden (Relief Organization of German Jews), modeled after the French Alliance Israélite Universelle, is founded in Berlin to provide charitable and educational assistance to Jews living in Eastern Europe and the Muslim world. It establishes a school system in Palestine, with instruction in Hebrew.

Berlin Art and Culture

The Berlin Secession is founded.

Gallery Cassirer is established by the cousins Bruno and Paul Cassirer. It opens with an exhibition of works by Liebermann, Edgar Degas, and Constantin Meunier.

Max Liebermann is elected to the Royal Academy.

Kaiser Wilhelm II demands to approve all new acquisitions of the National Gallery.

Café des Westens becomes the headquarters for Herwarth Walden's popular art club, Verein für Kunst.

Industrialization and mass immigration to the city cause Berlin's population to expand to 2 million, intensifying class and economic divisions in society.

Otto Brahm presents Ibsen's *Ghosts* at the Deutsches Theater, with Max Reinhardt in the cast.

Kaiser Wilhelm II's gift to Berlin—marble statues of Brandenburg rulers along the Siegesalle (Victory Avenue) in the Tiergarten—is unveiled.

Berlin's first cabaret, Überbrettl, is opened by Ernst von Wolzogen. Max Reinhardt launches his cabaret Schall und Rauch (Sound and Smoke).

Paul Cassirer opens Salon Cassirer, which becomes a showcase for modern art.

The Secession's Spring exhibition introduces the art of Van Gogh to Germany.

International Art and Culture

The Vienna Secession holds its first exhibition and launches its periodical, *Ver Sacrum*.

Mir Iskusstva (World of Art) group publishes its periodical introducing international modern art and literary movements in Russia.

Publication of H. G. Wells's *The War of the Worlds*.

From Delacroix to Neo-Impressionism by Paul Signac is published and translated into German.

Hugo von Hofmannsthal presents his verse drama *Der Tor und der Tod* (The Fool and Death).

Karl Kraus starts the satirical journal *Die Fackel* (The Torch) in Vienna.

Ancient Babylon is excavated by German archaeologist Robert Koldewey.

Charles Rennie Mackintosh completes main building of the Glasgow School of Art.

Gauguin's *Noa-Noa* is published as a book.

The World Exposition in Paris celebrates the recent openings of the Eiffel Tower and the Metro.

The Brownie Box affordable camera is introduced by Eastman Kodak.

In *The Interpretation of Dreams*, a founding document of psychoanalysis, Sigmund Freud presents his first published account of the Oedipus complex.

Death of Friedrich Nietzsche.

Vasily Kandinsky establishes the Phalanx association and art school in Munich.

Henry van de Velde takes over the Weimar Academy of Arts and Crafts, which later is integrated into the Bauhaus.

Pablo Picasso begins his Blue Period.

Thomas Mann publishes *Buddenbrooks*.

Publication of Frank Lloyd Wright's *The Art and Craft of the Machine*.

Jugendstil 1880–1914

Primarily associated with architecture and design, this late-nineteenth-century modernist movement was crucial to the work of fine artists from Paul Gauguin to Edvard Munch to Gustav Klimt. With roots in Symbolism, this distinctly organic and ornamental style also revealed an underlying exoticism. It spread throughout Europe and the United States, and spurred a variety of national designations: Jugendstil in Germany, Art Nouveau in France, Sezessionstil in Austria, Modernista in Spain, and Stile Liberty in Italy. The English Arts and Crafts movement, with its emphasis on fine craftsmanship and the stylized representation of natural forms, exerted a strong influence on the various practitioners of this new style. At the same time, each national expression of the style was indebted to particular local traditions, such as Rococo in France and Biedermeier in Germany. Munich became a hub of Jugendstil artists, and its Secession became their showcase. The School of Arts and Crafts at Weimar was also an important center for Jugendstil under the direction of the Belgian Symbolist Henry van de Velde, whose reductivist approach to ornamentalism encouraged artists to focus on the expressive potential of color or sinuous line. With its Symbolist affinities, Jugendstil was enormously influential for future abstract artists, such as Vasily Kandinsky and Gabriele Münter. It was also important for early German Expressionism and Die Brücke. With its emphasis on linearity and organic form, Jugendstil lent itself naturally to the graphic arts, as reflected, for example, in the work of E. M. Lilien. The style was popularized in Germany through illustrated books and journals, notably the Munich weekly satiricals *Jugend* and *Simplicissimus*.

World History and Politics	Jewish History and Culture

1902 Leon Trotsky escapes from Siberian prison to London.

The Triple Alliance is renewed between Germany, Austria, and Italy.

Theodor Herzl presents his utopian novel *Altneuland* (Old-New Land).

The Jüdischer Verlag (Jewish Publishing House) is founded by a group of cultural Zionists with strong modernist sensibilities, including Martin Buber and E. M. Lilien.

Gesellschaft zur Förderung der Wissenschaft des Judentums (Society for the Promotion of the Science of Judaism) is founded in Berlin.

HIAS (Hebrew Immigrant Aid Society) consolidates in the United States as an agency to aid immigrants during the mass migration of East European Jews to America.

Publication of *The Spirit of the Ghetto* by Hutchins Hapgood, illustrated by Jacob Epstein, on Jewish immigrant life on the Lower East Side of New York.

1903 Germany outlaws child labor.

The Russian Social Democratic Labor Party holds a congress, and divides between Mensheviks and Bolsheviks.

The Wright Brothers make their first flight in a motored biplane at Kitty Hawk, North Carolina.

The Kishinev pogroms climax a wave of anti-Jewish violence in Russia, leading to mass emigration of Jews.

End of the First Aliyah, the wave of immigration to Palestine from Eastern Europe and Russia that began in 1882, results in the settlement of more than 30,000 Jews.

At the Sixth Zionist Congress, the British offer of territory for Jewish settlement in Uganda is rejected.

Hermann Struck travels to Palestine and produces numerous etchings of holy sites, ancient cities, new communities, and the landscape.

1904 *Entente cordiale* is established between France and Great Britain regarding colonial interests in North Africa.

Japan's victory at war with Russia asserts its ascension as a global power.

In German Southwest Africa, the Hereros and Hottentots revolt.

A conference is held in Paris on the white slave trade.

Geneticist Theodor Boveri identifies chromosomes as carriers of genetic material.

Theodor Herzl dies at age forty-four.

In Germany, a branch of the Mizrahi organization is founded to reassert Orthodoxy in response to the growth of the Reform movement.

The Jüdischer Frauenbund (League of Jewish Women) is founded in Berlin.

Beginning of the Second Aliyah, the wave of immigration to Palestine that laid foundation for the labor movement, kibbutzim, and Hebrew press and literature.

The Jewish Theological Seminary establishes The Jewish Museum in New York.

U-Bahn subway service is inaugurated.

Bruno Cassirer establishes the journal *Kunst und Künstler* (Art and Artist) to promote modern art in Germany.

The Styx poems by Else Lasker-Schüler are published.

The telling of Jewish jokes in a performance at the Schall und Rauch cabaret leads to protests and police arrests.

Publication of the first installment of *Philosophy of the Spirit* by Benedetto Croce.

The premiere of Debussy's opera *Pelléas et Mélisande*, based on the 1892 Symbolist play by Maurice Maeterlinck, takes place in Paris.

The Flatiron Building is completed in New York.

Aby Warburg founds his library for the history of European art and culture in Hamburg.

Symbolism 1890–ca. 1900

A French literary movement coined by poet Jean Moréas in his 1886 manifesto, Symbolism began to inspire visual artists throughout Europe toward the *fin de siècle*. In reaction to the dry objectivity of Naturalism and Realism and the dispiriting effects of industrialization, writers and artists sought to imbue their work with the mysticism and exoticism of the Romantic era. Their goal was both to capture and elicit a transcendent idea or inner reality. More of a thematic than a stylistic movement, Symbolism was reflected in the visual arts in diverse ways. It can be perceived equally in the intense psychological portraits painted by Edvard Munch and Vincent van Gogh, and in Pierre Puvis de Chavannes's evocations of Arcadia. The pursuit of a more simple and pure sensibility led to an interest in so-called primitive religions. Together with Emile Bernard, Paul Gauguin formed the Nabis group (the name taken from the Hebrew word for prophet) at Pont-Aven in Brittany, where he depicted the Bretons in their age-old rituals. Rejecting the Impressionists' primarily visual observation of nature and social life, the Nabis termed their approach *synthetism*, since it sought to unite visual and emotive experience. Symbolist exhibitions were held in Paris in the 1890s by the Rosicrucian or Rose + Croix fraternity; and *Revue Blanche*, the Symbolist journal of 1891, brought together its practitioners from across Europe. It featured illustrations by Pierre Bonnard, Edouard Vuillard, and Henri de Toulouse-Lautrec, along with literary pieces by Marcel Proust, Henrik Ibsen, August Strindberg, and Oscar Wilde. Symbolism found a particularly strong following in Belgium, and was represented at the Berlin, Munich, and Vienna Secessions through the 1890s.

Max Reinhardt leaves the Deutsches Theater to become director of the Kleines Theater (formerly Schall und Rauch) and the Neues Theater. He produces Maeterlinck's Symbolist drama *Pelléas et Mélisande* to much acclaim.

Composer Rudolf Nelson opens the Roland von Berlin cabaret.

The Metropol Theater begins to produce revues about cosmopolitan life in Berlin.

Deutscher Künstlerbund is founded in Weimar as a union for all German secessions.

The Wiener Werkstätte is founded as the arts-and-crafts cooperative of the Vienna Secession; leading artists are Josef Hofmann and Koloman Moser.

Death of Paul Gauguin.

Wilhelm II and the Association of German Artists block the Secession's participation in the exhibition of German Art at the St. Louis World's Fair.

Jewish art patron James Simon donates important Renaissance works to the new Kaiser Friedrich Museum.

Samuel Lublinski's critique of the Naturalist movement, *Bilanz der Moderne*, is published.

The Wertheim department store opens, and becomes a model for similar emporiums in Europe.

Publication of Julius Meier-Graefe's *Entwicklungsgeschichte der modernen Kunst* (History of Modern Art).

Frank Wedekind's play *Die Büchse der Pandora* (Pandora's Box) is first performed.

Puccini's opera *Madame Butterfly* is presented in Milan.

Publication of *The Golden Bowl* by Henry James.

World History and Politics	Jewish History and Culture
1905 France legislates the separation of Church and State.	The Russian edition of *The Protocols of the Elders of Zion*, an anti-Semitic forgery, is published.
Germany and France clash over the status of Morocco.	Berlin becomes the headquarters of the Zentralverband jüdischer Handwerker Deutschlands, an umbrella group for Jewish artisanal organizations throughout Germany.
Germany and Russia sign pact for mutual military assistance.	
Czar Nicholas II's October Manifesto guarantees reforms in the wake of a workers' uprising.	*Zeitschrift für Demographie und Statistik der Juden* (Journal for Jewish Demographics and Statistics) is established to monitor population trends in the face of rising rates of conversion and intermarriage.
Albert Einstein formulates his Special Theory of Relativity, Brownian theory of motion, and photon theory of light.	
1906 The United States passes food inspection laws following the publication of Upton Sinclair's *The Jungle*.	Alfred Dreyfus's guilty verdict is overturned by the French court of appeals.
An international ban is imposed against night-shift work for women.	The Society for the Founding and Maintenance of a Jewish Museum is established in Prague.
Finland is first in Europe to grant women the right to vote.	The American Jewish Committee is founded by Louis Marshall and other prominent, mostly German Jewish, community leaders.
A major earthquake in San Francisco practically destroys the city.	Boris Schatz founds the Bezalel School of Arts and Crafts in Jerusalem.
1907 A second peace conference takes place in The Hague.	In Palestine, newspapers serving various immigrant communities proliferate.
Universal direct male suffrage is established in Austria.	Poale Zion (Workers Union) holds its first international conference in The Hague.
German astronomer Karl Schwarzschild presents his theory of the black hole.	Di Yunge, poets and writers devoted to creating a modern Yiddish literature in the United States, publishes its first little magazine, *Yugend* (Youth).
The United States Division of Forestry introduces the term *conservation*.	S. Y. Agnon arrives in Palestine. From 1913 he lives in Germany until he returns to Palestine in 1924.

First German welfare center for mothers is established in Berlin.

In a production of *A Midsummer Night's Dream* at the Neues Theater, Max Reinhardt employs the revolving stage. The same year, Reinhardt takes over the Deutsches Theater, marking the end of its Naturalist program.

Paul Cassirer mounts a major Van Gogh exhibition. The show also travels to Dresden, where it influences Die Brücke artists.

Construction of the Berlin Cathedral (the Dom) is completed.

Death of Adolph von Menzel.

Henri Matisse and André Derain are designated the Fauves at the Salon d'Automne.

Die Brücke (The Bridge), an association of Expressionist artists, is founded by Erich Heckel, Ernst Ludwig Kirchner, and Karl Schmidt-Rottluff in Dresden.

Max Liebermann begins his paintings of Amsterdam's *Judengasse* (Jewish Quarter).

Alfred Stieglitz opens Little Galleries of the Photo Secession, known as 291 for its Fifth Avenue address. As well as a venue for photography, it becomes an important showcase for modern art.

Richard Strauss's opera *Salome* is presented in Dresden.

Police censors close George Bernard Shaw's *Mrs. Warren's Profession* after its premiere in New York.

Nickelodeon movie houses open in the United States.

Otto Wagner completes the modernist Vienna Post Office Savings Bank.

Max Reinhardt founds the chamber theater Kammerspiele; the opening performance is Ibsen's *Ghosts*, with sets designed by Edvard Munch.

Kleines Haus presents Frank Wedekind's proto-Expressionist drama *Frühlings Erwachen* (Spring Awakening).

Censorship of movies is mandated by the police.

Sergei Diaghilev organizes an exhibition of Russian art in Paris.

Picasso paints Gertrude Stein's portrait. Stein completes "Melanctha," the experimental modernist narrative in *Three Lives*.

Death of Paul Cézanne.

Death of Henrik Ibsen.

Kaufhaus des Westens (KaDeWe) department store opens.

Schiller Theater is founded as a public "Volkstheater."

Märkisches Museum is completed.

Composer Rudolf Nelson opens the Chat Noir cabaret.

Deutscher Werkbund is established in Munich.

Color photography is invented by the Lumière brothers.

Oskar Kokoschka writes the Expressionist play *Mörder, Hoffnung der Frauen* (Murderer, Hope of Women).

Picasso paints *Les Demoiselles d'Avignon*.

L'Evolution créatrice (Creative Evolution) by Henri Bergson is published, presenting his vitalist philosophy of duration and the *élan vital*.

Pragmatism: A New Name for Some Old Ways of Thinking by William James is published.

Fauvism 1903–8

As opposed to a formal group with programmatic guidelines, the Fauves were a short-lived but highly influential association of Post-Impressionist French painters; leading artists were Henri Matisse, André Derain, Raoul Dufy, and Maurice Vlaminck. By exaggerating the Impressionist application of color in separate, visible brushstrokes to the point of delineating broad patches of intensely contrasting color, they went further in rejecting traditional perspective and the illusion of three-dimensionality. The style received its name—meaning the "wild beasts"—in critic Louis Vauxelles's review of the group's submissions to the 1905 Salon d'Automne, although the term was more reflective of the public's reaction to their work than to the painters' temperaments. In their subjects, the Fauves pursued the Impressionist celebration of nature and the lighter side of life, made explicit in titles such as Matisse's *Luxe, calme, et volupté* (1904–5) and *Bonheur de vivre: Joie de vivre*, or *Joy of Life* (1905–6). And while they rejected the melancholy and intense introspection of the Symbolists, the Fauves did explore so-called primitive cultures, notably the art of Africa. Matisse and Derain discovered African sculpture around 1905–6 and soon began to incorporate its dramatic angularity and exaggerated renderings of anatomy into their work. In their embrace of the exotic, as well as their explorations of the expressive potential in bold color and contrast, the Fauves influenced the German Expressionists, both Die Brücke and Der Blaue Reiter, as well as abstract artists from Robert Delaunay to the American Abstract Expressionists.

	World History and Politics	**Jewish History and Culture**
1908	Bosnia and Herzegovina are annexed by Austria-Hungary, with the support of Germany.	Delegates at the Yiddish Language Conference in Czernowitz proclaim Yiddish the Jewish national language.
	The revolution of the Young Turks threatens the supremacy of the Ottoman Empire.	The Kunstgewerbemuseum in Düsseldorf mounts Germany's first exhibition of Jewish ceremonial objects.
	Prussian woman are permitted to matriculate at the university.	Arthur Schnitzler addresses the anti-Semitism of the day in his novel *Der Weg ins Freie* (The Road into the Open).
		A writer of popular novels, Georg Hermann explores Berlin Jewish family life in *Henriette Jacoby*.
1909	An American exploration team is first to land at the North Pole.	The city of Tel Aviv is founded.
	The National Association for the Advancement of Colored People (NAACP) is founded.	Deganya is established as the first kibbutz.
	Called Bakelite, plastic is invented by Belgian-American chemist Leo Baekeland.	
	Fifty thousand people demonstrate for free elections in Prussia.	
1910	The Carnegie Endowment for International Peace is formed.	Buber delivers his treatise "Drei Reden über das Judentum" (Three Talks on Judaism), in which he stresses the theme of pathos.
	A revolution in Portugal establishes a republic.	Shulamit Conservatory is established as a music school in Tel Aviv.
	Slavery is outlawed in China.	Alberto Gerchunoff's book *Los Gauchos Judios* (The Jewish Gauchos) portrays life in Jewish agricultural settlements in Argentina.
	Appearance of Halley's Comet.	

Kaiser Wilhelm II and Hugo von Tschudi, director of the National Gallery, clash over acquisition of modern works for the museum.

Richard Dehmel publishes "Talent and Race," an imaginary conversation between a German writer and a Jewish painter.

Paul Cassirer establishes Pan Presse for contemporary graphics and bibliophile editions.

The Berlin Secession's acceptance of works by Die Brücke and other avant-garde artists provokes tension among the leadership.

Death of Walter Leistikow.

Jewish entrepreneur Paul Davidson opens the Union Theater, Berlin's first fashionable movie cinema, on the Alexanderplatz.

Der Neue Club holds public readings and performances of avant-garde works.

Peter Behrens completes the modernist steel and glass AEG Turbine Factory.

Hugo von Tschudi leaves Berlin to assume directorship of the Bavarian State Museums in Munich.

Herwarth Walden founds the journal *Der Sturm*, devoted to avant-garde literature, art, and music.

Die Brücke moves to Berlin.

The Neue Secession is founded by Max Pechstein.

Auguste Hauschner, leader of a progressive intellectual salon, sees the completed publication of her two-volume novel *Die Familie Lowositz*.

Max Reinhardt stages a theater-in-the-round presentation of *Oedipus Rex*, featuring huge crowd scenes.

Der Neue Club becomes the Neopathetisches Cabaret, actively promoting Berlin's modernist musicians and literati.

In his book *Berlin: Ein Stadtschicksal*, Karl Scheffler, art critic and editor of *Kunst und Künstler*, critiques the city's modernization as ugly.

Georges Braque's Cubist submissions to the progressive Salon d'Automne are refused by a jury that includes Matisse.

The Eight, a group of Realist painters of urban life, is founded in New York. They are later known as the Ashcan School.

Amedeo Modigliani exhibits in the Salon des Indépendants. The first painting he shows in Paris is called *La Juive* (The Jewess).

Wilhelm Worringer's *Abstraktion und Einfühlung* (Abstraction and Empathy) is published.

Nietzsche's *Ecce Homo* is published posthumously.

Picasso and Braque develop Analytic Cubism.

Kandinsky founds the Neue Künstlervereinigung (New Artists' Society) in Munich.

Gustav Klimt completes a mural cycle for Josef Hoffmann's Palais Stoclet in Brussels.

The Futurist Manifesto is written by poet Filippo Marinetti and published in *Le Figaro*.

Sergei Diaghilev founds the Ballet Russes.

Publication of Martin Buber's *Ekstatische Konfessionen* (Ecstatic Confessions).

Frank Lloyd Wright completes the Robie House in Chicago.

The Manifesto of Futurist Painters is signed.

Roger Fry coins the term *Post-Impressionism* in connection with the London exhibition of paintings by Cézanne, Gauguin, and Van Gogh.

Rainer Maria Rilke's novel *The Notebooks of Malte Laurids Brigge* explores the theme of subjectivity in modern life.

Diaghilev presents Igor Stravinsky's ballet *The Firebird*.

The tango is popularized in Europe and the United States.

German Expressionism 1905–24

Initiated at the turn of the century by artists such as Ernst Barlach, Käthe Kollwitz, Paula Modersohn-Becker, and Emil Nolde, German Expressionism was launched as a modern art movement by a group of young artists in Dresden, who, in 1905, named themselves Die Brücke (The Bridge), evoking their link to the new century. Ernst Ludwig Kirchner, Max Pechstein, Erich Heckel, and Karl Schmidt-Rottluff were joined by Nolde in their efforts to create and promote a revolutionary program for modern German art. Part of what motivated them to organize was the dominance of Germany's traditionalist national art association, the Allgemeine Deutsche Kunstgenossenshaft. Although they emerged from the bourgeoisie, Die Brücke preached an anti-bourgeois ideology. In their famously raw depictions of the underside of the modern city and its inhabitants, they absorbed the influences of Van Gogh, Edvard Munch, the Fauves, and the Italian Futurists, though the Brücke's disillusionment with urban life differed from the Futurist infatuation with the city. This ambivalence toward modernity led to an interest in so-called primitive culture and religion as well as folk and artistic traditions from the German past, such as the art of woodcutting.

In 1911 Die Brücke, now centered in Berlin, was challenged as the leading voice of Expressionism in Germany by Der Blaue Reiter (The Blue Rider), a group formed in Munich by Franz Marc, Vasily Kandinsky, and Gabriele Münter. Focused on spirituality and the capacity of art to convey and inspire sacred and mystical truths, Der Blaue Reiter promoted a transcendental type of Expressionism. For example, Kandinsky's belief in the expressive power of color and line are articulated in his paintings as well as his still-influential treatise *Concerning the Spiritual in Art* (1912). Der Blaue Reiter's program soon became an important catalyst for abstract art. Die Brücke and Der Blaue Reiter disbanded before the outbreak of World War I, but Expressionist currents persisted in the work of individual artists and in the Novembergruppe, the Dresdner Sezession, and the Arbeitsrat für Kunst (Workers Council for Art).

World History and Politics	**Jewish History and Culture**

1911

The Manchu dynasty is overthrown by Chinese revolutionaries, and a republic headed by Sun-Yat-Sen is proclaimed.

An international crisis is provoked by the arrival of a German gunboat at Agadir in Morocco. Germany renounces influence in Morocco, and receives some French colonies in the Congo.

Norwegian explorer Roald Amundsen is first to reach the South Pole.

A fire at the Triangle Shirtwaist Company in New York kills 168 people, mostly women, triggering mass protests and growth of the U.S. labor movement.

In his book *Die Juden und das Wirtschaftsleben* (The Jews and Modern Capitalism), Werner Sombart articulates the alien status of the Jews in Germany.

1912

The first Balkan war breaks out.

Germany, Austria, and Italy renew their alliance.

Laborers strike in England and the United States.

The luxury ocean liner *Titanic* sinks during its maiden voyage, resulting in the death of more than 1,500 of the 2,200 people aboard.

Habima Ha-Ivrit, a Hebrew Theater Company, is founded in Bialystok.

S. An-sky (Shlomo Zanvil Rapoport) leads 1912–14 ethnographic expedition through shtetl communities in the Ukraine. The encounter with Jewish folk traditions inspires An-sky's play *The Dybbuk* as well as artists such as El Lissitzky.

The Technion Institute is founded in Haifa; teachers and students protest the Hilfsverein's demand that the official language of instruction be German.

Franz Pfemfert founds *Die Aktion*, an Expressionist literary and political journal.

Carl Vinnen publishes *Ein Protest deutscher Künstler* (Protest of German Artists), which attacks the influence of French art in Germany.

Lovis Corinth is elected president of the Berlin Secession.

Robert Delaunay paints the *Window on the City* series of geometric abstractions.

Marcel Duchamp paints the first version of *Nude Descending a Staircase*.

Der Blauer Reiter is founded in Munich, with Kandinsky, Franz Marc, Paul Klee, August Macke, and Gabriele Münter as members.

Arnold Schönberg publishes *Manual of Harmony*.

Futurism 1909–29

Although it was launched in Paris and quickly gained an international following, Futurism was a distinctively Italian movement. Its core group of artists included Giacomo Balla, Umberto Boccioni, Carlo Carrà, Luigi Russolo, and Gino Severini. They aligned themselves with the poet Filippo Tommaso Marinetti, whose Futurist Manifesto was published on the front page of *Le Figaro* in 1909. A celebration of the dynamism of modernity, the treatise derided Italy's devotion to its cultural past and exalted modern Europe's industrial and technological advancements in transportation, mechanical production, even warfare. Marinetti championed the creation of a new language for literature, art, and everyday life that embraced the notion of *velocità*, or speed. In 1910 the painters created their own manifesto, which called for the representation of speed through the simultaneous fragmentation and merging of forms in space. Influenced by the Cubist faceting of objects, the Futurist approach differed in its focus on motion, which was also conveyed by the evocative titles of works such as Boccioni's *The Street Enters the House*, 1911, and Severini's *Dynamic Hieroglyph of the Bal Tabarin*, 1912. The Futurists were inspired by the burgeoning German Expressionist currents seeking to probe the many facets of urban modernity, notably in Berlin. Manifestos on sculpture, architecture, literature, music, dance, and theater soon followed; and the Futurist idiom was wide-ranging in its influence. Through a traveling exhibition in 1912, audiences across Europe were exposed to Futurism. In addition to the Expressionists, the movement was especially significant for the English Vorticists and the Russian Cubo-Futurists and Rayonists.

Herwarth Walden opens Der Sturm gallery with exhibitions of Der Blaue Reiter and the Italian Futurists.

Die Brücke disbands, as does the Neue Secession.

Der Kunstwart (Guardian of Art) publishes Moritz Goldstein's article "The German-Jewish Parnassus," provoking the "*Kunstwart* debate" on the paradox of Jewish assimilation in Germany.

Ludwig Meidner, Jakob Steinhardt, and Richard Janthur form The Pathetiker and exhibit together at The Sturm Gallery.

Death of Otto Brahm.

Picasso and Braque develop *papier collé* (collage).

Albert Gleizes and Jean Metzinger publish *Du Cubisme* (On Cubism).

Mikhail Larionov and Natalia Goncharova establish Rayonism in Russia.

Publication of Umberto Boccioni's *Technical Manifesto of Futurist Sculpture*.

Der Blaue Reiter Almanach is published.

Kandinsky presents his manifesto *Concerning the Spiritual in Art*.

"The Metamorphosis," a story by Franz Kafka, is published.

Rudolph Steiner establishes the Anthroposophical Society.

Arnold Schönberg composes the Expressionist classic *Pierrot Lunaire*.

Macchu Picchu is discovered by American archaeologist Hiram Bingham.

Publication of Emile Durkheim's *Elementary Forms of Religious Life*, a landmark work of cultural anthropology.

World History and Politics	Jewish History and Culture

1913

The second Balkan war breaks out.

Tensions arise between France and Germany over the Alsace-Lorraine Zabern Affair.

England swears in its first woman magistrate; suffragette demonstrations are held in London.

On the eve of President Wilson's inauguration, the National American Women's Suffrage Movement marches on the Capitol.

Danish physicist Neils Bohr develops his theory of atomic structure.

Grand Central Station in New York, then the largest railroad station in the world, is completed.

The blood-libel trial and acquittal of Mendel Beilis in Kiev generates anti-Semitic propaganda.

In response to nativist anti-Semitism, B'nai B'rith establishes the Anti-Defamation League (ADL) in Chicago.

Conservative congregations establish the United Synagogue of America as a counterpart to the Reform movement's Union of American Hebrew Congregations.

Hebrew Union College in Cincinnati establishes a museum of Judaica.

1914

The assassination of Archduke Franz Ferdinand, heir to the Austrian throne, ignites World War I, involving the Central Powers—Germany, Austria-Hungary, Turkey—against the Entente, or Allied Powers, including France, England, Russia, and eventually Italy, Japan, and the United States. New warfare includes poison gas, machine guns, tanks, and fighter aircraft.

In the first moving assembly line, Ford Motors produces the Model T.

The end of the Second Aliyah, or wave of immigration to Palestine, results in settlement of an additional 40,000 Jews.

Henrietta Szold is elected president of Hadassah at first convention of the organization formed in 1912.

The American Jewish Joint Distribution Committee is founded, developing into the pre-eminent Jewish overseas relief agency.

Paul Cassirer organizes the annual Secession exhibition, showing Matisse's *The Dance* and works by the German avant-garde.

Herwarth Walden organizes the *Erster deutscher Herbstsalon* (First German Autumn Salon), showcasing Italian Futurists, French Cubists, and other avant-garde art.

Ernst Ludwig Kirchner dissolves Die Brücke.

Philipp Stauff publishes the anti-Semitic essay "The Alien Element in German Art, or Paul Cassirer, Max Liebermann, etc."

Publication of the *Hebräische Balladen* (Hebrew Ballads) by Else Lasker-Schüler.

Publication of *Die moderne Jüdin* (The Modern Jewess) by Else Croner.

Café des Westens closes.

There are 206 movie theaters in the city.

The landmark New York Armory Show of European modernist art erupts in scandal.

Kasimir Malevich paints *Black Square on White*, ushering in the Russian Suprematist movement.

The Omega Workshop is founded by artists of London's Bloomsbury Group.

Chaim Soutine arrives in Paris from Vilna.

Igor Stravinsky's ballet *Le Sacre du Printemps* (The Rite of Spring) premieres in Paris.

The first volume of *Remembrance of Things Past* by Marcel Proust is published.

Death in Venice by Thomas Mann is published.

Charlie Chaplin makes his film debut.

The Woolworth skyscraper, then the tallest building in the world, is completed in New York.

Edmund Husserl's treatise on phenomenology, known as *Ideen* (Ideas), is published.

The Free Secession is founded by Paul Cassirer, Liebermann, and Slevogt.

Herwarth Walden presents an exhibition of Marc Chagall at Der Sturm gallery, and initiates a program of traveling exhibitions in Germany and abroad.

Ludwig Meidner's "Anleitung zum Malen von Grossstadtbildern" (An Introduction to Painting Big Cities) appears in *Kunst und Künstler*.

Paul Cassirer's press publishes the first compete edition of Van Gogh's letters to his brother Theo.

Ernst Lubitsch stars in the first of many films set in the Jewish retailing milieu.

Paul Cassirer founds the journal *Kriegszeit* (Wartime), published until March 1916, in which modern artists interpret the war.

The Vorticist Group is founded in London.

The German Jewish artists Rudolf Levy, Walter Rosam, and Eugene Spiro, identified with the School of Paris, return to Germany to join the army. Chagall and Mané-Katz return to Russia.

The French government confiscates the collection of German-Jewish art dealer Daniel-Henri Kahnweiler.

Walter Gropius builds the Fagus factory as a prototype of modern industrial architecture.

The University of Frankfurt is founded with a mandate to prohibit religious discrimination in faculty appointments.

August Macke falls in the war.

World History and Politics	**Jewish History and Culture**
1915 Germany blockades England and conducts a Zeppelin air raid on London. Poison gas first used by German troops at Battle of Ypres. Europe's largest railroad station is opened in Leipzig. The first transcontinental telephone connection is made between Alexander Graham Bell in New York and Thomas Watson in San Francisco. In the United States, Margaret Sanger is imprisoned for advocating birth control in a book.	In the United States, Jewish immigrant communities flourish. Approximately 1,200 *landsmanshaftn*—immigrant benevolent societies consisting of people from the same town or region—and 500 synagogues exist in New York City alone. Hermann Struck's volumes of lithographs, *In Russian Poland* and *Drawings from Lithuania, Belorussia and Poland*, are produced. They chronicle his first exposure to East European communities as an army officer during Germany's occupation of the region.
1916 Germany introduces steel helmets and gas masks to its arsenal. It conducts Zeppelin air raids on Paris; the Battle of Verdun results in massive casualties. Kaiser Wilhelm II's peace proposal is rejected by the Allies. Within Germany, nationalist fervor and racist agitation take hold. The Prohibition movement in the United States gains force. The Arab uprising against Ottoman rule in Arabia is led by T. E. Lawrence (Lawrence of Arabia).	The Zionist Organization of America is founded. The German Imperial Army orders the *Judenzählung*, a census of Jewish soldiers at the front. In reaction to wartime anti-Semitism, Martin Buber founds the Berlin journal *Der Jude* (The Jew). Louis Brandeis is the first Jew appointed to the U.S. Supreme Court. The Yiddish writer Sholem Aleichem (pen name of Sholem Rabinovich) dies in New York.
1917 The United States enters World War I. To replace male clerks sent overseas, the Navy hires 12,000 women. Lenin and Trotsky mobilize the "November Revolution," which establishes the Soviet Republic. Women are granted the right to vote. The dancer known as Mata Hari is executed as a German spy in Paris. Famine in Germany brings the "Winter of Turnips."	The Balfour Declaration expresses British support for "the establishment in Palestine of a national home for the Jewish people." Jerusalem is surrendered to the British by the Ottoman Turks. General Allenby occupies the city. The Habima theater opens in Moscow.
1918 Armistice ends World War I in November. The war leaves approximately 8.5 million dead, 21 million wounded, and 7.5 million prisoners or missing people. Kaiser Wilhelm II abdicates and flees to Holland, and the Weimar Republic is proclaimed. The Communist Workers' Party is founded in Germany by Rosa Luxemburg and Karl Liebknecht. Czar Nicholas II and his family are executed by the Bolsheviks. A worldwide influenza epidemic leaves 22 million dead by 1922.	The Hebrew University is founded in Jerusalem. Hadasssah establishes the first Jewish nursing school in Jerusalem. The Akademie für die Wissenschaft des Judentums, establishing the academic study of Judaism and Jewish culture, is founded in Berlin. Maurice Schwartz initiates the Yiddish Art Theater in New York, offering a wide range of plays, including Chekhov and Schnitzler in Yiddish and experimental "cubist" pieces.

The Denishawn School of Dance and Related Arts, founded by Ruth St. Denis and Ted Shawn, initiates modern dance instruction in the United States.

Sigmund Freud writes "Thoughts for the Times of War and Death," in which he champions the ethic of *Bildung* and derides wartime xenophobia.

Film director D. W. Griffith creates *The Birth of a Nation*.

World war brings food rationing, hunger, and public resentment.

Franz Marc is killed at the front; Der Sturm Gallery holds a memorial exhibition.

Der Sturm presents the first exhibition of Max Ernst.

Walden opens an art school.

Paul Cassirer publishes the journal *Bildermann*, which includes pacifist images.

Tristan Tzara and Jean Arp establish the Dada movement in Zurich, with Cabaret Voltaire as its headquarters.

Publication of James Joyce's novel *Portrait of the Artist as a Young Man*.

Publication of Carl Gustav Jung's *The Psychology of the Unconscious*.

Frank Lloyd Wright begins work on the Imperial Hotel in Tokyo.

Max Reinhardt directs the world premiere of Reinhard Sorge's Expressionist drama, *Der Bettler* (The Beggar).

Walden opens a Sturm theater and acting school, and publishes *Einblick in Kunst: Expressionismus, Futurismus, Kubismus*.

Cassirer Gallery mounts major exhibitions of Barlach and Kollwitz.

The Dutch De Stijl movement is founded by Piet Mondrian, Theo van Doesburg, and others.

Carlo Carrà and Giorgio de Chirico found the *Scuola Metafisica* (School of Metaphysical Painting).

Surrealism is named by Guillaume Apollinaire.

In New York, the Society of Independent Artists holds its First Annual Exhibition, rejecting Marcel Duchamp's ready-made *Fountain*.

Death of Edgar Degas.

Arbeitsrat für Kunst, the artists' group inspired by the November Revolution, is established by Bruno Taut. Members include Walter Gropius, Ludwig Meidner, Lyonel Feininger, and Erich Mendelsohn.

The Novembergruppe union of artists, architects, and writers is initiated by Max Pechstein and César Klein.

The Berlin Dada movement is founded by Richard Huelsenbeck.

After Cubism, a manifesto on Purism by Le Corbusier and Amédée Ozenfant, is published.

Kandinsky joins the Soviet Commissariat for Popular Culture.

Chagall is made Commissar of Fine Arts in Vitebsk; he is also given his first solo exhibition in Paris.

Apollinaire and Egon Schiele die of influenza.

Works by living German composers are banned by the New York Philharmonic. Karl Muck, German conductor of the Boston Symphony Orchestra, is arrested as an enemy alien.

Figure 198
Jakob Steinhardt
**Recollection of the War
(Kriegserinnerung)**, ca. 1919
Lithographic chalk on paper,
18½ x 19½ in. (48 x 49 cm)
The Marvin and Janet Fishman Collection,
Milwaukee

Selected Bibliography

Achenbach, Sigrid, and Matthias Eberle, eds. *Max Liebermann in seiner Zeit.* Exh. cat. Munich and Berlin: Bayerische Staatsgemäldesammlungen and Nationalgalerie Berlin, 1979.

Allen, Roy. *Literary Life in German Expressionism and the Berlin Circles.* Ann Arbor: UMI Research Press, 1983.

Antonowa, Irina, and Jörn Merkert. *Berlin/Moskau 1900-1950.* Exh. cat. Munich and Berlin: Prestel and Berlinische Galerie, 1995.

Aschheim, Steven E. *Brothers and Strangers: The East European Jew in German and German Jewish Consciousness, 1800–1923.* Madison: University of Wisconsin Press, 1982.

Barron, Stephanie, and Wolf-Dieter Dube, eds. *German Expressionism: Art and Society 1909–1923.* London: Thames and Hudson, 1997.

Bartmann, Dominik, ed. *Berliner Kunstfrühling: Malerei, Graphik und Plastik der Moderne 1888–1918 aus dem Stadtmuseum Berlin.* Exh. cat. Berlin: Stadtmuseum Berlin, 1997.

Bauschinger, Sigrid. *Else Lasker-Schüler: Ihr Werk und ihre Zeit.* Heidelberg: Lothar Stiehm, 1980.

Berding, Helmut. *Moderner Antisemitismus in Deutschland.* Frankfurt am Main: Suhrkamp, 1989.

Berlin Museum, *Stadtbilder: Berlin in der Malerei vom 17. Jahrhundert bis zur Gegenwart.* Exh. cat. Berlin: Berlin Museum, Nicolaische Verlagsbuchhandlung, and Verlag Willmuth Arenhövel, 1987.

Berlinische Galerie. *Berlin um 1900.* Exh. cat. Berlin: Berlinische Galerie/Akademie der Künste, 1984.

Blackbourn, David, and Richard J. Evans, eds. *The German Bourgeoisie: Essays on the Social History of the German Middle Class from the Late Eighteenth to the Early Twentieth Century.* London and New York: Routledge, 1993.

Braun, Günter and Waldtraut, eds. *Mäzenatentum in Berlin.* Berlin and New York: Walter de Gruyter, 1993.

Brenner, Michael. *The Renaissance of Jewish Culture in Weimar Germany.* New Haven: Yale University Press, 1996.

Breuer, Gerda, and Ines Wagemann, eds. *Ludwig Meidner: Zeichner, Maler, Literat 1884–1966.* 2 vols. Exh. cat. Stuttgart: Institut Mathildenhöhe Darmstadt, 1991.

Bronner, Stephen Erick, and Douglas Kellner. *Passion and Rebellion: The Expressionist Heritage.* New York: Columbia University Press, 1987.

Brühl, Georg, *Herwarth Walden und "Der Sturm."* Cologne: Du Mont, 1983.

Buber, Martin, ed. *Jüdische Künstler.* Berlin: Jüdischer Verlag, 1903.

Donath, Adolph. *Lesser Ury: Seine Stellung in der modernen deutschen Malerei.* Berlin: Verlag Max Perl, 1921.

Eberle, Matthias. *Max Liebermann 1847–1935: Werkverzeichnis der Gemälde und Ölstudien.* 2 vols. Munich: Hirmer, 1995–96.

Eliel, Carol. *The Apocalyptic Landscapes of Ludwig Meidner.* Exh. cat. Los Angeles: The Los Angeles County Museum of Art and Prestel, 1989.

Elsaesser, Thomas, ed. *A Second Life: German Cinema's First Decades.* Amsterdam: Amsterdam University Press, 1996.

Forster-Hahn, Françoise, ed. *Imagining Modern German Culture: 1889-1910.* Washington, D.C.: National Gallery of Art, 1996.

Frisby, David, and Mike Featherstone, eds. *Simmel on Culture: Selected Writings.* London: Sage Publications, 1997.

Fritzsche, Peter. *Reading Berlin 1900.* Cambridge, Mass.: Harvard University Press, 1996.

Gay, Peter. *Freud, Jews and Other Germans: Masters and Victims in Modernist Culture.* New York: Oxford University Press, 1978.

Gilman, Sander L., and Jack Zipes. *Yale Companion to Jewish Writing and Thought in German Culture, 1096–1996.* New Haven and London: Yale University Press, 1997.

Glatzer, Ruth, ed. *Das Wilhelminische Berlin: Panorama einer Metropole, 1890–1918.* Berlin: Siedler Verlag, 1997.

Gordon, Donald E. *Modern Art Exhibitions, 1900–1916.* 2 vols. Munich: Prestel, 1974.

——. *Expressionism: Art and Idea.* New Haven: Yale University Press, 1987.

Grochowiak, Thomas. *Ludwig Meidner.* Recklinghausen: Aurel Bongers, 1966.

Grunfeld, Frederic V. *Prophets Without Honour: A Background to Freud, Kafka, Einstein, and Their World.* New York: Holt Rinehart and Winston, 1979.

Hake, Sabine. *Passions and Deceptions: The Early Films of Ernst Lubitsch.* Princeton: Princeton University Press, 1992.

Hamburger Kunsthalle. *Munch und Deutschland.* Exh. cat. Hamburg: Hamburger Kunsthalle, 1994.

D'Harnoncourt, Anne. *Futurism and the International Avant-Garde.* Exh. cat. Philadelphia: Philadelphia Museum of Art, 1980.

Haxthausen, Charles W., and Heidrun Suhr, eds. *Berlin: Culture and Metropolis.* Minneapolis and Oxford: University of Minnesota Press, 1990.

Heller, Reinhold. *Art in Germany, 1909–1936: From Expressionism to Resistance—The Marvin and Janet Fishman Collection.* Exh. cat. Munich and Milwaukee: Prestel and the Milwaukee Art Museum, 1990.

High Museum of Art, Atlanta, Georgia. *Art in Berlin 1815–1989.* Exh. cat. Atlanta: High Museum of Art, 1989.

Jelavich, Peter. *Berlin Cabaret.* Cambridge, Mass.: Harvard University Press, 1993.

Jensen, Robert. *Marketing Modernism in Fin-de-Siècle Europe.* Princeton: Princeton University Press, 1994.

Junge, Henrike, ed. *Avantgarde und Publikum: Zur Rezeption avantgardischer Kunst in Deutschland 1905–1933.* Cologne/Weimar/Vienna: Böhlau, 1992.

Kocka, Jürgen, and Manuel Frey, eds. *Bürgerkultur und Mäzenatentum im 19. Jahrhundert*. Berlin: Fannei & Walz, 1998.

Kohut, Thomas. *Wilhelm II and the Germans*. New York and Oxford: Oxford University Press, 1991.

Korff, Gottfried, and Reinhard Rürup, eds. *Berlin, Berlin: Die Ausstellung zur Geschichte der Stadt*. Exh. cat. Berlin: Berliner Festspiele and Nicolai, 1987.

Lange, Annemarie. *Das Wilhelminische Berlin: Zwischen Jahrhundertwende und Novemberrevolution*. Berlin: Dietz Verlag, 1967.

Lasker-Schüler, Else. *Lieber gestreifter Tiger: Briefe von Else Lasker-Schüler*. Edited by Margaret Kupper. Munich: Kösel, 1969.

Lasker-Schüler, Else, and Franz Marc. *Mein lieber, wundervoller blauer Reiter: Privater Briefwechsel*. Edited by Ulrike Marquardt and Heinz Rölleke. Düsseldorf and Zurich: Artemis und Winkler, 1998.

Lowenstein, Steven M., Paul Mendes-Flohr, Peter Pulzer, and Monika Richarz. *Deutsch-jüdische Geschichte in der Neuzeit*. Vol. 3, *1871–1918*. Munich: C. H. Beck, 1997.

Mai, Ekkehard, and Peter Paret, eds. *Sammler, Stifter und Museen: Kunstförderung in Deutschland im 19. und 20. Jahrhundert*. Cologne/Weimar/Vienna: Böhlau, 1993.

Mangold, Ursula von. *Auf der Schwelle zwischen gestern und morgen: Begegnungen und Erlebnisse*. Weilheim: Wilhelm Barth-Verlag, 1963.

Marc, Franz, and Else Lasker-Schüler. *"Der Blaue Reiter präsentiert Eurer Hoheit sein Blaues Pferd": Karten und Briefe*. Edited by Peter-Klaus Schuster. Munich: Prestel, 1987.

Mendes-Flohr, Paul. *Jewish Intellectuals and the Experience of Modernity*. Detroit: Wayne State University Press, 1991.

The Metropolitan Museum of Art. *German Masters of the Nineteenth Century: Paintings and Drawings from the Federal Republic of Germany*. Exh. cat. New York: The Metropolitan Museum of Art, 1981.

Meyer, Michael, ed. *German-Jewish History in Modern Times*. New York: Columbia University Press, 1997.

Mosse, George L. *German Jews Beyond Judaism*. Bloomington and Cincinnati: Indiana University Press and Hebrew Union College Press, 1985.

Mülhaupt, Freya. *Herwarth Walden (1878–1941): Wegbereiter der Moderne*. Exh. cat. Berlin: Berlinische Galerie, 1991.

The Open Museum. *Jacob and Israel: Homeland and Identity in the Work of Jakob Steinhardt*. Exh. cat. Tefen Industrial Park, Israel: The Open Museum, 1998.

Paret, Peter. *The Berlin Secession: Modernism and Its Enemies in Imperial Germany*. Cambridge, Mass.: Harvard University Press, 1980.

Paris/Berlin: Rapports et contrastes France-Allemagne 1900–1933. Exh. cat. Paris: Centre Nationale d'Art et de Culture Georges Pompidou, 1978.

Perloff, Marjorie. *The Futurist Moment: Avant-Garde, Avant Guerre, and the Language of Rupture*. Chicago and London: The University of Chicago Press, 1986.

Pickar, Gertrud Bauer, and Karl Eugen Webb, eds. *Expressionism Reconsidered*. Munich: Wilhelm Fink Verlag, 1979.

Prinzler, Hans Helmut, and Enno Patalas, eds. *Lubitsch*. Munich and Lucerne: C. J. Bucher, 1984.

Raabe, Paul, and H. L. Greve. *Expressionismus: Literatur und Kunst 1910–1923*. Marbach am Neckar: Deutsches Literaturarchiv im Schiller-Nationalmuseum, 1960.

Roters, Eberhard, ed. *Berlin 1910–1933*. New York: Rizzoli, 1982.

Roters, Eberhard, and Bernhard Schulz, eds. *Ich und die Stadt: Mensch und Grossstadt in der deutschen Kunst des 20. Jahrhunderts in Deutschland*. Exh. cat. Berlin: Berlinische Galerie, 1987.

Scheffler, Karl. *Berlin: Ein Stadtschicksal*. 1910. Reprint. Berlin: Fannei & Walz, 1989.

——. *Max Liebermann*. Munich: Piper, 1922.

Schuster, Peter-Klaus. *Delaunay und Deutschland*. Exh. cat. Munich: Haus der Kunst, Staatsgalerie Moderner Kunst, 1985.

Schutte, Jürgen, and Peter Sprengel, eds. *Die Berliner Moderne 1885–1914*. Stuttgart: Philipp Reclam Jun., 1987.

Schweinitz, Jörg, ed. *Prolog vor dem Film: Nachdenken über ein neues Medium 1909–1914*. Leipzig: Reclam, 1992.

Selz, Peter. *German Expressionist Painting*. Berkeley and Los Angeles: University of California Press, 1974.

Simmel, Georg. *The Sociology of Georg Simmel*. Translated and edited by Kurt H. Wolff. New York: The Free Press, 1964.

Styan, J. L. *Max Reinhardt*. Cambridge and New York: Cambridge University Press, 1982.

Teeuwisse, Nicolaas. *Vom Salon zur Secession: Berliner Kunstleben zwischen Tradition und Aufbruch zur Moderne 1871–1900*. Berlin: Deutscher Verlag für Kunstwissenschaft, 1986.

Usai, Paolo Cherchi, and Lorenzo Codelli. *Before Caligari: German Cinema, 1895–1920*. Exh. cat. Pordenone: Le Giornate del Cinema Muto and Edizioni Biblioteca dell'Immagine, 1990.

Wehler, Hans-Ulrich. *Das Deutsche Kaiserreich 1871–1918*. Vol. 9 of *Die Deutsche Geschichte*. Edited by Joachim Leuschner. Göttingen: Vandenhoeck & Ruprecht, 1988.

Wesenberg, Angelika, ed. *Max Liebermann—Jahrhundertwende*. Exh. cat. Berlin: Ars Nicolai, 1997.

Wilhelmy, Petra. *Der Berliner Salon im 19. Jahrhundert (1780–1914)*. Berlin and New York: Walter de Gruyter, 1989.

Willett, John. *Expressionism*. New York: McGraw-Hill, 1970.

Index

Italicized page numbers indicate illustrations.
Artworks are indexed by the name of the artist.

A

Abrahamsohn, Otto. *See* Brahm, Otto

Acher, Matthias. *See* Birnbaum, Nathan

Adler, Egon, 80

Ahad Ha'am (Asher Ginsberg), 167, 173.

Die Aktion, 71, 72, 80, 140

Alexanderplatz, Construction
of the U-Bahn (Underground), *27*

Allgemeine Zeitung des Judentums, 161, 168

Altneuland (Old-New Land), 168, 171.
See also Herzl, Theodor

Amsler & Rutthardt (gallery), 55

Andreae, Edith, 203, *203*

Der Anfang (The Beginning), 82

Ansorge, Conrad, 67

Antoine, André, 210

Antokolski, Mark, 179

Apollinaire, Guillaume, 69

Arbeitsrat für Kunst (Workers Council for Art), 184

Archipenko, Alexander
Collage: Two Figures, 95

Der arme Teufel (The Poor Devil), 68

Arnhold, Eduard, 3, *54*, 55, 56

Arnold, Victor, 218, 230

Arnswaldt, Bertha von, 190, *196*, 196, 200, 203

Arnswaldt, Hermann Baron von, 196

Association of Berlin Artists, 35, 36, 38, 49

Association of German Artists, 49

Avenarius, Ferdinand, 20

B

Bahnhof Friedrichstrasse, *102*

Bahr, Hermann, 203

Balla, Giacomo, 131
Dynamism of a Dog on a Leash, 97

Baluschek, Hans, 40
Berlin Landscape, 40

Bar Kochba, 174, 182

Barlach, Ernst, 12, 42, 48, 52, 65, 66
Pulling the Net, 46
Resting Wanderer, 47
Tilla Durieux, 223

Basel Manifesto, 166

Beaurepaire, Gustav, 218

Beckmann, Max, 11, 42, 45, 137
Balloon Race, 45
Two Officers, *11*

Beer, Amalie, 193

Der Bettler (The Beggar), 222, 223.
See also Sorge, Reinhard

Bendemann, Eduard, 113, 116, 117, 179
*The Exile of the Jews into
Babylonian Captivity*, 113, *114*, 116

Benjamin, Walter, 26, 82, 205

Benn, Gottfried, 59, 64, 76

Beradt, Martin, 201

Bergmann, Shmuel Hugo, 182

Berlin Alexanderplatz, 71

Berlin Moderns, 76, 78

Berlin Secession,
32, *38*, *39*, 38-40, 41, 42, 43, 45, 48–55, 147,
150, 151, 153, 185, 202

Berlin State Museums, 35

Berliner Dom, *23*

Berliner Tageblatt, 19, *58*, 76

Bernstein, Carl, 3, 5, *197*, 198, 199,

Bernstein, Felicie, 3, 5, *196*, 198, 199, 200
Reception room in the Bernstein home, *198*
Music room in the Bernstein home, *199*

Bertens, Rosa, *219*

Bezalel School of Arts and Crafts, 158, 172

Bierbaum, Julius, 158

Der Bildermann, 12, *12*

Birkenfeld, Günther, 81

Birnbaum, Nathan, 167, 170, 172

Bismarck, Otto von, 16, 227

Bithell, Jethro, 80

Der Blaue Reiter (The Blue Rider), 52, 69

Bloch, Ernst, 191, 207n. 9

B'nai B'rith Lodge, 143n. 40, 180

Bnei Moshe, 173

Boccioni, Umberto, 69, 131, 140
Drawing After *States of Mind: Those Who Go*, 69
The Street Enters the House, 131, *132*
The Strengths of a Street, 131
Unique Forms of Continuity in Space, 90

Böcklin, Arnold, 42, 124, 129, 144n. 69

Bode, Wilhelm von, 35, 153, 157, 198, 199

Boelsche, Wilhelm, 169

Böhme, Jakob, 169

Bondy, Walter, 54

Boskamp, Katrin, 155

Brahm, Otto, 6, 9, 209–14, 216, 220–22

Brand, Adolf, 169

Brandes, Georg, 3, 199, 207n. 30

Brecht, Bertolt, 220

Brieger-Wasservogel, Lothar, 153

Brod, Max, 64, 182

Brouwer, Adriaen, 198

Die Brücke (The Bridge), 50, 52, 69

Buber, Martin,
6, 25, *25*–27, 62, 64, 109, 110, 112, 113, 115–17,
156, 165–67, 169–73, 172, 177–79, 182, 183,
191, 201, 206n. 9
Drei Reden über das Judentum
(Three Talks on Judaism), 182
Ekstatische Konfessionen
(Ecstatic Confessions), 27, 145n. 108
Jüdische Künstler (Jewish Artists), 156, 179

Budko, Joseph, 26, 181, 183, 185

Bund der Moderne, 59

Bunsen, Marie von, 192, 195, 203, 206n. 13

Burckhardt, Jacob, 171

Buruma, Ian, 28

C

C.-V.-Zeitung, 152

Café Bauer, 79

Café des Westens, 78–82, 133
The "Moderns" at their regular table, *58*, 76

Café Grössenwahn, 78

Café Jolicke, 79

Café Josty, 81

Café König, 79

Café Megalomania, 78, 81

Café Stephanie, 78

Caillebotte, Gustave, 3

Campendonk, Heinrich, 65, 80
The Balcony, 92

Carrà, Carlo, 131
The Swimmers, 96

Cassirer, Bruno,
6, 8, *32*, 41, 42, *42*, 43, 45, 55, 59, 66, 67, 151

Cassirer, Ernst, 43

Cassirer, Paul,
6, 7, 8, 9, 11, *33*, 33, 42, 43, *43*, 45,
46, 48–50, 52, 55, 56, 59, 65–67,
66, 129, 157

Cassirer, Richard, 43

Cassirer, Sophie, 42

Cassirer, Suzanne Aimée, 7, *44*

Centralverein (CV) (Central Organization
of German Citizens of the Jewish Faith),
163n. 25, 165, 181

Cézanne, Paul, 3, 35, 45, *45*, 52, 125

Chagall, Marc, 147, 181
The Flying Carriage, 100, *101*
The Poet, *101*

Chat Noir, 225, *225*

Chavannes, Puvis de, 109

Chronology (1890-1918), 236–53

Coblentz, Ida, 149

Cohen, Arthur, 26

Cohn, I. S., 225, 226

Conrad, Michael Georg, 169

Corinth, Lovis,
33, 36, 40, 40, 45, 48, 50, 51, 51, 52,
129, 185, 200, 207n. 33, 219

*Das Erlernen der Malerei: Ein Handbuch
von Lovis Corinth* (Painting: A Handbook
by Lovis Corinth), 48

*Exhibition of Lovis Corinth at Salon
Paul Cassirer* (poster), 50

Portrait of Makabäus-Hermann Struck, 51

Portrait of Sophie Cassirer, 42

Courbet, Gustave, 46

Croner, Else, 205

Cultural Zionists, 167-73. *See also* Zionism

Curtius, Ernst, 199

D

Daily Telegraph (London), 50

D'Annunzio, Gabriele, 171

Das muss man sehen (*You Gotta See It*), 228.
See also Freund, Julius

Daumier, Honoré, 35

Davidsohn, Hans. *See* Hoddis, Jakob van

Davidson, Paul, 229

Degas, Edgar, 35, 42, 45, 108

Dehmel, Richard, 67, 149, 149, 150, 152, 158

Delaunay, Robert, 69, 123, 132, 140

The City, 132, 134

Windows in Three Parts, 93

Delaunay, Sonia, 69

Democratic Zionist Faction
(Demokratische Fraktion), 167, 173

Derain, André, 52

Deutsche und französiche Kunst
(German and French Art), 10

Deutscher Werkbund
(German Association of Craftsmen), 176

Deutsches Theater,
65, 195, 210–14, 217, 220, 222, 230

Dilthey, Wilhelm, 171

Döblin, Alfred, 66, 67, 70, 70, 71, 82

Dohm, Hedwig, 200–202, 207n. 37

Dohme, Emma, 200

A Doll's House, 209. See also Ibsen, Henrik

Don Carlos, 214, 216

Donath, Adolph, 112, 117

Döring, Willy, *32, 41*

Dumont, Louise, 201, 207n. 41

Dürer, Albrecht, 157

Durieux, Tilla, 223, *223*

E

Eberle, Matthias, 104, 163n. 1

Der Eigene, 169

El Greco, 33, 45, 128, 129, 145n. 88

Laocoön, 129, 130

Engel, Otto, *32*

English Arts and Crafts movement, 179

Ephrussi, Charles, 3

Epstein, Jehudo, 179

Erdgeist (Earth Spirit), 219.
See also Wedekind, Frank

Erster Deutscher Herbstsalon
(First German Autumn Salon),
52, 69, 130, 131

Ewers, Hanns Heinz, 185

Eyde, Samuel, 195, 206n. 20

Eysoldt, Gertrud, 219, *219,* 220

F

Die Fackel (The Torch), 67, 75

Fauves, 125

Feilchenfeldt, Walter, 65, 83n. 18

Feininger, Lionel, 40, 50

The Bicycle Race, 91

Feiwel, Berthold, 166, 168, 172, *172, 173*

Fenneker, Josef

Der Fall Rosentopf (poster), *231*

Fidus, 169, 185

Fifth Zionist Congress,
156, 167, 178, *178,* 179

First German Autumn Salon.
See Erster Deutscher Herbstsalon

Fischer, Samuel, 28, 66, 83n. 18

Flaubert, Gustave, 61

Förster-Nietzsche, Elisabeth, 195, 206n. 20

Frank, Leonhard, 82

Frankfurter Zeitung, 209

Franz Liszt Foundation, 67

Franzos, Karl Emil, 199, 207n. 30

Free Secession, 52

Freie Bühne, 210, 211

Freud, Sigmund, 15, 24, 25

Freund, Julius, 209, 226–28

Friedlaender, Salomo (Mynona), 70

Friedländer-Fuld family, 43

Frisch, Ephraim, 169

Frühlings Erwachen (*Spring Awakening*),
222, *222, 227,* 228. *See also* Wedekind, Frank

Fürstenberg, Aniela, 198, 200, *201,* 200–203

Fürstenberg, Carl, 200, 202, 203

Fürstenberg, Hans, 203, 207n. 36

Futurist Manifesto, 69, 132

G

Galerie Fritz Gurlitt, 3, 55

Galerie Schulte, 55

Galliner, Arthur, 110

Gauguin, Paul, 109

Gaul, August, 6, 40, 150, 151, 163n. 9

Cat, 152

Otter with Fish, 152

Gay, Peter, 4, 16, 30, 59, 63, 64, 70

Géricault, Théodore

The Raft of Medusa, 137

Geiger, Ludwig, 161

George, Stefan, 64

German Social Democratic Party, 202, 211

Die Gesellschaft (Society), 59

Ghosts, 209, 210, 221, 222. See also Ibsen, Henrik

Giesenberg, Hermann, 196

Ginsberg, Asher. *See* Ahad Ha'am

Gipkens, Julius E.F.

Chat Noir (poster), *225*

Glicenstein, Henryk, 179

Gobineau, Comte de, 171

Goethe, Johann Wolfgang von, 23, 212

Gogol, Nikolai, 68

Goldman, Max. *See* Reinhardt, Max

Goldstein, Moritz, 8, 18, 20

Gombrich, Ernst, 4

Goncharova, Natalia

River Landscape, 98

Gorky, Maxim, 68, 219

Gottlieb, Maurycy, 179

Goyen, Jan van, 198

Graef, Gustav, 192

Grünewald, Matthias

Isenheim Altar, 129

Grunfeld, Frederic, 5

Gurlitt, Fritz, 183

Gurlitt, Wolfgang, 183

H

Hagemeister, Carl, 40

Halevi, Yehuda, 124

Hamburger Kunsthalle, 151, 155

Hanneles Himmelfahrt (Hannele Goes to Heaven),
211. *See also* Hauptmann, Gerhart

Harden, Maximilian, 28, 201

Hart, Heinrich, 62, 169

Hart, Julius, 62, *62*, 169

Harz, Benjamin, 153

Hauptmann, Gerhart, 28, 65, 210–12, 214, 218, 226

Hauschner, Auguste, 201–3, 207n. 39

Hausenstein, Wilhelm, 183

Haxthausen, Charles, 135

Hebräische Balladen (Hebrew Ballads), 75, 76

Heckel, Erich, 69

Heilbut, Emil, 152

Heimann, Moritz, 66

Heine, Heinrich, 16, 124, 160

Heine, Thomas Theodor
  Exhibition of the Berlin Secession (poster), 39

Helferich, Hermann, 152

Hermann, Georg (Georg Borchardt), 156, 163n. 25

Hermann, Kurt, *32, 41*

Herrnfeld, Anton, 228, 233

Herrnfeld, Donat, 228, 233

Hertel, Albert, 194, 206n. 16

Herz, Henriette, 189, 199, 206n. 1

Herzl, Theodor, 156, 166–68, 171, 172
  Altneuland (Old-New Land), 168, 171
  Der Judenstaat (The Jewish State), 171

Hesse, Hermann, 65

Heym, Georg, 64–66, 134

Hille, Peter, *62*, 80

Hiller, Kurt, 140

Hindenburg, Paul von, 152

Hirschfeld, Georg, 169

Hirschfeld, Magnus, 80, 169

Hirsh, Sharon L., 114

Hirszenberg, Samuel, 179

Hitz, Dora, 200, 207n. 33

Hoddis, Jakob van (Hans Davidsohn), 70, 82, 134, *135*, 140

Hodler, Ferdinand, 42, 45, 113, 114
  The Disappointed Souls, 113, 114

Hofmann, Ludwig von, 169

Hofmannsthal, Hugo von, 64, 78, 195, 206n. 20, 219, 223

Hohenlohe-Schillingsfürst, Chlodwig zu, 211

Hölderlin, Friedrich, 64

Hollaender, Viktor, 209, 226, 227

Holland, Bertha. *See* Arnswaldt, Bertha von

Holländer, Felix, 169

Horovitz, L., 200

Hoyos, Alexander Count, 195, 206n. 20

Humboldt, Wilhelm von, 23

Huyssen, Andreas, 61

I

Ibsen, Henrik, 209, 210, 212, 221, 222

Die Insel der Seligen (The Isle of the Blessed), 229

International Art Show (Munich), 153

Israels, Jozef, 163n. 31, 169, 179, 181

J

Jacobowski, Ludwig, 59, 61, 63, 71

Jacobsohn, Siegfried, 68, 221

Jacques Manasse, 225, 225, 226

Janthur, Richard, 127, 144n. 81

Jawlensky, Alexej, 46, 50

Jefferson, Allan, 70

Jewish Museum (Berlin), 157, 162, 179, 180, 183

Jewish Youth Movement, 174

Juda, 7, 167. *See also* Börries von Münchhausen

Der Jude (The Jew), 25–27, 183, 185

Der Judenstaat (The Jewish State).
  See also Herzl, Theodor

Jüdische Künstler (Jewish Artists), 156, 179.
  See also Buber, Martin

Die jüdische Moderne, 170, 174

Jüdische Rundschau
  (The Jewish Review), 174, 182

Jüdischer Almanach (The Jewish Almanac),
  164, 169, 179

Jüdischer Verlag, 169, 172, 173, 176

Jüdisches Lexikon, 157

Die Jugend (Youth), 174, 217

Jugendstil, 176, 179–81, 185, 194

Jungmann, Max, 167, 170

Justi, Ludwig, 158, 160

K

Kabale und Liebe, 220.
  See also Schiller, Johann von

Kafka, Franz, 15, 27, 28, 182

Kain: Zeitschrift für Menschlichkeit
  (Cain: Journal for Humanity), 130

Kaiser Friedrich, 200

Kaiser-Friedrich Museum, 153

Kaiser Wilhelm II. *See* Wilhelm II

Kalckreuth, Babette. *See* Meyer, Babette

Kalckreuth, Graf Leopold von
  Portrait of Paul Cassirer, 43

Kalckreuth, Stanislaus von, 193

Kammerspiele, 222

Kandinsky, Vasily, 50, 69
  Painting with White Border, 88

Kantorowicz, Gertrud, 191, 206n. 9

Kardorff, Konrad von, 40

Kastan, Isidor, 211

Katz, Jacob, 31n. 38

Kayssler, Friedrich, 214, *216,* 219

Kayzer family, 196

Kerr, Alfred, 28, *29,* 80, 201

Kessler, Harry Count, 33, 49, 195, 206n. 20

Kirchner, Ernst Ludwig, 69
  Portrait of Alfred Döblin, 70
  Three Nudes, 87

Klee, Paul, 50, 72

Das Kleine Journal, 211

Kleine Scala, 79

Kleines Theater, 216, 218, 220

Klimsch, Fritz, *32, 40, 41*

Klimt, Gustav, 39

Klinger, Max, 3, 42, 199

Klingsor, Tristan, 72

Koehler, Bernhard, 69

Kohn, Hans, 182

Kokoschka, Oskar, 30, 48, 52, 64, 65, 69, *69,* 70, 80
  Murderer, Hope of Women
    (cover of *Der Sturm*), 67
  Portrait of Max Reinhardt, 224
  Self-Portrait, 86

Kolb, Annette, 65, 83n. 18

Kolbe, Georg, 162
  Amazone, 47
  Portrait of Paul Cassirer, 33

Kollwitz, Käthe, 40, 162, 212
  The End, 212
  March of the Weavers, 210, 212
  Uprising, 41

Komet, 68

Die Kommenden (The Up-and-Coming),
  7, 9, 59, 67, 68, 169, *169,* 185

Kraus, Karl, 64, 67, 75, 79, 80

Kriegszeit (Wartime), 11

Kruse, Max, 219

Kubin, Alfred, 65

Kunst und Künstler (Art and Artist),
  43, *43,* 51, 67, 151, 159

Das Kunstblatt, 147

Die Kunstschau (The Art Show), 151

Der Kunstwart (Guardian of Art), 18–20, 174

L

Lachmann, Cäcilie. *See* Liebermann, Cäcilie

Lachmann, Hedwig, 201, 207n. 41

Landauer, Gustav, 169, 201, 202, *202,* 207n. 41

Landsberger, Franz, 105, 125, 144n. 77

Langbehn, Julius, 104

Lasker, Berthold, 62, 63, 67

Lasker-Schüler, Else,
  6, 9, 10, 30, 48, 59–61, *60,* 62, 63–72, *72, 73,*
  74–77, 80, 169, 181
  Hebräische Balladen
    (Hebrew Ballads), 75, 76
  Der Malik, 72, 81

Mein Herz: Ein Liebesroman mit Bildern und wirklich lebenden Menschen (My Heart: A Romance with Pictures and Real People), 78

Meine Wunder (My Miracles), 75

Die Nächte Tino von Bagdads (The Nights of Tino of Bagdad), 75

Der siebente Tag (The Seventh Day), 67

Snake Charmer in the Thebes Marketplace, 74

Thebes with Jussuf, 74

Theben (Thebes), 74, 81

Die Wupper, 65, 65, 66

Lebensreform (life-reform movement), 169, 176, 179

Lefèbvre, Jules Joseph, 108

Léger, Fernand, 69

Nude Model in the Studio, 94

Leibholz, Lise, 152

Leistikow, Walter, 6, 32, 36, 40, 41, 45, 49, 50, 57n. 3, 169

Grunewald Lake, 36

Lake in the Mark Brandenburg, 37

Lepsius, Sabine, 192, 199, 203, 204, 206n. 10

Lessing, Gotthold Ephraim, 66, 212

Lessing Theater, 221

Lewin, Georg. *See* Walden, Herwarth

Lewin, Victor, 67

Lewitan, Issak, 169

Lewysohn, Rudolf. *See* Nelson, Rudolf

Leyden, Ernst Victor von, 196

Leyden, Marie von, 195, 196, 203

Lichtwark, Alfred, 33, 55, 66, 150, 155

Liebermann, Benjamin, 148

Liebermann, Cäcilie, 161

Liebermann, Felix, 148, 161, 162

Liebermann, Georg, 148, 161

Liebermann, Joseph, 147

Liebermann, Louis, 148

Liebermann, Martha, 150, 161, 163n. 4

Liebermann, Max, 3, 6–9, 11, 12, 33–36, 34, 35, 40–43, 41, 45, 46, 50–52, 54, 56, 66, 67, 103–6, 140, 146, 147–62, 159, 169, 179, 199, 200, 202

Boy on Horse, 49

Evening at the Brandenburg Gate, 106, 107

Jewish Quarter in Amsterdam, 105, 106, 148, 148

Leisure Hour in the Amsterdam Orphanage, 36, 104

Portrait of Lovis Corinth, 40

Portrait of Max Slevogt, 44

Portrait of the Poet Richard Dehmel, 149

Portrait of Professor Dr. Carl Bernstein, 197

Samson and Delilah, 150, 150, 151

Self-Portrait with Brush and Palette, 34

Self-Portrait with Kitchen Still-Life, 159, 159–62

Suse Cassirer and Gerda Leistikow, 7

The Twelve-Year-Old Jesus in the Temple, 153–56, 154, 155

Vegetable Market in Amsterdam, 105

View of the Tiergarten from the Artist's Living-Room Window, 104

Women Plucking Geese, 36

Lilien, Ephraim Mose (E. M.), 6, 7, 10, 18, 26, 106, 153, 156, 167, 168, 172, 172, 173, 178, 179–81

Jüdischer Almanach (cover), 164

Die Kommenden (invitation postcard), 169

Ost und West (cover), 175

Postcard Commemorating the Fifth Zionist Congress, 178

Liliencron, Detlev von, 149

Lippmann, Friedrich, 199, 207n. 30

Liszt, Franz, 67

Loewe, Heinrich, 167

Loewenson, Erwin, 65

Loga, Valerian von, 200

Loos, Adolf, 79

Lowenstein, Steven, 63

The Lower Depths, 219. *See also* Gorky, Maxim

Lubitsch, Ernst, 6, 9–11, 209, 217, 229–34, 233

Lublinski, Samuel, 59–61, 63, 64, 80, 170

Lydia und Mäxchen, 67. *See also* Döblin, Alfred

M

Macke, August, 12, 69, 72

Greeting, 68

The Storm, 68

Maeterlinck, Maurice, 214, 219, 226

Der Malik, 72, 81

Manet, Edouard, 3, 35, 45, 123, 125, 198

A Café in the Place du Théâtre-Francais, 120, 123, 123

The Departure of the Folkstone Ferry, 199

White Lilacs in a Glass Vase, 199

Mangoldt, Ursula von, 196

Mann, Heinrich, 48, 65

Mann, Katia (Pringsheim), 207n. 37

Mann, Thomas, 59, 65–67

Marc, Franz, 12, 48, 69, 72, 80, 81

Atonement, 71

Dancer from the Court of King Jussuf, 72

Sleeping Shepherdess, 87

Stables, 93

Yellow Seated Female Nude, 71

Marckwald, Elsbeth, 161

Marées, Hans von, 109

Marinetti, Filippo, 69

Massary, Fritzi, 226, 227, 227

Matisse, Henri, 45, 52, 129

Mauthner, Fritz, 201, 202, 207n. 41

Medea, 220

Meidner, Ludwig, 6, 9, 12, 103, 123–29, 131–41, 181, 183, 184

Apocalyptic Landscape, 126–28, 134–38, 135, 136, 138

Battle, 89

Building the Underground, 126, 127, 127, 135

Coffeehouse Scene, 78

Construction Site Between Houses, 126, 126

Cosmic Landscape with Comet, 128

Explosion, 137, 138

Golus, 124

Jehuda ben Halevy, 124, 125

Landscape with Burned-Out House, 128

Mortify the Flesh, 124

My Nocturnal Visage, 139

Nude Self-Portrait at the Easel, 138, 140

Portrait of Jakob van Hoddis, 135

Self-Portrait, 132

Self-Portrait as Prophet, 137, 140, 141

Study, 137, 137

Südwestkorso, Berlin, Five O'Clock in the Morning, 134, 134

Meier-Graefe, Julius, 129, 145n. 88, 158, 200, 207n. 33

Mendelssohn, Moses, 15, 160

Mendelssohn-Bartholdy, Felix, 160

Mendelssohn family, 43

Menorah, 185

Menschheitsdämmerung (Twilight of Humanity), 70

Menzel, Adolph, 3, 34, 35, 147, 157, 163n. 2, 194, 206n. 16

Views of Workers Eating, 34

The Merchant of Venice, 220, 225

Metropol Theater (revues), 226–28, 231

Meunier, Charles, 108

Meunier, Constantin, 45, 108

Meyer, Babette, 192–96, 201, 206n. 13

Meyerbeer, Cornelie. *See* Richter, Cornelie

Meyerbeer, Giacomo, 160, 193, 194

Meyerbeer, Minna, 193

Meyerheim, Paul, 194

Michelangelo, 117

A Midsummer Night's Dream, 220, 220

Millet, Jean-François, 157

Minkowski, Maurycy

After the Pogrom, 115, 115

Minna von Barnhelm, 220. *See also* Lessing, Gotthold Ephraim

Die moderne Jüdin (The Modern Jewess), 205

Modigliani, Amedeo, 125

Moeller van den Bruck, Arthur, 185

Mommsen, Theodor, 3, 199, 207n. 30

Monet, Claude, 33, 35, 42, 45, 119, 133, 198

    Arrival of the Normandy Train, 120

Der Morgen (Morning), 68

Morgue, 64

Mörder, Hoffnung der Frauen
    (Murderer, Hope of Women), *67, 69*

Mosse, Rudolf, 55, 56

Motzkin, Leo, 167, 173

Mühsam, Erich, 62, 68, 82, 130

Müller, Georg, 183

Munch, Edvard, 34, 45, 149

    Frieze of Life, 222

    Set design for Ibsen's *Ghosts, 221, 222*

Münchhausen, Börries von, 7, 168, 185

Mundlak, Regina, 181

Munich Secession, 39

Münter, Gabriele, 69

Muther, Richard, 155

Mynona. *See* Friedlaender, Salomo

N

Narodniki, 167, 173

Natanson, Aniela. *See* Fürstenberg, Aniela

National Gallery (Berlin), 49, 50, 107, 116, 198

National Library (Jerusalem), 182

Neimann, Kurt, 78

Nelson, Rudolf, 209, 224–26, *225*, 233

    Jacques Manasse, 225

Neopathetiker, 67

Neopathetisches Cabaret, 64, *64*, 65, 127, 128

Der Neue Club, 64, *64*, 65, 70, 127, 132

Die Neue Freie Volksbühne
    (The New Public Theater Association), 59

Die Neue Gemeinschaft
    (The New Community), 9, 62, *62*, 169, 184, 185

Neue jüdische Monatshefte
    (New Jewish Monthly), 183

Das neue Pathos, 132, 184

Neue Synagoge
    (New Jewish Synagogue), *16, 17, 17*

Das neue Tagebuch (The New Diary), 147

Der neue Weg (The New Way), 68

Neues Theater, 219, 222

Neuestes!! Allerneuestes!!!
    (Get the Latest!! The Very Latest!!!), 226, *227*

New Secession, 50, 51, 52

Nietzsche, Friedrich,
    64, 128, 145n. 85, 149, 165, 171, 200

Nolde, Emil, 42, 45, 50, 51, 72

Nollendorf Casino, 168

Nossig, Alfred, 172, 179

Nostitz, Helene von, 193, 195

Novembergruppe, 184

O

Oedipus Rex, 223, 223

Oppenheim, Marie. *See* Leyden, Marie von

Oppenheim, Moritz Daniel, 106, 177

    Friday Night, 176

Oppenheimer, Franz, 149, 169

Oppenheimer, Julius, 149

Oppenheimer, Max, 55

Oppenheimer, Paula, 149

Oranienburger Strasse Synagogue.
    See Neue Synagoge

Orlik, Emil, 221

    Cézanne Exhibition at the Cassirer Gallery
    (poster), *45*

    Paul Cassirer, 66

    Sketch of impression of *Oedipus Rex, 223*

    Schall und Rauch (Sound and Smoke), *215*

Ost und West, 170, 175, 179, 185

Osthaus, Karl Ernst, 75

Ostwald, Hans, 152

P

Padilla, Désirée Artôt de, 199, 207n. 30

PAGU, 229, 230

Palukst, Abraham, 181

Pan, 149

Pan (journal), 66, 158

Pan Presse, 48

Panofsky, Erwin, 142n. 9

Pariser Platz, *147, 148,* 193

Parlaghy, Vilma, 4

    Kaiser Wihelm II, 4

Pasternak, Leonid, 179

Die Pathetiker, 127–32, 140, 183, 184

Pauli, Gustav, 55

Pechstein, Max, 50, *50,* 51-52

    *The New Secession—Exhibition of Works
    Refused by the Berlin Secession* (poster), *50*

Pelléas et Mélisande, 214, 219.
    See also Maeterlinck, Maurice

Pfemfert, Franz, 71, 82

Picasso, Pablo, 69

Pillars of Society, 209. See also Ibsen, Henrik

Pinthus, Kurt, 70

Pissarro, Camille, 35, 42, 133, 179

    Peasants Working in the Fields, 199

Portaels, Jean-François, 108, 112

Potsdamer Platz, *15,* 24

Pressa exhibition (Cologne), 180

The Pride of the Firm.
    See Der Stolz der Firma

Pringsheim, Hedwig. *See* Hedwig Dohm

Prinzess Café, 82

Professor Bernhardi, 221.
    See also Schnitzler, Arthur

Ein Protest deutscher Künstler, 10.
    See also Vinnen, Carl

Prussian Academy of Arts, 147, 161

Prussian Commission for the Fine Arts, 49

Przbyszewski, Stanislaw, 67

R

Rathenau, Walther,
    28, *28,* 35, 107, 193, 201, 203, 206n. 20

Rauch, Christian Daniel, 194

Reff, Theodore, 120

Reicher, Emanuel, 217

Reinhardt, Max,
    6, 9, 20, 65, 78, 190, 195, 206n. 20, 209,
    213–24, *216,* 224, 228–30

Reiss, Erich, 183

Rembrandt van Rijn,
    35, 104, 105, 108, 111, 117, 143n. 36,
    n. 37, n. 40, 181

    Jeremiah Lamenting the Destruction of Jerusalem,
    117, *117*

    The Return of the Prodigal Son, 111

Renoir, Pierre-Auguste, 33, 35, 46

Reuter, Gabriele, 200, 207n. 35

Richter, Cornelie,
    188, 193–96, *193, 194,* 203, 206n. 20

Richter, Gustav, *188,* 193, *193, 194, 194*

Richter, Hans

    Portrait of Herwarth Walden, 84

Richter, Raoul, 195, 206n. 20

Rilke, Rainer Maria, 59, 64, 67

Rodin, Auguste, 42

Roland von Berlin, 225, *225*

Romanisches Café, 81, 82

Rosenberg, Else, 201, 207n. 37

Der Rosenkavalier, 70. See also Strauss, Richard

Roslund, Nell. *See* Walden, Nell

Royal Academy of Arts, 35, 36

Russisch-jüdischer wissenschaftlicher Verein
    (Russian-Jewish Scientific Society), 167

S

Sabarsky, Serge, 4

Salome, 219, 219, 235n. 18. *See also* Wilde, Oscar

Sargent, John Singer, 42

Schadow, Johann Gottfried, 147

Schaffner, Jakob, 201

Schall und Rauch (Sound and Smoke),
    214, *215,* 216-18, 221, 226, 230

Schatz, Boris, 172

Schaubühne (The Stage), 68

Scheerbart, Paul, 65

Scheffler, Karl, 7, 33, 51, 157–60, 162

Scherbera, Jürgen, 81

Schiff, Gert, 142n. 1

Schildkraut, Rudolf, 220, *220*

Schiller, Johann von, 212, 214, 220

Schiller Prize, 212

Schinkel, Karl Friedrich, 194,

Schleich, Carl Ludwig von, 190, 197

Schlemiehl, 167

Schlesinger, Hedwig. *See* Dohm, Hedwig

Schmidt-Rottluff, Karl, 69

    Der Neue Club, Neopathetisches Cabaret, 64

    The Reader, 73

Schnitzler, Arthur, 59, 221

Scholem, Gershom, 151, 205

Schönberg, Arnold, 15, 64, 67

Schönheit (Beauty), 169

Schopenhauer, Arthur, 200

Schorske, Carl, 61

Schreyer, Lothar, 71

Schuhpalast Pinkus
    (Pinkus's Shoe Palace), 10, 230–32

Schultz, Franziska, 71

Schultz, Richard, 226

Schulz, Wilhelm

    Ninth Exhibition of the Berlin Secession
    (poster), *38*

Schwabach, Julius Leopold, 196

Schwabach, Leonie, 196, 203

Schwabach, Paul, 196

Schwarz, Karl, 157, 183

Schwarzes Ferkel, 149

Secession.
    See Berlin Secession; Free Secession;
    New Secession

Seidlitz, Woldemar von, 199, 207n. 30

Semi-Kürschner oder Literarisches Lexikon
    (Literary Dictionary), 33, 57n. 7, 152

Servaes, Franz, 107, 109, 115

Seurat, Georges, 109, 142n. 25

Severini, Gino, 131

    Festival at Montmartre, 99

Shaw, George Bernard, 68

Simmel, Georg,
    5, 21, 21–23, 119, 190, 191, 206n. 6

Simmel, Gertrud, 190, 191, 206n. 6

Simmel, Hans, 191, 204

Simplicissimus, 43, 217

Sisley, Alfred, 198

    The Seine at Argenteuil, 199

Skarbina, Franz, 36, 40

Slevogt, Max, 40, 44, 46, 48, 52

    Kunst und Künstler (cover), *43*

The Magic Flute (etchings), 48

    Portrait of Bruno Cassirer, 42

    Portrait of Suzanne Aimée Cassirer, 44

Solomon, Solomon J., 179

Sombart, Werner, 17, 18, 31n. 15, 200, 207n. 33

Soncino Society of Friends of the Jewish Book, 185

Sorge, Reinhard, 223

Sound and Smoke. *See Schall und Rauch*

Spiro, Eugen, 55

Spitzemberg, Hildegard von, 194, 195

Städtisches Museum, 161

Stauff, Philipp, 33, 34, 42, 53

    Semi-Kürschner, 33, 152

Steiner, George, 15

Steiner, Rudolf, 59, 169

Steinhardt, Jakob,
    6, 9, 12, 103, 106, 123, 125, 128–41, 181, 183–85

    Apocalyptic Landscape, 129, *131*

    Cain, 129, *129,* 130, 141

    The City, 131, *133*

    Coffeehouse, 78

    Job Amidst the Mountains, 130, *130*

    Pogrom, 183

    The Prophet, 130, 131, *182*

    Recollection of the War, 254

    Red and Glowing Is the Eye of the Jew, 184

    Self-Portrait, 131

    Two Jews, 127, 129

Steinlen, Théophile, 42, 129

Stenzel, Abraham, 80, 82

Stern, Ernst, 223

    Set design for Sorge's *Der Bettler*
    (The Beggar), *222*

    Set design for *Die Wupper, 65*

Stöcker, Adolf, 153, 217

Der Stolz der Firma
    (The Pride of the Firm), 230, *233,* 234

Stramm, August, 65

Straus, Oscar, 224

Strauss, Heinrich, 155

Strauss, Richard, 70

Strindberg, August, 149, 218

The Stronger, 218

Struck, Hermann,
    10, 26, 40, *51,* 52, 54, 57n. 18, 105, 106, 125,
    129, 157, 179, 181, 185

    Everyone Who Mourns Jerusalem Reaps Its Joy, 181

    Old Jew from Jaffa, 181

Stuck, Franz von, 124, 144n. 69

Der Sturm Gallery, 127, 130–32, 183

Der Sturm (The Storm),
    9, 12, 30, 52, 67, 67–72, 75, 78, 80, 81

Susman, Margarete, 191, 204, 206n. 8

Suttner, Berta von, 200, 207n. 35

T

Tel Aviv Museum, 157

Das Theater, 68

Théâtre libre, 210

Theben. See Lasker-Schüler, Else

Tiergarten, *23*

Tissot, J. James
    Abraham's Servant Meeteth Rebecca, 112, *112*

Toorop, Jan, 108

Toulouse-Lautrec, Henri de, 35

Tramer, Hans, 63

Treitschke, Heinrich, 16, 217

Treu, Georg, 198, 199

Trietsch, Davis, 167, *172, 173,* 174

Tschudi, Hugo von, 3, 33, 49, 50, 55, 56, 198–200

Tuaillon, Louis, 54

Tucholsky, Kurt, 68

U

U-Bahn, *27, 61*

Überbrettl, 214

Uhde, Fritz von, 155

Union Theater, *229, 230*

Unter den Linden, 26, *147, 148*

Ury, Lesser,
    6, 9, 10, 26, 55, 57n. 20, 103, 106–24, 132,
    140, 179–81, 185

    Bahnhof Friedrichstrasse
    (At the Friedrichstrasse Train Station),
    119, *119*

    Berlin Street Scene-Leipziger Platz, 122

    Café, 123, *123*

    David and Jonathan, 180

    Jacob Blessing Benjamin, 110, *110, 111, 111*

    Jeremiah, 112, 116, *116,* 117, 137, 179, 180

    Jerusalem, 109, 112, 112–14, 120

    Landscape, 121

    Man in Café, 122

    Moses on Mount Nebo, 180, *180*

    Night Impression, 120, *120*

    Portrait of Walther Rathenau, 28

    Rebecca at the Well, 112, *112,* 180

    Self-Portrait, 108

    Transience, 116, 117, 124

    View of the Nollendorfplatz, 192

    Volluvet, 109, *109*

V

Vallentin, Richard, 219

Van Gogh, Vincent, 33, 45, 48, 52, 125

Vanselow, Karl, 169

Varnhagen, Rahel Levin, 189, 196, 206n. 1

Veblen, Thorstein, 21

Velde, Henry van de, 33, 169, 194

Eine venezianische Nacht (A Venetian Night), 229

Verein für Kunst, 67, 78

Verhaeren, Emile, 127

Verlag für jüdische Kunst und
    Kultur Fritz Gurlitt, 183

Vienna Secession, 39

Vinnen, Carl, 10

Vlaminck, Maurice, 52

Vogeler, Heinrich, 71

Volkov, Shulamit, 160

Vollard, Ambroise, 45

Vollmöller, Karl, 229

Vor Sonnenaufgang (Before Sunrise), 210, 211.
    See also Hauptmann, Gerhart

Voss, Richard, 193

Vossiche Zeitung, 209

W

Wagner, Richard, 20, 194

Walden, Herwarth,
    6, 8, 9, 30, *30*, 52, 55, 59, 62, *62*, 66, 67–72,
    69, 78, 79, *81*, 82, 84, 85, 101, 127, 132, 169, 183

    Die vier Toten der Fiametta
    (The Four Dead of Fiametta), 67-68

Walden, Nell, 78, *101*

Wauer, William

    Portrait of Herwarth Walden, *85*

Weber, Max, 8

Die Weber (The Weavers), 210, 211

Wedekind, Frank, 64, 66, 67, 219, *222*, 226–28

Wegener, Paul, 223

Weidner, Albert, *62*

Die weissen Blätter (The White Pages), 66

Weizmann, Chaim, 167, *171*, *173*

Die Welt (The World), 174

Die Weltbühne (The World Stage), 68

Weltsch, Robert, 182

Der Weltspiegel, *58*, 76

Werefkin, Marianne von, 69

Werner, Alfred, 110

Werner, Anton von, 49, 56

    *The Mosse Family Banquet: Study for
    Dining-Room Mural at the Mosse Villa*, *55*

Wertheim Department Store, 226, *230*

Werther der Jude (Werther the Jew), 59

Westheim, Paul, 147

Whistler, James Abbott McNeill, 117

Wilde, Oscar, 219

Wildenbruch, Ernst von, 193

Wilhelm II,
    3, 4, 36, 40, 49, 53, 67, 70, 153, 211, 216

Wintergarten Theater, 229

Winz, Leo, 174

Wislicenus, Hermann, 108

Wittgenstein, Ludwig, 15

Wolff, Kurt, 64

Wolfskehl, Karl, 169

Wolzogen, Ernst von, 214, 224

Die Wupper, 65, *65*, 66.
    See also Lasker-Schüler, Else

YZ

Yerushalmi, Yosef, 115

Zech, Paul, 65

Der Zeitgenosse (The Contemporary), 59

Das Zelt (The Tent), 185

Zetkin, Clara, 202

Zickel, Martin, 214, *216*

Zion, 174

Zionism, 166–74. *See also* Cultural Zionists

Zlocisti, Theodor, 167, *167*, 172

Zola, Emile, 209

Die Zukunft (The Future), 28

Zweig, Arnold, 212

Zweig, Stefan, 127, 128, 168, 169

Contributors

Sigrid Bauschinger is Wolfgang Paulsen Professor of German Studies and Adjunct Professor of Judaic Studies at the University of Massachusetts, Amherst. She is the author, among other publications, of *Else Lasker-Schüler: Ihr Werk und ihre Zeit* (1980).

Inka Bertz is Curator of Collections at the Jewish Museum in Berlin. She is the author, among other publications, of "The Prophets' Pathos and the Community of the Shtetl: Jakob Steinhardt's Work Before and After World War I," in *Jacob and Israel: Homeland and Identity in the Work of Jakob Steinhardt* (1998). She has served as curator of the 1991 Berlin Museum exhibition "'Eine neue Kunst für ein altes Volk': Die jüdische Renaissance in Berlin, 1900 bis 1924" and other exhibitions.

Emily D. Bilski is an independent curator living in Jerusalem, specializing in nineteenth- and twentieth-century art. Her publications include *Art and Exile: Felix Nussbaum, 1904-1944* (1985) and *Golem! Danger, Deliverance and Art* (1988). She has served as curator of numerous exhibitions at The Jewish Museum, New York, including its permanent exhibition, "Culture and Continuity: The Jewish Journey."

Barbara Hahn is Professor of German Literature at Princeton University. Among her publications on women writers and intellectuals in Germany are *Unter falschem Namen: Von der schwierigen Autorschaft der Frauen* (1991) and, as editor, *Frauen in den Kulturwissenschaften: Von Lou Andreas Salome bis Hannah Arendt* (1994). She has edited the first volume of the critical edition of the writings of Rahel Levin Varnhagen, *Rahel Levin Varnhagens Briefwechsel mit Pauline Wiesel* (1997).

Peter Jelavich teaches modern European cultural and intellectual history at The University of Texas, Austin. He is the author, among other publications, of *Munich and Theatrical Modernism: Politics, Playwriting, and Performance, 1890-1914* (1985) and *Berlin Cabaret* (1993).

Paul Mendes-Flohr is Professor of Modern Jewish Intellectual History at The Hebrew University of Jerusalem. Most recently, he is the author of *German Jews: A Dual Identity* (1999) and co-author of *German Jewish History in Modern Times*, vol. 4 (1998). He is the editor of the German edition of the collected works of Martin Buber, the first volume of which will appear in 2000.

Peter Paret is Andrew W. Mellon Professor in the Humanities, Emeritus, School of Historical Studies, Institute for Advanced Study. Among his publications on the cultural history of art are *The Berlin Secession* (1980), *Art as History* (1988), *Imagined Battles* (1997), and, with Beth Irwin Lewis and Paul Paret, *Persuasive Images* (1992).

Chana C. Schütz is Senior Curator and Deputy Director of the Stiftung "Neue Synagoge Berlin-Centrum Judaicum" in Berlin. She is the author of *Preussen in Jerusalem* (1988), among other publications. She has served as curator of the 1992 exhibition "Jüdische Lebenswelten" as well as other exhibitions in Berlin.

Photography Credits